A Source Book on Early Monetary Thought

T0327649

A Source Book on Early Monetary Thought

Writings on Money before Adam Smith

Edited by

Edward W. Fuller

Palo Alto, CA, USA

Cheltenham, UK • Northampton, MA, USA

Published by
Edward Elgar Publishing Limited
The Lypiatts
15 Lansdown Road
Cheltenham
Glos GL50 2JA
UK

Edward Elgar Publishing, Inc.
William Pratt House
9 Dewey Court
Northampton
Massachusetts 01060
USA

A catalogue record for this book
is available from the British Library

Library of Congress Control Number: 2020944726

This book is available electronically in the **Elgar**online
Economics subject collection
http://dx.doi.org/10.4337/9781839109997

ISBN 978 1 83910 998 0 (cased)
ISBN 978 1 80037 000 5 (paperback)
ISBN 978 1 83910 999 7 (eBook)

Printed and bound by CPI Group (UK) Ltd, Croydon, CR0 4YY

Contents

Foreword

Money is the quintessential social institution. Society is nothing but a complex network of exchange relationships. The emergence of money exponentially increases exchange relationships, both quantitatively and qualitatively. In this way, money fosters society. Further, it is in the framework of exchange relationships that other vital human institutions are formed and refined. Institutions like language, morality, law, and accounting emerge spontaneously in the context of the exchange relationships that are only possible because of money. Money is the fundamental societal institution on which all others ultimately depend.

Given the overwhelming significance of money to society, monetary theory is the most important area of study in all of the social sciences. As economists of all schools have recognized, economic ideas ultimately determine the course of humankind. And ideas about money are the most momentous of all economic ideas. For better or worse, the future course of human civilization hangs on whether good or bad ideas on money triumph.

Just as monetary theory holds a cardinal place in the social sciences, the history of monetary thought holds a special place in the general history of thought. Indeed, it is impossible to truly understand the history of thought or the history of human institutions without some understanding of the history of monetary thought. For historians of economic thought in particular, there is no more important space than the history of monetary thought.

Therein lies the importance of the current book. This volume is an anthology of key contributions to monetary thought in the 20 centuries before Adam Smith. Such a collection has been sorely needed. Here, for the first time, we have a single volume that provides an extensive overview of the history of monetary thought.

The future of Western civilization depends on the institution of money. If the institution of money regresses, other vital human institutions are sure to follow. Sound money is essential to the continuing progress of humankind. But sound money starts with sound ideas—specifically, sound monetary theory. The history of indispensable ideas on money can be found within this volume.

Jesús Huerta de Soto
Madrid, Spain
February 2020

Foreword

Prior to the marginalist revolution of the 1870s, during which the Austrian school of economics was born, the crowning achievement of economics was classical monetary theory. This theory originated over the course of two nineteenth-century monetary controversies involving mainly British economists. The so-called "bullionist controversy" took place during the first decade of the nineteenth century. It concerned the question of whether or not the legal suspension of convertibility of bank notes into gold was the cause of the domestic price inflation, the rise in the price of gold bullion above its par value with the British pound, and the depreciation of the pound on the foreign exchanges. The "bullionists," led by David Ricardo and his lesser known predecessor Lord King, were hardcore anti-inflationists who argued that the expansion of the supply of inconvertible bank notes mainly by the Bank of England caused these events and that the remedy was to end the suspension of specie payments by the Bank and return to the gold standard. Their opponents, the "anti-bullionists," were pro-inflationists and comprised largely bankers and merchants. They argued that the increased supply of inconvertible bank notes had nothing to do with rising commodity prices, the high price of gold bullion, and depreciated exchange rates. The anti-bullionists instead blamed these things on the scarcity of commodities and the unfavorable balance of payments caused by bad harvests and the war with France.

The bullionists triumphed in the debate and their views were reflected in the famous Bullion Report issued by Parliament in 1811 that initiated the legislative movement to return to full convertibility of all bank notes in 1821. Most important for our purposes is that the bullionists, in defending their position in the controversy, developed a systematic way of thinking about money and banking that formed the core of classical monetary theory.

Despite the bullionists' triumph and the subsequent restoration of the gold standard, however, Great Britain experienced financial panics and recessions in 1825–26 and then again in 1837 and 1839. These episodes set the stage for a debate between the British Currency School and the British Banking School. The controversy actually began in the mid-1830s, heated up in the 1840s, and lingered on through the 1850s. The central point at issue was whether the convertibility of bank notes into gold was in and of itself sufficient to prevent the recurrence of financial crises and economic downturns. The Banking School argued that it was, while the Currency School countered with the "currency principle."

According to this principle, under a "mixed currency" composed of both gold and bank notes convertible into gold, financial crises and contractions of real output and employment could only be avoided if the money supply expanded and contracted exactly as a "purely metallic currency" would. In practice this meant that banks could only issue additional notes in exchange for a deposit of gold of equal denomination. For Great Britain, which lacked gold mines, the currency principle implied that the money supply would decrease and increase pound for pound with the ebb and flow of gold through the balance of payments. In this way an increase in real output in Great Britain, for example, would increase the demand for money and cheapen domestic prices, thereby encouraging exports and creating a surplus in the balance of payments. This would draw in additional gold and expand the money supply to satisfy the increased monetary demand. If the growth rate of real output in Great Britain lagged behind that of other nations, the reverse would occur and the decline in the demand for money would increase spending and domestic prices and cause a balance-of-payments deficit, an outflow of gold, and the contraction of the supply of gold and bank notes in domestic circulation. Thus the domestic money supply would only expand and contract in response to genuine changes in the demand for money by the public. With the Bank of England and the private banks completely deprived of the power to increase the money supply by arbitrarily creating and lending out unbacked bank notes or "fiduciary media," there would be no more inflationary booms culminating in banking panics and the onset of business bankruptcies, declining production, and sharp spikes in unemployment.

This was the vision and hope of the Currency School, which marked its members as the true heirs of the bullionists. Unfortunately, while further developing bullionist monetary theory, leading proponents of the currency principle—namely, Robert Torrens, Lord Overstone (S. J. Loyd), and George W. Norman—made a critical error. They failed to recognize that bank *deposits* were—no less than bank *notes*—money substitutes and, therefore, a part of the overall money supply. By ignoring this fact, the Currency School failed to apply the currency principle to bank deposits, leaving banks free to arbitrarily increase the money supply by expanding credit via the creation of unbacked deposits. Consequently, the triumph of the Currency School in the policy arena with the enactment of the currency principle into law in Peel's Act (also known as the Bank Charter Act of 1844) was a victory in name only. Financial crises and the boom-bust cycle continued to disrupt the British economy during the next several decades, and in each instance Peel's Act was suspended and the Bank of England was permitted to issue additional notes without 100 percent gold backing. The repeated cyclical fluctuations and suspensions discredited the Currency School and classical monetary theory in general and, by the last quarter of the nineteenth century, Banking School doctrines came to dominate the literature on money and banking and the currency principle sank into oblivion.

It was not until 1912, in his treatise *Theorie des Geldes und der Umlaufsmittel*—translated into English in 1934 as *The Theory of Money and Credit*—that Ludwig von Mises revived and reconstructed classical monetary theory by jettisoning the cost-of-production theory of value and integrating money with the subjective theory of value and prices. Mises also elaborated the Currency School's explanation of financial crises and recessions into a full-blown theory of the business cycle valid for closed as well as open economies. In so doing Mises also breathed new life into the currency principle while perfecting it by including bank deposits along with bank notes and gold in the money supply. Mises upheld the revised currency principle as the only means for preventing the recurrence of business cycles.

What were the main propositions of classical monetary theory? First, and most important, the classical economists conceived money as a commodity subject to the same laws of value as any other commodity. They thus applied supply and demand analysis to explain the purchasing power or "price" of money in the short run while tracing out the long-run forces that caused its purchasing power to tend to equal the costs of production of the money commodity in the long run. Classical monetary theorists therefore did *not* characterize money as a mere token which was arbitrarily selected and assigned value by the political authorities or by social convention to function as a claim to goods. Rather, they maintained that money was a useful commodity chosen by market participants to serve as a medium of exchange, which had a value of its own that was naturally determined in exchange with other commodities. In addition, classical monetary theorists demonstrated that the modern mainstream concept of an "optimal" supply of money in a "closed" economy, that is, in the entire world or in an isolated country, is meaningless because any supply of money (beyond some technical minimum) confers the full benefits of a medium of exchange. In other words, the supply of money would never be inadequate to meet "the needs of trade" no matter how much the supplies of goods and, therefore, the demand for money increase.

Classical economists also deduced that the global supply and distribution of a commodity money such as gold proceeded according to definite economic laws. In elaborating the mechanism by which money under the gold standard was distributed to different countries and regions according to their relative demands for money, they developed a sophisticated monetary approach to the balance of payments and exchange rates. This approach treated the flow of gold through the balance of payments as part of the process by which prices in all countries adjusted to a change in the demand for or supply of money in any one country and thus ensured that the purchasing power of money was internationally equalized. This balance-of-payments adjustment process also served as a central component in the classical economists' explanation of how the issue of fractionally backed bank notes and deposits brought about alternations of inflationary expansions and deflationary contractions of economic activity in an open economy. This analysis was one of the crucial building blocks for the Austrian theory of the business cycle later developed by Ludwig von Mises and Friedrich A. Hayek.

Finally, classical monetary theorists viewed inconvertible paper currency as a "disordered" or "sick" money. They saw it as inherently inflationary money, money that was prone to continuous depreciation since it could be issued without limit by governments and banks. With inconvertible money there also was no method, like that provided by the currency principle, to determine whether bank notes were being "overissued," even if government and banks tried to act prudently. Perhaps most important, during the time that classical monetary theory prevailed and even for many years after, those writers who promoted paper fiat money and inflationism as a deliberate policy were forced into the "underworlds" of monetary cranks, as John Maynard Keynes once complained.

Now the bullionists and adherents of the Currency School were admittedly brilliant and insightful men, but they did not create classical monetary theory out of whole cloth in a mere half century. In fact, almost all of the essential elements of the classical theory described already existed when they wrote. The outstanding achievement of the British classical economists was to synthesize and integrate these elements into a coherent explanation or theory of contemporary monetary developments.

The great contribution of the book that you are about to read is the light it sheds on the prehistory of classical monetary theory, which stretches back more than two millennia and originates in the writings of Aristotle. Edward Fuller, the book's editor, has done yeoman work in identifying and compiling the most important and illuminating contributions to this prehistory in the form of 37 selections from 30 different writers. His judicious choice of readings clearly demonstrates that classical monetary theory as outlined above was not a purely British creation but was heavily indebted to Aristotle and his medieval European commentators, including Albert the Great, Thomas Aquinas, and Jean Buridan, as well as late Spanish scholastics of the sixteenth-century School of Salamanca.

The transmission of this monetary tradition from the Catholic Romance countries to Protestant countries is illustrated with selections from seventeenth-century Protestant "scholastics" Hugo Grotius, Samuel Pufendorf, and John Locke, who, thanks to their acquaintance with the writings of their Catholic predecessors, were steeped in the Aristotelian tradition. Also well represented among the readings are the immediate predecessors of the classical school. These eighteenth-century British, French, and Italian writers fully grasped all the diverse strands of Aristotelian monetary thought and began to synthesize them into a systematic theory of money in their treatises, tracts, and essays. It is noteworthy that these authors, from Isaac Gervaise and Richard Cantillon to David Hume and A.R.J. Turgot, were all reacting to the monetary fallacies propagated at the beginning of the century by the forefather of modern macroeconomics, the fiat-money inflationist John Law. It is thus no accident that the contemporary proponents of the Austrian approach to money, banking, and the business cycle are the leading critics of mainstream macroeconomic theories and policies, for the Misesian theory of money is the culmination of the Aristotelian tradition.

I know of no other book of readings in monetary theory before Adam Smith—and certainly none currently in print—that offers the range of coverage or thematic coherence that this book does. Fuller has made a major contribution to monetary thought by uncovering the Aristotelian roots of sound monetary theory. The book is must reading not only for economic specialists in the history of monetary theory but for all those interested in learning about the development of the long and venerable tradition that gave birth to Austrian monetary theory.

Joseph T. Salerno

Academic Vice President, Mises Institute

April 2020

Acknowledgments

The editor and publishers wish to thank the authors and the following publishers who have kindly given permission for the use of copyrighted material.

Christian's Library Press, Acton Institute, Juan de Mariana; translated by Patrick T. Brannan, *A Treatise on the Alteration of Money*, 2011.
Christian's Library Press, Acton Institute for excerpts: "The Origin and Functions of Money," Martín de Azpilcueta; translated by Jeannine Emery, *On Exchange: An Adjudicative Commentary*, 2014, 27–31; "The Value of Money," Martín de Azpilcueta; translated by Jeannine Emery, *On Exchange: An Adjudicative Commentary*, 2014, 93–108; "On How the Same Amount of Money May Have a Different Value in Different Places," Luis de Molina; translated by Jeannine Emery, *A Treatise on Money*, 2015, 95–8; "Sale-Purchase," Leonardus Lessius; translated by Wim Decock and Nicholas De Sutter, *On Sale, Securities, and Insurance*, 2016, 5–10; "The Equal or Just Price of Saleable Goods," Leonardus Lessius; translated by Wim Decock and Nicholas De Sutter, *On Sale, Securities, and Insurance*, 2016, 15–19.
Franciscan Institute Publications, *A Treatise on Contracts*, Peter John Olivi; translated by Ryan Thornton and Michael Cusato, OFM, 2016.
Hackett Publishing Company for excerpts: "Commentary on Aristotle's Poetics," Aquinas; translated by Richard J. Regan, 50–3, 56–60 62–3.
The Ludwig von Mises Institute for excerpts: "An Essay on Economic Theory: An English Translation of Richard Cantillon's Essai sur la Nature du Commerce en Géneral," ed. Mark Thornton, translated by Chantal Saucier, 2010, 115–81; and "The Turgot Collection: Writings, Speeches, and Letters of Anne Robert Jacques Turgot, Baron de Laune," ed. David Gordon, 2010, 44–53.
Springer Nature BV for excerpt: "Copernicus on the Money Question," Copernicus, *Collected Works The Minor Works*, 1985, 176–95.

Every effort has been made to trace all the copyright holders but if any have been inadvertently overlooked the publishers will be pleased to make the necessary arrangement at the first opportunity.

1. Introduction: The Aristotelian Monetary Tradition

Edward W. Fuller

It is impossible to overstate the significance of Aristotle in the history of monetary thought. Of course, Aristotle did not give posterity a complete theory of money. But every major contribution to monetary thought in the history of economic science has been built on the foundation laid by Aristotle. At its core, the modern theory of money is an Aristotelian theory of money. Thus it is impossible to fully understand monetary theory today without understanding its Aristotelian origins.

Aristotle (384–22 BC) was born in Stagira, Macedonia, or what is today northern Greece. Aristotle's father, Nichomachus, was physician to the king of Macedonia. Aristotle went to Athens in 367 and studied in Plato's Academy for 20 years. He left Athens after Plato's death in 347 and became tutor to Alexander the Great. In 334, he returned to Athens and founded his own school, the Lyceum. He stayed at the Lyceum until just before his death. He was forced to flee Athens after the death of Alexander the Great in 323, and he died on the island of Euboea of natural causes in 322.

Unfortunately, Aristotle's philosophy was lost in the West after the sixth century. As legend has it, Emperor Justinian shut down the pagan schools of philosophy in 529 AD, and the pagan philosophers fled east with Aristotle's works. Knowledge of Aristotle's works was only regained in the West after the First Crusade (1095–99), which restored contact between the East and West. Eventually, ancient Greek and Arabic versions of Aristotle's works found their way to Europe. The recovery of Aristotle's thought is generally placed from about 1150 to about 1250. The reintroduction of Aristotle in the West ignited the greatest intellectual revolution in the history of humankind. No doubt, it was the recovery of Aristotle that set the stage for the Renaissance—the rebirth of reason in Europe.

Initially, the Catholic Church saw Aristotle as a threat. He had argued that the Earth was uncreated and eternal, and this contradicted the account of creation found in the Bible. The church initially banned Aristotle's works. But his monumental system of philosophy was too powerful to be ignored. Soon enough, the church realized that the proper course was to reconcile Aristotelianism with Catholicism. Albert the Great (c. 1200–80) and Thomas Aquinas (1225–74) were the best minds in Europe, and they got to work harmonizing Aristotelianism with Catholicism. More than anyone else, these two men were responsible for bringing Aristotle back to the West. In this way, Albert and Aquinas opened the door for the Renaissance.

Aristotle's writings on money are contained in two works: the *Nicomachean Ethics* and the *Politics*. A work called *Economics* was attributed to Aristotle in the Middle Ages, but the work is not authentic and is not about economic science. The *Nicomachean Ethics* and the

Politics must be considered the germs of the modern theory of money. Thus it is necessary to understand the history of these works and their translations.

The *Nicomachean Ethics* was not written for publication but was rather a set of notes from Aristotle's lectures. It is a revision of his earlier work, the *Eudemian Ethics* (c. 350 BC). Book V of the *Nicomachean Ethics*, which contains his material on money, is identical to Book IV of the *Eudemian Ethics*. Still, the *Eudemian Ethics* was not translated into Latin until long after the *Nicomachean Ethics*, meaning the *Nicomachean Ethics* is the relevant work for those interested in the history of economic thought.

Robert Grosseteste (1175–1253) completed the Latin translation of the *Nicomachean Ethics* by 1247. Unfortunately, Grosseteste's translation was problematic, and it created much trouble for Aristotle's medieval interpreters. Importantly, Grosseteste mistranslated the Greek word *chreia* into the Latin *opus*, meaning "work" or "labor." However, *chreia* means "need," while the Greek for "work" is *ergon*. Grosseteste was aware of the issue. In his notes, he also translated *chreia* into the Latin *utilitas*, meaning "utility," and the Latin *indigentia*, meaning "need" or "demand." Still, Grosseteste translated *chreia* as "work" in his translation of the *Nicomachean Ethics*. Grosseteste's mistranslation of *chreia* made it seem as though Aristotle had a labor theory of value.

Albert the Great is perhaps the most underappreciated figure in the history of monetary thought. He is best remembered as Aquinas's master, but Aquinas did not advance beyond Albert's work on money. In fact, Albert's commentaries were far more influential than Aquinas's with early monetary thinkers. Shockingly, Albert's writings on money are still available only in Latin.

Albert obtained a copy of Grosseteste's translation in 1248, and he produced two commentaries on the *Nicomachean Ethics* in the following decades. Albert's *First Commentary* was completed around 1252, and it set the pattern for commentaries by Aquinas and others. Albert is often wrongly associated with the labor theory of value because of his *First Commentary*. As noted, however, Grosseteste was responsible for injecting the labor theory into Aristotle, not Albert. Albert finished his *Second Commentary* around 1262, and this work cleared up the confusion over the word *chreia*. Here Albert established the meaning of *chreia* as the Latin *indigentia*, meaning "need" or "demand." Thus the *Second Commentary* contains the Aristotelian utility theory of value, not the labor theory. Albert deserves much credit for putting value theory back on track after Grosseteste. Following Albert, no medieval economic thinker argued that labor was the sole determinant of value.

Aquinas wrote his commentary on the *Nicomachean Ethics* in 1271. Aquinas's commentary is very similar to Albert's *Second Commentary*, and his goal was to clarify. His main contribution was to popularize the monetary thought of Aristotle and Albert. Along with Albert, Aquinas played the key role in establishing the utility theory of value in medieval economics. Aristotle's *Nicomachean Ethics* and the commentaries by Albert and Aquinas contain the seeds of the modern theory of supply and demand. The quantity theory of money is the application of the theory of supply and demand to money. It is the most elementary proposition in the theory of money, and its history begins with Aristotle's *Nicomachean Ethics* and the commentaries of Albert and Aquinas.

Aristotle's *Politics* is the other foundational work in the history of monetary thought. Aristotle developed the *Politics* after his work on ethics, and it dates to around 350 BC. It contains more commentary on money than the *Nicomachean Ethics*. In the *Nicomachean*

Ethics, Aristotle defines money as a medium of exchange, recognizes the double coincidence of wants, and notes that the purchasing power of money can change. But he elaborates in the *Politics*. He explains there that money emerges out of barter, and he lists some of the characteristics of good money.

The *Politics* was translated into Latin after the *Nicomachean Ethics*. The translator was the Flemish Dominican William of Moerbeke (c. 1215–86), who produced two translations. The first translation was probably produced around 1255, but it was never completed. The second translation was probably completed around 1261. Although the second translation was superior to the first, Moerbeke had a rough Latin style, and his translation was generally of poor quality. Albert probably wrote his commentary on the *Politics* around 1263, and Aquinas probably completed his commentary in 1272.

The French theologian and philosopher Peter John Olivi (1248–98) discovered subjective-utility theory. While Aristotle, Albert, and Aquinas were utility theorists, Olivi was the first to stress that subjective utility, not some ambiguous notion of objective utility, is relevant to price determination. Although he did not systematically treat money, Olivi used gold in his discussion of supply and demand. He realized that the price of gold is lower when there is a great abundance of it and higher when there is a lack of it. By using gold in his analysis, Olivi hinted at the quantity theory of money.

Aristotle, Albert, and Aquinas were the three founding fathers of monetary theory. But the work of Jean Buridan (1300–58) represents a huge leap forward in monetary thought. Like Albert's and Aquinas's writings, Buridan's writings on money are contained in his commentaries on the *Nicomachean Ethics* and the *Politics*. Not only does his work contain the theory of supply and demand, but he explained that money loses its value as the supply of money increases. Though Albert and Aquinas warned against debasing money, Buridan went further and argued that inflation benefits government at the expense of the people. For his contributions, Buridan can be considered the founder of the modern theory of money. Amazingly, his seminal writings on money have never appeared in English.

This brings us to the great Nicholas Oresme (1320–82). Unlike the writings of Albert, Aquinas, and Buridan, Oresme's writings on money were not commentaries on Aristotle. Thus Oresme was the first to write a treatise specifically dedicated to money. Unfortunately, however, Oresme's place in the history of monetary thought is the subject of controversy. In an effort to elevate Oresme, some scholars have argued that Buridan borrowed heavily from Oresme. Oresme was Buridan's greatest student, and some have claimed that Oresme produced his *Treatise* before Buridan's commentaries on Aristotle. Such scholars have downplayed the significance of Albert, Aquinas, and Buridan and have deemed Oresme the great figure in the history of monetary thought. The evidence shows that these scholars are incorrect and that it was Oresme who borrowed from his master Buridan. No one can deny the greatness of Oresme's *Treatise on Money*. Still, his work's status in the history of economic thought is somewhat inflated. His enduring contribution was introducing Gresham's law into economics.

There were no major contributions to monetary thought for over a century after Oresme. Europe experienced a great depression from 1340 to 1450, and the Black Death occurred during this period. The great depression and the Black Death stifled intellectual development, including the development of monetary thought. The next great contribution to monetary thought came from Gabriel Biel (1420–95) a century and a half after Oresme. Biel followed Aristotle and Oresme, meaning he must be considered an author in the Aristotelian tradition.

Like Oresme, he criticized inflation in the harshest possible terms and argued that any government that inflates tyrannically oppresses the people.

Nicolaus Copernicus (1473–1543) is one of the greatest figures in the history of the
natural sciences, but he also made important contributions to economics. Copernicus is
widely considered the first thinker to explicitly state the quantity theory of money. However,
Copernicus does not seem to have gone far beyond Buridan. He argued that money loses its
value through abundance and that increasing the money supply causes the price of everything
to rise. However, he never seems to have stated the quantity theory as a general law. Although
his *Essay* is a fantastic contribution with a brilliant analysis of inflation, it seems the quantity
theory had not yet been achieved.

Now we come to the School of Salamanca. The great Aristotelian-Thomist Francisco de
Vitoria (1483–1546), the father of international law, established the School of Salamanca in
the early 1500s. Although he did not leave any writings on economics, Vitoria was a known
advocate of the theory of supply and demand. Around this time, large quantities of precious
metals began flowing into Europe from the New World. The influx of precious metals caused
the purchasing power of money to decline in Europe, especially in Spain. The Spanish scholars
of the School of Salamanca wanted to explain the fall in the purchasing power of money, and
they were armed with Vitoria's supply-and-demand framework. The stage was set for the
quantity theory of money.

The first important contribution on monetary thought from the School of Salamanca comes
from Luís Saravia de la Calle (c. 1500–60). In his work *Instructions for Merchants*, he stated
a general law: the abundance (scarcity) of goods, merchants, and money raises (lowers) prices.
Here Saravia de la Calle expressed the law of supply and demand. Moreover, he included
money in his formulation. He did not explicitly state the quantity theory of money, but he
certainly pointed the way.

Martín de Azpilcueta (1491–1586) was the first thinker to explicitly state the quantity theory
of money. As noted, thinkers such as Buridan, Oresme, Biel, and Copernicus had approached
the theory. But Azpilcueta was the first to state the theory as a general law: the purchasing
power, or price, of money is determined by the supply of and demand for money. Incredibly,
he also explicitly stated the purchasing power parity theory of exchange rates. For his contributions, Azpilcueta must be considered one of the towering figures in the history of monetary
economics. After Azpilcueta, the quantity theory was articulated by all the major economic
writers in the School of Salamanca, including Tomás de Mercado (1525–75), Francisco García
(f. 1583), and Luís de Molina (1535–1600).

There are two important figures outside of Spain from the sixteenth century: Sir Thomas
Smith (1513–77) in England and Bernardo Davanzati (1529–1606) in Italy. Smith has
been described as the first English thinker to express the quantity theory. Smith appeals to
Aristotle, meaning the earliest English writings on money have Aristotelian origins. Like
Smith, Davanzati is commonly labeled as an early quantity theorist. In reality, neither Smith
nor Davanzati matched Azpilcueta. Still, they both realized that increasing the money supply
causes the prices of all goods to rise and that this makes some people richer while making
others poorer. On top of that, they argued that unnatural increases in the money supply cause
economic turmoil. Hence the works of Smith and Davanzati foreshadowed monetary explanations of depressions.

This brings us to Leonard Lessius (1552–1623). Although he was Flemish, Lessius was a Jesuit in the Spanish tradition of Vitoria, Azpilcueta, and Molina. Lessius's seminal contribution to economic science is the loanable-funds theory of the interest rate. He realized that the interest rate is the price of a loan. Since it is a price, the interest rate is determined by supply and demand on the market, or the bourse. Specifically, the interest rate is determined in the loan market by the supply of and demand for money loans. Lessius's development of the loanable-funds theory of the interest rate gives him a special place in the history of economic science.

Juan de Mariana (1536–1624) was one of history's great opponents of inflation. Following Buridan, Oresme, and Biel, he argued the purpose of money is to facilitate the exchange of goods and services. Citizens are the owners of the goods and services exchanged for money, meaning they are also the rightful owners of society's stock of money. Since government does not own society's stock of money, any government that manipulates the money supply behaves tyrannically. Not only is government inflation unjust, but it undermines trade—the foundation of society—and thereby disrupts social order. For Mariana, inflation poses an existential danger to the preservation and proliferation of humankind.

The shorter and less original contributions of Hugo Grotius (1583–1645) and Samuel Pufendorf (1632–94) bridge the gap between the Catholics and Protestants. The Flemish Jesuit Lessius played the key role in transmitting Catholic ideas on money to the Protestants in Northern Europe, and he did so through Grotius and Pufendorf. While Grotius obsessively cited all his predecessors, the Lutheran Pufendorf was fiercely anti-Catholic. Although influenced by the Catholics, he refused to cite them. Via his translator Gershom Carmichael, Pufendorf had a major influence on the thinkers of the Scottish Enlightenment, including Adam Smith. But Pufendorf's refusal to cite the Catholics, along with Smith's own disinclination to cite others, meant knowledge of the Catholic influence on Protestant economics was lost.

John Locke (1632–1704) and Dudley North (1641–91) marked the beginning of English dominance in economics. Both Locke and North explicitly stated the quantity theory of money, and both opposed inflation. Beyond that, Locke and North endorsed the loanable-funds theory of the interest rate. They argued that the interest rate, like all prices, is determined by the market forces of supply and demand. Like all price controls, attempts to fix the interest rate by law are futile. Any such attempt will create shortages, black markets, and, in the end, an even higher interest rate. As with all prices, the interest rate must be free to find its own level in the market.

Isaac Gervaise (d. 1739) was the first to explain the price-specie-flow mechanism—the most fundamental theory in international monetary economics. Gervaise wrote in the aftermath of John Law's disastrous banking experiment in France, and he developed the price-specie-flow mechanism to show that bank money causes domestic and international disequilibrium. When banks in France inflate the money supply, this will cause French prices to rise relative to prices in other nations. Higher prices in France will lead domestic and foreign buyers to purchase fewer French goods and more non-French goods. But this means gold and silver, or specie, will flow out of France and into other nations. As their reserves dwindle, French banks will be forced to contract the supply of bank money. And the contracting money supply will cause French prices to fall back toward equilibrium with other nations. In the end, banks cannot enrich the nation by increasing the money supply.

Richard Cantillon (1680–1734) is the father of modern economics. Obviously, many thinkers wrote on economic problems before Cantillon. But these writers never viewed economics as an independent science of its own. Instead, they wrote on economic problems in connection with other subjects, such as religion, ethics, law, and politics. Cantillon's famous *Essay on Economic Theory* (1730) is the first book devoted entirely to economics; it is the first systematic treatment of economic science as a whole. Cantillon expressed the theory of supply and demand, the quantity theory, the loanable-funds theory, and the price-specie-flow mechanism. Beyond that, he was the first to show that banks influence the interest rate when they lend newly created money on the loan market.

Jacob Vanderlint (d. 1740) was an early advocate of the quantity theory of money in England. Like Gervaise and Cantillon, Vanderlint recognized that money creation by banks causes price inflation. Further, he articulated the price-specie-flow mechanism, and he used the mechanism to argue that money creation by banks causes mischief in foreign trade. For these reasons, Vanderlint passionately opposed bank-money inflation.

Along with his master Carmichael, Francis Hutcheson (1694–1746) was the founding father of the Scottish Enlightenment. Hutcheson's writings on money follow closely those of Grotius and Pufendorf, who were influenced by the Aristotelian-Thomists in the School of Salamanca. Although it is not original, Hutcheson's work is historically significant, for he transmitted Aristotelian ideas on money to his great students David Hume and Adam Smith.

Ferdinando Galiani (1728–87) is the grandfather of the marginal revolution of the 1870s, and his work *On Money* (1751) was the greatest monetary treatise of the eighteenth century. During Galiani's lifetime, the labor theory of value rose to dominance in the English-speaking world. Unlike many of his more famous English contemporaries, Galiani advocated the utility approach to value theory. He developed a marginal theory of utility and came close to expressing the law of diminishing marginal utility. Galiani applied his utility theory of value to money and, significantly, to interest. Galiani's praise of Aristotle, Aquinas, and Davanzati shows that he was firmly in the Aristotelian tradition.

David Hume (1711–76) is one of the most influential monetary theorists of all time. In philosophy, he was a thorough skeptic and opponent of natural law. However, Hume's monetary work was in the Aristotelian tradition of Grotius and Hutcheson. A staunch advocate of the quantity theory, Hume stressed that the quantity of money in society is irrelevant. Hume explained that there is no such thing as an optimal money supply; any size of the money supply is optimal. There is never any need to increase the money supply, because all it does is reduce the purchasing power of money. Hume is widely considered the first to express the price-specie-flow mechanism. Although Gervaise, Vanderlint, and Cantillon achieved it earlier, Hume deserves credit for clarifying and popularizing the theory. Finally, like Gervaise, Vanderlint, and Galiani, the quantity theory and price-specie-flow mechanism led Hume to advocate 100 percent reserve banking.

Joseph Harris (1702–64) was England's greatest authority on coinage. His large work *An Essay upon Money and Coins* (1757–58) represents the great consolidation of English views on money prior to Adam Smith. Here we find the quantity theory, the price-specie-flow mechanism, and a critique of bank money. A fierce opponent of inflation, he insisted that the standard of money must never be altered under any circumstances. Finally, like Hume, he advocated 100 percent reserve banking.

A.R.J. Turgot (1727–81) and Étienne Bonnot de Condillac (1714–80) were two of the most significant French economists of the eighteenth century. Turgot's greatest contributions to economics were in the area of interest. He stated the loanable-funds theory of the interest rate with greater clarity than any of his predecessors, and his work on interest was not surpassed until after the marginal revolution of the 1870s. Condillac published his great work *Commerce and Government* in 1776, just one month before Adam Smith published *The Wealth of Nations*. Along with Cantillon's *Essay*, Condillac's work is the most important general treatise on economics in the period before *The Wealth of Nations*. Turgot and Condillac relied greatly on Cantillon. Cantillon had drawn on Locke, who had been heavily influenced by Grotius, who in turn was heavily influenced by the Aristotelian-Thomists in the School of Salamanca. All this means that there is a line from Turgot and Condillac all the way back to Aristotle.

Adam Smith is widely considered the father of economics. However, the writings in this volume should make one point abundantly clear: Smith did not singlehandedly invent economics. There were many important economic thinkers who came before Smith, and it could be argued that, on certain points, some earlier thinkers were more advanced than Smith. This is not to diminish Smith's role in the history of economic science. He is a central figure. It just means that Smith did not invent economics out of whole cloth. He was familiar with the economic thought of Grotius, Locke, Hutcheson, Cantillon, Hume, and Turgot. Through these authors, the Aristotelian tradition influenced Adam Smith.

Unfortunately, however, Smith departed from the Aristotelians by adopting the problematic labor theory of value rather than the utility theory. Hutcheson was Smith's teacher, and Hutcheson passed down the Aristotelian utility theory to Smith. Indeed, we find the utility theory of value in Smith's lectures. Smith's adoption of the labor theory of value in *The Wealth of Nations* represented a step back from the utility theory advocated by the Aristotelians that came before. In short, we find the greatest problem in Smith's work precisely where he deviated most from the Aristotelian tradition. The problematic labor theory of value created problems for his theory of money and banking.

The following pages contain the most important writings on monetary thought from Aristotle up to the time of Adam Smith. Regrettably, many of these writings have remained inaccessible to those interested in monetary thought. This volume makes these inaccessible contributions available in one convenient place.

2. Aristotle: *Nicomachean Ethics* (c. 350 BC)[1]

Some think that reciprocity is without qualification just, as the Pythagoreans said; for they defined justice without qualification as reciprocity. Now reciprocity fits neither distributive nor rectificatory justice—yet people want even the justice of Rhadamanthus to mean this: Should a man suffer what he did, right justice would be done—for in many cases they are not in accord; e.g. if an official has inflicted a wound, he should not be wounded in return, and if someone has wounded an official, he ought not to be wounded only but punished in addition. Further, there is a great difference between a voluntary and an involuntary act. But in associations for exchange this sort of justice does hold men together—reciprocity in accordance with a proportion and not on the basis of equality. For it is by proportionate requital that the city holds together. Men seek to return either evil for evil—and if they cannot do so, think their position mere slavery—or good for good—and if they cannot do so there is no exchange, but it is by exchange that they hold together. This is why they give a prominent place to the temple of the Graces—to promote the requital of services; for this is characteristic of grace—we should serve in return one who has shown grace to us, and should another time take the initiative in showing it.

Now proportionate return is secured by cross-conjunction. Let A be a builder, B a shoe-maker, C a house, D a sandal (Figure 2.1). The builder, then, must get from the shoemaker the latter's work, and must himself give him in return his own. If, then, first there is proportionate equality of goods, and then reciprocal action takes place, the result we mention will be effected. If not, the bargain is not equal, and does not hold; for there is nothing to prevent the work of the one being better than that of the other; they must therefore be equated. (And this is true of the other arts also; for they would have been destroyed if what the patient suffered had not been just what the agent did, and of the same amount and kind.) For it is not two doctors that associate for exchange, but a doctor and a farmer, or in general people who are different and unequal; but these must be equated. This is why all things that are exchanged must be somehow commensurable. It is for this end that money has been introduced, and it becomes in a sense an intermediate; for it measures all things, and therefore the excess and the defect—how many shoes are equal to a house or to a given amount of food. The number of shoes exchanged for a house [or for a given amount of food] must therefore correspond to the ratio of builder to shoemaker. For if this be not so, there will be no exchange and no intercourse. And this proportion will not be effected unless the goods are somehow equal. All goods must therefore be measured by some one thing, as we said before. Now this unit is in truth demand, which holds all things together (for if men did not need one another's goods at all, or did not need them equally, there would be either no exchange or not the same exchange); but money has become by convention a sort of representative of demand; and this is why it has the name

---

[1]   Translated by Benjamin Jowett, 1132b22–1133b28.

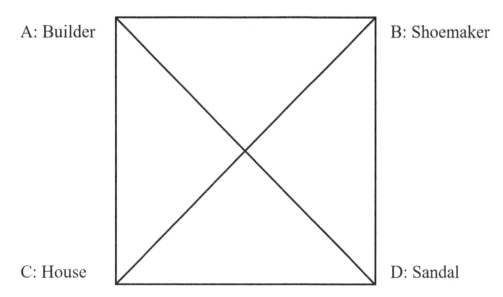

A: Builder   B: Shoemaker

C: House   D: Sandal

Figure 2.1

'money' (*nomisma*)—because it exists not by nature but by law (*nomos*) and it is in our power to change it and make it useless. There will, then, be reciprocity when the terms have been equated so that as farmer is to shoemaker, the amount of the shoemaker's work is to that of the farmer's work. But we must not bring them into a figure of proportion when they have already exchanged (otherwise one extreme will have both excesses), but when they still have their own goods. Thus they are equals and associates just because this equality can be effected in their case. Let A be a farmer, C food, B a shoemaker, D his product equated to C. If it had not been possible for reciprocity to be thus effected, there would have been no association of the parties. That demand holds things together as a single unit is shown by the fact that when men do not need one another, i.e. when neither needs the other or one does not need the other, they do not exchange, as we do when someone wants what one has oneself, e.g. when people permit the exportation of corn in exchange for wine. This equation therefore must be established. And for the future exchange—that if we do not need a thing now we shall have it if ever we do need it—money is as it were our surety; for it must be possible for us to get what we want by bringing the money. Now the same thing happens to money itself as to goods—it is not always worth the same; yet it tends to be steadier. This is why all goods must have a price set on them; for then there will always be exchange, and if so, association. Money, then, acting as a measure, makes goods commensurate and equates them; for neither would there have been association if there were not exchange, nor exchange if there were not equality, nor equality if there were not commensurability. Now in truth it is impossible that things differing so much should become commensurate, but with reference to demand they may become so sufficiently. There must, then, be a unit, and that fixed by agreement (for which reason it is called money); for it is this that makes all things commensurate, since all things are measured by money. Let A be a house, B ten minae, C a bed. A is half of B, if the house is worth five minae or equal to them; the bed, C, is a tenth of B; it is plain, then, how many beds are equal to a house, viz. five.

That exchange took place thus because there was money is plain; for it makes no difference whether it is five beds that exchange for a house, or the money value of five beds.

3.   Aristotle: *Politics* (c. 350 BC)[1]

There is another variety of the art of acquisition which is commonly and rightly called an art of wealth-getting (or money-making), and has in fact suggested the notion that riches and property have no limit. Being nearly connected with the preceding, it is often identified with it. But though they are not very different, neither are they the same. The kind already described is given by nature, the other is gained by experience and art.

Let us begin our discussion of the question with the following considerations. Of everything which we possess there are two uses: both belong to the thing as such, but not in the same manner, for one is the proper, and the other the improper use of it. For example, a shoe is used for wear, and is used for exchange; both are uses of the shoe. He who gives a shoe in exchange for money or food to him who wants one, does indeed use the shoe as a shoe, but this is not its proper use, for a shoe is not made to be an object of barter. The same may be said of all possessions, for the art of exchange extends to all of them, and it arises at first from what is natural, from the circumstance that some have too little, others too much. Hence we may infer that retail trade is not a natural part of the art of getting wealth; had it been so, men would have ceased to exchange when they had enough. In the first community, indeed, which is the family, this art is obviously of no use, but it begins to be useful when the society increases. For the members of the family originally had all things in common; later, when the family divided into parts, the parts shared in many things, and different parts in different things, which they had to give in exchange for what they wanted, a kind of barter which is still practised among barbarous nations who exchange with one another the necessaries of life and nothing more; giving and receiving wine, for example, in exchange for corn, and the like. This sort of barter is not part of the wealth-getting art and is not contrary to nature, but is needed for the satisfaction of men's natural wants. The other form of exchange grew, as might have been inferred, out of this one. When the inhabitants of one country became more dependent on those of another, and they imported what they needed, and exported what they had too much of, money necessarily came into use. For the various necessaries of life are not easily carried about, and hence men agreed to employ in their dealings with each other something which was intrinsically useful and easily applicable to the purposes of life, for example, iron, silver, and the like. Of this the value was at first measured simply by size and weight, but in process of time they put a stamp upon it, to save the trouble of weighing and to mark the value.

When the use of coin had once been discovered, out of the barter of necessary articles arose the other art of wealth-getting, namely, retail trade; which was at first probably a simple matter, but became more complicated as soon as men learned by experience whence and by what exchanges the greatest profit might be made. Originating in the use of coin, the art of getting wealth is generally thought to be chiefly concerned with it, and to be the art which

---

[1]   Translated by Benjamin Jowett, 1256b40–1258b8.

produces riches and wealth, having to consider how they may be accumulated. Indeed, riches is assumed by many to be only a quantity of coin, because the arts of getting wealth and retail trade are concerned with coin. Others maintain that coined money is a mere sham, a thing not natural, but conventional only, because, if the users substitute another commodity for it, it is worthless, and because it is not useful as a means to any of the necessities of life, and, indeed, he who is rich in coin may often be in want of necessary food. But how can that be wealth of which a man may have a great abundance and yet perish with hunger, like Midas in the fable, whose insatiable prayer turned everything that was set before him into gold?

Hence men seek a better notion of riches and of the art of getting wealth, and they are right. For natural riches and the natural art of wealth-getting are a different thing; in their true form they are part of the management of a household; whereas retail trade is the art of producing wealth, not in every way, but by exchange. And it is thought to be concerned with coin; for coin is the unit of exchange and the limit of it. And there is no bound to the riches which spring from this art of wealth-getting. As in the art of medicine there is no limit to the pursuit of health, and as in the other arts there is no limit to the pursuit of their several ends, for they aim at accomplishing their ends to the uttermost (but of the means there is a limit, for the end is always the limit), so, too, in this art of wealth-getting there is no limit of the end, which is riches of the spurious kind, and the acquisition of wealth. But the art of wealth-getting which consists in household management, on the other hand, has a limit; the unlimited acquisition of wealth is not its business. And, therefore, from one point of view, all riches must have a limit; nevertheless, as a matter of fact, we find the opposite to be the case; for all getters of wealth increase their hoard of coin without limit. The source of the confusion is the near connexion between the two kinds of wealth-getting; in both, the instrument is the same, although the use is different, and so they pass into one another; for each is a use of the same property, but with a difference: accumulation is the end in the one case, but there is a further end in the other. Hence some persons are led to believe that getting wealth is the object of household management, and the whole idea of their lives is that they ought either to increase their money without limit, or at any rate not to lose it. The origin of this disposition in men is that they are intent upon living only, and not upon living well; and, as their desires are unlimited, they also desire that the means of gratifying them should be without limit. Those who do aim at a good life seek the means of obtaining bodily pleasures; and, since the enjoyment of these appears to depend on property, they are absorbed in getting wealth: and so there arises the second species of wealth-getting. For, as their enjoyment is in excess, they seek an art which produces the excess of enjoyment; and, if they are not able to supply their pleasures by the art of getting wealth, they try other causes, using in turn every faculty in a manner contrary to nature. The quality of courage, for example, is not intended to make wealth, but to inspire confidence; neither is this the aim of the general's or of the physician's art; but the one aims at victory and the other at health. Nevertheless, some men turn every quality or art into a means of getting wealth; this they conceive to be the end, and to the promotion of the end they think all things must contribute.

Thus, then, we have considered the art of wealth-getting which is unnecessary, and why men want it; and also the necessary art of wealth-getting, which we have seen to be different from the other, and to be a natural part of the art of managing a household, concerned with the provision of food, not, however, like the former kind, unlimited, but having a limit.

And we have found the answer to our original question, whether the art of getting wealth is the business of the manager of a household and of the statesman or not their business?—viz. that wealth is presupposed by them. For as political science does not make men, but takes them from nature and uses them, so too nature provides them with earth or sea or the like as a source of food. At this stage begins the duty of the manager of a household, who has to order the things which nature supplies—he may be compared to the weaver who has not to make but to use wool, and to know, too, what sort of wool is good and serviceable or bad and unserviceable. Were this otherwise, it would be difficult to see why the art of getting wealth is a part of the management of a household and the art of medicine not; for surely the members of a household must have health just as they must have life or any other necessity. The answer is that as from one point of view the master of the house and the ruler of the state have to consider health, from another point of view not they but the physician has to; so in one way the art of household management, in another way the subordinate art, has to consider wealth. But, strictly speaking, as I have already said, the means of life must be provided beforehand by nature; for the business of nature is to furnish food to that which is born, and the food of the offspring is always what remains over of that from which it is produced. That is why the art of getting wealth out of fruits and animals is always natural.

There are two sorts of wealth-getting, as I have said; one is a part of household management, the other is retail trade: the former is necessary and honourable, while that which consists in exchange is justly censured; for it is unnatural, and a mode by which men gain from one another. The most hated sort, and with the greatest reason, is usury, which makes a gain out of money itself, and not from the natural object of it. For money was intended to be used in exchange, but not to increase at interest. And this term interest, which means the birth of money from money, is applied to the breeding of money because the offspring resembles the parent. That is why of all modes of getting wealth this is the most unnatural.

4.   Albert the Great: Commentary on Aristotle's *Nicomachean Ethics* (c. 1262)[1]

But the concept, which the Pythagoreans call reciprocity, refers in exchanges only to those things which are called exchangeable. Then the exchangeable things are those in which, on the basis of a voluntary agreement, one thing can be exchanged for another. In fact, such an exchange in political matters is defined by a legal concept that is called reciprocity: and, if it is not lawful, the exchange between citizens will be dissolved; thus, it is necessary to accept reciprocal proportionality and not always by the equality of the matter; because the contract cannot be judged on just one thing, but on three things, as Tullius affirms. In fact, sometimes the politician puts the market at the disposal of the public, stating what must be sold at what price, since, if done another way, due to the urgent need of merchandise, the citizens would often suffer excessive harm; so, as it is regulated in the times of shortage, a bushel of wheat is sold at a certain price and not more. Sometimes, these exchanges happen with an interfering bond, without any deceptive scam, and then it is not the equivalent that is given for the merchandise, but what has been negotiated. Sometimes the exchanges are established for the equality of the matter, so that he who sells shall have the equivalent of what the other person buys. Therefore, in these cases, it is necessary to bear in mind that a just reciprocity does not always mean a transaction settled in the same way, but sometimes an equal exchange, occasionally an outcome of negotiation, at times of a judgment.

Yet, in these exchanges it is not possible to change a thing for another one, such as a house for a bed, or a bushel of wheat for sandals, since they are neither equivalent nor of equal necessity. For the person who exchanges wheat does not always need sandals so badly as to exchange wheat for the sandals. In fact, this exchange does not happen through the equality of the exchanged things, but rather according to the proportion of the value of one thing compared to the value of the other thing, the proportion having been established on the basis of need, which is the reason of the exchange. In fact, owing to a proportional reciprocity, the city can endure; actually, the city will not endure unless the needs of the citizens are catered to, but they cannot be replenished without the economic exchange of one thing for another. In reality, nobody can supply, by himself, for his every need; if, in fact, he has his own wheat, he lacks sandals and a house and a bed; even if he produces one thing, he cannot excel in another one; because of this everyone needs someone else, and, owing to such exchange, the city can survive.

But this is proven: because everyone requires something in the city, because in the city he either fares well or badly. As a matter of fact, those who fared badly lack things because they are not able to obtain things from others who also fared badly; because, if those who fare badly

---

[1]   Translation produced by Edward W. Fuller.

cannot exchange goods, their lot is not a city life, but servitude, because, obviously, they suffer bad treatment through the will of others, just like slaves suffer from their masters. City life, however, is not slavery, but a sort of liberty and democracy. If, in fact, acting by the law, it is mandatory to reciprocate by the proportion that we previously mentioned, the city survives owing to the liberty of exchange and it will endure; and a politician must aim at it. Because they fared well, they then seek to have their needs catered to by those people by whom they fared well, so that everything is done proportionally by the way of retributions and thankful deeds. But if it does not happen this way, then there is no just repayment: with just retribution, however, the city endures. Because of that the legislators zealously act so that the sacred favor remains in the cities, and just repayment immediately occurs to everyone without any waste of time. We call it the sacred favor, because it is sacred by the law: favor refers in this case to a proper retribution through proportionality; actually, this is characteristic of favor according to which we accept it, and that way the citizens remain grateful and friendly. Truly, it is necessary for the person who receives the favor to compensate the person who did the favor; and, right after, for the person who at first did the favor, he should again start doing a favor to the person who has compensated him. In reality, this course and the repayment of favors help the city to endure: in truth, the correspondence of favor triggers repayment through the aforementioned proportionality. In fact, the favor of someone goes to another person, and the favor of the other person goes back to the first one.

This is made evident in the description of Figure 4.1. Imagine that the builder of a house is represented by A, the shoemaker making a sandal is represented by B, the need of the builder towards the shoemaker, and vice versa, by the line AB; let the house, which is the work of the builder, be represented by G, let the dependence of the house on the builder be represented by the line AG; and the sandal, which is the work of the shoemaker, shall be represented by D, the dependence of the sandal on the shoemaker shall be represented by the line BD; the exchange of the house with the sandal, and vice versa, shall be represented by the line GD, then the transfer of the house to the shoemaker shall be represented by the diagonal GB, while the transfer of the sandal to the builder shall be represented by the diagonal AD. The builder then does not lack the house, since he himself has the skill to build a house; the house certainly does not pass to him, since he has it. Similarly, the builder does not lack a shoemaker, nor vice versa; since both are men, and they both are perfect in their humanity. Similarly, the house does not lack a sandal, nor vice versa; because they are both supplying the need. But the builder lacks the sandal, since he does not have it; and correspondingly, the shoemaker lacks the house. If, then, the exchange happens due to the need, it shall happen not via the sides of the square, but via the diagonal. We put this description in four points, that are the points of the disjointed proportion; but, below, we shall demonstrate it in three, that are the points of the continued proportion, so that the knowledge shall be more complete according to both proportions. In fact, according to this description, it is necessary that the builder gets the goods from the shoemaker, and vice versa the builder shall reimburse the shoemaker according to what reciprocity is owed by the same shoemaker; because, otherwise, it will not be corresponding in terms of labor and expenses. If, therefore, first shall be the thing that in such an exchange is equal, stipulated or judged according to proportionality; then the reciprocity shall occur; and the city is saved and endures. We call the prior action a purchase by a fair price, and that which happens next we call the payment of the price. If this does not take place in these exchanges, the equality of the proportion is not preserved; since it has not been preserved, the city will not endure, since

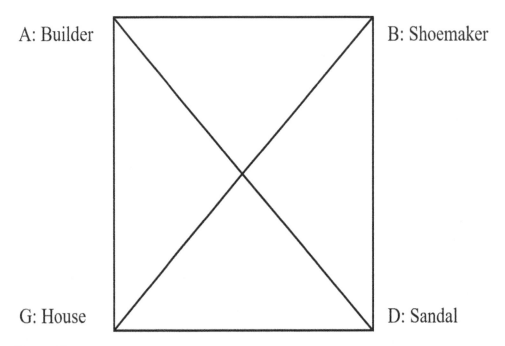

A: Builder   B: Shoemaker

G: House   D: Sandal

Figure 4.1

it is not repaid for its labor and expenses. As a matter of fact, like Eustratius says, there is no exchange of the city in which every citizen does the same thing, because, if everyone did the same thing, everyone would have what all others have, and all would be the same. But the human need requires many things and very different ones that cannot be acquired by just one person; it is, then, necessary that many things are produced by many people. Therefore, Tullius says that the city is built like a human body: in the human body, even if there is only one ruler, that is the heart, there are many operating parts that are assigned various tasks which cannot be carried out by just one part, and the parts help one another by reciprocal favors, and so the body endures in its consistency. In these occasions, there is nothing that prevents the work of one person from being better than the work of another person, and from having a big difference according to labor and expenses. But the exchange does not happen unless there is equality of the proportion. Hence, it is necessary to equalize to the proportion those things that are different. But this principle is present also in all mechanic arts; in reality, everyone would perish, if the person who does a contract did not receive what was promised in the contract. Actually, the city cannot be made of only one kind of artisan. As a matter of fact, there is no exchange between two doctors, but rather between a doctor and a farmer; and, universally speaking, the exchange happens between two totally different artisans, and not those who perform the same work. But it is necessary that those are equalized in some way; that is, because the exchange does not happen unless by the equality of proportion. But it is not possible to proportionate those who aim at the same thing; truly, the line does not have any value for the proportion; and if they are taken so, per se, as the substance of the bed and the substance of the house, they can never be proportionate. Therefore, it is necessary that those things shall be taken not as absolute, but as comparable, according to the value of need, as otherwise there shall be no exchange of these things. In this manner, those who need something and those who have something to offer may meet at the same point; as a result the equality of the proportion may be achieved.

Since those things are juxtaposed with regard to the comparison of their value according to the need for them and their usefulness, money has been invented, because it is the measure of everything, by its number, through its addition and its subtraction; and then, equally, money becomes the intermediary, according to which all the other things are measured. In reality, money measures everything. It measures overabundance and scarcity; and it is measured with the help of money, which measures how many sandals are equivalent to the house that the builder exchanges, and which is equivalent to food, the bushel of wheat, or something else that is exchanged due to the need of food. In this proportion, however, it is necessary, just like the builder gives his labor and the expenses of his work to the shoemaker according to the excess, that a specific amount of sandals, and additional money, are exchanged for a house or food; for a house if it is purchased from the builder, for food if it is purchased from the farmer. If this rule is not observed, there shall be no exchange nor a dealing between the shoemaker and the builder or the farmer; there shall be no exchange unless, in this part, the goods are brought to the equality of the proportion. But they will not be proportionate, unless they are measured in one way, as has been previously mentioned, because they are not proportional per se. Thus, it is necessary that all the things that can be exchanged are measured in some way.

This concept that we call work or need (demand) has been accepted as truth by everyone. Some people, instead, call it use or utility. In fact, this work provides everything that enables us to survive and live in the city. In truth, if nobody needed anything reciprocally in their works, or if nobody lacked similarly, so that, for example, the work of just one person seemed necessary, while the work of someone else seemed not, unless if it were enjoyable for games, there would be no exchange, or there would not be the one that we previously stated; since a thing is exchanged for a thing according to its value, that is according to necessity, thanks to the opposite sides of the proportion when we compare work to work, money is invented. This concept is demonstrated in this way because in this way it takes this name of money.

As a matter of fact, it is called *numisma* not by its nature, since it is made of gold or silver or any other metal, but from the Greek word *nomos*, that is a measure through a number. But this measure is regulated by us, just like an arm is instituted as a measure of cloth, and a barrel as a measure of oil, and a bushel as a measure of wheat; and there are no things that could be measured by themselves; in all these cases we have the faculty of adding and subtracting in order to precisely know the quantity of the measured object. But, with regard to money, we also have the faculty to easily exchange the money for everything that we need. Therefore, the concept that is called reciprocity is just and may be performed when it is equalized by the value of the money: just like the shoemaker compares the builder, so the work of the shoemaker has the same value as the work of the farmer; and as we mentioned before, when these things are exchanged, in that they go from one person to the other, it is necessary that they are brought back proportionally, as has been demonstrated on the square and diagonals in Figure 4.2. As, for example, the farmer to the food, likewise the shoemaker to the sandal, according to the need of the population; and as the farmer to the shoemaker, likewise the food to the sandal, by the same way of need. And as the farmer has himself an association with the food, so does the shoemaker with the sandal; in fact, these both happen via the exchange of the work that is called use or utility. And along the diagonals, like the dealing of the farmer with the sandal, so

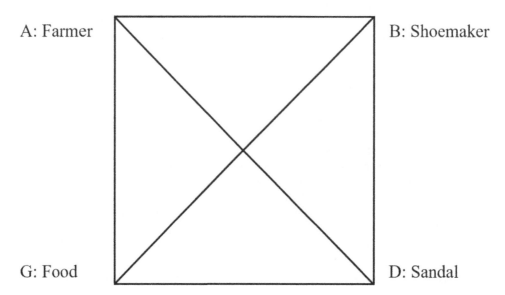

Figure 4.2

occurs the dealing of the shoemaker with the food; and in both cases, the need is catered to by both: this is called the image of proportionality.

But, as we said, work contains all the things that can be exchanged, and we also said that work is utility or demand, we did not talk about the things that can be exchanged by the fact that each one is taken for what it really is; truly, each object is not measured by the value of its nature. But, as we stated before, it is necessary to take it according to its utility, that is, how much it is worth to satisfy the need when used; actually, in such a way, everything is just one thing: and thereby it may be measured in one way, because the measure is not based on the nature of all things, but on their position. Then, this is called money. If, in fact, the things exchanged are not measured in this way, inconveniences would occur, for example the exchangers will both have surpluses and shortages: the farmer, that does not want anything but a sandal, in exchange for a bushel of wheat, without the equalization of the money, will have an overabundance in labor and expense since he is a farmer; but he will have a shortage in the reciprocity, the sandals that are less valuable. On the other hand, the shoemaker, receiving food, will have both excellences: in reality, he has an overabundance of food, because he receives more than he gives back; in fact, the farmer and the work of the farmer, in his labor and expenses, exceeds the shoemaker and his work. Thus, the shoemaker, receiving the work of the farmer, exceeds him; but giving a sandal in return, he is found wanting. Hence, since these things, before the exchange, are not proportionate, it is necessary that they will be made proportionate by money, provided both can be exchanged. This way, if each and every person can produce something, by the value of their work they are equal and able to exchange recip-rocally: in fact, this equality can happen in these cases: let us say that the farmer is represented by A and, under him, food by G, the shoemaker by B and his equalized work by D, and let the lines and the diagonals be drawn like it has been done in Figure 4.3.

A: Farmer 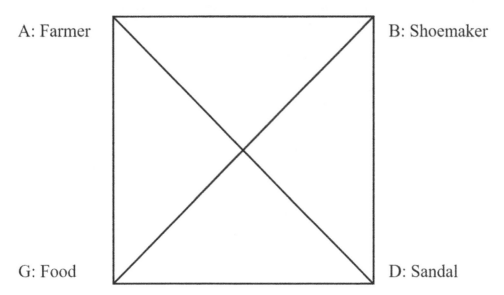 B: Shoemaker

G: Food   D: Sandal

Figure 4.3

If it is not equalized in this way, there shall be no true reciprocity. If, then, there is no reciprocity, there shall be no exchange.

For the fact that work, like one entity, in all these cases contains all the things that can be exchanged, it is represented in this way: since both artisans, or just one of them, are not reciprocally in need, they will not exchange goods, but each one will keep what he has produced for his own sake. Reciprocal need, however, occurs when one needs a thing that the other person owns (produces), and vice versa. For example, when one person lacks wine and the other person has it, he gives a measure of wheat that is in overabundance, so that he shall make an exchange of wheat for wine, and so it is necessary that the things that can be exchanged shall be equalized in some way. And since they are not exchanged unless there is necessity, but the necessity is various, it is necessary that the thing, with regard to which every exchange happens, supplies for all needs, be they present or future ones. In fact, often exchanges happen as a supply for a future necessity even for those who now do not lack anything in this moment. And this supply is money, since it is our guarantee for every necessity when we lack something. Actually, for the person who possesses money through a civil statute, it is necessary that he takes, in money, everything that he does not have.

Money, however, is not always equal, but sometimes goes above and is worth more; after that it is worth less or, by chance, it loses value; and, for that, it is not a guarantee of future necessities. Among the things that are in exchange, money remains more stable.

Therefore, it is a necessity that all the things that can be exchanged must be measured by money: thus, there always will be an exchange. If there is an exchange, a deal always succeeds. In reality, the money equalizes the things that can be exchanged, like the measure equalizes the measured things through addition and subtraction. In fact, we already said that if there is no exchange of goods, there shall not be any exchange of citizens. There cannot be an exchange of goods that have not been reduced to equality of proportion. There cannot be equality, however, without a measurement. But there cannot be a measurement without the proportion of the measurer. This is, then, necessary, for it is necessary to find, first and foremost, a measurer of things that can be exchanged.

Thus, by the veracity of the nature of each of these things, due to the difference in their nature, it is nearly impossible that all these things would be measured according to just one criterion which would be the measure of all things: because in this way each thing will not be measured according to its nature. Because of need, then, it is mandatory that all the things that can be exchanged shall be sufficiently measured in one way. Therefore, there shall be one measure of all the related things to one: and if they cannot be compared by their nature, it is necessary that they shall be compared by the institution of the law. Consequently, the money is named *nomos*, that is measure or rule. In fact, as a first and universal thing it measures all the things that can be exchanged, because all the things are measured via addition and subtraction. For example, let a house worth 5 *mina* be represented by A; let a bed worth 1 *mina* be represented by B. Then, the bed shall be the fifth part of the house not by its nature, but by the value of money. It will be immediately clear how many beds are equal to a house, because five beds, after four beds are added to a single one, can be exchanged for a house. Because there was, then, this exchange among citizens, that, for example, two or three things were exchanged for one more valuable thing, before money was invented, by this way of dealing, it is evident that exchange was the reason money was invented; because in this exchange it does not change if five beds are exchanged for a house, or if the price of five beds is given for the house. So, then, what is just and unjust has been determined by us. This image is accordingly described, so that it shall be among the three terms of the continued proportion, for example that the value of the house shall be A, the value of the bed G, B, instead, is the money in the middle, by which those things will be reduced to equality. This is in numbers: five, four and one. Thus, in this way, B, C, G, that is four, by one are equalized to five: in this way, the abundance of five is reduced to equality of one, having had a middle part added.

5.   Albert the Great: Commentary on Aristotle's *Politics* (c. 1263)[1]

First, Aristotle discusses the question whether money-making (wealth-getting) and household-management are the same thing (as some people thought). In the second part, he shows that money is an element and object of exchange, and describes household-management. In the third part, based on previous definitions, he concludes that money-making is not the same as household-management, as is well known, and as it was doubted from the beginning. The chapter ends at this point.

He takes up the first issue, saying that there is an activity or ability which it is rational to call money-making. It seems to Solon that there is no limit to wealth or possession. As he later says, there is no limit for wealth, for desire does not have boundaries. And he clarifies the issue and its reason, saying that money-making naturally complements household-management, as many think. Both activities furnish the necessary means to live and to prosper. As activities that serve to the same end, they are certainly similar. Money-making, like household-management, serves to support a family, to live, and to thrive. Because of this connection, the two terms are close to each other.

And he immediately adds a definition to the issue, even if he seems to offer a better definition later. And in this definition he makes a twofold distinction: thus, first he defines the barter exchange that was once used to trade things between people. Then he defines the exchange that was used after money was invented. He divides the first part into four. First, he explains the principle that was employed in this kind of exchange transaction. Then he explains the exchange that occurred in houses existing at that time. In the third part, he discusses the exchange that was made in cities existing at that time. In the fourth part, he explains why money was introduced.

He immediately adds a solution to the problem. He differentiates money-making and household-management, saying they are not the same, but also not far from each other. And he adds a distinction of one from the other: thus, household-management is natural and appointed to uphold nature. It is natural and derived from nature. Money-making is not natural and is not derived from natural activity, but came into practice from experiment and craft, that is daily practice. It is not natural for humans to wish to gain money. They want money for other things, in order to obtain products necessary for the household, as it is said in the *Ethics*: "money is loved because it is a supplier of future needs."

Then he proposes a general rule that should be proved by the fact that money multiplies by craft and experiment, and not in a natural manner. He proposes a general rule, saying: if a certain thing has a double usage, or utility, and both of the usages or utilities of the thing are

---

[1]   Translation produced by Edward W. Fuller.

derived from its nature, but are not similarly derived from it, then the first usage is concordant with the natural purpose of the thing; the second one, however, is not concordant with the natural purpose. For instance, the purpose of footwear is to cover feet. There is the second usage of footwear: for the sake of trade. Shoes may be exchanged for money of a certain value, or wheat, or wine, or something else essential, and they may be exchanged with someone who has an excess of wheat, wine, or money but needs shoes. Thus, this is the use of shoes not according to their natural purpose, because the shoes are not made for this purpose, but for the sake of covering feet. And he adds, this is why we talk about the double usage of footwear: for the purpose of covering feet and for exchange. For indeed, one who lacks shoes acquires them for money. Money is the measure of every value, as it is said in the fifth book of the *Ethics*. And he adds the reason for this, saying: thus, the shoes are not made for the sake of exchange, but to be used according to their natural purpose. It is the same case with all the other items of possession, such as pastries, bread, woven fabrics, and everything else. And all of them have a double use, one consistent with their nature, but one not consistent with their natural purpose.

And he adds that the exchange of goods, which pertains to household-management, is in all these things. As he says, trade and exchange occur everywhere. Then he explains how the exchange of goods between humans came into being, saying that it arose from what was natural; it was appointed to secure living, and well-being. Then he adds the reason why goods need to be exchanged, saying that some people had an excess of things, such as wine or shoes, they had more of those things than sufficient, but they did not have enough of other goods, and for this reason they wanted to exchange the things they had in excess for those they lacked. This is, then, the primary reason barter exchange came into being. And clearly, monetary exchange developed out of barter. The one that is an exchange of money for money, this kind of exchange is not natural because it does not serve to ensure living and well-being. This also is not why money was invented, since it was invented as the measure of value of the things that pertained to living and well-being, and not in order to be exchanged for money.

And then he shows the course of these things in the exchange between people. He says, in the first exchange, that is the economic exchange that pertains to the household matters, it is worthy of consideration what was not, in fact, its object. Since those who inhabited the same house, shared the same goods, and had the same occupation, they did not have to exchange anything, neither goods, nor money. But exchange was taking place on a larger scale, between one house and another, one man and another, one city and another, and even between those who lived in suburbs, a city, or a house, and were producing many goods, were exchanging in their surrounding the excess of things they produced for those things they needed but lacked. Thus those, that is those living apart, that had the excess of some things but lacked other ones, exchanged their own goods for products they accepted as their own. Because of such an exchange, it was necessary to establish payments according to the demand, on an arithmetic basis, as is noted in the fifth book of *Ethics*. Such an exchange occurs on the principle of equivalence and agreement, and "if the repayment does not follow on the basis of equivalence and agreement, they turn to court," as Aristotle says in the fifth book of *Ethics*. He is predisposed towards justice. And adds that when people started to exchange goods with each other, they exchanged things of equal value, and the things they exchanged pertained to living and well-being, as is still the case among many barbarians who exchange goods for goods because they do not use currency.

Such is this kind of barter exchange, of things for things, that nothing else is exchanged apart from the most necessary things. Money does not belong to the things that are most necessary for survival. Its purpose is to obtain the essentials, not multiplication of money. He also adds, naming the reason for this state of things, that the supplementation is consistent with nature. Nature itself appointed those things as necessary to survive, which is to say that exchange resulted in sufficiency. Since things that were in abundance were exchanged for things that were lacking, in this manner, sufficiency for living and well-being was achieved in the end.

However, from this natural and definite barter exchange another kind was created that is not natural, but one that rather serves to exchange goods for money according to reason and law, in that the essentials are exchanged for money. And he narrates how it happened: as the number of people in villas and cities was increasing, people needed means to travel, to pay for the toils of their journeys and the dangers on the roads. Also people needed money to pay taxes, which were needed by the people who collected them, which were also needed to be sent in exchange to people who were abundant in them. And from the necessity of these acquisitions the use of money arose, because money travels back and forth with ease, and is a measure of all value, as well as a supplier for the future needs. And he adds the reason for this, saying that all the things that are necessary according to their nature—such as wheat, wine, wool, and the like—are not easy to transport the far distances between lands. Money was created because of this need to exchange all necessary products. People created it on the basis of an agreement between each other, so that they could give and receive whatever they needed in order to live and thrive. And he names the following reason, saying that money had a feature that was very convenient, since there was a need to measure all exchangeable things according to their usefulness for life and well-being. And he gives an example on metals, saying: imagine everything may be exchanged for iron, silver, gold, copper, and alloys. Then he demonstrates the history of the metal's monetary use over time, adding: first, they were simple bullion, that is without any imprinted image or stamp, and exchanged only on the basis of their size and weight. Then, however, when it turned out that it is not always possible to weigh them, they started to furnish coins with images and stamps, since it was necessary that they freed themselves from the measure of weight, as it was hindering the exchange: the symbol, however, that is an image or stamp, was placed on a coin, to indicate its quantity and purity of metal, as it was known how many coins made up a *marcha*, and how many *marchae* made up a *libra*, and how many *librae* made up the value of this or that thing.

Once the history of exchange before the invention of money used for exchanges, purchases, and sales has been presented, he shows the fate of exchange after the invention of money, which is both unnatural and infinite. It is unnatural, because it belongs to things which are not appointed to sustain nature, and infinite, because it is used to satisfy desire, which is in itself infinite. And this is what he says, stating that once money was established, which is the measure of everything's value, and a supplier of every future need, from the necessary exchange, which people need in order to exchange superfluous goods for the necessary ones they lack, then the other kind of exchange was established, which exchanges money for money, silverware for silver, golden things for gold. And, as he said, there is the progress of exchange, natural and definite. He demonstrates its development and raises three points: first, how it developed, and how it was practiced. Secondly, he shows in what way it is unnatural. Thirdly, he shows in what way it is infinite.

He says, therefore: the currency was invented to be the measure of value of everything that may be exchanged. And this is what he adds: there is necessary exchange, which people need in order to exchange superfluous goods for the necessary ones they lack. But the other kind of exchange, money for money, was established for the sake of its multiplication. Then he adds a remark about its development in the practice of people. First, therefore, it was done in a simple manner, one amount of money was exchanged for the same amount of money, as the Lord says (*Luke* 6:35): "lend, expecting nothing in return." Then for the practice, because obviously in the time they were exchanging, some were already able to save money, by means of experimentation, they began to artificially lend with interest—that is, less for more—in order to get compensated for their loan by receiving more: this is how they exchanged money. That is, they exchanged money for compensation and, as it is known from experience, interest amasses gain, and that is how money multiplied.

Because of this it seems to be an investigation into how money accumulation arose from lending, exchange, or any other manner: this is indeed the actual purpose of wealth and money.

And he referred to wealth, because it is much more concerned with real goods than with money. Many common people see wealth as a great amount of money, and think that wealthy people are those who own a great amount of money. Because of this, they think exchange is about money, and not about wheat, wine, and other things necessary to live and thrive. This is the opinion of common people.

And he immediately contradicts the common opinion. He says, a long time ago, when everything was judged by the wise according to the natural order, money seemed to be a nonsense, it seemed to be a luxury, as it was just a law, that is instituted by the law, and not by nature. And he adds the following as the reason for this state of things: because when the necessary goods were exchanged, first wheat, wine, wool, and other products necessary to survive, then people started to exchange money, which was not worth anything, that is money was not useful to anything necessary to live. And he adds another argument, saying that, often, a person with an abundance of money lacks the food necessary to survive. He obviously cannot use money as food, and he cannot organize the exchange of the necessary goods with money. Indeed, as common people say, and not without sense, it is exceedingly unbeneficial that there are such riches, as even having them in abundance, a rich man may die of hunger. Then he evokes an example from poetry, known from Ovid, and in Greek from Homer. As they say, Midas wished that everything he touched turned into gold, and when Jupiter granted him that wish, all the food that was given to him turned into gold after he touched it. He died from hunger, because gold cannot be used for survival.

Because of this, the wise, who are intent on keeping the natural order of things, who are searching for true riches, allow money to be used in exchange for goods. For according to them, money was invented to exchange goods that are necessary to live and not in order to multiply money. And this kind of wealth that serves to survive and thrive is compliant with nature and is economic—that is, it serves household-management. However, the exchange of money for money to multiply money is not at all concordant with nature. Although lawful, it is a desire to extend wealth by means of exchanging money for money, and not an exchange of goods necessary to live and prosper. To many it seems to be about the multiplication of money. As the Poet says: "Today the supreme ruler is money."

Then Aristotle adds this reason, saying: money is the object and limit of exchange, because it was instituted to be the measure of value of everything exchangeable.

And because the wealth acquired by commercial money-making concerns money, it is infinite. For there is no limit to acquisition. And he proves this statement by means of a comparison with arts. In every art the end is desirable, but an artisan does not designate the end to his art; he only desires it and his desire is infinite. For instance, the end of medical art is health, so the desire for health is infinite, but the artisan does not put an end to those means through which he may pursue the end. And he adds that although they want very much to reach the end, they do not put any limit on its attainment. And then he instantly adds in what manner the desire for other possessions that are necessary to live and prosper is limited. He says, all the things that have an appointed end, and are not infinite, end in sufficiency, that is when there is enough it is an end. This is why the end of wealth is infinite. The end of money-making for household-management is when a person and his family has sufficient means. And this is not the same as commercial money-making. For this reason, household-management is different than commercial money-making because its purpose is to provide sufficiency at home, which is also its end. Thus, household-management is finite, while commercial money-making is infinite.

And he concludes, adding: because of this, that is the sufficiency of possessions for the needs of a household, it seems that all the necessary wealth has an end. However, those who aim to increase their money holdings seem to act to the contrary. And he adds that all people who act on greed wish to infinitely increase their wealth, and instead of things for necessary use, they have coins, because money is the measure of the value of all things for necessary use, and because of this they want to infinitely increase their wealth.

Furthermore, the two types of money-making are close to each other in meaning. Nevertheless, they have different purposes. Even though both are used to provide sufficient means to live and prosper, and their purpose is acquisition, it is not in the same manner. And he adds a differentiation between the one and the other. The purpose of household money-making is the sufficiency of necessary goods to live and prosper and this is where the acquisition ends, while the purpose of commercial money-making is infinite acquisition, and because of this it does not have an end. For indeed, it seems that such people acquire not for the sake of usage but out of greed, and they always persist in acquiring, and save whatever they have acquired, and increase the money by new acquisitions, and so on forever.

And he adds the reason for this insatiable desire, saying: the reason for this disposition, that is the desire dictated by greed, is an effort to live and not an effort to live the good life. For indeed, very few things suffice to live the good life, while endless possessions only drive us towards living according to desire. And then he adds: thus, there is an infinite desire. They also say that (*Ecclesiastes* 5:10): "Whoever loves money never has money enough." On the other hand, they say: those people who strive to live the good life seek only that which is necessary to cater for the bodily needs, that is necessary to live, and these things are definite, and for this reason such possessions are definite. On this basis he concludes with regard to commercial money-making. Because commercial money-making for the sake of possession makes life about acquisition and money, they are driven by the desire to have money rather than the desire to live the good life.

Based on what was stated above, he concludes that there are two kinds of money-making: household and commercial. The former is natural and definite, while the latter is unnatural and infinite. Because of this the commercial activity tends towards excess, since it seeks the actual excess rather than the satisfaction of real needs. That is, such people seek overabundance to live according to desires, although not for money, with which they acquire things for another reason than natural usage, because they appoint everything they have to their gain, including virtues and sciences, in order to live according to desires. Because it is not the purpose of fortitude, and as well as other abilities and virtues pertaining to it, to multiply money, but the purpose of fortitude is courage. Fortitude is not the purpose of the military or medical sciences. Their main purpose is, respectively, military victory and bodily health. Nevertheless, all these arts and sciences also earn money. But like household money-making, they are definite, as there is an end to all skills and all their works. And for this final end they all head, as it is said (*Ecclesiastes* 10:19): "All things obey money." And also (*Sirach* 10:9): "Nothing is more wicked than one who loves money, for such a person puts his own soul up for sale."

And he adds an epilogue about which it is said that we suffer an infinite need. It is also said that household-management is concordant with nature, because it is about food sufficient to survive and live well. And since what is about food is concordant with nature, it is not infinite but has an end. This is not true for commercial money-making.

Then he comes back to the question posed at the very beginning, whether commercial money-making is a part of household-management or politics. He solves it in the following manner: now it is clear on the basis of what has been said to which of the two, politics or household-management, money-making belongs. And he gives a reason that does not pertain to anything related to household-management or politics. Whatever is given or accepted, is the object of household-management which, however, does not produce those things, because it is not the purpose of household-management to make them. But it uses money, given or acquired. For this reason, money-making, which is the acquisition of money, does not belong to household-management, but it is necessary that the money and other supplies useful for household-management are produced by the commercial money-makers for the sake of other skills and activities, which then may be used by a household-manager.

And he demonstrates this by making two comparisons, one related to nature, the other to art. The comparison with nature introduces two further terms: a comparison with politics, as politics that subordinates citizens to justice does not "produce" them, but takes ready ones produced by nature and adjusts them by means of laws and social norms to the form defined by justice, and this is how it uses ready humans. And this is what he says: politics does not make men, but uses the ones already made by nature, and shapes them with laws and rules. And he instantly evokes the second comparison with nature. In the same way it is necessary to naturally obtain the food used by the household-manager to feed the family from earth or sea, or something else, as was demonstrated in the previous chapter, because people and animals take food from different sources, as he says in his book on *Animals* that "certain animal species thrive in the places that abound in their food." The household-manager is thus responsible for serving food and other necessary goods to the family, but not its acquisition. The household-manager only predicts what will be needed and then uses it as his instruments in arranging the household. And he proves it by means of a comparison with arts, referring to art with the obvious example of textiles: for indeed textile art is not tasked with producing wool, but with using it, and it takes wool from another source. It is, however, the task of textile art to recognize whether the wool is useful and suitable, or whether it is inferior and unsuitable. And likewise, it is the task of the housekeeper to recognize what is useful and suitable, and what is inferior and unsuitable in supplying the family, that is in providing them with food, clothes, and other necessary goods. On the basis of the arguments stated above, it is clear that commercial money-making is not a part of household-management, but provides the things that are useful to the housekeeper in managing the house.

To make the solution more convincing, he introduces another question. Someone may believe money-making is a part of household-management, while medical art is not. And then he evokes an argument in favor of the contrary, which is: it is necessary to heal those who are at home, otherwise they will not be able to make an exchange. In other words, it is necessary that they have something that is useful to others, without which the exchange will not be possible. And he at once proceeds to the solution, solving it through a distinction. He asks: how are health and politics related to household-management? The politician and the house-keeper should provide the necessary means so that a doctor can uphold the family in health, and cure the sick. In this way, medicine is related to the politician and housekeeper. But the doctor, who recognizes the causes of illnesses and cures them, should use both purgative and alternative medicine. And medicine is, in turn, useful to the politician and housekeeper. They must employ the doctor to provide cures. By means of this solution, he confirms the solution of the main question, adding: the same is true about money-making. In one way it pertains to the housekeeper, but in another way it does not pertain to him, but to the subservient means, which he manages, such as food and other necessary goods.

And he proves it: the things used by the housekeeper existed naturally. And he adds the reason for it. Nature should produce food in such quantity, so that it could be easily found, as has already been said, both in viviparous as well as oviparous animals. There are indeed things that provide food for themselves. In other words, there are things which are arranged in the way that they have food, such as egg yolk or cow milk. And similarly, it is necessary to have a housekeeper who would use goods and distribute them to the family. And the money-making activity is compatible with the nature of everything that derives from fruit or animals, since money was invented for the sake of exchange between buyer and seller. Money was not invented for the sake of money multiplication, which is not consistent with the nature of money. Instead, it is an aberration induced by human greed that often impedes good associ-ation between citizens and inhabitants of households.

And he adds a distinction of activities that are called money-making: for there are two kinds of it, as has already been said. One involves exchanging money for money, and this is not the purpose for which money was invented. The other kind involves exchanging money for food and clothes and other necessary goods that are of use to a housekeeper, and for this purpose money was invented. And he names the properties of both, saying: the one that exchanges money for necessary goods according to nature is essential and praiseworthy. The other one, however, that is the one that converts money into money, is justly censored. And he adds the reason why it is censored: for indeed the exchange of money for money is unnatural, because it does not convert money into naturally necessary things. This was demonstrated with the example of King Midas, who, having turned everything he was provided with into gold, died from hunger. So this kind of exchange differs from the other one. And he adds another reason to attack the exchange of money for money. Usury is reasonably despised. Usury is the mutual establishment and acquisition of money. Usury creates money, and does not result in the acqui-sition of any goods. As Augustine says in his book, *Of the Good of Marriage*, "money takes its name from cattle (*pecunia*), because it was initially invented for the sake of purchasing cattle." But because, as has already been said, it was difficult to exchange one thing for another, money was invented, which is the measure of value of all exchangeable things. Afterwards, however, greed transfigured the nature of this exchange, and the exchange of money for money began, for which purpose it was not invented. So usury was born. Usury is a sort of profit that relies on unnatural exchange. In Greek it is called *tokos*, which in Latin means birth. And this is what he adds: it multiplies by itself within its kind—that is, money bears money. This is where the name *tokos* originates. And he adds a reason: similar births occur among some species. And he adds a further explanation: it is called *tokos* because money is created from money.

And he concludes all of this with a proposal that this kind of usury should not be a part of household-management, because such an acquisition is inconsistent with nature.

6.   Thomas Aquinas: Commentary on Aristotle's *Nicomachean Ethics* (c. 1271)[1]

We must say that, in regard to justice in exchange, there should always be an equality of thing to thing, not, however, of action and passion, which implies corresponding requital. But in this, proportionality must be employed in order to bring about an equality of things because the work of one craftsman is of more value than the work of another, e.g., the building of a house than the production of a penknife. Hence, if the builder exchanged his work for the work of the cutler, there would not be equality of thing, given and taken, i.e., of house and penknife.

Then, he proves his statement, saying that justice in exchanges includes reciprocation according to proportionality. This can be shown by the fact that the citizens live together amicably because they have proportionate kindliness towards one another. Accordingly, if one does something for another, the other is anxious to do something in proportion in return. Obviously, all citizens desire that reciprocation be done to them proportionately. By reason of this all men can live together because they do for one another what they themselves seek. Therefore, they never seek in regard to evil that corresponding requital be done to them proportionately. But if they do not seek this in regard to evil, for example, when one man does not take vengeance on another who injures him, a kind of servility seems to result. Indeed it is servile when a man cannot gain by his own activity something that he does not desire in an evil way.

We may even say that men not only do not desire that corresponding requital, when unjust, be done to them proportionately, but they do not desire that it be done when just. In this way if corresponding requital is not done them in a proportionate way, proper retribution will not be effected. But men live together because one makes a return to another for the favors he has received. So it is that virtuous men promptly express gratitude to their benefactors as if it were a sacred duty to make them a return in this way; repaying a favor is characteristic of gratitude. It is fitting that a man should be of service to one who has done him a favor, i.e., bestowed a gratuitous kindness, and that he be not content to give only as much as he received but that in return he begins to offer more than he got so that he himself may do a favor.

Next, he makes known the form of proportionality according to which reciprocation ought to be made. First he gives an example in the shoemaker and the builder; then he shows that the same is found in other arts. He says first that a conjunction by means of a diagonal shows how to make compensation or reciprocation according to proportionality. To understand this draw A, B, G, and D, make two diagonals intersecting one another, viz., AD and BG. Let A represent a builder, B a shoemaker, G a house that is the work of the builder, and D a sandal that is the work of a shoemaker (Figure 6.1). It is necessary at times that the builder should take

[1]   Translated by C.I. Litzinger.

from the shoemaker his product, a sandal. But the builder himself ought to give his product as a recompense to the shoemaker.

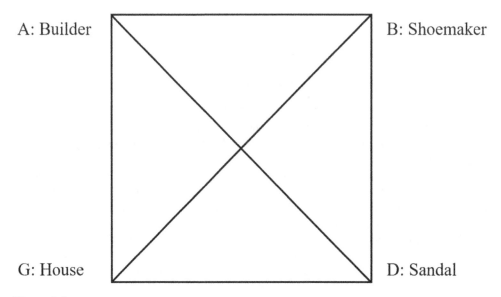

A: Builder　　　　　　　　　　　　　　　　　　B: Shoemaker

G: House　　　　　　　　　　　　　　　　　　D: Sandal

Figure 6.1

Therefore, if first an equality according to proportionality is found so that on one side a certain number of sandals be fixed as equal to one house (for a builder incurs more expense in building one house than a shoemaker in making one sandal), next, corresponding reciprocation is had so that the builder may receive many sandals equal to one house and the shoemaker one house, there will be recompense—as was said—made according to proportion by a diagonal conjunction.

The reason is that a proportionate number of sandals are given to the builder, and the house to the shoemaker. But if compensation is not made in this way, there will not be an equality of things exchanged—and so men will not be able to live together—since nothing hinders the work of one craftsman from being worth more than the work of another, a house than a sandal. For this reason these things must be equated one with the other according to the previously mentioned proportionality, so that a just exchange may take place.

Then he shows that the same thing is found in the other arts. He affirms that what was said about the builder and the shoemaker must be observed also in the other arts, so that reciprocation and exchange may take place according to diagonal proportionality. Indeed the arts would be destroyed if a workman did not receive according to the quantity and quality of what he produced—a thing that must be discovered in the way indicated. It is not common for men practicing one art, for example, two doctors, to exchange their work with one another, but very often men practicing different arts do, for instance, a doctor and a farmer, both entirely different and unequal. These must be equated in the preceding way.

After Aristotle has proposed the form of proportionality, with which reciprocation is identified in exchange, he now shows in what way this form of proportionality can be observed. First he explains his intention. Then he clarifies the previous statements. He discusses the initial point in a twofold manner. First, he shows that to preserve the form of proportionality perfectly it is necessary to make everything commensurate. Next, he explains how a just reciprocation in exchanges may be effected by a commensuration of this kind. He treats the first point under three aspects. Initially he explains the nature of that which measures all things. Then he shows how such a commensuration is established in exchanges. Last, he indicates the nature of this commensuration.

He says first, in order that the products of the different workmen be equated and thus become possible to exchange, it is necessary that all things capable of exchange should be comparable in some way with one another so that it can be known which of them has greater value and which less. It was for this purpose that money or currency was invented, to measure the price of such things. In this way currency becomes a medium inasmuch as it measures everything, both excess and defect, to the extent that one thing exceeds another, as was pointed out before. It is a mean of justice—as if someone should call it a measure of excess and defect.

Next, he shows how exchange takes place according to the preceding commensuration. Although a house is worth more than a sandal, nevertheless, a number of sandals are equal in value to one house or the food required for one man during a long period. In order then to have just exchange, as many sandals must be exchanged for one house or for the food required for one man as the builder or the farmer exceeds the shoemaker in his labor and costs. If this is not observed, there will be no exchange of things and men will not share their goods with one another. But what has been said, that a number of sandals are exchanged for one house, is not possible unless the sandals are equated with the house in some way.

He indicates the nature of this commensuration made by means of money. He states that for this reason it is possible to equate things because all things can be measured by some one standard, as was pointed out. But this one standard which truly measures all things is demand. This includes all exchangeable things inasmuch as everything has a reference to human need. Articles are not valued according to the dignity of their nature, otherwise a mouse, an animal endowed with sense, should be of greater value than a pearl, a thing without life. But they are priced according as man stands in need of them for his own use.

An indication of this is that if men were not in need there would be no exchange, or if they did not have a similar need, i.e., of these things, exchange would not be the same because men would not exchange what they have for something they did not need. That demand really measures everything is evident from the fact that money originated by arrangement or a kind of agreement among men on account of the necessity of exchange, i.e., exchange of necessary goods. There is an agreement among men that what a person needs will be given him in exchange for currency. Hence currency is called money (*numisma*)—nomos means law— since currency is not a measure by nature but by law (*nomos*). It is in our power to change currencies and make them useless.

Then he shows how just reciprocation takes place in exchanges according to the preceding commensuration. First, he explains his proposition; and then he puts it in a diagram. He says first that the norm measuring all things by need according to nature and by currency according to human convention will then become reciprocation when everything will be equated in the way just mentioned. This is done in such a manner as the farmer (whose work is raising food for men) excels the shoemaker (whose work is making sandals), in the same proportion the work of the shoemaker exceeds in number the work of the farmer, so that many sandals are exchanged for one bushel of wheat. Thus when exchange of things takes place, the articles to be exchanged ought to be arranged in a proportional figure with diagonals, as was stated previously. If this was not done, one extreme would have both excesses; if a farmer gave a bushel of wheat for a sandal, he would have a surplus of labor in his product and would have also an excess of loss because he would be giving more than he would receive. But when all have what is theirs, they are in this way equal and do business with one another because the equality previously mentioned is possible for them.

Next, he puts in a diagram what has been said about the proportional figure. Take then (as in the previous example) a square A, B, G, D, and two diagonals AD and BG intersecting one another. Let A represent the farmer and G the food, his product, e.g., a bushel of wheat. Let B represent the shoemaker and D his equated product, i.e., as many sandals as have the value of a bushel of wheat. There will then be a just reciprocation if A is joined with D and B with G (Figure 6.2). If there is not such a compensation men will not share their goods with one another.

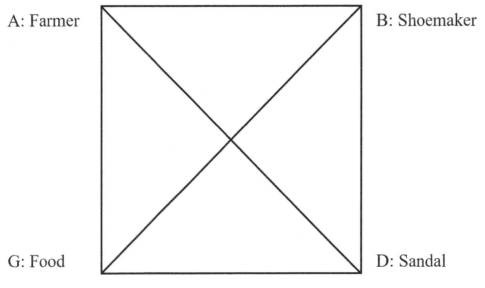

Figure 6.2

He explains more fully what has already been mentioned. First he shows how things are made commensurate; and next how the things made commensurate may be exchanged. He discusses the first point from two aspects. First, he shows that necessity is a measure according to reality; and then how currency is a measure according to the provision of law. He says first the statement that human need contains everything as a certain measure is explained in this way. When men are so situated among themselves that either both, or at least one, do not need a thing possessed by the other, they do not engage in mutual exchange. But exchange does take place when a man owning grain is in need of wine which his neighbor has, and thus gives the grain for the wine, so that a quantity of grain is allotted according to the value of the wine.

Then he shows clearly how currency serves as a measure. On this point we must consider that if men always needed immediately the goods they have among themselves, they would have no need of any exchange except of thing for thing, e.g., wine for grain. But sometimes one man (who has a surplus of wine at present) does not need the grain that another man has (who is in need of wine), but perhaps later he will need the grain or some other product. In this way then for the necessity of future exchange, money or currency is, as it were, a surety that if a man has no present need but may want in the future, the thing he needs will be available when he presents the currency.

The particular virtue of currency must be that when a man presents it he immediately receives what he needs. However, it is true that currency also suffers the same as other things, viz., that it does not always obtain for a man what he wants because it cannot always be equal or of the same value. Nevertheless it ought to be so established that it retains the same value more permanently than other things.

Next, he explains how, by the measure of currency, there is exchange of things which are made commensurate in currency. He discusses this point from three aspects. First he shows in what manner there is exchange of goods that are measured in currency. Then, he discloses under what aspect currency serves as a measure. Last, he puts in terminals what was said. He states first that, because currency as a measure ascertaining quantity retains its value longer, all goods must be evaluated in currency. In this way exchange of goods can take place and, consequently, association among men. Money equates exchangeable goods, as a certain measure making them commensurate. He clarifies what has been said by stating that association is not possible if there is no exchange. But exchange is impossible unless an equality is established in goods, which in turn cannot exist without commensuration.

Then he shows in what way currency is used as a measure. He says that it is impossible that things so greatly different be made commensurate according to reality, i.e., according to the peculiar nature of the things themselves. But they can be sufficiently contained under one measure by comparison with the needs of men. Hence there must be some one criterion that measures all things of this kind and is not a measure by reason of nature but because so fixed by men. Therefore, this is called money owing to the fact that it makes all things commensurate insofar as they are measured by money.

He explains in terminals what has been said, stating: let A be a house worth five *minae*, B a bed worth one *mina*, and in this way the bed will be one fifth the value of the house. Hence it is obvious how many beds are equal in value to one house, viz., five. Likewise it is obvious that barter took place before there was currency, since five beds have been exchanged for one house. But it makes no difference whether five or the value of five beds are given.

7.   Thomas Aquinas: Commentary on Aristotle's *Politics* (c. 1272)[1]

After Aristotle has determined about one kind of acquiring property (i.e., acquiring food and other necessities of life), he here determines about another kind of acquiring property called money-making (wealth-getting). And regarding this, he does two things. First, he lays out its condition. Second, he determines about it. Regarding the first, he determines three things about the second kind of acquiring property. For he first determines its name, saying that we call it money-making, namely, because it consists of acquiring money. Second, he says that, since there is no limit to acquiring money, it seems to human beings that, because of the second kind of acquiring property, there is no limit to the wealth and acquisition of property they may acquire. For many think that this way of acquiring property is one and the same as the first kind of acquiring property, because of their close association. Third, he lays out the relation of this kind of acquiring property to the first kind, saying that it is neither the same as, nor far different from, the first kind. And he shows that it is not the same because the first kind of acquiring property (i.e., acquiring food and other necessities of life) is natural, and the second kind (i.e., acquiring money) is not. For nature did not invent money, but experience and skill introduced it. And so he said that the two kinds are not far apart, since one can possess even the necessities of life for the sake of money, and vice versa.

Then he begins to determine the nature of money-making. And since money was invented to facilitate exchanges, he does three things regarding this. First, he shows how exchange is related to the things exchanged. Second, he determines about natural exchange. Third, he determines about monetary exchange. Therefore, he says first that, in order to consider money-making, we should begin as follows. Each thing has two uses, which are the same in that each use is of the thing as such and not incidental to another use, but differ in that one use is the proper use of the thing, and the other is a common rather than a proper use. For example, shoes have two uses. One use is proper, namely as covering for the feet, since shoes were made for this use. The other use, namely, exchange, is not proper, since shoes were not made in order that human beings exchange them for something else. But human beings can use shoes in exchange for bread or food. And using shoes in exchange, although not a proper use of shoes, nonetheless uses them as such and not as incidental to another use, since the one who exchanges them uses them according to their worth. And as he has said about shoes, so should we understand about all other things that human beings can own.

Then he determines about natural exchange, doing three things in that regard. First, he shows of what things this exchange consists. Second, he shows how it was introduced. Third, he shows how it is related to nature. Therefore, he says first that all things can be exchanged.

---

[1]   Translated by Richard J. Regan.

And the first exchange was of things that nature bestows for the necessities of human life, since some people have more of these things and others less (e.g., some have more wine, and others more bread). And so human beings needed to exchange such things until each had what was sufficient for each. (And so it is clear that, since money is not from nature, as he has said, commerce (i.e., exchange of money) is not from nature.)

Then he shows how this exchange of necessary things was introduced. He says that there was no need of such exchange in the first association (i.e., an individual household), since all the necessities of life belonged to the head of the household, who provided everything. But when there was a larger association, namely, a neighborhood or political community, those of the same household, among whom there could be no exchange, shared in all things, and those of separate households shared in many other things as well. Therefore, there needed to be exchanges of different things, namely, that if one were to receive from another what the other had, the latter would recompense the former with what the latter had. And many foreign peoples who do not use money still practice barter, and they exchange only things that are advantageous for life (e.g., giving and receiving wine, wheat, and the like).

Then he infers from the foregoing that such exchanges are not contrary to nature, since they concern things that nature provides. And it is not a kind of money-making, since it is not transacted by the use of money. And he proves that it is not contrary to nature, since it supplies self-sufficiency (i.e., that human beings by such exchanges have things necessary to support human life adequately).

Then he determines about monetary exchange, doing two things in that regard. First, he shows how reason invented this kind of exchange, since it is not from nature. Second, he shows that it is unlimited. Regarding the first, he does three things. First, he determines about the original invention of monetary exchange. Second, he determines about an additional kind of monetary exchange. Third, he determines about the money-making that concerns such exchanges.

Therefore, he says first that another system of exchange, invented by reason, developed out of the original exchange of mutually necessary things. For the mutual assistance of human beings by exchanges came to involve more foreign trade, namely, people began to make exchanges with remote persons as well as neighbors, importing things that they needed and exporting things of which they had a surplus. Therefore, the use of money was invented because of the need of exchange, since human beings could not easily transport natural necessities (e.g., wine, wheat, or the like) to remote parts of the world. And so, in order to make exchanges in remote parts of the world, people established mutually to give and receive something that could be easily and expeditiously transported but would of itself have utility. Metals (e.g., bronze, iron, silver, and the like) are such. For they are intrinsically useful insofar as one makes vases or other implements out of them, and yet they could be easily transported to remote places, since a small amount of them, because of their rarity, were worth a great deal of other things. Just so, human beings who have to make a long journey now carry silver or gold coins instead of bronze ones for their expenses.

Because of the aforementioned need of exchange at remote places, the value of metal was first determined only by its weight and size, as, for example, some peoples use forms of bulk silver. But later, in order to free human beings from the need to measure and weigh metal, they printed a mark to signify that the metal is of such and such amount. Just so, some localities use standard signs to measure wine and grain. Therefore, it is clear that coins were invented for the exchange of necessary things.

Then he determines about an additional, different kind of exchange. He says that, after money resulted from the aforementioned exchange, an exchange that was necessary for acquiring necessary things from remote places, a kind of monetary exchange was introduced by which money is exchanged for money. And he calls the latter exchange commerce, namely, the occupation merchants engage in. And this was first done simply and as if by chance (e.g., some merchants in foreign lands in the course of transferring money spent more than they took in). And so something involving skill later arose by experience, namely, that human beings weigh where money was exchanged, and how they could make the greatest profit. And this belongs to commercial skill.

Then he determines about money-making, doing two things in this regard. First, he infers from the foregoing the matter and activity of this skill. Second, he answers a question. Therefore, he infers from the foregoing that, since money began to be exchanged for money for the sake of profit in a skillful way, we call the skill regarding money money-making. And its activity is to be able to weigh from what sources a person could make a great deal of money. For money-making is directed to making a great deal of money and wealth as its end.

Then he resolves a question about the foregoing. For, inasmuch as he had said that money-making produces wealth and money, one could ask whether money and wealth are altogether the same thing. Regarding this, therefore, he does three things. First, he posits the opinion of certain people. Second, he introduces arguments to the contrary. Third, he infers determination of the truth of the matter. Therefore, he says first that human beings very often think that wealth is nothing but a great deal of money, since all money-making and commerce, the end of which is to multiply wealth, is about money as its proper matter.

Then he posits the contrary opinion, saying that it sometimes seems fatuous to say that none of the things in accord with nature (e.g., wheat, wine, and the like) are wealth, and that all wealth consists of money, which law introduced. And he introduces two arguments for this. The first is that, given the diverse situations of human beings, no wealth without worth or benefit for the necessities of life is true wealth. But if the situation of the human beings who use wealth is altered (e.g., if it should please a king or community that coins have no value), money is of no value and offers nothing for the necessities of life. Therefore, it is foolish to say that wealth is absolutely nothing but a great deal of money.

He posits the second argument as follows. It is unfitting to say that one who is rich needs food or dies of hunger. But it can happen very often that a human being with much money needs food and dies of hunger. Just so, the famous story says that someone called Midas, because of his insatiable desire for money, asked and begged of a god that everything offered to him be made of gold, and so he, having much gold, died of hunger when all the food offered him was converted to gold. Therefore, money is not true wealth.

Then he concludes by determining the truth of the matter, saying that those who correctly understand the matter because of the aforementioned arguments hold that wealth and money, or money-making, are different things. For some wealth, namely, the wealth concerning things necessary for life, is in accord with nature, as he has said, and such acquisition of wealth properly belongs to household management. But the money-making that is commerce multiplies money only by exchanging money, not in every way. And so all such money-making consists of money, since money is the beginning and end of such exchange, in which money is given for money. Therefore, it is clear regarding this that those who abound in things necessary for life are in truth richer than those who abound in money.

After Aristotle has shown how law introduced the money-making kind of exchange, he shows here how such acquisition of money is unlimited. And regarding this, he does two things. First, he shows what he proposes. Second, he assigns the reason for the foregoing things. Regarding the first, he does two things. First he shows what he proposes. Second, he resolves a difficulty arising from this.

Therefore, he says first that the wealth acquired by this kind of money-making, namely, commerce, all of which concerns money, is unlimited, and he proves this by the following argument. In any skill, the desire of the end is unlimited, and the desire of means to the end is limited by the rule and measure of the end. For example, medical skill aims at health without limit when it brings about health as much as possible. But it administers medicine in the measure that is useful for health, not as much as possible. And the same is true in other skills. And the reason for this is because the end as such is desirable, and what is intrinsically such, if it should be greater, will be more such. For example, if something white blinds vision, something whiter blinds vision more. But money is the end of commerce, since the aim of commerce is to acquire money, and only a means of household management to its end (i.e., household governance). Therefore, money-making seeks unlimited money, but household management seeks a limited amount of money.

Then he resolves a difficulty arising from the foregoing. And regarding this, he does two things. First, he raises a question. Second, he answers it. Therefore, he says first that it seems, because of the aforementioned argument, that there needs to be a limit of wealth in household management. But if one should consider what happens in practice, the contrary seems to be true, since all household managers, wanting to have money for things useful for living increase money without limit.

Then he resolves the foregoing difficulty, saying that the reason for the aforementioned difference seems to be the close relationship of the two kinds of money-making. That is to say, there is a close relationship between the money-making that serves household management, which seeks money for the exchange of necessary things, and commerce, which seeks money for its own sake. For the activity of both kinds of money-making is the same, namely, the acquisition of money, but not in the same way. In household money-making, the acquisition of money is directed to another end, namely, governance of the household, but in commercial money-making, namely, commerce, increasing money is the end. And so, since commerce is closely related to household management, it seems to some household managers that what belongs to merchants, namely, to be zealous to maintain and increase money without limit, is their duty.

Then he assigns the reason for what he had said, that household managers sometimes persist in increasing money without limit. And because some abuses result from the reason he assigns, he divides this section into three parts by the three abuses that he posits. Therefore, he says first that the reason for this disposition, namely, that household managers seek to increase money without limit, is because human beings are eager to live howsoever, not to live well, which is to live virtuously. For, if they were to strive to live virtuously, they would be content with things sufficient to sustain nature. But since they omit this effort and want to live according to their own will, each of them strives to acquire things with which to satisfy the individual's desire. And because the desire of human beings has no limit, they desire without limit things whereby they can satisfy their desire.

There are also others who are anxious to live well but add to living well what belongs to physical pleasures, since they say that human beings enjoy the good life only by living immersed in such pleasures. And so they seek things whereby they can enjoy physical pleasures. And since it seems to human beings that abundant wealth can bring this about, their every care seems to be to acquire a great deal of money. And we should consider that he assigns the reason why things belong to the household manager from the aim of human life, since the household manager has the good life of its members as his goal. Therefore, the first abuse is that human beings strive to acquire money without limit because they do not have the right endeavor for the good life.

Then he posits the second abuse. For household managers are anxious about acquiring money. Therefore, another kind of money-making, namely, commerce, is added to the care of the household besides the care that is proper to household management, namely, the acquisition of things necessary for life. But since they strive excessively to enjoy physical pleasures, they seek things that can conduce to such excess, namely, abundant wealth. And so the second abuse is that unnatural and unnecessary money-making is included in household management.

Third, he posits the third abuse, saying that, since human beings sometimes lack enough financial skill to be able to acquire things to satisfy their excessive desire for physical pleasures, they strive to acquire money in other ways. And they abuse their faculties (i.e., their virtues, skills, or position) in ways contrary to their nature. For example, courage is a virtue, and its proper function is to make human beings bold for attacking and withstanding, not to accumulate money. And so, if one uses courage to accumulate wealth, one does not use it in accord with nature. So also, military skill is for the sake of victory, and medical skill for the sake of health, but neither skill is for the sake of money. But some use military and medical skills to acquire money and so make both into instruments to make money (i.e., to acquire money), subordinating such skills to money as the end to which all other things need to be directed. And so *Eccl.* 10:19 says: "All things yield to money."

Therefore, he summarily infers from the foregoing what he said about unnecessary money-making, namely, the money-making that acquires money without limit as its end. And money is also the reason why human beings need it, namely, because of their unlimited desire. He also spoke about necessary money-making, namely, the money-making that is different from the foregoing kind. For necessary money-making acquires money up to a limit because of another end, namely, to provide for the necessities of life. And household management, properly speaking, concerns things in accord with nature (e.g., things pertaining to food), and this money-making is limited, unlike the first kind of money-making. Or one can understand that necessary money-making differs from unnecessary money-making. Necessary money-making is household management, and no other things are exchanged.

He had previously raised the question whether money-making is a part of household management or subordinate to it, and he distinguished money-making from other acquisitions of property. Now he answers the question. And regarding this, he does two things. First, he shows that money-making is subordinate to household management. Second, he shows how one kind of money-making is praiseworthy and another kind contemptible. Regarding the first, he does three things. First, he answers the previously posed question. Second, he raises another difficulty. Third, he makes clear something he previously said. Therefore, he says first that the foregoing can now show the answer to the initial question, whether money-making belongs to household managers and statesmen or is altogether extraneous. And the truth is that money-making is not the same as household management, as he has said before, but subordinate to it, since one needs money in order to govern the household.

And he proves this by the fact that there needs to be in the household and the political community both human beings and the things necessary for them. But political science does not produce human beings. Rather, it receives them as produced by nature and then uses them. Therefore, likewise, nature, not political science or household management, produces food, whether from the land (e.g., crops), or from the sea (e.g., fish), or from anything else. Therefore, producing or acquiring such food is not the proper and immediate task of political science or household management. Rather, their proper task is to distribute those things in the household as circumstances require. Just so, we perceive that it belongs to the weaver to use wool and to know which wool is suitable for his task, and which wool is bad and unsuitable, not to make the wool. Therefore, both nature, which produces human beings and food, and the money-making that acquires things serve household management, just as both nature, which produces wool, and the buying that acquires it serve the weaver's skill.

Then he raises a question as follows. Since members of the household need health, as they need things necessary for life, such as food and clothing, why is medical skill not, like money-making, part of household management? And he answers that it belongs to the household manager and the ruler of a political community to consider health in one way, namely, by using the advice of doctors for the health of their subjects. But it belongs to the doctor, not to household managers or rulers, in another way, namely, by considering what things preserve or restore health. Likewise, it also belongs to the household manager to consider money in one way, namely, by using money already acquired and the services of those who acquire it. But it does not belong to the household manager to consider whence and how money can be acquired. Rather, the latter belong to a subordinate skill, namely, money-making.

Then he shows what he had said before, namely, that nature produces necessary things. And he says, as he has said before, that the things that household management and political science use need especially to pre-exist from nature, from which subordinate skills also receive them. And he proves this by the fact that it is the function of nature to give food to what nature generates. For we perceive that the residue of generation from what was produced is food for the thing generated. For example, it is clear that animals are generated from menstrual blood, and nature converts what is left over from this material into milk and prepares food for the offspring. And so, since human beings are constituted out of things from nature, other things from nature are food for them. And so there is a natural kind of money-making (i.e., one that acquires food or money for food from natural things, namely, produce and animals). But it is not in accord with nature that one acquires money from money itself and not from natural things.

Then, with the two kinds of money-making stipulated, he shows which kind is praiseworthy, and which kind contemptible. And he says that we call one kind commerce, namely, the one that acquires money out of money and for the sake of money, and the other kind is household management, namely, the one that acquires money from natural things (e.g., crops and animals), as he has said. The second kind is necessary for human life and so also praiseworthy. But the first, namely, commerce, is transformed from what is a necessity of nature to what desire demands, as he has said, and so rightly despised. For such money-making is contrary to nature, since it is neither from natural things nor directed to satisfy the needs of nature. Rather, it derives from the transfer of money from one to another, namely, insofar as human beings make money from money.

And although the money-making that is commerce is justly despised, there is another kind of acquiring money that is most reasonably despised and odious. And this money-making is lending money for a fee (i.e., charging a fee, as those who profit excessively by lending money do). For this acquisition of money is made from money itself, not in the original way established for acquiring money, since money was created to facilitate transfer of goods (i.e., exchanging them), as he said before.

And there is another kind of money-making, interest (called *tokos* in Greek), whereby money increases itself. And so the Greeks called it *tokos*, since that means offspring. For we perceive that things generated by nature are like the things generating them. And so there is a kind of generation when money increases from money. And so also such acquisition of money is the most contrary to nature, since it is according to nature that money is acquired from natural things, not from money. Therefore, one kind of money-making is praiseworthy, and three kinds contemptible, as he has said.

After Aristotle has taught knowledge about the origin of money-making and its properties and parts, he here determines things that belong to its use. And he speaks first of his aim. Second, he asserts what he proposes. Therefore, he says first that, since we have adequately determined about money-making in the things that belong to knowing its nature, we need briefly and in passing to posit the things that belong to its use, namely, how we should use it. For all such things belonging to human actions enjoy free (i.e., unhindered) consideration, since it is easy to consider them in general. But one needs to have experience about them in order to be able to make perfect use of them.

Then he determines things that belong to the use of money-making. And regarding this, he does two things. First, he distinguishes the kinds of money-making. Second, he posits some useful examples of money-making. Regarding the first, he does two things. First, he assigns the kinds of money-making necessary for human life. Second, he assigns the unnecessary kinds. And he has said before that the money-making, whereby human beings acquire money from things that nature provides for the necessities of life, is necessary. And he posits two parts of such money-making. The first is the money-making whereby human beings can acquire money by buying and selling such things.

And regarding this part, he says that these kinds of money-making are useful (i.e., useful examples), and so human beings should be knowledgeable about such goods that they acquire: which of them are the most valuable, where they are sold at the highest price, and how they are sold (e.g., when and under what other conditions). And he explains what acquirable goods he is speaking about. For example, there is the acquisition of horses, cattle, birds, and other animals. And one who wishes to make profit from these things needs to know which of these are the most valuable, and where they are. For some are plentiful in some places, and others in other places, namely, so that one buys where they are plentiful and sells where they are valuable.

8.   Peter John Olivi: *A Treatise on Contracts* (c. 1295)[1]

ON PURCHASES AND SALES

Regarding contracts for sales and purchases, eight questions are asked.

1st Question

First, it is asked whether, licitly and without sin, things can be sold for more than they are worth or bought for less.

Initial arguments

It seems so, because otherwise nearly the whole community of buyers and sellers would sin against justice, since nearly everyone wants to sell high and buy low.

Also, it is licit for me to put the price that I want on my own good, nor does any law compel me to give or to exchange a good of mine except for a price that is pleasing to me and set by me, just as, conversely, no one is forced to buy the good of another beyond a price that is pleasing to them. And if the contract for selling and buying is purely voluntary, the setting of the price of the things for sale will then be purely voluntary as well; consequently, a law and judgment will obtain that is purely voluntary, as the common saying goes, "A thing is worth as much as it can be sold for."

Also, according to the order of law, justice, and charity, the common good is preferred and ought to be preferred to the private good; but it is indeed expedient for the common salvation of human beings after the Fall that the setting of the price of things for sale not be at an exact point nor according to the absolute value of things, but rather be freely set by the common consent of each party, namely between those selling and those buying. In fact, this involves less risk for the sin and fraud. Otherwise, that setting of price could hardly be done without sin, since the exact and absolute value of things is rarely clear to anyone in a certain and full way. Therefore, etc.

Opposing arguments

On the contrary, to deceive others—both to intend and to attempt to deceive them—is a sin and contrary to the right and natural desire of human beings, the fidelity of friendship, and the purity of truth and justice, since, by nature, no one likes to be deceived. Moreover, it belongs

---

[1]   Translated by Ryan Thornton and Michael Cusato.

to the rectitude of divine law, of charity, and of natural law that we do to no one what, by a right and natural desire, we do not want done to us. However, the falsity or deceitfulness and fraud which exists in deceiving and in the will to deceive is contrary to the divine will and to those laws of God by which He wants us to be faithful and truthful towards all. But the one who knowingly sells a thing for more than it is worth greatly deceives the buyer and intends to deceive them, since generally no buyer wants or is presumed to want to buy a thing for a price higher than it is worth. Similarly, the one who knowingly buys a thing for less than it is worth deceives the seller and intends to deceive them, since generally everyone wants and is presumed to want to sell their things at a price that is not less than they are worth. Therefore, etc.

Also, commutative justice consists in a real equality or equivalence of the things exchanged, just as the justice of returning to each person what is their own or what is owed to them also consists in a real equivalency between that which is returned and that which is owed, namely so that you do not return less, but exactly as much as you owe. Therefore, it is contrary to the equality of commutative justice to knowingly sell something for more than it is worth or to buy it for less than it is worth.

Distinctions

It must be said that the value of things is taken in two ways. First, according to the real goodness of its nature, and in this way a mouse or an ant is worth more than bread, because these things have a soul, life, and sense, but bread does not. In a second way, the value of things is taken with respect to our use, and in this way the more some things are conducive to our uses, the more they are worth, and in this respect bread is worth more than a mouse or a toad. However, since the acts of buying and selling are ordered to use in human life and are themselves a certain kind of use, in these cases the value of things for sale is consequently understood and measured in the second way, not the first.

In turn, it must be known that this kind of value for things sold and used is measured in three ways. In a first way, the value is measured according to which a thing is better adapted and more effective for our utility from its own real qualities and properties; in this way, a good loaf of bread made from wheat is worth more to us as food than one made from barley, and a strong horse is worth more to us for transport or for combat than a donkey or a rouncy.

In a second way, the value is measured according to which things are more necessary to us from their rarity or difficulty in being found, since by their very scarcity, we have a greater need for them and less of an ability to get and use them. Accordingly, the same wheat is worth more at a time of general shortage or famine and scarcity than at a time when it is in great abundance among all. And thus, the four elements, namely, water, earth, air, and fire, have a lower price among us on account of their supply than gold or balsam might, even though they are of themselves more necessary and useful for our life.

In a third way, the value of things is measured according to the greater or lesser pleasure of our will in having things of this kind. Indeed, to "use" (in the sense that it is taken here) is to take or to have something in the power of one's will; for that reason, not a small part of the value of things for use is measured from the pleasure of the will—whether it is more or less pleased in using this or that thing and in having that thing at its disposal. Accordingly, one horse is more pleasing to one person and another horse to another, one ornament or jewel to one person and another to another; in this way, one person appraises highly something that is worthless to another and considers it precious and expensive, and vice versa.

Also, as a third point, it must be known that this type of measurement regarding the value of things for use can hardly or never be made by us except by means of a conjectural or probable opinion; and this measurement is made not at an exact point or within a calculation and measure that cannot be divided into more and less, but within some appropriate latitude about which, indeed, persons and judgments differ in their estimation. For that reason, the measurement includes different degrees, little certitude, and much ambiguity in accord with the way of things known through opinion, although some things are more and some less certain.

Response

These points noted, it must be said that things cannot be licitly sold for more than they are worth nor bought for less, their value having been measured with respect to our use and according to the probable judgment of human estimation which measures the value within the limits of an appropriate latitude.

Nonetheless, it is not necessary to always predicate a mortal sin in the exceeding of these limits, unless it is so great and so immoderate that in the contract itself inequality and injustice should prevail over equality and justice. Accordingly, it is stipulated in civil law that if the buyer or seller is defrauded by more than half of the just price, that contract is null and it must be voided by judges. Because in the case that something strictly worth only 10 solidi should be sold for more than 20 solidi, the excess is clearly immoderate.

I understand this on the condition that the person defrauded would be ignorant of such an excess, because if knowing and attending to the quantity of the excess they consent to such a price and contract, they are not then defrauded. Instead, just as they can give a good of theirs away without any price (if they so want), they can give it away for a hundredth of its just price. Nor in this is any injustice done to them, unless their consent were to proceed clearly or presumably from such a lack of seriousness or a defect of their will that it ought to have no or insufficient force in law and justice, or if they were to do this compelled by such a great need or some other necessity that it could not be considered to come from just a pleased and free will; and in that case, to contract with them in such a way would not only be contrary to justice, but also contrary to charity and natural compassion.

To the arguments

To the objections of each part, a response must be made. To the first argument of the first part, it must be said that this is not true for the community of the just, but only for the community of the unjust and the greedy. For the just person does not want to sell or buy anything contrary to the just price, and the one who is perfectly just wants absolutely nothing of injustice to be there. But the one who is imperfectly just does not want injustice to prevail over justice in their case, and inasmuch as they unduly want something for an unjust price, so much so do they have within themselves something of the vice of injustice.

To the second argument, it must be said that although I am not compelled by law to sell my own good, I am nevertheless compelled in the act and contract of selling to observe the form and rule of law and justice. For that reason, in the act of selling, it is not licit for me to put and to receive an unjust price on my good, since then I am not establishing a price simply for my own good, but for a good to be exchanged with someone else. This kind of establishment of price entails, efficaciously or through the exchange, the reception of a price that is more than it is worth; however, to receive something more than something is worth entails an inequality.

To the third argument, it must be said that if the consent of each party to such a price or its setting could not be considered involuntary by reason of ignorance or inexperience or because of some other need compelling the person to this in some way, then the argument follows and its conclusion is true, but otherwise it does not. For even though our estimation in setting the price or the value of things is not at an exact point, nevertheless it can and ought to be measured within fitting limits, otherwise it would exceed a fitting and probable measure as well as the rule of reason.

But to the first argument of the other part, it must be said that whenever the value of things pertaining to our use is estimated and set in a probable manner by the free and experienced consent of those contracting, neither one deceives the other, unless by accident and in spite of their intention. Rather, it is actually contrary to their intention, since it is by way of such an estimate and such a contract that the one party intends to guarantee equality for their partner, even though the opposite can sometimes occur on account of the uncertainty of estimation.

To the second argument, it must be said that commutative justice does not consist in a real equivalence of things measured according to the absolute value of their natures, but only in an equivalence with respect to our use and utility, as described in the way discussed above.

2nd Question

Second, it is asked whether a price can be set according to the value of the utility for those buying something or receiving some service in return for payment. For example, if a drink or medicinal herb has the value of freeing me from death and of restoring my health, which is beyond price, can the one who gives it justly demand from me a price equivalent to the healing, that is to say, beyond price?

Initial arguments

It seems so, because, just as was said above, the value and price of things for sale is measured with respect to our use and utility rather than according to the absolute value of their natures.

Also, the equity of commutative justice is that I confer as much utility upon you as you confer upon me.

Response

It must be said that if the price of things necessary for our life were to be set according to the equivalence of what they specifically confer upon us, the price of these things would be, as it were, beyond price. For in the case of one suffering from thirst and about to die if they do not have water, a cup of water is worth an infinite amount of gold and much more. Therefore, because in civil and human contracts the ultimate measure is the common good of all, equity in the setting of prices was and is to be measured with respect to the common good, namely as it is expedient for the common good since nothing is more unjust than to prejudice the common and universal good in favor of private and individual advantage.

Indeed, a refutation of a counter-argument for individual good is contained quite forcefully and quite broadly in this very argument, which can be elucidated all the more specifically from the proposed case. Because if I have the utmost need for a drink of water or for a little fire, I am obligated to give you as much as my life is worth, which is what these things confer upon me. By that same argument then, in a similar case, you will be obligated to give me as much for a drink of water, which would certainly be an unjust and unbearable burden. Moreover, this type of equity would root out at the core all compassion and humanity, and chiefly in cases that have need of even greater compassion and humanity. And may it never happen that virtuous and true equity should thus oppose compassion and the common bond of all humanity!

Conditions for the general setting of price
Therefore, it must be known that because the price of goods and services must be set with respect to the order of the common good, one must attend, first and foremost, to the general setting of price and the estimation commonly done by civil communities. And it is proven to generally take into account four conditions.

First, it takes into account a certain natural order of things for use. Just as certain things are the matter, as it were, and the materials for other things, like the elements are for composites, so too is their use lower among us than their more noble composites, as is seen in the use of water with respect to that of wine and in the use of earth with respect to that of bread or wheat. Likewise, just as certain things are by their nature more quickly corruptible or poorly and hardly moveable, but others are more durable and more moveable, so too in our uses some things are more quickly consumed; in fact, the use of some things constitutes their very consumption, as in food and drink. Some things, however, are more durable and more moveable in their use, as is clear in the use of a horse or gold.

In turn, just as some things are more beautiful and pleasing than others by nature, so too are they generally more agreeable to the use of our will and our senses, as in the colors of dyes, cloth, and precious stones, in the smell of spices, and in the various sounds of musical instruments. Thus, because in these things the general order of nature accords with the general order of our use, it follows that the general estimation in prices prefers the last to those that go before in this order of nature.

Second, it takes into account the general course of supply and lack of scarcity and abundance. From this comes the common saying that "everything rare is expensive and precious" and that "too much abundance and familiarity breeds contempt." Indeed, the more rare and difficult it is for us to get to and have something, the more we estimate it to be something quite wonderful and even high beyond our means. We admire things that are hard for us to obtain and things that are unusual; for that reason, when gold or wheat are generally in great abundance, they are not estimated at as high a price as when there is generally a great lack of them. The same is also true when there is a general supply or lack of doctors or lawyers, manual laborers or ditch diggers.

Third, it takes into account the labor as well as the risk and the industriousness in making goods or services available. For all things being equal, we value more in price merchandise or toilsome services made generally available or done through greater labor and risk. From this comes the fact that in those lands which are generally quite distant from French or overseas merchandise, the same merchandise is generally at a higher price. That merchandise which likewise requires greater industriousness is generally estimated at a higher price as well, all things being equal. And although they work more with their body, a ditch digger or stone cutter is not given a price for their work like that of the architect, who with higher expertise and industriousness order directs the ditch digger and stone cutter as to what must be done. On account of this too, wheat has a higher price than wild herbs that are more effective for medicine, since these are not collected with such intense and lengthy labor and industriousness, nor is the quantity of them that is sufficient generally obtained through great expenditures.

Fourth, it takes into account the general degree and order of offices and the dignities associated with them. From this comes the fact that a military leader is given higher wages than a knight, and a knight higher wages than a squire or foot soldier; the reason for which is three.

The first of these reasons is taken from what was said above, namely that to properly carry out higher offices a greater experience, industriousness, and thoughtfulness is required. Furthermore, both because experience and such industriousness is generally acquired through great and lengthy study, through experience and labor, with many risks and expenditures and because those qualified for this type of work are rare and few in number, they are consequently thought worth a higher price.

The second reason is because it serves the honor and utility of the civil community that its preeminent members be provided for quite reverently and copiously; with a certain perceptible superiority and dignity. However, these preeminent individuals, especially if they belong to an evangelical state, ought to give an example in their very selves and to practice works of humility and holiness, rather than the worship of temporal things.

The third reason is because higher offices require as often more expenses. For instance, the leader of an army, in order to properly direct the whole army and the sequence of battles, is in need of more than any one of their subordinates.

Therefore, when these four aforementioned circumstances have generally been taken into account, prices are and must be reasonably set according to what is more manageably and beneficially expedient for the community, all things considered. Moreover, private individuals in their private contracts or in the collection of their expenses ought to follow the form and rule of common estimation and setting of price, lest a part be in discord with its whole in a shameful, unruly, and disobedient way and lest someone for their own pleasure prejudice the common utility and, consequently, common justice and compassion.

To the arguments
To the first argument then, the response to the contrary is clear from what was said above, because the price of things for use is measured with respect to our use within the order of and in relation to the common good and the common use of a thing, and not in relation to something contrary or harmful to them.

To the second argument, it must be said that I ought to return to you as much as you confer upon me according to the rule of the common good among those who commonly estimate and not in any other way for the reasons mentioned before. Otherwise, this would not be the equity of virtuous justice, but rather a cruel and inhuman iniquity.

9.   Jean Buridan: Commentary on Aristotle's *Nicomachean Ethics* (c. 1336)[1]

BOOK V – QUESTION XVI

Is human need a measure of things that can be exchanged?

1st Argument

We argue no, because the measure must be of the same kind as what has to be exchanged, as it is written in Chapter Ten of the *Metaphysics*. Yet, human need is not the same as things that have been exchanged.

2nd Argument

Moreover, the measure must be simple and indivisible, as it is written in Chapter Ten of the *Metaphysics*. Human need is not as such, since men can have several kinds of needs.

3rd Argument

Furthermore, a measure includes in itself what is measurable. Yet, the human need does not include in itself things that can be sold because, when we have them, we are not in need.

Argument Against

On the contrary, Aristotle says: it should be noted that human need is the natural measure of exchanges.

1st Evidence

It is proven that the quality or value of a thing is considered in relation to the purpose for which this thing has been produced. According to Aristotle, in Chapter Two of the *Metaphysics*, nothing is good if it is not in accord with its final cause. However, the natural purpose for which commutative justice regulates external exchanges is to provide for human needs. For instance, if I am out of wheat you have in abundance, and if you are out of wine, which I have

---

[1]   Translation by Chantal Saucier and Edward W. Fuller.

in abundance, we can trade wine for wheat, and thus both our needs are satisfied. Therefore, what provides for human needs constitutes the real measure of exchanges. However, what is supplied appears to be measured by the need. In fact, the value of what is supplied is greater when it provides for greater needs. Thus, the more important the capacity and hollowness of barrels, the more wine is needed to fill them; this is why, etc.

2nd Evidence

Furthermore, this is proven by experience because, when there was a shortage of wine, the less we had, the more expensive it became.

3rd Evidence

Also, wine is more expensive when it is not available in large quantities than when it is available in large quantities because of the fact that we have less of it. The same goes with other things.

4th Evidence

Also, in exchange, the prices of things exchanged are not determined according to their natural value because, in this case, a lot of things would be worth more than all the gold in the world. Instead, we determine value according to whether it is useful or not, or satisfies our needs.

1st Doubt

However, on the opposite, we reject the idea that a poor man should pay more for wheat than a rich man, because he has less wheat than the rich man.

2nd Doubt

In addition, a lot of the things that we need, and which the rich are using not for their needs, but for superfluous pleasure and regalia, are very expensive.

3rd Doubt

Moreover, we have doubts about the way in which tradeable things are measured in terms of needs.

Response to the 1st Doubt

Firstly, it is worth noting that it is not the need of this or that man that measures the value of exchanges, but the needs of all those who can exchange among themselves. Otherwise, we would have to say that the poor, in comparison to what he has in abundance, pays a higher price than the rich for what he lacks. Actually, the poor would provide more effective labor for one bushel of wheat than would the rich for twenty, but he would not contribute more money because he lacks money. Generally, as the poor lacks wheat, he also lacks external goods.

Response to the 2nd Doubt

Secondly, it should be noted that both the rich and the poor are understood in two different ways. On the one hand, it is about having more or less property by fate. This is how common men distinguish them. On the other hand, it is to have what is sufficient or insufficient; this is how real wealth and real poverty are described by Seneca in a letter addressed to Lucilius: "The poor is not someone who has less, but someone who wants to have more." He proves this by saying, "What really matters to someone? How much he hides in a safe or an attic, how he multiplies or increases his assets, if he rises above others, if he counts not what he has acquired, but rather what he must acquire." Furthermore, he adds, when speaking of wealth, that, "You're looking for the appropriate limit of wealth." He replies, "Firstly, to have what is necessary, and secondly, to have what is sufficient." Therefore, it is clear that the wealthy do not have needs, but the poor, on the contrary, always have needs. However, in regarding the common attitude of the rich and the poor, Aristotle says in Chapter One of the *Rhetoric* that, they all covet wealth because of their needs, but at times, the rich covet unnecessary pleasures because of their power. This is why, in reality, they both have needs, and are therefore poor. On this topic, Aristotle in Chapter One of the *Rhetoric* says they both have two kinds of needs: by necessity, as is the case with the poor, or by excess, as is the case with the rich. We therefore have to say that, not only does the lack of necessities measure exchanges for the poor, but also the lack of excesses measures exchanges for the rich.

Response to the 3rd Doubt

Thirdly, it is worth noting that a measure is equal to a quantity. That is to say that the measure can be equaled to the measured object by reducing it to the unit. As such, one is the measurement of a number, the ounce is a weight of measurement, a quarter of a barrel is the measurement for wine, and brass is the measurement for bread. Aristotle wrote about this in Chapter Ten of the *Metaphysics*. These measurements are actually of the same type as the objects being evaluated, and are indivisible and simple, whether by sense perception or according to what has been instituted, or in any similar manner. The measurement according to the similarity of proportion, for instance, when we measure a movement in space or in time, is otherwise. In fact, if a movement A is in a time B, and a movement C is in a time D, we will argue thus: since A is in B, and C is in D; therefore, in one place, through the transmutation of proportion, as A is in C, and B is in D; but time B is twice time D, therefore movement A is twice movement C. This is an example of movement being measured by space. I therefore conclude that human needs determine exchanges according to similitudes of proportion, and not according to quantity. However, depending on whether we have more or less needs, depending on whether the thing we lack is more or less valuable, depending, on the one hand, on the quantity, the value of the good is measured by the value, the need by the need, the time by the time, and the movement by the movement. For instance, by knowing the value of a quart of wine, we can, by returning to the unit, determine the value of a quarter barrel. And, I will measure the human needs of the community by the needs of the individuals.

Response to the 1st and 2nd Arguments

As such, in regard to these arguments, it should be said that the first two proceed by measuring the equality of quantity.

Response to the 3rd Argument

As far as the third argument is concerned, it should be noted that the common need depends on the existence of things that are lacking, and that only a few people acquire. That is why the measurement by quantity is not valid in this case.

That is all as far as this question is concerned.

BOOK V – QUESTION XVII

Is money necessary to measure exchanges?

1st Argument

We argue no, because from one measurable thing, there must be a single measure according to a single criteria, which is used to calculate that thing. Yet, tradeable things cannot be measured by money according to any calculation criteria, except that they are suitable for human use, and thus have a different measure, that is, human needs. Therefore, they cannot be measured by money following any calculation criteria.

2nd Argument

Similarly, if money was the measure for tradeable things, it would follow that, for equal amounts, I would always receive equal goods. However, this is false because for ten pounds, I sometimes get one barrel of wine, and sometimes two or three.

3rd Argument

In the same vein, from the fact that trade is necessary for human subsistence, as it has been said earlier, and because nature is not lacking in things that are necessary, it thus follows that everything necessary for exchange is found in nature. However, as Aristotle says, money does not come from nature. On the contrary, it is up to us to transform it and make it useful. Therefore, money is not necessary or is not a measure that is necessary for exchanges.

Argument Against

Aristotle appears to be saying the opposite. In Chapter One of the *Politics*, he says that, because it is not always possible to transport natural things to remote areas in order to acquire what we lack, the use of money was created for this purpose. Firstly, it is important to study the necessity of money for exchanges. Secondly, it is important to study how tradeable things are measured by money.

1st Article

As far as saying that money is necessary in exchanges for both ideal communication and for the survival of men, I think it is simply necessary for the survival of the population of people we have today. This conclusion is proven in several ways.

1st Evidence

Firstly, certainly by the distance to places where these goods are found. For instance, there is wheat in Artois, but there is no wine to trade for wheat. If Artesians want to get wine from Gascony for their wheat, transporting their wheat to Gascony would lead to an increase in price greater than what the wheat would be worth, and they would get nothing or only a small quantity of wine. It became necessary to have something small enough that could easily be transported, and of great value to enable the exchange between wheat and wine. The answer is money, that I will accept in exchange for my wheat, and through which I will bring back some wine. Guilders are the most suitable for this type of exchange.

2nd Evidence

Secondly, it is proven by the time differences. For instance, I currently have plenty of wine, while next year I will lack it. I cannot preserve this wine that I have because it would spoil. It is therefore necessary for me to exchange it for something that I could easily store at no cost and with no degradation: that is money. Aristotle presents this argument in the following terms: "If for now, you lack nothing, for future exchanges, if you lack something, money will be a guarantor for you."

3rd Evidence

Thirdly, it is proven by the multiplicity of our needs. For instance, this poor man wants to obtain what he needs through his labor. He therefore works three days for a rich man. He lacks bread, meat, milk, salt, turnips, etc. The rich man does not have all these things, but he has precious stones. It therefore appears necessary that, for his work, he receives something that is divisible. From one part he will obtain milk, bread from another part, and so on for other needs. For this, small units of currency are necessary.

4th Evidence

Fourthly, it is also proven by the indivisibility of some tradeable things of great value. For instance, I have a horse and I need some clothes, shoes, and food. I would not give my horse to the shoemaker because he does not have clothes, or to the peasant because I would probably not get shoes. Besides, the peasant and the shoemaker are probably not in need of a horse. I therefore need to sell the horse for money, and I will use a part of it to buy clothes, another part for shoes, and the rest to buy wheat. In a nutshell, upon examination, many other needs for money will appear.

For these necessities, as some people say, money entails some conditions. One of them is that it has to be in small amounts because mistakes are not likely with what can be evaluated easily. The second is that the money should be minted with the mark or stamp of a prince. Otherwise, the money could be imitated or counterfeited. In this way, the equality in exchanges would be eliminated. The third is for it to have a predetermined weight. Otherwise, a predetermined price cannot be applied to tradeable things. The fourth is that, it has to be stable and not corrupt because otherwise, it could not provide for future needs on its own. The fifth is that, it has to be made from a precious material to account for a great value in its own region, and to be easily transported to a remote area. The sixth is that, it should be divisible into small amounts, especially for the poor, because they often need low-cost things.

2nd Article

In regard to the second article: some people say that princes dictate the value of money, and that, depending on the fixed value, tradeable things are measured by them. That is why Aristotle said that money does not exist by nature, but by name, and that we can render it useless. However, speaking in such general terms is not necessary, because if there was no money left, and the king was minting some money again, it is true that he could impose a name, i.e., call it penny or obol. But it would not be up to the king to set the value of the penny or the obol. In fact, if the king said that the penny was worth a quart of wine, it would be unfair because one wine can be better than another, and more so in a given region than in another. Therefore, let's first make sure that the value of the money is measured by human need. However, it turns out that we never lack gold or silver for human necessities. But the rich lack it for their excessive extravagance or in their external spending. That is why we see that gold and silver bars are almost as valuable when they are minted. As the value of money would have been determined in relation to human needs, all tradeable goods could be appreciated proportionally to money. In fact, as they are in proportion to human needs, they will also be in proportion with the money, which is itself proportionate to human needs. It is however true that, no matter what the current money is, if the king minted another money, he could establish it in relation to the previous price. For instance, he could say a new penny is added and worth three old ones. However, if its value in material is not based on its relation to human needs, the king would sin seriously, and enrich himself unjustly at the expense of the entire community. He would only be absolved of his sin in the case of a war threatening the community, or in case of some other general necessity.
In regard to these arguments, it should be said that:

Response to the 1st Argument

Regarding the first argument, that human need is the only primary and natural measure of exchanges. However, it is not a disadvantage if there is another intermediate measure that, when evaluated according to the first, would ensure that other things can be measured.

Response to the 2nd Argument

As far as the other argument is concerned, we concede that money is not an exact measure for saleable things, if it is not based on the relationship between itself and these things for human needs.

Response to the 3rd Argument

In regard to the argument that follows, we can say that the population as large as it is now, cannot be well fed without many things, and nature cannot provide it all without art. This is why nature is not lacking in necessary things, as it gave us a reasoning ability through which we can acquire any know-how, and consequently, obtain all the necessary things. This concludes this question.

10. Jean Buridan: Commentary on Aristotle's *Politics* (c. 1349)[1]

BOOK I – QUESTION XI

Are altering and exchanging money lawful in a well-governed city?
  We argue.

1st Main Argument

Firstly, altering money is unlawful because what leads to seditions and divisiveness is unlawful. This is the case with altering money. The consequent is well known, and the major too. The minor one is obvious by experience because it leads to controversies and complaints, conflicts and wars against the prince and the lord.

2nd Main Argument

Secondly, what reduces the common good while increasing the fortune of one person is unlawful in a good city. This is what happens when money is altered. The major is notorious, and the minor is obvious because each time money is altered, the lord's assets increase, while the common good gets ruined.

3rd Main Argument

Thirdly, if its disappearance or absence would not prevent the city from achieving the goal for which the money is established, it is unlawful. This is the case with altering money. The consequence is obvious, the major is notorious, and the minor is manifested because money's purpose is for the circulation of goods, and such circulation can be achieved through the use of a common money.

4th Main Argument

Fourthly, any innovation not done by necessity is considered harmful to a city. Yet, altering money is an innovation that is not done for a good reason or necessity. The consequent is in moral philosophy. The minor is manifested because altering the money is useful to the lord.

---

[1]   Translation by Chantal Saucier and Edward W. Fuller.

5th Main Argument

We argue still that altering money is unlawful, and especially alteration by the money changer. This is done as follows: the money changer's alteration is done counter to the use and natural order of money. The consequent is obvious, and the antecedent is clear because money's natural order and purpose are both the circulation of other goods. As such, the money changer's arts or exchange of money can only be money for money, and consequently, there is an abuse.

Argument Against

We reject that changing and altering money are lawful in a well-governed city. The consequent is obvious, what is unlawful is not permissible in a good city, and the antecedent is evident by experience.

This eleventh question will comprise three articles. The first is going to emphasize some aspects of money institutions, and their essence. The second will focus on various ways through which the money is exchanged and altered. And in the last one, we will provide answers to the question asked in the beginning.

1st Article

In regard to the first article, it should be noted that:

1st Note

Firstly, as there are four causes for each effect, there are four causes of money: the efficient, the material, etc. The material cause is what the money is made of. Such a material must be very rare and precious because a small amount of it must be of a great value. The final cause is that, through money, man should be able to obtain things that are necessary for life. The formal cause refers to the type of money, and its weight stamp for a given value. The efficient cause makes reference to the prince who is to govern the city or the community of citizens.

1st Consequence

As a corollary, mandating that money be used for another purpose than the circulation of natural goods is, therefore, to abuse the money.

2nd Consequence

Secondly, it follows that a material, which can be easily found and which men possess in abundance, is not a valuable material for the money. This is obvious because it has to be very rare.

3rd Consequence

Thirdly, it follows that, if the money is not a rare and precious material, and if it does not have as much weight and value as it needs, then this money is not well regulated.

2nd Note

It should be noted secondly that in any city, it is good to have diverse currencies and materials. This is obvious because merchants sometimes have to travel to remote areas, and therefore, they need a money made out of a precious material that can easily be transported.

3rd Note

Thirdly, it should be noted that the material for money is put at our disposal in two ways: by nature, for instance minerals and gold, and through alchemy, that is, by changing the material into something else. This point has three proposals. First proposal: alchemy is not necessary to make money. This is obvious, because what makes money lose its value is unnecessary. This is the case with alchemy. The consequence is obvious, and both the major and minor are manifested because the money material would thereby become common and not rare. Second proposal: alchemy is prohibited by law and rightly so. This is just, because an art which harms the common good must be prohibited. This is the case with alchemy. The consequence is obvious. Both the major and minor are manifested because the harm to the city lies in the fact that evil men gain a lot of money through alchemy. Third proposal: we acknowledge that nature prohibits alchemy. This is obvious because many alchemists have naturally become poor. The consequence is obvious because nature brought order to so many things that should not be done. However, there are doubts. The first is to determine if the institution of money is necessary in the city, and the second is to determine if a great quantity of money constitutes real wealth.

1st Doubt

We argue against the first doubt because if this were so, the circulation of goods would mainly be achieved with money, but that is not the case. The consequent is obvious, and the major results from what we have said, while the minor is manifested because men could exchange wheat for wine, etc. Consequently, this institution depends on willingness.

1st Note

Firstly, it is worth noting that, though necessity can be interpreted in several ways, it is however understood here as that without which a goal cannot be achieved in a good and orderly manner.

2nd Note

Secondly, it is worth noting that the goal achieved by the money cannot be reached in a good and orderly manner through the alteration of natural goods. This is obvious because merchants have to go to various regions where they often cannot bring along natural goods.

In response to this question, the conclusion reveals that the institution of money is necessary. This is obvious according to what has been said.

Response to the 1st Note

About these arguments, and in regard to the first one, we stand against the minor because it is difficult for merchants to take their goods along with them.

Response to the 2nd Note

Regarding the second argument, we say that necessity is understood in a different way, as we have seen.

2nd Doubt

We argue in the affirmative for the second doubt. Firstly, because we say that a rich man is a happy man. Secondly, this is also true because real wealth is that without which the money goal cannot be achieved. That is why Aristotle says that money is a guarantor for man.

Argument Against

We argue against that, what makes men starve to death is not considered real wealth. Yet, this is caused by a large quantity of money. The consequent is obvious, and both the major and minor are manifested through the example of Midas who wished that everything he touched be transformed into gold. He died of starvation after his wish was granted.

1st Note

In this regard, it is worth noting that someone is said to be wealthy when he has what is necessary for life. Consequently, in order to determine what real wealth is, it is important to find out what is necessary for life.

2nd Note

Secondly, it is worth noting that this question's title can be understood in two different ways: on the one hand, knowing if a great quantity of money is a real wealth in itself; on the other hand, knowing if real wealth can happen by accident. First proposal: a large amount of money is not considered real wealth. This is obvious through Aristotle's reasoning, which is presented in the aforementioned argument against. Second proposal: a large amount of money is real wealth by accident. This is obvious through the second argument against presented above.

Accordingly, it follows that only real goods are real wealth. This is obvious because only real goods support life.

Response to the 1st Note

In regard to the reasoning after the argument against: for the first, we say that natural wealth is real wealth because it is sought after by wise and well-advised men. It is not the case with the accumulation of money.

Response to the 2nd Note

It is said thus for the second.

2nd Article

As to the second article, we need to know in what ways and under which circumstances the alteration of money is lawful or unlawful?

1st Note

Firstly, it is worth noting that five points are to be taken into account when it comes to money: the material, weight, type, name, and usage. The material has to be precious, rare, and sometimes supplied by nature only, and sometimes by art; the type is obtained by printing the image; the weight is obtained by what determines whether it will be this or that weight; the name refers to what it is called; the usage refers to how people use it in this or that area.

2nd Note

Secondly, in regard to the material of money, it is worth noting that the alteration can be done in two ways. The first way is through a total alteration, and this is also done in two ways: sometimes only by the prince's wish without increasing the welfare of the community; sometimes by oversupplying the material. That is to say that the material becomes very common and cheap. Therefore, such an alteration is considered lawful. The second way is the partial alteration, that is, when the material is not pure gold. This is also done in two ways: sometimes only through the prince's wish with no benefit for the community, and this is therefore considered an unlawful alteration; sometimes by a state mandate, that is, in a bid to tax merchants, and this cause is therefore considered lawful.

3rd Note

Thirdly, in regard to the weight, it is also worth noting that a multiple alteration is possible, that is, reducing or increasing it. If this alteration reduces the price, and without benefit to the community, it is considered unlawful. However, if the material remains the same and the weight is reduced so that the price falls, then the alteration is lawful, and not otherwise, as it is obvious.

4th Note

Fourthly, in regard to the stamping of the image, it is worth noting that, as all the other things have been determined, there are neither many disadvantages nor advantages for the state in this alteration. It follows in this case, that whether the prince's stamp is valuable or not, the stamp is good or not.

5th Note

Fifthly, in regard to the name and use of money, it is worth noting that their alteration does not cause any major damage.

6th Note

Sixthly, it is worth noting that the alteration of money can also be done in an alternate way. This is because sometimes the money can be strong, i.e. when its value is increasing, and sometimes the money is said to be weak, when its value is decreasing. As such, it is necessary to advise according to each case.

7th Note

Seventhly, it is worth noting that only changing the money's name does not produce great benefits or cause damage, except for the fact that contributions, taxes, and duties are estimated according to the money's name. The first part is quite obvious, while the second is obvious because if the money's name is changed in this manner, there would be fraud and deceit.

8th Note

Eighthly, it is worth knowing that altering the money can only be done lawfully by the person who is authorized to regulate it. This is obvious because the money receives its value from the lord.

9th Note

Ninthly, it is worth noting that everything that concerns the city has to be done for the honor and good of the governing of the whole community. Consequently, whoever takes care of their private good to the detriment of the common one is committing a mortal sin. Yet, it is worth noting that the good has a double aspect, notably, the primary good, which is the good of the soul, and the second, which is the good of the body. Therefore, in comparing the primary good with the second one, the private good should be preferred. However, in comparing the second private good with the second common one, the common good should be preferred.

1st Conclusion

Based on these preliminary elements, the first conclusion is that, altering the money can only be done by the prince. This is obvious because the prince alone can regulate the money. The consequent is clear because only the person entitled to institute it is also entitled to change it. The antecedent is known, and here, the prince has to be understood not as a single man, but as those who must govern.

2nd Conclusion

The second conclusion is that, it is always unlawful to alter the money for private benefit, whether it is done by the prince or by somebody else, and especially in the case where the alteration would be detrimental to the state. This is obvious because there are many disadvantages. Furthermore, this kills friendship, and gives rise to disputes. It is well noted: "in the case where it would be detrimental to the state," because if the stamp is altered, it would not cause much damage.

3rd Conclusion

The third conclusion is that, for the good of the community, altering the money is lawful in many cases. This conclusion is obvious because otherwise, the money alteration would not be authorized in a well-governed city. Yet, it is difficult to list all the distinctive ways to alter the money. However, first of all, regarding the alteration of the material, it is lawful for it to be changed if there is a shortage of material, and in order to obtain contributions from the entire community for a common utility. Furthermore, in regard to the weight, if following the reduction of the weight, we are unable to have many francs, it is permissible to change the weight.

Doubt

However, there is a doubt. In fact, it is said that only the prince is entitled to change the money.

Argument Against

On the opposite side, we argue that the prince is sometimes very unjust, and favors his private interest. The consequent is obvious because if this is the case, the city should not tolerate it, and the antecedent is quite notorious.

1st Note

As far as this doubt is concerned, and when speaking from a moral point of view of the prince, it is first worth noting that, there may be two types of princes: the one who is prince by election, and the one who inherits the throne.

2nd Note

It should secondly be noted that there are two types of princes: one with unlimited powers, who is not subject to the law, such as a king or emperor, and the one with limited powers, such as a governor, a bailiff, or a similar person.

3rd Note

It should thirdly be noted that, in regard to the elected prince, if he is unjust, and if this is known by all, one should not submit to such a person, and he should always be overthrown. This is obvious because such a person is not worthy of honor, and because only a good prince should be honored.

1st Conclusion

Consequently, it follows that no one can be a prince unless he is virtuous. This is Aristotle's conclusion when he says that there must be a greater virtue in the prince than in his subjects. Again, the prince must be an example of virtue for his subjects. Therefore, a tyrant cannot be prince.

2nd Conclusion

Altering the money only concerns the prince who has the characteristics of a good prince. This is obvious because such a prince is worthy of his function.

3rd Conclusion

Altering the money does not concern a man called prince by name, who does not meet the requirements of a good prince. This is obvious according to the first conclusion.

For these reasons, it is said that in such a case, such a man shall only be designated as prince, but shall not be the prince.

3rd Article

As far as the third article is concerned, we need to answer the question specifically concerning the money changer's alteration: is it lawful?

1st Argument

Firstly, it is proven that no, an alteration that is rightly reprehensible is not just. Yet, the money changer's alteration is of this kind. The consequent is obvious, and the major too, because no fair thing is reprehensible, and it is the case with the minor, too, according to Aristotle.

2nd Argument

Secondly, the alteration is also not lawful if one receives more than he gives in the exchange. Yet, this is the case with the money changer's alteration. The consequent is obvious, and the major too, because this is unjust, and the minor is evident by experience, because the money changer receives more than he gives.

3rd Argument

Thirdly, the alteration that is brutal and against nature is considered unlawful. And, the alteration of the money changer is of this kind. Therefore, the consequent is obvious, and both the major and minor appear, because using something otherwise, and for other purposes than that for which it has been created, is an abuse and against nature. Yet, this is what the money changer does, because he changes money for money. However, money is established for another purpose, notably to acquire things that are necessary for life, such as wine, wheat, etc.

1st Argument Against

Firstly, we argue on the opposite that the money changer's exchange of money for money is necessary for life's basic needs. The consequent is obvious because what is necessary for life is lawful. Furthermore, the antecedent appears because when merchants go to remote areas, they cannot avoid trading money, as this is obvious.

2nd Argument Against

Secondly, an exchange is also considered lawful if the person exchanging gives something on their own free will. This is the case with the money changer.

1st Note

In order to better understand, it should first be noted that there are two types of exchanges for the money changer: on the one hand, there is the one in which the money changer receives more than he gives, and on the other hand, the one in which the person changing receives exactly as much as he gives.

2nd Note

Secondly, it should be noted that the first exchange is of two types: one is actually for the good of the state as a whole, and the other is when the money received by the person who is changing is not regulated in accordance with the common good, but the private one.

3rd Note

Thirdly, it should be noted that the value of a thing should not be considered according to the dignity of that thing, but according to what it brings to human use. This is obvious because wheat is more valuable in dignity than money. This is evident in itself.

4th Note

Fourthly, it should be noted that the value of something should not be established or received according to what is necessary to the buyer or seller, but according to what is necessary for the whole community. The first part is obvious because it would be detrimental to the community if the buyer gave more than what he is supposed to pay, and this practice would be harmful to many people.

1st Conclusion

From this preliminary information, we draw a first conclusion. The money changer's exchange, where the person who is changing receives more than he gives, and acts for what is considered necessary and good for the community, is lawful. This conclusion is verified because the exchange is considered lawful if it is intended for the common good, and it is as such.

2nd Conclusion

The money changer's exchange, where the person who is changing receives more than he gives, and acts for his private interest, is unlawful and against justice. This is verified because the exchange through which one gets accustomed to vice is considered unlawful; and this is the case with such an exchange.

3rd Conclusion

The money changer's exchange, where the person who is changing receives more than he gives, and acts for their private interest, is unlawful and against justice. The consequent is obvious, and both the major and minor appear because, in such a community, greediness increases on a daily basis, and this is what Seneca says: "The more effort we put in accumulating money, the more we covet it."

4th Conclusion

The money changer's exchange, where the person who is changing receives as much as he gives, is lawful if it is not done to the detriment of the community. This is verified because the exchange is considered lawful when equality is achieved, and is not done to the detriment of the community or state. Yet, this exchange is as such. The consequent is obvious, and the major appears because there is distributive justice. The minor is evident in itself. It is well specified: "When it is not done to the detriment of the community and the city, because otherwise, it would not be lawful."

1st Doubt

However, we then wonder if, in the exchange, the person who is changing money can lawfully receive less than he gives.

Response to the 1st Doubt

We answer that such an exchange is unlawful, if this happens by ignorance, that is, if he did not take any precaution, or maliciously, in that he would not get very wealthy and his heirs would not have much to inherit. The first part is obvious, because this would be done to the detriment of someone else. The second part is obvious because, conversely, in the event he does it in order to help the poor, it is lawful.

2nd Doubt

The following case is submitted: money has a certain value in a given region, but it is less valuable in another one. In this case, we need to know whether it is lawful for him to receive more than he gives.

Response to the 2nd Doubt

We answer that, in all such exchanges, circumstances always have to be taken into account. If the money changer is acting to help others, it is lawful. However, if it is to increase his wealth or to the detriment of the community, it is unlawful.

With this preliminary information, we respond to the main arguments of the third article.

Response to the 1st Argument

For the first argument, we will acknowledge that the exchange is unlawful if the person who is changing receives more and acts as such in his personal interest. However, in other cases, if he is acting to fulfill vital needs and for the common good, it is lawful.

Response to the 2nd Argument

For the second argument, we will also acknowledge that the exchange is unlawful, but all things considered, we say for the minor that the money changer does not receive more than he gives. Actually, the person exchanging buys goods, and in this acquisition, he is providing both effort and zeal, and that is worth something. However, what the money changer receives by acquiring money with money is worth more than that. We can say otherwise, by negating the major, because such an exchange is done for the benefit of the state.

Response to the 3rd Argument

In regard to the third argument, when we say that an exchange against nature is considered unlawful, I am negating the minor. To this end, one needs to know that regulating money can be understood in two ways: on the one hand, in order to save it, and this is considered an abuse; on the other hand, not for the money per se, but for vital needs, as it is obvious for the merchant who has to exchange money.

In regard to the arguments against:

Response to the 1st Argument Against

For the first argument, we stand by what has been said.

Response to the 2nd Argument Against

For the second argument, the major is negated as a whole because, in this case, we would have to say that the person who goes to the loan shark voluntarily gives more, as it will be obvious in the following question.

In regard to the arguments on the main question:

Response to the 1st Main Argument

For the first main argument, when it is said, "are considered lawful those through which, etc.," the major is recognized, as well as the minor, when such an exchange is done by the prince's sole wish, for no good reason, because people are then complaining.

Response to the 2nd Main Argument

For the second main argument, when it is said, "This is considered lawful," the major is recognized, but in some cases the minor is not. Actually, the common good sometimes increases with such an alteration.

Response to the 3rd Main Argument

For the third main argument, when it is said, "must not be left aside that by which, etc.," the major is recognized if that goal is achieved. As far as the minor is concerned, we say that it is not as good because sometimes the material is too vile or the money is lighter.

Response to the 4th Main Argument

For the fourth main argument, when it is said, "any innovation is harmful," the major is recognized, and the minor is negated, because, in a few cases, it is very harmful, and in others, it is not.

Response to the 5th Main Argument

For the fifth main argument, we say that this argument is resolved by the third article.

Does real wealth consist of money?

1st Argument

Firstly, we argue that yes, the real wealth of the city are the things that allow it to obtain what it wants, when, how, and where. And, this is the case with money. The major is obvious, and the minor is proven, since the coin is a guarantor for everybody. In Chapter 5 of Aristotle's *Ethics*, the state is nothing more than a group of citizens.

2nd Argument

Secondly, we argue that yes, real wealth is something the person governing is seeking in a rational manner. And, this is the case with money. The major is obvious because the person who is governing otherwise is not seeking wealth based on considerations of rationality. The minor appears because the person governing in a rational manner must seek it.

3rd Argument

Thirdly, we argue that yes, real wealth consists of things without which the city would wither away. Yet, the city's wealth is as such. The major is obvious, as well as the minor, because we see that, if there were no men fighting against usurpers, the state would have to be diverted to other uses.

4th Argument

Fourthly, we argue that yes, real wealth consists in what tends to satisfy men's needs. Yet, this is the case with money. The major is obvious in itself, and the minor is proven by experience. Moreover, the Poet says, "Love money."

Argument Against

We argue on the opposite that, as a result, dignities would be distributed according to each person's wealth. The consequent is false, and contrary to Aristotle's view in Book 3. The consequence is obvious because, if real wealth consisted of money, it would lead to what has just been said. Furthermore, this is demonstrated by Albert who says that real wealth is not found in money, because the desire to possess wealth is insatiable.

There are two articles on this issue: in the first one, we will answer the question, and in the second one, we will be expressing some doubts.

1st Article

In regard to the first article,

1st Note

Firstly, it should be noted that, as Aristotle writes in the beginning of his first book, there are two types of wealth: the first is natural and consists of what is needed to meet the vital needs, and subsistence of human life, such as wine and wheat; the other is artificial wealth, such as money.

2nd Note

Secondly, it should be noted that money can be considered in two ways: the first is when men seek it for money itself, and the second is when men seek it for another purpose. The first pursuit is irrational because it is contrary to reason to want something for itself when its purpose is otherwise. The second pursuit is a virtue.

3rd Note

Thirdly, it should be noted that money is clearly not real wealth because, if that was the case, it would not vary according to men's changing conventions. This is obvious, and this is why Aristotle says that money is not real wealth.

4th Note

Fourthly, it should be noted that strictly speaking, real wealth, i.e. the city's wealth, is one that is for the public interest, and one through which the city's government fulfills a just purpose. This hypothesis is obvious according to Albert.

5th Note

Fifthly, it should be noted that men have two parts: the first is the inferior part, consisting of the senses, and the other is the superior part, the part dictated by reason (this is mentioned at the end of the book of *Ethics*). On this basis, it is concluded that only what is desired by men's superior faculty is desirable, and the rest is not.

1st Conclusion

This being said, here is the first conclusion:

1st Note

Firstly, money is not real wealth. This is proven because real wealth does not change with men's changing conventions. However, this is not true of money.

2nd Note

Secondly, it is not real wealth if, even when in abundance, it cannot prevent men from starving to death. Yet, money is as such. The major comes from Aristotle, and the minor is obvious because, in some cases, it may be impossible to get commodities, even if we have money. Indeed, many have perished because of it.

3rd Note

Thirdly, it is not real wealth because we say of the man who owns it that he is really rich. Yet, this is the case with the person who has money. That is why the Poet says, "The wealthy patient has money, but not health."

4th Note

Fourthly, it is not real wealth if it does not meet vital needs. Yet, this is the case with money. The consequent is obvious, as well as both the major and minor for each part.

5th Note

Fifthly, it is not real wealth if it generates never-ending desires for more. Yet, this is the case with the desire to have money. The major is obvious because the desire to have real wealth is not endless; nature likes moderation. The minor is obvious in the beginning of this. Hence, the difference between natural and artificial wealth is clear.

2nd Conclusion

The city's real wealth is not in money. This is proven because money is not real wealth. The consequent is obvious, and the antecedent is proven by the previous conclusion. We will see later what real wealth consists of.

2nd Article

And so, if the city's real wealth does not consist of money, we can wonder, how can the one governing seek it in a rational manner? We answer that, if the person governing is just, he will not seek this wealth, except by accident when fulfilling another purpose. For instance, first reason: that a certain amount of money be dedicated to the city's defense; second reason: to beautify the city; third reason: for money to not be transferred from one region to another; fourth reason: in order to obtain food necessary for human life through something in the image of the king; fifth reason: in order to promote more unity and harmony in the city, and as a result of this, money should be collected for the good of citizens; sixth reason: to demonstrate that the good of all citizens is not to be gratified equally in the city, at least not by a public gratification.

Albert records these six reasons, notwithstanding this: these are not considered as real wealth for the city, as it is sufficiently proven by previous conclusions.

Response to the Four Arguments

In regard to the arguments prior to opposition, they proceed on their own path, and the answers to these arguments clearly follow from previous conclusions.

Response to the Argument Against

In regard to the argument after opposition, it is consistent with these conclusions.

11. Nicholas Oresme: *Treatise on Money* (1358)[1]

CHAPTER 1: WHY MONEY WAS INVENTED

"When the Most High divided to the nations their inheritance, when He separated the sons of Adam, He set the bounds of the people." Next, men were multiplied on the earth, and possessions were divided to the best advantage. The result of this was that one man had more than he needed of one commodity, while another had little or none of it, and of another commodity the converse was true: the shepherd had an abundance of sheep and wanted bread, the farmer the contrary. One country abounded in one thing and lacked another. Men therefore began to trade by barter: one man gave another a sheep for some corn, another gave his labour for bread or wool, and so with other things. And this practice persisted in some states, as Justin tells us, till long afterwards. But as this exchange and transport of commodities gave rise to many inconveniences, men were subtle enough to devise the use of money to be the instrument for exchanging the natural riches which of themselves minister to human need. For money is called "artificial riches" seeing that a man who abounds in it may die of hunger; as appears from Aristotle's example of the greedy king, who prayed that everything he touched should turn to gold, which the gods granted, and he perished of hunger, as the poets tell. For money does not directly relieve the necessities of life, but is an instrument artificially invented for the easier exchange of natural riches. And it is clear without further proof that coin is very useful to the civil community, and convenient, or rather necessary, to the business of the state, as Aristotle proves in the fifth book of the *Ethics*, although Ovid says: "From earth we mine a source of future ill, First iron and then gold, more deadly still." For that is caused by the perverse greed of wicked men, not by money itself; which is a convenience for human intercourse, and whose use is essentially good. Whence Cassiodorus says: "However common money seems to us from our constant use of it, we should consider how good reason our forefathers had to amass it." And he says in another place that, "It is certain that moneyers were established for the particular use of the public."

CHAPTER 2: THE MATERIAL OF MONEY

Now, since money is an instrument for the exchange of natural riches, as appears from the preceding chapter, it follows that it must be a fit tool for the work. This implies that it must be easy to handle and to feel with the hands, light to carry and that a small portion of it should purchase a larger quantity of natural riches, with other conditions which will appear later. Coin must therefore be made of a precious and rare material, such as gold. But there must be

---

[1] Translated by Charles Johnson.

enough of such material. Wherefore, if there is not enough gold, money is also made of silver; and where these two metals do not exist or are insufficient, they must be alloyed, or a simple money be made of another metal, without alloy, as was formerly the case with copper, as Ovid tells in the first book of the *Fasti*, saying: "Men paid in copper once: they're now for gold, And the new money elbows out the old." A like change the Lord promised by the mouth of Isaiah: "For brass I will bring gold, and for iron I will bring silver." For these metals are the fittest for coining. And, as Cassiodorus says: "Aeacus and Indus, king of Scythia, are said to have been the first to discover, one gold and the other silver, and to be praised for delivering them to man's use." And therefore so much of them ought not to be allowed to be applied to other uses that there should not be enough left for money. It was this consideration that led Theodoric, king of Italy, to order the gold and silver deposited according to pagan custom in the tombs, to be removed and used for coining for the public profit, saying: "It was a crime to leave hidden among the dead and useless, what would keep the living alive." On the other hand it is inexpedient that the material of money should be too plentiful; for that, as Ovid says, was the reason for the disuse of copper. That may be the reason why Providence has ordained that man should not easily obtain gold and silver, the most suitable metals, in quantity, and that they cannot well be made by alchemy, as some try to do; being, if I may say so, justly prevented by nature, whose works they vainly try to outdo.

CHAPTER 3: OF THE VARIETY OF MATERIALS AND OF ALLOY

Money, as was said in Chapter 1, is the instrument of trade. And since both for communities or individuals, trade must sometimes be large, or in bulk, sometimes smaller, and more generally petty, or retail, it has been convenient to have precious money, made of gold, easy to carry and to count, and suitable for large transactions. It was also proper to have silver money, less precious, suitable for giving change and for adjustments of price, and for buying goods of lower value. And since a particular country is not always furnished with silver in proportion to its natural riches, besides which, the portion of silver which would be justly due for a pound of bread or the like, would be too small to hold in the hand, money came to be coined of a cheaper metal together with the silver, and that is the origin of our "black" money, which is suitable for petty dealings. And thus, where silver is not abundant, the best plan is to have three materials for money, gold, silver and the "black" alloy. But it should be observed and laid down as a general rule that no alloy should be permitted except in the least precious metal used for small change. For instance, where the money consists of gold and silver, the gold should never be alloyed if it can be coined pure. The reason is that all such mixture is naturally suspect because the proportion of pure gold in it cannot readily be determined. Consequently coins should not be alloyed except for the necessity above mentioned. And this should only be done where the suspicion is least, or the fraud is of least importance, that is in the less precious metal. Again, no such mixture should be made except for the common good, on account of which money was invented and by which it is regulated as is shown above. But there is no necessity nor common advantage in alloying gold money where silver is also in use; nor can it honestly be done, nor has it been done in any well-governed community.

CHAPTER 4: OF THE FORM OR SHAPE OF MONEY

When men first began to trade, or to purchase goods with money, the money had no stamp or image, but a quantity of silver or bronze was exchanged for meat and drink and was measured by weight. And since it was tiresome constantly to resort to the scales and difficult to determine the exact equivalent by weighing, and since the seller could not be certain of the metal offered or of its degree of purity, it was wisely ordained by the sages of that time that pieces of money should be made of a given metal and of definite weight and that they should be stamped with a design, known to everybody, to indicate the quality and true weight of the coin, so that suspicion should be averted and the value readily recognised. And that the stamp on coins was instituted as a guarantee of fineness and weight, is clearly proven by the ancient names of coins distinguishable by their stamp or design, such as pound, shilling, penny, halfpenny, *as*, *sextula* and the like, which are names of weights applied to coins, as Cassiodorus says. Shekel, likewise, is the name of a coin, as appears in Genesis, and also of a weight as appears in the same book. The other names of coins are not "proper" (i.e. derived from the essence), but accidental, or denominative from a place, a design or an authority, or in some other way. But the pieces of money which are called coin (*nummisma*) should be of a shape and quantity suitable for handling and counting, and of a material capable of being coined, malleable and fit to receive and retain an impression. Hence not all precious substances are fit for coins: gems, lapis lazuli, pepper and the like are not naturally fit, but gold and silver eminently are so, as we said before.

CHAPTER 5: WHO HAS THE DUTY OF COINING?

Furthermore, it was ordained of old, with good reason, and to prevent fraud, that nobody may coin money or impress an image or design on his own gold and silver, but that the money, or rather the impression of its characteristic design, should be made by one or more public persons deputed by the community to that duty, since, as we have said, money is essentially established and devised for the good of the community. And since the prince is the most public person and of the highest authority, it follows that he should make the money for the community and stamp it with a suitable design. This stamp should be finely wrought and difficult to engrave or counterfeit. It should also be penal for a foreign prince or any other to coin money of like design but of lower weight, so that common people could not distinguish one from the other. This should be a crime; nor can anyone have such a privilege, for it is forgery; and it is a just cause for war.

CHAPTER 6: WHO OWNS THE MONEY?

Although it is the duty of the prince to put his stamp on the money for the common good, he is not the lord or owner of the money current in his principality. For money is a balancing instrument for the exchange of natural wealth, as appears in Chapter 1. It is therefore the property of those who possess such wealth. For if a man gives bread or bodily labour in exchange for money, the money he receives is as much his as the bread or bodily labour of which he (unless he were a slave) was free to dispose. For it was not to princes alone that God gave freedom to possess property, but to our first parents and all their offspring, as it is in Genesis. Money, therefore, does not belong to the prince alone. But if anyone objects that our Saviour, when a penny was shown Him, asked: "Whose is this image and superscription?" and when it was answered "Caesar's", gave judgment: "Render therefore unto Caesar the things which are Caesar's, and unto God the things that are God's" (as though He meant "The coin is Caesar's because Caesar's image is stamped upon it"), it is clear to anyone who reads the context that He does not say that the money was due to Caesar because it bore Caesar's image, but because it was "tribute." For, as the apostle says: "Tribute to whom tribute is due; custom to whom custom." Christ therefore showed that the stamp was the means of knowing to whom the tribute was due, namely the person who fought the battles of the state, and by reason of his dominion had the right to coin money. Thus, money belongs to the community and to individuals. And so says Aristotle in the seventh book of the *Politics* and Cicero about the end of the old *Rhetoric*.

CHAPTER 7: WHO BEARS THE EXPENSE OF COINING?

As money belongs to the community, it should be coined at the expense of the community. The most appropriate way of doing this is to distribute the expense over the whole coinage by causing the material, such as gold, when it is brought to be coined or sold for coined money, to be bought for less money than it could be coined into and at a certain fixed rate: e.g. if a mark of silver can be coined into sixty-two shillings, and two shillings are needed for labour and other necessaries in minting, the mark of silver will be worth sixty shillings and the other two will be paid for the minting. But the rate should be fixed high enough to cover the cost of coining at all times. And if the money can be made at a lower price, it is reasonable that the balance should go to the distributor or ordainer, to wit, the prince or the master of the mint, as a sort of pension. But this rate should be a moderate one, and need only be quite small if money is adequately plentiful, as shall be said later. And if such a rate or pension were excessive it would be to the damage and prejudice of the whole community, as any man may easily see.

CHAPTER 8: ON ALTERATIONS IN COINAGE IN GENERAL

First of all we must know that the existing laws, statutes, customs or ordinances affecting the community, of whatever kind, must never be altered without evident necessity. Indeed, as Aristotle says in the second book of the *Politics*, an ancient positive law is not to be abrogated in favour of a better new law, unless there is a notable difference in their excellence, because changes of this kind lessen the authority of the laws and the respect paid them, and all the more if they are frequent. For hence arise scandal and murmuring among the people and the risk of disobedience. Especially if such changes should be for the worse, for then they would be intolerable and unjust. Now it is the case, that the course and value of money in the realm should be, as it were, a law and a fixed ordinance. This is indicated by the fact that pensions and yearly rents are reckoned according to the value of money, i.e. in a certain number of pounds or shillings. From which it is clear that a change in money should never be made, unless perhaps under eminent necessity or for the obvious advantage of the whole community. Wherefore Aristotle, in the fifth book of the *Ethics* speaking of coin, says: "It aims at remaining of the same value."

But alteration in money (considering the matter generally) may be regarded as being made in various ways: first, to put it shortly, in form or shape; then, in bimetallic ratio; in value and denomination; again, in quantity or weight, and lastly in material substance. For money may be altered in any one or more of these five ways. We had better, then, discuss these ways, and reasonably inquire whether money can justly be altered in any of them and, if so, when, by whom, how and for what reason.

CHAPTER 9: CHANGE OF FORM

The impressed form or stamp of the money can be altered in two ways. One is without demonetising the old money; as, if a prince should inscribe his own name on the money issued during his reign, allowing the old money to pass current. This is not strictly an alteration, nor is it a great matter if it is done, unless another alteration is involved.

The form may be changed in another way, by making new money and demonetising the old. That is definitely an alteration and can justly be made for one of two reasons. One is, if a foreign prince or false coiners maliciously copy or counterfeit the moulds or die of the money and there is found in the realm a forged, false money, like the good in colour and form. Then, if no other remedy could be applied, it would be well to change the moulds and the form of the stamp. Another reason might be if perchance the old money was too much injured by age or reduced in weight. Its currency should then be forbidden and the new and better money should be given a different stamp, so that the common people should be able to know one from the other.

But I do not think that the prince should be able to demonetise the old money except for one of these reasons, for such a change would otherwise be unnecessary, scandalous and to the damage of the community. Nor does it appear that the prince could be induced to make such a change but for one of two reasons: either because he wishes to have no other name than his own inscribed on the coins, which is a slight to his predecessors, and empty ambition; or because he wants to get a larger profit by coining more money, as was mentioned in Chapter 7, and that is covetousness and to the prejudice and loss of the whole community.

CHAPTER 10: CHANGE OF RATIO

Ratio is the comparison or habitual relation of one thing to another, just as in the proportion of gold money to silver money there ought to be a definite relation in value and price. For as gold is naturally more precious and scarcer than silver, and more difficult to find and to get, gold of the same weight ought to excel silver in value by a definite proportion. The ratio, for instance, might be twenty to one, and thus one pound of gold would be worth twenty pounds of silver, one mark twenty marks, one ounce twenty ounces and so forth. And another proportion is possible, such as twenty-five to three, or any other. But this proportion ought to follow the natural relation in value of gold to silver, and a ratio should be fixed, not to be arbitrarily changed, nor justly varied except for a reasonable cause and an alteration arising from the material, a thing which rarely happens. Thus, if it were notorious that less gold was being found than before, it would have to be dearer as compared with silver, and would change in price and value. But if there were little or no material change, the prince would not be free to make such a change in price. For if he were to alter the ratio arbitrarily, he might unfairly draw to himself his subjects' money, for instance, by fixing a low price for gold and buying it for silver, and then raising the price when he sold his gold or gold money; or by doing the same with silver. It would be like fixing a price for all the corn in his kingdom, buying it and selling again at a higher price. Everyone can clearly see that this would be an unjust exaction and actually tyranny: indeed, it could appear outrageous and worse than that which Pharaoh did in Egypt, of which Cassiodorus says:

> We read that Joseph gave leave to buy corn, to meet the deadly famine, but set such a price that the people, hungry for relief, sold themselves into slavery to him to buy themselves food. What a miserable life it must have been for those to whom the bitter bread of relief seemed to take away their freedom, where the freed man groaned no less than the captive wept. I believe the holy man to have been compelled by the necessity both of satisfying a greedy prince and of helping a perishing people.

But the monopoly of coinage of which we spoke would be even more tyrannous, being more involuntary and not for the need of the community, but literally to its harm. But if anyone should say that corn is not a fair parallel, because certain commodities are the private property of the prince for which he may set his own prices, as some say is the case with salt and *a fortiori* with money, we answer that a monopoly or *gabelle* of salt, or any public necessity, is unjust. And that princes who have made laws to give themselves this privilege are the men of whom the Lord says, in the words of the prophet Isaiah: "Woe unto them that decree unrighteous decrees, and write grievousness which they have prescribed." Again, it is clear from our first and sixth chapters, that money is the property of the commonwealth. Therefore, and lest the prince should unfairly put forward the reason given in this chapter for altering the ratio, the community alone has the right to decide if, when, how and to what extent this ratio is to be altered, and the prince may not in any way usurp it.

CHAPTER 11: CHANGE OF NAME

As was said in Chapter 4, there are certain names or non-essential denominations of money which indicate the author or the place of coinage, and these have little or nothing to do with our subject. But others are essential or proper to coin, e.g. penny, shilling, pound and the like, which denote the value or weight and were given by our forefathers after deep thought and with great mystery. Of which Cassiodorus says:

> It is remarkable on how rational a plan money was brought together by the ancients. They would have six thousand pence to be a shilling (*solidus*), in order that the round shape of radiant metal, like a golden sun, might correspond numerically with the age of the world. But the number six (*senarius*) (which learned antiquity defined not undeservedly as perfect) it signified by the name of ounce (*uncia*), the first degree of measurement, and multiplying it by twelve to match the months, brought it up to a pound to correspond with the year. What a wise invention! How far-seeing were our elders! It was most ingenious to devise measures for human use and at the same time symbolise so many of the secrets of nature. That, therefore, is deservedly called a pound which has been so weightily considered.

But although we now apply these names differently to our coins, they must not be changed to no purpose. Suppose, for example, that there are three kinds of coins, the first worth a penny, the second a shilling and the third a pound. Then if the description of one is altered but not that of any other, that will change their proportionate value. So, if anyone were to call or fix the value of the first kind at two pence without altering the others to match, the proportionate value would be changed, a thing which is not lawful (as appears in the preceding chapter), except in very rare cases with which I am not concerned at present. It is necessary, then, that if the proportion is to remain unchanged, and one coin changes its denomination, the others should be changed in proportion, so that if the first coin is called two pence, the second shall be two shillings and the third two pounds. And if no other change were made, it would be necessary for goods to be bought or priced at proportionately higher rates. But such a change would be to no purpose, and must not be made, because it would be scandalous and a false denomination. For that would be called a pound which really was not a pound, which is, as we have said, improper. But no other impropriety would ensue, except where pensions or rents were appointed in terms of money. For in that case it is immediately apparent that besides the impropriety which we have named, such rents by this change would either be reduced or would increase unreasonably and unjustly and to the damage of many people. For where some people's pensions or rents were inadequate, they should be augmented by another special measure, and not this prejudicial and hurtful one. Therefore this change of denomination should never be made; least of all should the prince attempt to make it.

CHAPTER 12: CHANGE OF WEIGHT

If the weight of a coin is changed and its value proportionately altered and also its denomination and its form, a new variety of money is created, as if a penny were made into two halfpence, involving neither loss nor gain. This may lawfully sometimes be done by reason of a real change in the value of the material, a thing which very rarely happens, as was said in Chapter 10, speaking of another kind of change. But I am now speaking of a definite alteration of the weight or quantity of money without any change of name or value. And it seems to me that such a change is plainly unlawful, especially in a prince, who cannot do it without disgraceful injustice. Because, in the first place, the prince's image or superscription is placed by him on the coin to guarantee the weight and standard of the material, as was proved above in Chapter 4. Consequently, if the weight is not true, this is at once seen to be a foul lie and a fraudulent cheat. For measures of corn and wine and other measures are frequently stamped with the king's public mark, and any man tampering with these is held to be a forger. In exactly the same way, the inscription on a coin indicates its weight and the purity of its material. Can any words be too strong to express how unjust, how detestable it is, especially in a prince, to reduce the weight without altering the mark? Cassiodorus says on this point, in the fifth book of his *Variae*: "For what is so criminal as to permit oppressors to sin against the very nature of the balance, so that the very symbol of justice is notoriously destroyed by fraud?"

Secondly, the prince can in this way get possession of other people's money, nor can there be any other reason why he should make such a change. For he would receive money of good weight, recoin it and pay out coins of short weight. And this is the very thing which God forbids in sundry places of Holy Scripture. Of this Solomon says: "Divers weights and divers measures, both of them are alike abomination to the Lord." And in Deuteronomy it is said that: "All that do such things … are an abomination unto the Lord." Therefore riches thus gathered to their Lord's hurt are soon consumed, because, as Cicero says, "Ill-gotten goods never prosper."

CHAPTER 13: CHANGE OF MATERIAL

The material of money is either simple or mixed, as appeared in Chapter 3. If simple, it may be abandoned as insufficient; for instance if little or no gold could be found, it must cease to be coined: and if it again were found in sufficient plenty, money would again begin to be coined of it, as has sometimes happened. Again, a particular material might have to cease to be coined because it was too abundant. It was for that reason that copper money formerly went out of use, as was said in Chapter 3. But such causes occur rarely, and in no other way is a material for money, pure or mixed, to be abandoned or newly adopted. But if the material be mixed, it should be so only in the less precious of the metals which are coined pure (as was proved in Chapter 3), and in black money, that the pure may be distinguished from the mixed. And the mixture (or alloy) must be made in a fixed proportion, such as ten parts of silver to one, or to three, of some other metal, as is convenient, as we said in Chapter 3. And this proportion may be altered on account of a real or corresponding proportion or variation in the nature of the material, and in two ways. Either owing to the lack of material, like having no silver, or conspicuously less than before, in which case the proportion of silver to the other metal in the black money may be diminished; or, if silver were much more abundant than before, the quantity of silver in the mixture should be raised. But, as has been said, such causes are very rare and, if the case occurs, such a change in proportion should be made by the community, for greater safety and to prevent fraud, as was said in Chapter 10 of the change in the (bimetallic) ratio. But in no other case should the mixture, or its proportion, be changed, least of all by the prince, for the reasons given in the last chapter, which are directly applicable to the present question since the stamp on the coin denotes the genuineness of the material and its proportions, and so to change these is to falsify the coinage. Besides, some coins are inscribed with the name of God or of some saint and with the sign of the cross, which was devised and appointed of old as a witness of the genuineness of the money in material and weight. If the prince, then, despite this inscription, should change the material or the weight, he would seem to be silently lying and forswearing himself and bearing false witness, and also transgressing that commandment which says: "Thou shalt not take the name of the Lord thy God in vain." Also he misuses the "word" money, for Uguccio says: "*Moneta* is so called from *moneo* (to warn)" because it warns us against fraud in metal or weight. Again, a prince by this means could wrongfully draw to himself the wealth of his people, as was said in the last chapter on change of weight, and many other anomalies would result. This fraud indeed would surely be worse than that of change of weight, because it is more cunning and less apparent and does more harm and injury to the community. And for this reason, where such alloy or black money exists, the community ought to keep in some public place or places a sample of this proportion or quality of alloy, to prevent the prince (which God forbid) or the moneyers secretly committing this fraud in the alloy, just as examples of other measures are frequently kept in charge of the community.

CHAPTER 14: COMPOUND CHANGE OF MONEY

There is a compound change of money when more simple changes than one are combined, as by changing at the same time the (bimetallic) ratio or the mixture of materials and possibly the weight as well. There would thus be a number of possible combinations of the five simple changes already described. And since no simple change ought to be made except for the real and natural causes mentioned which very rarely occur, it is obvious that the occasion for a compound change will even more rarely, or perhaps never, happen. And if it should, *a fortiori* such a compound change must never be made by the prince, because of the dangers and disadvantages already named, but only by the community. For if so many abuses result from simple changes wrongly made, as we have said, much greater and worse would follow from a compound change. For money ought to be true and just in substance and in weight, as is shown us in the Holy Scriptures, where it is said of Abraham that he bought a field for which he gave 400 shekels of silver of approved public money. If then the money were good and were not unnecessarily altered, since it would last a long time, there would not be any need to make a great deal of it nor to have many moneyers at the public expense. And this would be to the public advantage, as was suggested in Chapter 7. On the whole then, we must conclude from the premises that no change of the money, simple or compound, is to be made on the sole authority of the prince, especially where he wishes to do it for the sake of the profit and gain to be got from the change.

CHAPTER 15: THAT THE PROFIT ACCRUING TO THE PRINCE FROM ALTERATION OF THE COINAGE IS UNJUST

I am of opinion that the main and final cause why the prince pretends to the power of altering the coinage is the profit or gain which he can get from it; it would otherwise be vain to make so many and so great changes. I propose therefore to give fuller proof that such gain is unjust. For every change of money, except in the very rare cases which I have mentioned, involves forgery and deceit, and cannot be the right of the prince, as has previously been shown. Therefore, from the moment when the prince unjustly usurps this essentially unjust privilege, it is impossible that he can justly take profit from it. Besides, the amount of the prince's profit is necessarily that of the community's loss. But whatever loss the prince inflicts on the community is injustice and the act of a tyrant and not of a king, as Aristotle says. And if he should tell the tyrant's usual lie, that he applies that profit to the public advantage, he must not be believed, because he might as well take my coat and say he needed it for the public service. And Saint Paul says that we are not to do evil that good may come. Nothing therefore should be extorted on the pretence that it will be used for good purposes afterwards. Again, if the prince has the right to make a simple alteration in the coinage and draw some profit from it, he must also have the right to make a greater alteration and draw more profit, and to do this more than once and make still more, and also to make one or more compound alterations, constantly making more profit in the ways already described. And it is probable that he or his successors would go on doing this either of their own motion or by the advice of their council as soon as this was permitted, because human nature is inclined and prone to heap up riches when it can do so with ease. And so the prince would be at length able to draw to himself almost all the money or riches of his subjects and reduce them to slavery. And this would be tyrannical, indeed true and absolute tyranny, as it is represented by philosophers and in ancient history.

CHAPTER 16: THAT SUCH A PROFIT IS UNNATURAL

Although all injustice is in a way contrary to nature, to make a profit from altering the coinage is specifically an unnatural act of injustice. For it is natural for certain natural riches to multiply, like grains of corn, "which," as Ovid says, "when sown, the field with ample interest repays." But it is monstrous and unnatural that an unfruitful thing should bear, that a thing specifically sterile, such as money, should bear fruit and multiply of itself. Therefore when profit is made from money, not by laying it out in the purchase of natural wealth, its proper and natural use, but by changing it into itself, as changing one form of it for another, or giving one form for another, such profit is vile and unnatural. It is by this reasoning that Aristotle proves, in the first book of the *Politics*, that usury is against nature, because the natural use of money is as an instrument for the exchange of natural wealth, as has frequently been said. Anyone therefore who uses it otherwise, misuses it against the natural institution of money, for he causes money to beget money, which, as Aristotle says, is against nature. And, besides, in these changes by which profit accrues it is necessary to call something which in truth is not a penny, a penny, and which is not a pound, a pound, as has already been said in another connexion. But it is clear that this is no less than to disturb the order of nature and of reason, of which Cassiodorus says

> Pay your shilling, and keep something back if you are strong enough; deliver a pound, and make it less if you can. In all such cases, as the names themselves show, you pay in full, or you are not giving what you say you give. You cannot by any means use the names of whole units and yet make fraudulent deductions. Is not such a violation of nature's secrets, such an attempt to obscure the greatest certainties, plainly a cruel and disgraceful wound to truth itself? Weight and measure are the first things to prove, for all is chaos where there is deceit in the unit of measurement.

Again, it is said in the book of Wisdom that God ordered all things by measure, weight and number; but in changing of money there is no profit unless fraud is committed in these most certain things, as I have declared before. Therefore he who seeks to profit from such changes of money sins against God and against nature.

CHAPTER 17: THAT PROFIT FROM THE CHANGE OF MONEY IS WORSE THAN USURY

It seems to me that there are three ways in which profit may be made from money, without laying it out for its natural purpose; one is the art of the money changer, banking or exchange, another is usury, a third alteration of the coinage. The first way is contemptible, the second bad and the third worse. Aristotle mentioned the first two, but not the third, because in his times such wickedness had not yet been invented. That the first is contemptible and disreputable, Aristotle proves by the reasons given in the last chapter, for this is as it were to make money beget money. He also calls exchange "obolostatic," what we commonly call *Poitevinage*. It was for that reason that Saint Matthew, the apostle who had been a money changer, did not return to his former calling after our Lord's resurrection, as Saint Peter, who had been a fisherman, did. And in giving this reason, the Blessed Gregory says: "It is one thing to earn a living by fishing, and another to amass money from the profits of receipt of custom. For there are many trades which can scarcely if ever be practised without sin, etc." For there are certain vulgar crafts which defile the body, such as cleaning the sewers, and others which, like this, defile the soul. As to usury, it is certainly bad, detestable and unjust, and Holy Scripture says so. But it remains to show that gaining money by altering the coinage is even worse than usury. The usurer has lent his money to one who takes it of his own free will, and can then enjoy the use of it and relieve his own necessity with it, and what he repays in excess of the principal is determined by free contract between the parties. But a prince, by unnecessary change in the coinage, plainly takes the money of his subjects against their will, because he forbids the older money to pass current, though it is better, and anyone would prefer it to the bad; and then unnecessarily and without any possible advantage to his subjects, he will give them back worse money. And even if he makes better money than before, it is only with a view to a future debasement, and that he may give them (meanwhile) less of the good money than the corresponding value of the old. In either case he keeps back part for himself. In so far then as he receives more money than he gives, against and beyond the natural use of money, such gain is equivalent to usury; but is worse than usury because it is less voluntary and more against the will of his subjects, incapable of profiting them, and utterly unnecessary. And since the usurer's interest is not so excessive, or so generally injurious to the many, as this impost, levied tyrannically and fraudulently, against the interest and against the will of the whole community, I doubt whether it should not rather be termed robbery with violence or fraudulent extortion.

CHAPTER 18: THAT SUCH ALTERATIONS OF MONEY ARE ESSENTIALLY NOT PERMISSIBLE

Sometimes, lest worse befall and to avoid scandal, dishonourable and bad things such as public brothels are allowed in a community. Sometimes also, from necessity or for convenience, some contemptible business like money-changing is permitted, or some evil one, like usury. But there seems to be no earthly cause why so much gain should be allowed from alteration of the coinage for profit. It does not avoid scandal, but begets it, as appears in Chapter 8, and it has many awkward consequences, some of which have already been mentioned, while others will appear later, nor is there any necessity or convenience in doing it, nor can it advantage the commonwealth. A clear sign of this is that such alterations are a modern invention, as was mentioned in the last chapter. For such a thing was never done in cities or kingdoms formerly or now well governed. Nor have I found any mention of it in history except that in a letter of Cassiodorus written in the name of Theodoric, king of Italy, a slight change of weight, which a certain treasurer had made in paying some soldiers, is severely blamed and thoroughly censured. Writing of this to Boetius, the king says: "Wherefore let your prudence, learned in philosophic doctrines, expel wicked lying from the company of truth, lest anyone should be tempted to diminish its integrity." And, a little later, he continues: "The wages of labourers must not be docked, but payment must be made in full to him of whom faithful service is required." If the Italians or Romans did in the end make such alterations, as appears from ancient bad money sometimes to be found in the country, this was probably the reason why their noble empire came to nothing. It appears therefore that these changes are so bad that they are essentially impermissible.

CHAPTER 19: OF CERTAIN DISADVANTAGES TO THE PRINCE RESULTING FROM ALTERATIONS OF THE COINAGE

Many great disadvantages arise from such alterations in the coinage, some of which specially affect the prince, others the whole community, and others particular parts of the community. Many of these have lately been seen to occur in the realm of France, and some have already been named, which must nevertheless be recapitulated. First, it is exceedingly detestable and disgraceful in a prince to commit fraud, to debase his money, to call what is not gold, gold, and what is not a pound, a pound, and so forth as in Chapters 7 and 8. Besides, it is his duty to condemn false coiners. How can he blush deep enough, if that be found in him which in another he ought to punish by a disgraceful death? Again, it is a great scandal, as was said in Chapter 8, and contemptible in a prince, that the money of his kingdom never remains the same, but changes from day to day, and is sometimes worth on the same day more in one place than in another. Also, as time goes on and changes proceed, it often happens that nobody knows what a particular coin is worth, and money has to be dealt in, bought and sold, or changed from its value, a thing which is against its nature. And so there is no certainty in a thing in which certainty is of the highest importance, but rather uncertain and disordered confusion, to the prince's reproach. Also it is absurd and repugnant to the royal dignity to prohibit the currency of the true and good money of the realm, and from motives of greed to command, or rather compel, subjects to use less good money; which amounts to saying that good is evil and vice versa, whereas it was said to such from the Lord, by his prophet: "Woe unto them that call evil good and good evil." And again, it is a disgrace to a prince to dishonour his predecessors, for we are all bound by the Lord's commandment to honour our parents. But he seems to detract from the honour of his ancestors when he cries down their good money, and has it, and with it their image, cut up and in place of the gold money which they coined makes money which is partly brass. This seems to be foreshadowed in the first book of Kings where we read that King Rehoboam took away the golden shields which his father Solomon had made, in exchange for which he made brazen shields. That same Rehoboam lost five-sixths of his people because he tried at the beginning of his reign to overtax his subjects. Furthermore, the king ought exceedingly to abhor tyrannical acts, of which as we have said before alteration of the coinage is one. And that is prejudicial and dangerous to all the king's posterity, as shall be shown more at length later.

CHAPTER 20: OF OTHER DISADVANTAGES TO THE COMMUNITY AS A WHOLE

Among the many disadvantages arising from alteration of the coinage which affect the whole community is one which was the main subject of Chapter 15, namely that the prince could thus draw to himself almost all the money of the community and unduly impoverish his subjects. And as some chronic sicknesses are more dangerous than others because they are less perceptible so such an exaction is the more dangerous the less obvious it is, because its oppression is less quickly felt by the people than it would be in any other form of contribution. And yet no tallage can be heavier, more general or more severe.

Again, such alterations and debasements diminish the amount of gold and silver in the realm, since these metals, despite any embargo, are carried abroad, where they command a higher value. For men try to take their money to the places where they believe it to be worth most. And this reduces the material for money in the realm.

Again, foreigners frequently coin similar counterfeit money and bring it to the country where the debased coin is current and thus rob the king of the profit which he thinks he is making. It may be, too, that some of the material is consumed in the constant melting and remelting which goes on where such alterations are made. There are thus three ways in which the material of money is lessened by these alterations. They cannot therefore last long unless the material is abundant in mines or otherwise, and so the prince would at last be unable to coin enough good money. Again, because of these alterations, good merchandise or natural riches cease to be brought into a kingdom in which money is so changed, since merchants, other things being equal, prefer to pass over to those places in which they receive sound and good money. Furthermore, in such a kingdom internal trade is disturbed and hindered in many ways by such changes, and while they last, money rents, yearly pensions, rates of hire, cesses and the like, cannot be well and justly taxed or valued, as is well known. Neither can money safely be lent or credit given. Indeed many refuse to give that charitable help on account of such alterations. And yet a sufficiency of metal for coin, merchants and all these other things mentioned are either necessary or highly useful to humanity, and their opposites are prejudicial and hurtful to the whole civil community.

CHAPTER 21: OF DISADVANTAGES TO PART OF THE COMMUNITY

Some sections of the community are occupied in affairs honourable or profitable to the whole state, as in the growing of natural wealth or negotiating on behalf of the community. Such are churchmen, judges, soldiers, husbandmen, merchants, craftsmen and the like. But another section augments its own wealth by unworthy business, as do money changers, bankers or dealers in bullion: a disgraceful trade as was said in Chapter 18. These men, then, who are as it were unwanted by the state, and some others such as receivers and financial agents, etc., take a great part of the profit or gain arising from changes in coinage and by guile or by good luck, draw wealth from them, against God and Justice, since they are undeserving of such riches and unworthy of such wealth. But others, who are the best sections of the community, are impoverished by it; so that the prince in this way damages and overburdens the larger and better part of his subjects and yet does not receive the whole of the profit; but the persons above mentioned, whose business is contemptible and largely fraudulent, get a large part of it. Again, when the prince does not announce beforehand the date and the scheme of the alteration which he means to make, some persons, by their own cunning or through their friends, secretly foreknow it, and buy up merchandise with the weak money to sell again for the sound, get rich quickly and make an excessive and undue profit against the lawful course of normal trade. And this seems to be a kind of monopoly to the prejudice and damage of all the rest of the community. Furthermore, by such changes rents assessed in terms of money are necessarily unjustly lessened or unjustly raised, as was said before in Chapter 11 on change of name. The prince, also, by such variations and sophistications of coin, gives scoundrels an opportunity to coin false money, either because they consider that the prince has already done so and it is thus less against their conscience, or because the forgery is less quickly found out and they can more easily commit more crimes in these conditions than if good money were constantly current. Besides, in these circumstances, what innumerable perplexities, obscurities, errors and insuperable difficulties occur in accounts of expenditure and receipts! Hence also arise matters for lawsuits and various issues, insufficient payments of debts, frauds, disorders, manifold abuses and sundry disadvantages more than I can describe and possibly worse and greater than some that have been mentioned. And no wonder, for as Aristotle says: "One error has many consequences" as may easily be seen.

CHAPTER 22: WHETHER THE COMMUNITY CAN MAKE SUCH ALTERATIONS

Since the coinage is the property of the community as was shown in Chapter 6, it appears that the community can dispose of it as it pleases. It can therefore alter it after any fashion, make what gain it will from it and treat it as its own, especially if it needs a large sum of money for war or for the ransom of its prince from captivity or some accident of the kind. For in that case it might raise the sum by an alteration of the coinage, nor would this be unnatural or like usury, because it would not be done by the prince but by the community to which the money belonged. For in this way many of the objections to the alteration of the coinage already made would drop and have no place. And it appears not only that the community might do this, but also that it ought, assuming that the contribution is necessary, for such an alteration seems to unite almost all the good conditions required by any tallage or contribution. For it brings in much profit in little time, is very easy to collect and assess or share without employing a large staff or risking fraud in collection and is cheap to collect. Nothing, either, can be devised more fair or proportional, since he who can afford most pays most. And it is, for its amount, less seen or felt and more endurable without danger of rebellion or popular discontent. For it is universal: neither clerk nor noble can escape it by privilege or otherwise, as many try to escape other contributions, causing envyings, dissensions, litigation, scandals and many other evils which do not arise from such an alteration of the coinage. Therefore, in the case presupposed, it can and should be done by the community.

But in this matter it seems to me now, with all respect for wiser heads, that it may be laid down that the money needed by the community should be exported to, or spent in distant lands and among people with whom there is no intercourse, and also be so much as to cause a notorious lack of the materials for money in the community for a long time. And if so, the sum may be raised by lightening or alloying the coin, because if this were not done, the alteration would have to be made later for the reason and in the way given in Chapter 13. But if the sum be not so great or be otherwise expended, or in any other way be such as not to cause a notable and long lack of material for money in the community, I maintain that besides the disadvantages hinted at in the present chapter, such an alteration of the coinage would involve more, and worse things than those above explained, than would any other contribution. And the worst danger would be lest the prince should at last assume the right to do this and then all the before-mentioned evils would come back again. Nor does it matter that, as we began by saying, the money belongs to the community, because neither the community nor anyone else has the right to misuse or unlawfully use his own property, as the community would be doing if it made such an alteration in the coinage. And if the community, rightly or wrongly, should make such a change, the money must with all speed be brought back to its due and permanent state, and all taking of profit from it must cease.

CHAPTER 23: AN ARGUMENT THAT THE PRINCE MAY ALTER THE COINAGE

It is usually said that in an emergency all things belong to the prince. Therefore in an imminent or instant emergency, he may take as much of the money of his realm as he chooses, in any way he likes, for the defence of the commonwealth or of his own position as prince. And alteration of the coinage is an appropriate and fitting way of doing this, as may be proven from what is said in the previous chapter. Again, supposing that the prince has no right at the common or ordinary law so to alter the coinage and take such a profit from it, it might be said that he can do so in virtue of a prerogative, for instance a special privilege from the Pope, or the Church, or the Roman Emperor, or even from the community, granted to him of old as a heritage for his services.

The money, also, is the property of the community, as appears from Chapter 6, and the community can change it as was said in the last chapter; therefore it can, or could, grant the authority to make such a change to the prince, renounce the right to ordain or change the coinage and give part of the money to the prince to take in any way he pleased. Again, if by the common law it rests with the community, as has been said, to regulate the coinage, and it, owing to popular discord, has failed to agree on a plan, may it not compromise by leaving the regulation of the coinage henceforward and forever to the will of the prince? It may surely do so, and allow him on this account to take a profit from the change or regulation of the coinage. It was said, too, in Chapter 7 that a certain "pension" ought to be fixed to cover the expense of coining and that the prince may have something out of or in excess of that "pension" for himself: therefore, by parity of reasoning, he may have or take more and more from this and consequently as much as he would get from an alteration in the coinage. He may, therefore, in the same way, raise that profit by such alterations. Besides, the prince ought to have a large settled revenue from the community with which to maintain a noble and honourable estate as becomes princely magnificence or royal majesty. These revenues, then, must be attached to the princely dominion or the prerogative of the royal crown. It is therefore possible that a considerable part of these revenues was formerly charged on the coinage, so that it would be lawful for the prince to make a profit by altering the coin. It is also possible that if this right were taken away the rest of the revenue would not be enough for a princely state. Consequently, to propose to take from him the power of altering the coinage, is an attack on the honour of the king, a disherison of the prince, it is indeed impoverishing him and robbing him of his magnificence, not only unjustly, but disgracefully to the whole community which cannot with decency have a prince unless he maintains his dignity.

CHAPTER 24: REPLY TO THE PREVIOUS CHAPTER AND MAIN CONCLUSION

Although there might possibly be many difficulties in meeting the first argument, I will pass over them briefly, as it occurs to me now that, lest the prince should pretend such an emergency when there is none, as Aristotle says tyrants do, it should be determined by the community or the better part of it, expressly or tacitly, when, what and how great an emergency threatens. I mean by "expressly," that the community should be assembled, if there is the opportunity; "tacitly," if the emergency is so imminent that the people cannot be called together and so plain that it is subsequently notorious. For in such a case the prince may take some part of the property of his subjects, not by changing the coinage, but by way of a loan to be repaid in full later. On the second point, that the prince may have a privilege to change the money, first, I will not discuss the Pope's powers, but I think he never has made or would make such a grant since he would be giving a licence to do evil, which no possible good deeds could qualify a man to receive. As for the Roman Emperor, I say that he never had power to give any prince the privilege to do what he could not lawfully do himself, e.g. such a change in the money, as appears from what has been said. As to the community, it has been said in Chapter 22 that it cannot change the money except in a particular case, and then, if it should entrust the task to the prince, within reasonable limits which are apparent from that chapter and from others, the prince would still not be doing it of his own authority but as the executor of a public ordinance. In answer to another argument, that the community which owns the money may divest itself of its right and transfer it to the prince, it seems, in the first place, that no well-advised community would do such a thing; and secondly that it is unlawful even for itself to alter the coinage or to misuse its own property in any way, as was said in Chapter 22. Again, a community of citizens which is naturally free would never knowingly reduce itself to slavery or submit itself to the yoke of a tyranny. If, therefore, it were cheated or terrified and coerced into granting the prince such alterations without foreseeing the resulting evils, and that this would amount to slavery, it can immediately or otherwise revoke the grant. Again, anything belonging to anyone as of natural right cannot justly be transferred to another; but that is how money belongs to the free community, as is clear enough from Chapters 1 and 6. So, just as the community cannot grant to the prince authority to misuse the wives of any of its citizens he will, it cannot give him such a privilege over the coinage as he can only misuse, by exacting a profit from changing it, as appears from several earlier chapters. The same argument applies to what was added about a disagreement in the community in the regulation of the coinage and its compromising in so far on the prince's decision. I admit it can do so for some purposes and on some occasions; but not by giving him the power to take such undue profit from the said unnecessary alterations. To another argument, borrowed from Chapter 7, that the prince may have some profit from the coinage, the answer is easy, namely that this is a small and limited pension, which is not to be at all augmented by alteration of the coinage, but is independent of any change. In reply to another argument, that the prince may have revenues and ought to have a magnificent and honourable estate, such revenues can and should be appropriated and drawn from other sources than such undue alterations from which, as has previously been shown, such great evils and disadvantages arise. And supposing that some part of such revenue is charged on the coinage, it must be fixed and limited in amount, say two shillings or so on every mark coined and so forth, which would not involve any alteration or unreasonable and enormous increase in profit arising from the detestable changes of which we have spoken.

The general conclusion from all this is that the prince cannot make these changes or receive profit in this way either by the regular common law or by privilege, gift, grant, bargain or any other authority or means whatever, nor can it be his right in virtue of his lordship or otherwise. Also that the denial of such a right is no disherison or infringement of his majesty as is falsely alleged by flatterers, intriguers and traitors to the commonwealth. Again, since the prince is bound not to do this, he deserves no pension or gift for refraining from such an improper exaction, for this seems nothing less than a ransom from slavery, which no king or good prince ought to exact from his subjects. Also, supposing, but not admitting, that he may have the privilege of drawing a profit from the coinage as a return for coining good money and maintaining its standard, even so he must forfeit the privilege if he so abuses it as to change and debase the money for the greedy and disgraceful enhancement of his own profit.

CHAPTER 25: THAT A TYRANT CANNOT BE LASTING

In this and the following chapter I propose to prove that raising money by such alterations of the coinage is dishonourable to the kingdom and to the damage of all the king's posterity. You must know, therefore, that the difference between kingdom and tyranny is that a tyrant loves and pursues his own good more than the common advantage of his subjects, and aims at keeping his people in slavery; a king, on the contrary, prefers the public good to his own and loves above all things, after God and his own soul, the good and public freedom of his subjects. And this is the true usefulness and nobility of the princely power, whose lordship is the nobler and the better, as Aristotle says, the more it is over freer and better men, and endures the longer for the king's steadfastness in following that principle. As Cassiodorus says: "The art of governing is to love the interests of the many." For whenever kingship approaches tyranny it is near its end, for by this it becomes ripe for division, change of dynasty or total destruction, especially in a temperate climate, far from a slavish barbarism, where men are habitually, morally and naturally free, not slaves, nor habituated to tyranny; to whom slavery would be unprofitable and unacceptable, and tyranny nothing less than unnatural and therefore short-lived, since as Aristotle says: "Things contrary to nature most quickly decay." So, too, Cicero says: "That no empire is strong enough to last if it is full of fear." And Seneca in his tragedies says: "No-one can prolong enforced empires; moderate empires last." Wherefore the Lord by his prophet reproached the deposed princes, saying: "With force and with cruelty have ye ruled them." And the same thing is said elsewhere, for Plutarch says to the emperor Trajan that, "the state is a body, living as it were by a gift of the gods, actuated by the decision of the highest justice, and governed by the restraint of reason." The state or kingdom, then, is like a human body and so Aristotle will have it in Book V of the *Politics*. As, therefore, the body is disordered when the humours flow too freely into one member of it, so that that member is often thus inflamed and overgrown while the others are withered and shrunken and the body's due proportions are destroyed and its life shortened; so also is a commonwealth or a kingdom when riches are unduly attracted by one part of it. For a commonwealth or kingdom whose princes, as compared with their subjects, increase beyond measure in wealth, power and position, is as it were a monster, like a man whose head is so large and heavy that the rest of his body is too weak to support it. And just as such a man has no pleasure in life and cannot live long; neither can a kingdom survive whose prince draws to himself riches in excess as is done by altering the coinage, as appeared in Chapter 20. Again, as in a chorus unison has no power to please and excessive or improper dissonance destroys and spoils the whole harmony, but a proportional and measured difference of tone is needed to produce the sweet melody of a joyous choir: so also, generally, equality of possessions or power in all sections of the community is inconvenient and inconsistent, but too great a disparity destroys and spoils the harmony of the state, as appears from Aristotle in *Politics*, Book V. But especially if the prince, who is, as it were, the tenor and leading voice in singing, is too great and is out of tune with the rest of the commonwealth, the sweet melody of the kingdom's constitution will be disturbed. And this, as Aristotle says, is another difference between a king and a tyrant. For a tyrant wishes to be more powerful than the whole community over whom he rules by force: but a king's moderation is restrained by the fact that he is greater and more powerful than any of his subjects, but of less power or wealth than the whole community, and so stands in the middle. But because the king's power commonly and easily tends to increase, the greatest care and constant watchfulness must be used, indeed extreme and supreme prudence is needed, to keep it from degenerating into tyranny, especially because of deceitful flatterers who have always, as Aristotle says, urged princes to be tyrants! For they cunningly deceive the simple ears of princes (as we read in the book of Esther), who judge other men's characters by their own, and by their suggestions kings' minds are turned to evil. But since it is hard to avoid them or to root them out, Aristotle gives another rule by which a kingdom may long survive. That is that the prince should not enlarge his dominion over his subjects, should not overtax them or seize their goods, should allow or grant them liberties and should not interfere with them or use his plenary powers but only a power regulated and limited by law and custom. For few things, as Aristotle says, should be left to the decision of a judge or a prince. For he adduces the example of Theopompus, king of the Lacedaemonians, who, after having given back to the people many powers and imposts, when his wife wept and reproached him, saying, "He should be ashamed to hand on to his sons a less profitable kingdom than he had received from his father," replied, "I leave them a more permanent one." Surely an oracle of God! How weighty a saying, fit to be written in golden letters in kings' palaces! "I leave them a more permanent one": as he might have put it, "I have made the kingdom greater in duration than I have made it less by limiting its power." A greater man than Solomon is here. For if Rehoboam, whom I mentioned above, had received from his father Solomon a kingdom so limited, he would never have lost ten of the twelve tribes of Israel, nor would he have been reproached thus in Ecclesiasticus: "Thou didst profane thy seed, to bring wrath upon thy children; and I was grieved for thy folly; so that the sovereignty was divided."

It has thus been proved that a dominion which is turned from a kingdom to a tyranny is bound to have a speedy end.

CHAPTER 26: THAT THE TAKING OF PROFITS FROM ALTERATION OF THE COINAGE INJURES THE WHOLE ROYAL SUCCESSION

I propound the thesis that the alterations before-mentioned are dishonourable to the king and prejudicial to the royal house. To prove this I lay down three premises:

First that that is a reproach to a king and to the prejudice of his successors by which a kingdom is exposed to destruction or to being given over to strangers. Nor could a king grieve or weep enough who should be so unhappy, so wretched as by his carelessness or misgovernment to do anything that brought him or his heirs to lose a kingdom ennobled by so many great deeds and so long gloriously maintained. Nor would it be without danger to his glorious soul, if by his fault his people should suffer so many plagues, so many great misfortunes as usually accompany the fall or the conquest of kingdoms.

Secondly, I submit that tyranny exposes a kingdom to ruin, as was set forth in the last chapter and since, as it is written in Ecclesiasticus, "Sovereignty is transferred from nation to nation, because of iniquities and deeds of violence and greed of money," while tyranny is iniquitous and violent. Furthermore, to come to particulars, God forbid that the free hearts of

Frenchmen should have so degenerated that they should willingly become slaves; and therefore a slavery thrust upon them cannot last. For, though the power of tyrants is great, it does
violence to the free hearts of subjects and is of no avail against foreigners. Whoever, therefore,
should in any way induce the lords of France to such tyrannical government, would expose the
realm to great danger and pave the way to its end. For neither has the noble offspring of the
French kings learned to be tyrannous, nor the people of Gaul to be servile; therefore if the royal
house declines from its ancient virtue, it will certainly lose the kingdom.

Thirdly, I submit, as a point already proved and often repeated, that to take or augment
profit by alteration of the coinage is fraudulent, tyrannical and unjust, and moreover it cannot
be persisted in without the kingdom being, in many other respects also, changed to a tyranny.
Wherefore, it not only brings disadvantages of its own, but involves many other evils as either
its conditions or its consequences. For this course can only be the advice of evil-minded men,
ready to counsel any fraud or tyranny, if they see a prince inclined to it or willing to listen to it.

To sum up my argument, I say that a thing which tends to bring a realm to ruin is disgraceful and harmful to the king and his heirs, my first premise; that it extends and changes to
a tyranny, my second; and that it does so by alteration of the coinage, my third. Consequently
a tax levied by means of such changes is against the king's honour and injures his posterity,
which was to be proved.

All this, as I said before, is tentative and subject to correction by experts. For, as Aristotle
says: "Civil matters are usually doubtful and uncertain." If anyone, therefore, in his love of
truth, chooses to contradict or oppose what I have written, he will be doing well. And if I have
spoken evil let him bear witness of the evil, but with reason, lest he be seen needlessly and
wilfully to condemn what he is not able effectually to refute.

12. Gabriel Biel: *On the Power and Utility of Moneys* (1495)[1]

To understand what follows we must note first of all that, according to Aristotle in Book V chapter 9 of *Ethics* and Book I of the *Politics*, the use of money was invented by necessity. For commodities cannot be exchanged directly, although mankind, numerous as it is, cannot exist without their exchange since all men do not possess in abundance all the necessaries of life. Added to this is the remoteness from each other of the localities in which exchangeable commodities are found and the difficulty in transporting them. Moreover there is the long interval of time during which such articles cannot be preserved without decay. There is also the necessity, owing to the multiplicity of human needs, that an exchangeable commodity should be divisible into numerous parts, so that many necessaries may be procured through it by different individuals. So, too, there is the need of certain indivisible articles of exchange of great value and utility to man, such as horses, houses and the like. It was necessary, therefore, to find some medium, small in quantity, so that it may be transferred readily from place to place, and its depreciation or diminution easily weighed. It should be marked with the stamp of the prince or of the one in authority, lest, if everyone should issue money, its value might vary and be unknown or falsified. In this event equality in exchanges would not be preserved. It should be of fixed weight, so that its value may not vary; permanent in its nature and free from decay, in order that it may be suitable for future provision; precious in material, so that great value may be stored in a small space, thus making it easy to carry from place to place. It should be divisible according to its value into numerous smaller parts to meet the needs of those who require many low-priced articles. Such then is money either from its own nature or from man's design relative to human need. For the more pressing is man's need of any commodity, the higher is its value and the greater the increase in its price. Therefore in accordance with the relation of money and exchangeable commodities to human need money becomes the definite measure of all exchangeable and salable wares.

In the second place we must note that money can be falsified in three ways related to its substance, namely its metallic composition, the amount of its weight and its public form, as Panormitanus states in the chapter, Quanto, *de iureiur*. This statement is found also in the gloss on the same chapter. In each of these three ways money can be falsified. It can be falsified in its composition, because it does not have its legal *liga* owing to the admixture of a cheaper material, or because the metal regularly used [as an alloy] is in excessive quantity. *Liga* is the kind of mixture or grade of metal. Money is false in weight if it does not have the legal weight. In this connection we should note that a coin should have as much weight as the material from which it is made, with a proper deduction for the expense and labor of minting. Such is the

---

[1]   Translated by Robert Belle Burke.

view of Innocent, although Bartolus does not agree with him. The latter holds that the expense of minting should be defrayed from the public treasury. Innocent's reason is based on the fact that no one is required to coin money at his own expense. Moreover, this opinion of Innocent is held generally, as Angelus maintains in his *Summa* on the word *falsarius*, and I so understand it.

The legal weight is the weight depending on the quantity of substance properly determined for such coin. For example, if it is determined the florin should have gold weighing a *dragma*, which is the eighth of an ounce, then the florin is false in weight if it does not have an amount of gold weighing a *dragma*. Therefore, since weight follows naturally the quantity of substance in a body, and quantity of substance is not distinguished from substance, falsification of weight is a diminution of substance, whether this results from rasure of the coin, or more subtly from the use of artificial corrosive water, or from some other cause not easily detected by the eye. Moreover, the correct determination of weight requires that the determined weight of money shall be of the same value as that of its material before minting. Therefore, money should have as much value from its weight as its material had before minting, and no more. The expense of minting is, of course, to be deducted as stated above.

Falsification in form occurs when a change is made in the name, device or image of he that issued the money. Therefore he that has authority to issue money, stamp on it a certain form, an image, circumscription or some device. If any part of this predetermined form is omitted, or if anything is added to it, the money is falsified in form. Moreover, the form of money is in a way a testification to its genuineness and legality, namely that it is of genuine substance and legal weight, as Nicholas Oresme states in his treatise on money. Therefore, on the money of Christian princes or states there is frequently placed an image of God, or of a saint with his name, or the sign of the Cross, which in olden times was designed as a testimony to the genuineness of money in material and weight. He adds also:

> If, therefore, a prince under this inscription changes the material or weight, he seems tacitly to utter a lie, commit perjury, and give false witness. For he himself abuses this word money, since money, according to Ugutio is derived from *moneo*, because it warns that there should be no fraud in metal or weight.

Such is his statement.

In the third place we must note in regard to the alteration of money that an alteration of this kind can be made in a number of ways, sometimes in the material, sometimes in the form, sometimes in the value, sometimes in the name. Money is altered in material when, for example, owing to a lack of material or to an overabundance a new money is formed in another material, or in another mixture or *liga* of the former material.

Money is altered in form when the impression of the figure is altered in the image or stamp, or when there is a change in the circumscription. Money is altered in value when, for example, a change is made in substance, composition or weight; or, these remaining unchanged, another value is fixed; as, for example, if the florin up to the present has had a value of twenty-six *grossi*, and it is decided that in the future it should be worth eighteen or twenty-four.

Money is altered in name when names are changed, whether they are accidental, to wit, such as do not indicate the weight or value of money; for example, names of its author or of the place where it was coined and the like; or essential, as those that are given to coins of determined value or weight like the *obulus, denarius, solidus, libra, florenus*.

These changes can sometimes be effected in such a way that the former money remains in circulation and retains its own value. Sometimes, however, they involve a repudiation and prohibition of the former currency. Moreover they result at times from a reasonable cause owing to the needs of the state and to its advantage. In accordance with these principles a change can sometimes be effected lawfully, sometimes culpably and unlawfully.

First conclusion: He that falsifies money in substance, form or weight commits a mortal sin, if he inflicts a loss on his neighbor or on the state.

This conclusion is that of Hostiensis and it is taught generally. It is manifest also from text of the chapter, Quanto, *de iureiur*, where we read that an oath concerning the maintenance of a debased currency is not binding, since an oath ought not to be a bond of iniquity. It is, therefore, iniquitous to keep false money and much more so to falsify money. Moreover, it is evident that the sin is a mortal one, because it is theft since it is an act depriving another of his property without his consent, as we state below. This is also clearly shown by the Extravagant of John XXII who excommunicates all such in the Kingdom of France. Moreover, the common middle term proves that the guilty person is required to make restitution, because everyone causing a loss unjustly is required to indemnify the loser if he can be found. But he that fraudulently falsifies money has caused a loss unjustly to his neighbor or to the state; therefore he is required to make restitution to the injured party if he can be found, or to the poor if he cannot be found. The major premise is clear from the chapter, Si culpa, *de iniu. et dam. da.* The minor premise is likewise quite clear. Moreover the qualification, "If he inflicts a loss on his neighbor," is expressly stated in the conclusion, because if a man should falsify money in form, but in such a way that its value is not lessened, he would not commit a sin, because he would not thus be causing a loss. So, too, if he should falsify money by rasure or by breaking it with no intention of passing such coin.

Second conclusion: He that alters money to the loss of the state is required to compensate for the loss inflicted by an act of restitution.

This is proved because such a man inflicts a loss unjustly; therefore, etc. The antecedent is proved because he that causes a loss on property not his own does so unjustly. But he that alters money, causing thereby a loss to the state, inflicts a loss on property not his own, because he inflicts a loss on the state, which is not his. The qualification, "If he inflicts a loss on the state," is expressly stated, because if money should be altered for a reasonable cause to the advantage of the state, restitution would be out of the question.

There are three causes for the lawful alteration of money. The first is the introduction of false coinage. For example, if a foreign prince or a counterfeiter should malevolently fashion or counterfeit prescribed forms or stamps by which he endeavored to introduce a debased currency, less in value than the old money, yet such that its difference from the true money could not be detected by the people; and if there was no other convenient way by which the false money could be driven out, then a change in the form of the true money would be expedient. Its correct value, however, should be retained, so that it could thus be distinguished from the false money that had been introduced.

The second cause: If the old money should be depreciated by excessive length of service and lessened in substance and weight by constant handling, new money should then be coined, differing from the old money in lawful weight, and the circulation of the old depreciated money could be forbidden.

The third cause is a scarcity of metal, which in that event cannot be procured at the regular price at which it sold before the dearth. The money should then be altered, either by determining another value for it in comparison with money of another material, or by making new money of less weight than the old and of equal face value. For example, if a *dragma* of uncoined gold for some reason should rise in price, so that it would then be worth thirty *grossi* of silver instead of twenty, its former value; then either the florin having a *dragma* should also be changed in value, so that even if its former value was twenty-one *grossi*, its new value should be fixed at thirty-one *grossi*: or new golden currency should be coined of less weight. The weight, however, should be sufficient to give the coin an intrinsic value of twenty *grossi*. There should also be some difference in form to distinguish the new from the old. This perhaps would prove more expedient for the state, so that the fixed prices of other commodities and incomes and pecuniary valuations should remain unchanged, and thus no one be defrauded. Moreover, it would make little difference whether the circulation of the old money continued. Nothing would be prohibited. The required ratio, however, should be maintained to other inferior moneys and to the prices of salable articles and to the values of incomes or appraisals.

A fourth cause might be added. A gain, not to the minter but to the state, following as a result from the new money might be expedient or necessary. Of this we shall speak below under the Doubts.

Outside of these causes a change in the value of money is condemned and is unjust, because it inflicts a loss on the state and robs the subjects, whether this change be in material, weight, voluntary composition, value or essential names. If, however, a change should be made in the form alone, or in accidental names, and not in value, such a change could be tolerated. A change even in value is tolerable if authorized beforehand by the state. If this change resulted from pride, ostentation, contempt of others or from another sinister motive, it would not lack guilt. No restitution, however, would be required. Therefore, our decision is that there be no alteration of money except such as arises from a great and a reasonable necessity.

Third conclusion: He that knowingly pays out false money for true and lawful money is a forger and is required to make restitution for the losses inflicted.

He is proved to be a forger because he employs falsehood to deceive his neighbor. Therefore the consequent holds from the definition of a *falsarius*. The antecedent is obvious. That he is bound to make restitution is proved, because he inflicts a loss on individual and state. Therefore he is bound to make restitution. The consequent holds from the common middle term and from the chapter adduced above, Si culpa, *de inur. et da. da.*

Fourth conclusion: He that passes knowingly money not current or otherwise depreciated for good and current money defrauds his neighbor and is bound to make restitution.

This conclusion is in the dictum of Angelus in the *Summa* and is that of Anthoninus. It is proved by the same middle terms as the one before. For such a man deceives his neighbor by giving him something bad for something good. Moreover, the word knowingly is expressly stated in the two preceding conclusions, since if his act is owing to ignorance, let us suppose, of the value of the money he is passing, he is absolved at least from guilt and also from making restitution so long as his ignorance lasts. If, however, later on he discovers his error, he will be required to make restitution, because whether knowingly or ignorantly I inflict a loss on my neighbor, I am bound to make good his loss, after the loss inflicted has been brought to my attention.

He that passes false money as defined in either Conclusion three or four is not excused on the plea that false or depreciated money of this kind was given to him for good money, since another's guilt and one's own error should not harm a third person. For guilt should hold fast its own agents, not others. He, therefore, that accepts false money, broken money or money whole but depreciated, for good money lays himself open to the charge that he did not examine it with due care. If, however, he knowingly accepted bad money, that he might pass it for good money, his fault is greater, and also the need of restitution.

Fifth conclusion: He that transfers money from a certain place where it is reckoned of less value to a place where its value is greater, does not commit a sin if he is not otherwise guilty of fraud.

This conclusion is due to Anthoninus. His proof is that any man may by his labor seek for gain without loss to another. But he that transfers, as stated in the conclusion, money purchased by him where it is less valuable to a place where it is more valuable employs his industry without loss to anyone else, provided, however, that he does not shave it nor diminish its value. Therefore the conclusion follows.

Three doubts follow.

In regard to what precedes our first question is: Who should coin money? To this Panormitanus replies on the chapter, Quanto, *de iureiura.*, that the prince alone, that is, the emperor, should have this power and no one else without his official authorization. He recognizes exceptions, however, in the case of an inferior prince or state, or in general an inferior power that had exercised this right for so long a time that memory knew not to the contrary; as stated in the chapter, *Super quibusda de var. sig.*; or in the case of one who had exercised imperial rights. For example, the kings of Spain are said not to be subject to imperial control, because they snatched their kingdom from the jaws of the enemy. Anthoninus also holds this view. The reason for his main point rests on the fact that, since money, as we have already assumed, was invented and introduced for the good of the community, it is fitting that money should be coined by the ruler of the community. But such is the prince or one having authority from him.

Although it is the privilege of the prince to coin money and to stamp it with his own image and name, for this reason money in circulation among the people is not his, nor is he himself the owner of the money current in his dominion. For money is the medium of exchange for natural riches and the equivalent of them. Therefore money belongs to those that have the natural riches. For when a man gives his bread or the labor of his own body for money the money is his own after he has received it, just as the bread and labor were his and at his free disposal.

Moreover, Nicholas Oresme says that although coining money is the prerogative of the prince, authority to fix the value of money or the ratio of one denomination of money to another should not be vested in the prince but in the community to which the money belongs. For example, the community should determine the ratio of the florin to the *grossus*, or of the *grossus* to the *obulus*, namely that the florin is worth so many *grossi* and the *grossus* so many *obuli*. This I take to mean that the prince has not the power to fix the value of money according to his own wish but according to the just and natural ratio of gold to silver and of silver to such a *liga*. Determination in regard to this matter is vested in the community.

We therefore conclude that, if a prince should reject valid money, in order that he may buy it up more cheaply and melt it and then issue another coinage of less value, attaching the value of the former currency to it, he would be guilty of stealing money and is required to make restitution. This is the opinion of Hostiensis and Panormitanus. It is quite obvious, because he sells a cheaper article at a higher price, which is contrary to justice. Moreover, in this way he would be able to acquire unjustly all the money of his subjects. For example, if he should depress gold to a low price and buy it for silver, and then after increasing the price sell the gold money for silver at a higher price. The case would be similar if he placed a price on all the grain in his dominion and bought it up, and afterwards should sell it at a higher price also determined by him. Such an act would be a most unjust and tyrannical oppression of his people. The sale of corn by Saint Joseph under the sway of Pharaoh is not a case in point, since from the time that the corn ceased growing it became dearer and commanded a higher price than formerly until Joseph had stored it up in granaries when there was an abundant supply of it. For man's need measures the price of a commodity, as Aristotle in Book V of the *Ethics* maintains. Moreover, if perchance the price was excessive, Cassiodorus remarks, "I suppose that the holy man was constrained by necessity to satisfy a greedy prince and aid his people in danger."

The second doubt is concerning the question whether a prince may under certain circumstances alter money for his own gain: or more generally, whether a prince may make a profit out of money by fixing a greater value for the money than its material before coinage was worth, the necessary expenses being deducted by lessening either the weight or the *liga* under the former valuation. In brief, the answer is that in one case alone may a prince realize a gain from money, namely, provided that gain is used to promote public welfare as indicated in the second conclusion. The case is in point where a prince requires a subsidy for the defense of the state, which his subjects are bound to grant. Then some alteration in the money might be made, lessening either the weight or material under the same value, so that in this way the people might feel the burden less. There is the proviso, however, that the gain is not extended beyond the absolute need of the prince as stated above. But this alteration should not be made without the consent of his subjects, to whom, as we said, the money belonged. For anyone may renounce his right according to VII q.1. Quam periculosum. So also the community. Innocent maintains that the consent of the majority of the magnates is sufficient, but Panormitanus in the passage adduced expresses his doubts on this point, since it is a matter concerning individuals. Angelus, therefore, says that the consent of the individuals concerned is required.

The consent of the people does not, however, suffice to put in circulation depreciated money of this kind outside the kingdom in question. For a prince may not relieve his own needs at the expense of those who are not his subjects. On this point all are fairly in agreement.

Some think that in case a large sum of money must be collected for ransoming a prince or for defense, etc., an alteration in the coinage is the better and more expeditious method. They reason that this is the easier way to collect quickly the required funds without fraud and undue exactions from the subjects. It is, moreover, felt less and for this reason more easily borne without protest and without the danger of a rebellion on the part of the people. It is the most general form of taxation embracing all classes, clergy, laity, nobility, plebeians, rich and poor alike. But whether these reasons are valid or not, I leave to the diligent reader.

There are, however, in this method two obligations that of necessity must be met. First, that such money be current only among the subjects of that particular realm, who are bound to aid their own prince and state; since others would suffer wrong if such money should be put in circulation among them. Second, that after the collection of the required amount the currency is restored to its former status, since cause and effect should cease together.

The third doubt is relative to the question whether he that sets apart the better and heavier *denarii* and has them melted, commits a sin and is required to make restitution. Angelus replies in his *Summa*, following Hostiensis, Johannes Andreas and others under this distinction:

> If coiners, since they cannot make all the coins equal, some of the *denarii* being under weight, allow others to be over weight, in order that there may be an equalization of the legal weight in a large number of pieces, which is impossible in individual ones: then those men that select the better coins are forgers and are required to make restitution to the community, because they have lessened the value of the coinage as a whole. If, however, all the *denarii* are of legal weight, but some exceed it; and if those men shave the better, not, however, below the legal weight, they are not in my opinion forgers, although they are wrong-doers, and in no way should they be advised to continue the practice. If, however, they are unwilling to abstain from it, I do not suppose they are on this account outside the pale of salvation.

He seems, therefore, to think that such a wrong doer commits a venial, not a mortal sin. I do not clearly understand his point of view, unless the trifling nature of the offense is its excuse since the selection is infrequent and few coins are involved. If, however, a man makes a practice of this, he inflicts a serious loss on the minter who has improvidently exceeded the legal weight, or on him in whose name the minter coins the money. He should accordingly be required to make restitution to him. The case is similar to that of the man who has bought below the regular price where there is a fixed market, and the seller has made a mistake in number or weight. Thus has the minter made a mistake in the weight. If, however, the offense should happen rarely, its trifling nature would be its excuse; just as the theft of an insignificant article, a single apple for example, is excused.

13. Copernicus: *Essay on the Coinage of Money* (1526)[1]

Although there are countless scourges which in general debilitate kingdoms, principalities, and republics, the four most important (in my judgment) are dissension, abnormal mortality, barren soil, and debasement of the currency. The first three are so obvious that nobody is unaware of their existence. But the fourth, which concerns money, is taken into account by few persons and only the most perspicacious. For it undermines states, not by a single attack all at once, but gradually and in a certain covert manner.

Coinage is imprinted gold or silver, by which the prices of things bought and sold are reckoned according to the regulations of any state or its ruler. Therefore money is, as it were, a common measure of values. That which ought to be a measure, however, must always preserve a fixed and constant standard. Otherwise, public order is necessarily disturbed, with buyers and sellers being cheated in many ways, just as if the yard, bushel, or pound did not maintain an invariable magnitude. Hence this measure is in my opinion the coin's face value. Although this is based on the metal's purity, nevertheless intrinsic value must be distinguished from face value. For, the denomination of a coin may exceed its metallic content, and the other way around.

Coinage was introduced for a necessary reason. Things could have been exchanged for gold and silver by weight alone, because mankind's common judgment prizes gold and silver everywhere. But to carry weights around all the time was very inconvenient. The purity of the gold and silver, moreover, was not instantly recognizable by everybody. Accordingly, people ordained that a coin should be marked with a universally recognized symbol to indicate that it contained the proper amount of gold or silver, and to instill confidence in its reliability.

In the next place, copper is usually mixed with coins, especially those made of silver. This is done, I believe, for two reasons. First, the coinage is less vulnerable to the schemes of crooks and those who would melt it down if it consisted of pure silver. Secondly, when silver bullion is broken down into little pieces and the smallest coins, it keeps a convenient size when it is alloyed with copper. A third reason may be added, namely, to stop it from disappearing sooner by being worn down through constant use, and to make it last longer by strengthening it with copper.

The face value of a coin is just and proper when the coin contains slightly less gold or silver than may be bought with it, since only the expenses of the minters should be deducted. For, the symbol should add some value to the metal.

Money loses its value most of all through excessive abundance, if so much silver is coined as to heighten people's desire for silver bullion more than for coined money. For in this way

---

[1]   Translated by Edward Rosen and Erna Hilfstein.

the coinage's market value vanishes when with it it is not possible to buy as much silver as the money itself contains, and is found a greater advantage in destroying the coin by melting the silver. The solution is to mint no more coinage until it recovers its par value and becomes more desirable than silver.

This face value is corrupted in many ways. Firstly, the metal alone may be defective, when for the same weight of coin more than the right amount of copper is alloyed with the silver. Secondly, the weight may be defective, even though the proportion of copper and silver is correct. Thirdly, and this is the worst, both defects may be present at the same time.

The value of a coin deteriorates also by itself as the coin is worn down through long use. Only for this reason should it be renewed and replaced. This is indicated if somewhat less silver is found in the coin than is bought with it. This is the condition in which depreciation of the coinage is properly perceived.

Having discussed money in a general way above, let me turn to Prussian money in particular by first showing how it became so debased. It circulates under the names mark, skoter, and the like, which are also names of weights. As a weight, a mark is 1/2 pound. As a coin, however, a mark consists of 60 shillings, all this is very well known. But lest ambiguity, as between weight and coin, give rise to misunderstanding, wherever "mark" is used, let it be understood as denoting the coin. On the other hand, where weight is involved, I shall interpret the term "pound" as a weight of marks, but a "mark" by weight as 1/2 pound.

Now in the old records of proceedings and official correspondence we find that when Conrad of Jungingen was Grand Master, that is just before the battle of Tannenberg, 1/2 pound, that is, 1 mark by weight of pure silver cost 2 Prussian marks, 8 skoters. That was when three parts of pure silver were alloyed with a fourth part of copper, and from 1/2 pound of this pure material they made 112 shillings. To this amount add 1/3, which is 37 1/3 shillings, making a total of 149 1/3 shillings. The total weighs 2/3 pound, that is, 32 skoters, containing of course three parts (which are 1/2 pound) of pure silver. Its price, however, as was just said, was 140 shillings for 1/2 pound. But the remainder of 9 1/3 shillings, which was missing, was made up by the money's face value. Its face value was therefore suitably linked with its intrinsic value.

Such coins of Winrich, Ulrich, and Conrad are still found now and then in strongboxes. Then after the defeat of Prussia and the aforementioned battle of Grunwald/Tannenberg, the damage to the Order began to be more and more apparent in the coinage day after day. For although the shillings of Heinrich look like those just mentioned, they are found to have no more than 3/5 silver. This mistake grew worse until the proportion was reversed and three parts of copper began to be alloyed with a fourth part of silver, so that "silver coinage" would no longer be the proper designation, but rather "copper coinage." Yet it kept the weight of 112 shillings to 1/2 pound.

It is not in the least advisable to introduce a new, good coinage while an old, debased coinage remains in circulation. How much worse was this mistake, while an old, better coinage remained in circulation, to introduce a new, debased coinage, which not only spoiled the old coinage but, so to say, swept away! When Michael Rusdorf was the Grand Master, they wanted to eliminate this mistake, and restore the coinage to its former, better state. They minted new shillings, which we now call "groats." But since the old, debased coins apparently could not be withdrawn without loss, they continued to circulate alongside the new coins, by an extraordinary error. Two old shillings were exchanged for one new one. It then came to pass that two kinds of marks were inflicted upon the people, namely, the new or good mark consisting of the new shillings, by contrast with the old or light mark consisting of the old shilling, with 60 shillings to each of the marks. However, the pennies remained as they had been, with only 6 pence being exchanged for 1 old shilling, but 12 pence for 1 new shilling. For it can easily be surmised that originally the shilling was equal to 12 pence. For just as we usually say *mandel* for the number 15, so in most parts of Germany the word *schilling* is still used for the number 12. The term "new shilling," on the other hand, lasted right down to a time within our memory. How they finally became groats, I shall explain below.

As regards the new shillings, then, at 60 shillings to the mark, 8 mark contained 1 pound of pure silver, as is quite evident from their composition. For they consist 1/2 of copper, and 1/2 of silver. At 60 shillings to the mark, 8 of these marks weigh nearly 2 pounds. The old shillings, on the other hand, although equal to the new shillings in weight, as has been said, were worth half as much. For since the old shillings contained only 1/4 silver, 16 marks were produced from 1 pound of pure silver and weighed four times as much.

Later, when the country's status changed, cities were granted the right to mint coins. As they exercised their new privilege, currency increased in quantity, though not in quality. Four parts of copper began to be alloyed with a fifth part of silver in the old shillings, until 20 marks were exchanged for 1 pound of silver. And so those new shillings, since they were now worth more than twice as much as the recent shillings, were made into skoters, reckoned at 24 to the light mark. Hence, 1/5 of the money's value in the mark perished.

Afterwards, however, the new shillings, having become skoters, disappeared because they were accepted also throughout the mark of Brandenburg. It was decided to recover them by evaluating them at a groat, that is, 3 shillings. This was a very bad miscalculation, quite unworthy of so distinguished a body of notables, as though Prussia could not get along without those groats, even though they were worth no more than 15 pence of the coinage then in circulation, while its value was already depressed also by its abundance.

The groat in fact differed from the shilling in that it was worth 1/5 or 1/6 less than the standard. Through its false and unfair evaluation it dragged down the value of the shilling. Maybe the wrong previously inflicted by the shillings on the groats by forcing them to become skoters had to be avenged in this way. But woe to you, O Prussia, you who pay the penalty for a maladministered state by your ruin, alas! Thus, although the money's market value and intrinsic value were gradually vanishing at the same time, nevertheless there was absolutely no interruption in the coining of money. The costs of minting did not cover the difference by which the later coinage would be equalized with the older coinage. Hence, a coinage always worse than the previous coinage was superimposed on it. This depressed the worth of the earlier coinage and drove it out, until the shilling's face value coincided in due proportion with the groat's intrinsic value, and 24 light marks were equivalent to 1 pound of silver.

But at least some small remnants of the money's worth must have persisted in the end, since no consideration was given to restoring it. Yet this practice or abuse of counterfeiting, clipping, and tampering with money was ingrained so long that it could not stop, nor has it stopped to this very day. For what kind of money it will become hereafter and what its condition is now, it is shameful and painful to say. For it has fallen so low today that 30 marks contain hardly 1 pound of silver. Then what remains in the absence of help except that hereafter Prussia, drained of gold and silver, will have an exclusively copper currency? Consequently, imports of foreign merchandise and all foreign trade will soon end. For what foreign merchant will want to exchange his goods for copper coins? Lastly, which of our merchants will be able to buy foreign merchandise in foreign lands with the same money? Yet those in authority scornfully disregard this immense misfortune of the Prussian state. To their very dear country they owe, not to mention the deepest devotion, after piety to God, even their very lives. Yet by their thoughtless indifference they let their country slip wretchedly downhill further and further day after day and crash.

While, then, such grave evils beset Prussian money and consequently the whole country, its calamities benefit only the goldsmiths and those who know the purity of metal by experience. For from the mixed coinage they collect the old pieces, from which they melt down the silver and sell it. From the inexperienced public they constantly receive more silver with the coinage. But after those old shillings now disappear completely, the next best are selected, while the inferior mass of money remains behind. Hence arises that widespread and incessant complaint: gold, silver, food, household wages, workmen's labor, and whatever is customary in human consumption soar in price. But, being inattentive, we do not realize that the dearness of everything is produced by the debasement of the coinage. For in line with the quality of money everything, especially gold and silver, rises and falls, prices being based not on brass or copper, but on gold and silver. For we declare that gold and silver are, as it were, the foundation of money, on which its value rests.

But maybe someone will argue that cheap money is more convenient for human needs, forsooth, by alleviating the poverty of people, lowering the price of food, and facilitating the supply of all the other necessities of human life, whereas sound money makes everything dearer, while burdening tenants and payers of an annual rental more heavily than usual. This point of view will be applauded by those who were heretofore granted the right to coin money and would be deprived of the hope of gain. Nor will it perhaps be rejected by merchants and artisans, who lose nothing on that account since they sell their goods and products in terms of gold, and the cheaper the money is, the greater is the number of coins they receive in exchange.

But if they will have regard for the common good, they will surely be unable to deny that sound money benefits not only the state but also themselves and every class of people, whereas debased coinage is harmful. Although this is quite clear for many reasons, we learn that it is so also through experience, the teacher of objective truth. For we see that those countries flourish the most which have sound money, whereas those which use inferior coinage decline and fall. Certainly Prussia too prospered when 1 Prussian mark as coin was worth 2 Hungarian florins and when, as was said above, 2 Prussian marks, 8 skoters, were exchanged for 1/2 pound, that is, 1 mark by weight of pure silver. But in the meantime, as its coinage was debased more and more day after day, our fatherland too declined, and as a result of this plague and other misfortunes it was brought down almost to its final destruction. Moreover, those places which use sound money, as is well known, have flourishing trades, excellent craftsmen, and an abundance of commodities. On the other hand, where cheap money prevails, through listlessness, lethargy, and slothful idleness the development of the fine arts as well as of the intellect is neglected, and the plentifulness of all goods is also a thing of the past. The memory of man has not yet forgotten that grain and produce were bought in Prussia with a smaller number of coins while sound money was still being used. Now, however, as it is being debased, we experience a rise in the price of everything related to food and human consumption. Hence it can be seen that cheap money fosters laziness more than it helps poor people. An improvement of the currency will not be able to impose a heavy burden on tenants. If they seem to pay more than usual for their land, they are going to sell the products of their fields, their livestock, and that kind of output at an even higher price. For the adjusted evaluation of the money will balance the mutual exchange of giving and receiving.

Therefore, if it is decided to let Prussia at last recover at some future time from its previous depression by restoring its currency, the most urgent task will be to avoid the confusion arising from the differences between the various mints where the coinage is to be struck. For, multiplicity interferes with uniformity, and maintaining standardized production in several mints is harder than in one. It would therefore be advantageous to have for all of Prussia one common mint producing coinage of every denomination. On one side, the device will be the arms or insignia of the lands of Prussia, surmounted by the crown to signify the overlordship of the kingdom of Poland. But the other side will display the arms of the duke of Prussia with the crown of the kingdom resting thereon.

If, however, this could not be done because of the opposition of the duke of Prussia on the ground that he wants to have his own mint, let two places be designated at the most, one in his Royal Majesty's territory and the other in the duke's domain. Let the first mint strike coins showing the royal insignia on one side, and on the other the arms of the lands of Prussia. Let the second mint, however, issue coins stamped with the royal insignia on one side, and on the other side the duke's. Let both coinages be subject to royal control, and by His Majesty's order be used and accepted throughout the entire kingdom. This arrangement will produce no small effect on the reconciliation of attitudes and participation in trade.

It will be essential, moreover, that these two coinages should be of a single standard, intrinsic value, and face value, and remain forever, under the watchful supervision of the leaders of the state, in agreement with the regulation to be established now. It is also essential that in both places the rulers should expect no profit from the minting of the coinage. Only as much copper should be added as would make the face value exceed the intrinsic value, so that it would be possible to recover the loss of the expenses of the minting operation and remove the opportunity of melting down the coinage.

Furthermore, let us hereafter avoid falling into our present age's confusion arising from the mixture of new coinage with old. It seems necessary, when the new coinage is issued, to abolish the old coinage, wipe it out completely, and exchange it at the mints for the new coinage in proportion to its intrinsic value. Otherwise the work of renewing the money will be in vain, and the subsequent confusion will perhaps be worse than the earlier. For again the old coinage will spoil the value of the new coinage. The mixture will of course make the aggregate's weight less than is right and its quantity excessive. The result will be the dislocation described above. In this regard, somebody may think that the solution is to assign to the remaining old coins a value as much beneath the new coinage's as their intrinsic value is inferior or lower. But this cannot be done without a great error. For not only the groats and shillings but also the pennies are now so different in their many kinds that individual coins can hardly be rated according to the condition of their intrinsic value and differentiated from one another. Consequently, the resulting variety of money would produce inescapable confusion and aggravate the difficulties, problems, and other annoyances of those who engage in business and enter into contracts. It will therefore always be better to withdraw the old coinage completely from circulation when money is being renewed afresh. For so small a loss will have to be borne calmly once, if that can be called a loss which gives rise to increased production and steadier serviceability as well as enhancing the state.

To raise the Prussian coinage, however, to its original worth is very hard and perhaps impossible after so drastic a collapse. Although any renewal of the coinage is a matter of no small difficulty, still under the conditions prevailing at the present time it seems possible to restore it satisfactorily, at least with 1 pound of silver returning to 20 marks. The program would be as follows. For the shillings, take 3 pounds of copper, but as regards pure silver take 1 pound minus 1/2 ounce or as much as has to be deduced to cover the expenses of minting. From the molten mass mint 20 marks, which will buy 1 pound, that is, 2 marks by weight of silver. According to the same proportion, skoters or groats and pennies may be struck as desired.

Gold and silver, as was said above, are the basis of coinage, in which its worth resides. Most of what has been set forth about silver coinage can be transferred also to gold coinage. It remains to explain the ratio for the mutual exchange of gold and silver. Accordingly, it is first necessary to examine the relative value of pure gold to pure or unalloyed silver, in order to proceed downward from the general to the particular and from the simple to the compound. In the next place, the ratio of gold to silver is the same in bullion form as in coinage of the same standard. Furthermore, the ratio of gold coin to gold bullion is the same as the ratio of silver coin to silver bullion of the same standard of alloy and weight. Now the purest gold coins found among us are the Hungarian florins. For they have the least alloy, and perhaps only as much as was necessary was deducted for expenses in the mints. Hence they are rightly exchanged for pure gold of the same weight, with the authority of the symbol making up for the deficiency of the florins. It therefore follows that the ratio of pure silver bullion to pure gold bullion is the same as the ratio of that silver to Hungarian florins, the weights being unchanged. But 110 Hungarian florins of proper and uniform weight, namely, 72 grains, make 1 pound (by a "pound" I always mean the sum of 2 marks by weight). By this reasoning we find that generally among all people 1 pound of pure gold is worth as much as 12,741 pounds of pure silver. Yet we observe that 11 pounds [of silver] once equaled 1 pound of gold. For this reason, apparently, it was ordained of old that 10 Hungarian gold pieces should weigh 1/11th of a pound. But if the same price continued today for that weight, we would have a convenient interchangeability of Polish and Prussian money on the basis of the aforementioned ratio gold: silver = 1:11. For if 20 Prussian marks were made from approximately 1 pound of silver, 1 gold piece would equal exactly 2 marks or 40 Polish groats. But after it became customary to exchange 12 parts of silver for 1 part of gold, the weight and price disagree, so that 10 Hungarian gold pieces are worth 1 pound of silver plus 1/11th of a pound. Therefore, if 20 Prussian marks are made from 1 1/11 pounds of silver, the Polish and Prussian coinages will be matched in the correct ratio, groat for groat, with 2 Prussian marks equal to 1 Hungarian gold piece. The price of silver, however, will be 9 marks, 10 shillings, or thereabouts, for 1/2 pound.

On the other hand, if a debased coinage and the ruin of the fatherland are definitely desired, and so slight a restoration and adjustment seem too hard, and it is decided that 15 Polish groats should remain equal to 1 Prussian mark, and 2 marks, 16 skoters, to 1 Hungarian gold piece, that too will be accomplished with no great trouble in the manner described above, if 24 Prussian marks are made from 1 pound of silver. This was certainly the situation recently when the price of 1/2 pound of silver was still 12 marks, the amount of money for which 6 Hungarian florins were exchanged.

This is said by way of an example and guideline. For there are countless ways of establishing a currency, and it is not possible to explain all of them. But a general agreement after mature deliberation will be able to make this or that decision, which will seem most advantageous to the state. But if the currency is correctly related to the Hungarian florin, and no mistake is made, other florins will also be easily rated according to their content of gold and silver in comparison with the Hungarian florins.

Let these remarks about the restoration of the coinage be sufficient at least to make clear how its value has fallen and how it can be restored. This, I hope, is evident from what was said above.

With reference to the restoration and maintenance of the currency, the following recommendations seem worthy of consideration.

Firstly, the currency should not be renewed without the deliberate advice and unanimous consent of the Councilors.

Secondly, only one place, if possible, should be designated for a mint. There coins should be struck in the name, not of one city, but of the whole country with its insignia. The validity of this recommendation is proved by the Polish coinage, which for this reason alone maintains its value over so vast an extent of territory.

Thirdly, when new money is issued, the old coinage should be demonetized and abolished.

Fourthly, it should be a permanent rule, without change and without exception, to strike only 20 marks, and no more, from 1 pound of pure silver, minus what must be deducted for the expenses of the operation. The Prussian coinage will in this way be definitely adjusted to the Polish, with 20 Prussian groats as well as 20 Polish groats being worth 1 Prussian mark.

Fifthly, an excessive multiplicity of coinage should be avoided.

Sixthly, money should be issued in all denominations at the same time, that is, skoters or groats, shillings, and pennies should be minted simultaneously. How big should the proportion of each denomination be? Should groats as well as shillings be struck? Should silver pennies also [be minted], worth 1/4 or 1/2 or even 1 whole mark? These questions are to be decided by those concerned, except that whatever the distribution, the decision should be made in such a way as to last forever after. Attention must also be paid to the ordinary pennies, since they are now worth altogether so little that a whole mark of pennies by weight contains hardly more than the silver in 1 groat.

Lastly, a difficulty arises from contracts and obligations made before and after the renewal of the money. In these matters a way must be found not to burden the contracting parties too much. This was done in former times, as is clear from what is copied out on the other side of this sheet.

14. Luís Saravia de la Calle: *Instructions for Merchants* (1544)[1]

CHAPTER 2: ON THE JUST PRICE

Excluding all deceit and malice, the just price of a thing is the price which it commonly fetches at the time and place of the deal, in cash, and bearing in mind the particular circumstances and manner of the sale, the abundance of goods and money, the number of buyers and sellers, the difficulty of procuring the goods, and the benefit to be enjoyed by their use, according to the judgement of an honest man.

I have said 'in the place', because the mere change from one place to another raises or lowers the price, according to whether the merchandise is abundant or scarce there. Thus we see by experience that in seaports fish is cheaper than elsewhere. Things are cheaper in the places where they are produced than in those to which they have to be sent.

I have said also 'in the place'. For we have to consider the place where the contract is arranged, not where the goods are situated. Merchandise in one place is consigned from another where the contract is drawn up, and ownership is transferred from there. If I buy spices in Genoa being myself in Milan, and I agree on the price and pay for the goods in Milan, the just price is the price current in Milan, as Sylvester observes. I have said 'at the time', for time alone raises or lowers the price of a thing. Thus it is clear that wheat is commonly worth more in May than in August, solely on account of time.

I have said 'bearing in mind the manner of the sale'. For an eager seller generally sets a lower price on his goods than one who is reluctant. Hence we see that a man who has bought a length of cloth from the merchant's house at its just price will find that in his hands the cloth will be worth less, since he will be inviting merchants and purchasers with it. As the Latin proverb says, *ultronee merces vilescunt*, goods willingly sold are worth less and fall in price.

I have said 'the abundance of merchants and money'. For in truth this is the principal reason why things are cheap or dear, and to this are reduced the three already mentioned: time, place, and manner of sale. The mere abundance or scarcity of goods, merchants, and money raises or lowers the price, as bargainers at fairs know by experience. For if a thing is worth more at one time or place than at another, or sold eagerly or reluctantly, it is because of the abundance or scarcity of goods, merchants, and money. If a great deal of merchandise is brought from many parts to the place where the goods are situated, then the latter will be cheap. This is why eggs are cheaper in a village than a city: because in a village there are more eggs, fewer buyers, and less money. And if in August wheat is cheaper than in May, this is because wheat is more

---

[1]   Translated by Marjorie Grice-Hutchinson.

abundant in August than in May. And if goods sold eagerly are worth less, it is because buyers are few. If many people wanted to buy them, they would not be sold for less than the cost price. So that in order to determine the just price we need only consider these three things: abundance or scarcity of goods, merchants, and money—of things which people want to barter and exchange for money. This doctrine is founded on Aristotle's dictum, *precium rei humana indigentia mensurat*, the price of things is measured by human needs. Thus we see that houses and estates are worth much less after wars and pestilences than before, because there are fewer people to buy them, although the property has not in itself deteriorated. Also, at the end of markets and fairs goods are worth less than when they are in full swing, because many buyers have left and the owners are unwilling to wait for others. From this we infer that the reason why a particular individual wishes to sell does not raise or lower the price.

CHAPTER 3: HOW THE JUST PRICE MAY BE KNOWN

Those who measure the just price by the labour, costs, and risk incurred by the person who deals in the merchandise or produces it, or by the cost of transport or the expense of travelling to and from the fair, or by what he has to pay the factors for their industry, risk, and labour, are greatly in error, and still more so are those who allow a certain profit of a fifth or a tenth. For the just price arises from the abundance or scarcity of goods, merchants, and money, as has been said, and not from costs, labour, and risk. If we had to consider labour and risk in order to assess the just price, no merchant would ever suffer loss, nor would abundance or scarcity of goods and money enter into the question. Prices are not commonly fixed on the basis of costs. Why should a bale of linen brought overland from Brittany at great expense be worth more than one which is transported cheaply by sea? Or take the cloth which I brought home from the fair on my horse and which cost me more than that which I carried in the cart. I have both bales in my shop and sell them at the same price, and it would be unjust to ask more for one than for the other, when both were woven at the same time and are of the same quality, colour, and so on … Why should a book written out by hand be worth more than one which is printed, when the latter is better though it costs less to produce? Finally, why, when the type of Toulouse is the best, should it be cheaper than the vile type of Paris? The just price is found not by counting the cost but by the common estimation …

The public officials who fix the just price of goods do not consider costs but the scarcity or abundance of goods in the city. This is why first fruits are dearer, because of their scarcity, not because they cost more to bring to market. Both early and late fruits come from the same orchard and tree.

15. Martín de Azpilcueta: *On Exchange* (1556)[1]

CHAPTER 3: THE ORIGINS AND FUNCTIONS OF MONEY

Regarding section nine, we state that the exchange or barter of goods that are not money (as was said most correctly by Paul the jurisconsult) is a much earlier operation than buying and selling, which began after money was introduced. Before money came into existence, if someone owned a good and was in need of another, he looked for someone who had it and wanted to exchange it for his possession. This was the case, for example, when someone had wine and wool, but not wheat or shoes, and looked for someone with wheat and shoes who wanted to exchange them for his wine and wool. This is the case even today with some foreigners with whom the Spanish and others deal.

After a time, money was discovered, which was certainly a very necessary discovery on the one hand. On the other, I am not sure whether today it destroys souls because of greed; bodies because of wars, travels, and terrifying pilgrimages; and even itself and the fleets where it travels because of horrifying storms and shipwrecks. The main use and purpose in creating money was as a means of payment in order to buy and sell with it the necessary things for human life, so that it would become a common standard of goods to be sold. After this, coins of a metal or value started being bartered for coins of another metal or another value, such as the thick one for the thin one and the thin one for the thick one. Later, because the currency of a land was worth less there than somewhere else (as today almost all the gold and silver currency from Spain is worth less there than in Flanders and France), the art of exchanging started, which is the art of dealing with currency. By giving and taking one for another, money started getting transferred from where it was worth least to where it was worth most. As happens in our time, many people have increased their fortune by taking *ducats* to Flanders and France in groups of two, four, and ten—some in small barrels, pretending they are olives, and some in wine barrels—and making a big profit with each one. In turn, they brought from those places merchandise that was worth little there but had great value here, thus helping with one but hurting us much with the other.

Aristotle thought it was wrong to exchange and trade with money because he did not think this third use of money was natural or brought any benefit to the republic or had any other purpose but that of profit, which is an end without an end. Saint Thomas said that any art of exchange whose main purpose was only to obtain profit was illicit. Saint Thomas himself, however, declares that the art of exchange is licit if its purpose is a moderate profit to support oneself and one's home and if the art of exchange brings about some benefit to the republic. We say that if it is exercised as it should be and the purpose of the profit is directed to honestly

---

[1]   Translated by Jeannine Emery.

and moderately support oneself and one's home, then it is licit. It is not true that using money to obtain a profit by exchanging it goes against its very nature because, even if it is a different use than the first and main one for which it was created, it is still apt for a less principal and secondary use. This happens, for example, when shoes are used to make a profit, which, although it is a different use than the primary one for which they were created (which was to wear on feet), does not go against their very nature.

Money has eight different purposes. The first three are the ones already mentioned. The fourth is to display one's riches, showing it to everyone or putting it in the marketplace where it is dealt with or exchanged. The fifth is to use it as medals and clothing decorations. The sixth use is to cheer with its presence. The seventh use is to cure some illnesses with its broth as, they say, is one of the properties of gold powder. The eighth use is as security for a debt. For these last five purposes, it is possible not only to lend and exchange money but even to rent it out. Thus, money may be given by way of many contracts: by way of price for a purchased good; by way of merchandise sold for another money; by way of innominate contract of barter exchanging it for something else or for money; by way of lending called *mutuum*, when something else is given back and not the same thing; by way of lending called *commodatum*, in order to get back the same thing given; by way of security for what is owed; and by way of rental of a sum so that the same amount that was given is returned after the person who borrows it takes advantage of its use by showing his riches, or enjoying its presence, or using its broth, or giving it as security, and so forth.

It can be taken by as many ways as it can be given. Because the nature of the aforementioned contracts, by which it is possible to give and take money, is diverse, so there are diverse law regulations that determine if and when they are licit or not. If money is given by way of buying and selling, it cannot be given but for what something else is worth. The same goes for when it is given by way of exchange or barter.

If it is given by way of loan or if it is given as security for one's own loan (whether the same or another is given back), neither a small nor a big sum can be charged. If rented out to enliven or honor with its presence or to cure with its broth or to use as security for someone else's debt, an honest rent may be taken because the nature of this contract is not to transfer the ownership but only the appraised use of money according to the amount of time for which it was taken. It is more important to understand what truly happens than what is feigned to happen. Every time one of these contracts is carried out truthfully and another is feigned, one should judge not by the rules of the feigned one but by the rules of the true one. Thus, if the exchanger truly lends his money, he cannot take anything for this operation, even if he feigns he is exchanging it or renting it out.

   …

CHAPTER 12: THE VALUE OF MONEY

The next thing that we say regards the seventh motive of why money increases or decreases its value. That happens when there is a great lack or need (or an abundance of it). It is worth more where and when there is a great lack of it than where there is a great abundance, as declare Calderini, Laurencio Rodulfo, and Silvestre, with whom Cajetan and Soto agree.

From them follow several opinions:

First, this is what most of the good and evil men of Christendom think, and thus it seems to be the voice of God and nature.

Second, and very obviously, all merchandise becomes more expensive when there is a great need and small quantity of it. Money, inasmuch as it is a thing that may be sold, bartered, or commuted by means of another contract, is merchandise for the reasons we gave above and may also become more expensive when there is a great need of it and yet not enough to satisfy this need.

Third, all other things being equal, in those countries where there is a great lack of money, less money is given for marketable goods, and even for the hands and work of men, than where there is an abundance of it. This we can see from experience in France where there is less money than in Spain. Bread, wine, wool, hands, and work cost less. Even in Spain, when there was less money, much less was given for saleable goods, and the hands and work of men, than later when the discoveries of the Indies covered it in silver and gold. The cause for this is that money is worth more where and when there is a lack of it than where and when there is an abundance. That which some say, that the lack of money reduces the price of everything, is born of the fact that its more than sufficient increase makes everything appear much lower, just as a small man next to a very tall man appears smaller than if he were next to his equal.

Fourth, the lack of gold coins may surely increase their value, so that more silver coins, or coins of another metal, have to be offered for the gold coins, as we see now that because of the lack of gold coins, some give 22 and even 23 and 25 *reales* for a *doubloon*, which by the kingdom's price and law is not worth more than 22.

We have even seen in Portugal 11½ silver *ducats*, and even 12, offered for 10 *ducats* of another kind. The shortage of silver coins may increase their value so that more gold coins or metal coins have to be given than before for the silver ones. Even the shortage of small copper coins or other cheap metals may have their value increase so that more gold or silver has to be given than before for them. This we have seen in Portugal where, when there was an abundance of *cetis*, 106 *maravedis* in *cetis* were given for 1 *teston*, which is not worth more than 100. Then, when there was a shortage of *cetis*, we gave 1 *teston* for 94 in *cetis*. So, it seems that when money in general is scarce, the price of the different coins in general increases.

Fifth, there is a law that establishes this. After saying that the reason why there is arbitrary action in asking in one place for something that must be paid somewhere else is because something is worth more in one place than in another (mainly if it is bread, wine, or oil), the law goes on to say the following about money: "Although the value of money also seems to be one and the same everywhere, nevertheless in some places it is more abundant and lighter usuries are found, and in other places it is more scarce and more severe usuries are found."

There are many arguments against this opinion and, because of these, we used to think it was unreasonable. The first objection against it is that no matter how much or how scarce money is, a *ducat* is never worth more or less than 11 *reales* and 1 *maravedi* here or in Rome, Flanders, or León. It is never worth more or less than what the pope, the king, or custom has appraised it for, and it will not be taken for a higher value from the person who sells you something. Also, it is objected that in holding the above opinion, we are forced to say what some people believe, namely, that there are two types of *ducats* and *escudos*: the first is the one used by merchants for their exchanges, which rises or falls according to the abundance or shortage of money. Consequently, depending on the situation, either many or few want to give or take in exchange. The second type are those *ducats* and *escudos* intended to be spent by the people and even by the merchants themselves in those expenses that are not exchanges, which always have a fixed price. This seems a tenuous belief because the Roman, ecclesiastical, or secular jurisdiction never considered it. Since merchants do not have the power to increase or decrease public money, it sounds like something fleeting—a trap, a veil, and cover of usuries to feign *ducats* or *escudos*—to give them an imagined value so that no one who sells bread, wine, meat, fish, cloth, or any other thing will take them except by way of exchange to pay them back in another fair or place. There does not seem to be a solid reason why, except for a lack of money in general, that a greater quantity of *ducats* and *escudos* are imagined only for exchanging them without there being another use for spending them. Thus, in exchanging them, a cloud is formed in order to cover the loan that is carried out with usury under it. Also against the earlier opinion is the fact that money considered as money seems to be the price of all other merchandise but is not itself merchandise, and its price is not appraised in each kingdom, and thus, may not increase more than wheat when it is appraised by the republic.

Regardless of these objections and Doctor Medina's contrary opinion (which, at one time, we thought was better), we hold the first opinion because of the new reasons and considerations in favor of it. To the first objection, which seems insoluble, we may respond that even if or when there is a shortage of money in general, a *ducat* should not be worth more *reales* than when there is an abundance of money, neither should the *real* be worth more *quartos*, nor the *quartos* more *maravedis*. All money is worth more because more saleable goods may be found for a fraction of what they were worth before, all else being equal. This is not to say that the increase in the price of money is due to the decrease in the other thing's prices, because it is this decrease that follows the increase in the price of money, as we have considered in the third argument above.

To the second objection, which seems insoluble, we may respond by denying that it is necessary in order to defend this opinion to introduce imagined and chimerical *ducats* and *escudos*, which as Plato's ideas, find themselves in specie and genre, and not individually, as the arguments rightly conclude. It is confirmed effectively with the consideration that whoever says this must confess that almost as many imaginary *ducats* must be fabricated as places money is given and taken for in the fair. There is almost a different price for each place: one for Flanders, another for Rome, another for León, another for Lisbon, another for Valencia, another for Zaragoza, and so forth. A comical thing adding to this consideration is that it seems it has not been said enough that the *ducat* or *escudo* are not worth as much in the fair if they are not worth as much for such and such a place. Even those who say this mean that the *ducat* is given for such and such a place for the barter or price that is given for it in one place.

To the third objection, we answer by denying that money considered as money should always be considered as the price of things, because, even considered as money, it may be commuted by buying, bartering, or with a contract specifically provided for by the law or an innominate contract, as was said above. Although it is true that its main and principal use and end for which it was created was as a price and measure of saleable goods, its secondary and less principal use and end, which is that of making a profit with it by dealing money for money, is not to be price but merchandise, just as the principal use and end of shoes is to put them on and wear them, but the secondary one is to make a profit by dealing with them through buying and selling them. As far as the value is concerned, we will respond to it below.

The following conclusions are derived from the above:

First, that the gold coin, because of the specific shortage of it, may be worth more than it would be worth if there were an abundance of it; and the silver coin, because of the specific shortage of it, as well as the metal one, for its shortage, and all coins in general for their general shortage.

Second, there is no need to feign merchants' imaginary *ducats* or *escudos* that are different from those the people use. Without them, it is still possible to clearly set a price for a *ducat* or *escudo* for one party and for the other. Moreover, it is more advisable not to feign them so that those who lend and give money unjustly do not have the chance to be repaid at the value they decide to fix, as Doctor Soto tacitly expressed.

Third, the exchange that many carry out is usury, who according to them give to some people *ducats* or *escudos* from one fair to the next to be paid at the price that they are worth when they are given, or at the price that the merchants' ones are worth in the market when they are to be paid, because there are no such *ducats* or *escudos* in the world, and because, if they existed, they would be as diverse in value as the cities between which they are exchanged. For between some cities, they are exchanged for an equal value, such as many times happens from Medina to Lisbon. For others, at 10 or 20 *maravedis*; for others at 30; and for others at 40 and 50. They even give them sometimes at the price they get for exchanging them in the city where they are worth the most. Moreover, the reason that justifies the commutation of a sum of money that has to be given in a faraway city does not justify the commutation of a similar amount that has to be given in the same city, for the reason we will state below. Although it should be confessed that whoever finds someone who takes his money for a true exchange and does not gain a profit with him because of giving it to his neighbor or another close person who greatly needs it, may in such manner earn with it what he is prevented from earning with the other person, for the reason we gave above.

Fourth, the value of money may not only increase or decrease inasmuch as it is a piece of metal, but even inasmuch as it is money and price of the rest of things. The majority of the eight motives because of which money increases or decreases are motives that pertain to money as money and price of saleable goods and conclude that inasmuch as it is money and price, it is worth more in one land than in another, and even in one land more at one time than in another.

Fifth, there is a need to explain that compelling argument against this that is based on the price, whose solution above we restate here. The argument is that money is appraised, and things are appraised, as wheat is usually, that do not increase due to a lack of it. Some of the aforementioned respond that even it is appraised inasmuch as it is price. It is not appraised inasmuch as it is merchandise. This is not satisfactory, however. For the reasons stated above, it is evident that even inasmuch as it is money and price, it may increase or decrease. Silvestre declares that money is appraised inasmuch as it is price of other saleable goods but not inasmuch as it is price of money itself. He does not explain why there is such difference. Others believe that money should never be sold, and thus some would say that there is not a higher price in its commutation. On the one hand, this goes against the common practice, which refers to buying and selling money. On the other hand, it is not convenient to those who hold this position at all. If they confess that there is barter and that you cannot barter but for what something is worth, that its value increases for its greater worth due to its great lack, and that more should be given the more it is worth, they have to forcefully confess that its value increases regardless of its price, and thus have the same need of explaining the argument based on its price as do those who say you can buy it.

Thus, we answer again, conceding that money is appraised for one end and not for another. It is appraised in order to compel the person who sells something or to whom something is owed to take the money for said price so that he cannot be compelled to take it for more. It is neither appraised in order that the person who has it cannot take less for it if he so desires, nor in order that he cannot take more if he gains an advantage by this. This solution cannot reassure the consciences of those who commute it for a higher price for the shortage of it without there being an advantage in keeping it, even if the person with whom one is commuting it obtains an advantage in getting paid. The seller cannot sell the thing more expensively for the personal gain that this may bring to the buyer, although he may sell it more expensively for the benefit he loses in selling it, according to what Saint Thomas and Scotus said. We see every day the dealers who frequently obtain a benefit from saving their money when there is great lack of it (even if it means only buying some things at a cheaper price). We see even those who are not dealers commute at present the *doubloons* for 24 and 25 *reales*, when they are actually appraised at 22, for the great lack of them. Though it might be said that the *doubloons* are worth more for the intrinsic value of their gold, which is much higher than that of the *coronas*, we would not be able to say the same of the rest of the other coins, though they increase or decrease every day, as Bartolus and Panormitanus say, whom no one contradicts. Therefore, it seems safer to respond that money is appraised so that, all else being equal, it is not worth more in one place, but not such that it cannot be worth more when it changes so much that there is a great lack and need of that appraised money, which seems so to wise and good men, at least in order to commute it for other money, as Silvestre says.

Sixth, it is not unusual that money (even inasmuch as it is money) is worth more in one fair than in another and more in one part of the same fair than in another part. It may be that in one part it is worth less because few people want to take it for true exchange, and many want to give it; and in another part it may be worth more because of there being many who want to take it for true exchange and few who want to give it. The price of money increases for a great need or lack of it. We say "true exchange" because we believe that the price of money should not be increased when there are a great many people who want to take it for feigned and illicit exchanges, as deception and fraud should not bring profit to the one who commits them. No merchandise becomes more expensive when there are many who want to steal it or illicitly usurp it, although it does become more expensive when there are many who want to justly buy it or barter it. As Doctor Soto stated wisely, money should not be more expensive at the fair for a lack of it or for an absence of people who want to give it when this lack is born of the illicit conspiracy of those who have to give it and of the exchangers who openly or covertly decide not to give it until it is more expensive. Nor should it be more expensive because at the beginning of the fair, when everything is cheaper for everybody, they took most of it, and then, as they are in possession of most of it, do not want to give it except as they please. In this case, those who are not guilty may give it in good conscience according to its lack, but not those who are guilty—something that happens more often than it should.

Seventh, it would be even less surprising if the *ducat* were worth more in Portugal than in Castile, although there is doubt if it is. First, because the person who in Portugal owes 400 *reales* may pay them with a *ducat* worth 11 *reales*, and the person who owes and to whom is owed 400 *maravedis* here cannot pay them here or there with 1 *ducat*. This means that the *maravedis* from here are worth more than the *reales* from there, but the *ducat* is worth the same here as there and there as here. In His Majesty's provision to moderate exchanges, whose content we referred to earlier, it is established that 370 *maravedis* from here are worth 400 *reales* over there.

We think the opposite is truer, that is, that the *ducat* from here and from there is worth more there than here; also that the *real* from here is worth more there than here because the *ducat* is worth 400 *reales* from there and the *real* 36, and here the *ducat* is worth only 375 *maravedis* and the *real* 34. That the *reales* from there and *maravedis* from here are equal is inferred from the fact that as a *real* is worth in Portugal 6 *cetis*, so the *maravedi* (now in use) is worth 6 *cornados*, which apparently are equal to the *cetis*, as the holy Archbishop Don Diego de Leyva y Covarrubias seems to efficiently prove. Today, in the kingdom of Galicia (where there are *cetis* as in Portugal) 6 *cetis* are worth 1 *maravedi*. In Portugal, too, they are worth 1 *real*. Also, what those who object to this view allege is not pertinent. We deny that the person who owes in Portugal 400 *reales* does just payment here with 1 *ducat* if he is not satisfied with it. We even deny that there is just payment when the one to whom you owe there 11 *reales* receives another 11 that you pay him here. We also deny that the person who owes here 400 *maravedis* does just payment there with 400 *reales*.

Also, it is possible to respond to the provision to moderate exchanges that such words were included there by accident. If you reply that its determination is based on it, we will say that it is based on someone else's acts and that the opposite may be proved. We believe that even if this is accepted in these kingdoms for their benefit, it will be not be accepted in the foreign ones, even if those kingdoms belong to His Majesty, because it will harm them.

Eighth, it is extremely important that whoever lends in Portugal 100 *ducats* is able to take for them in Medina more than 100 for the only reason that they are worth more there than here.

Ninth, whoever lends 100 *ducats* in Medina should not receive 100 in Lisbon because they are worth more there than here, and whoever lends may not take more than what he lent.

Tenth, what has been said about Medina and Lisbon in these two last conclusions should also be said of any other two cities where the same currency is worth more in one of them than in the other. Thus, the person who lends 100 *ducats* in Flanders, Rome, or León (where the *ducats* are worth more than in Castile) should be paid more than 100 in Castile. So also the other way around: the person who lends 100 in Castile should not get paid 100 in Rome, concerning which Doctor Soto notably agrees. Just as it would be usury to lend you a load of wheat in Salamanca (where it is worth 2 *ducats*) so that you pay it to me in Galicia where it is worth 4, so it would be usury to lend you here a *ducat* worth 375 *maravedis* so that you pay it back to me somewhere else where it is worth 400. Just as it is injustice (although it is not usury, but injustice) that for a load of wheat that I lent to you in Galicia where it was worth 4 *ducats* you pay me with another one here in Salamanca where it is not worth more than 2, so it is injustice that for 100 *ducats* that you lent me in Rome or Lisbon where they are worth 400 I give you but 100 in Medina where they are not worth more than 375.

Eleventh, he who lends a certain quantity of wheat, wine, and oil where it is worth more should get back a greater amount if he is paid where they are worth less, depending on how much more it is worth where he lends than where he is being paid. He who lends where something is worth less, should receive a smaller quantity if he is paid where it is worth more, depending on how much more it is worth where he is getting paid than where he lends. Thus, he who lends *ducats* where they are worth more, should receive as much more if he is paid where they are worth less as the greater value of those *ducats* amounts to. So, too, the other way around: he who lends *ducats* where they are worth less, should receive as much less if he is paid where they are worth more as that greater value amounts to.

Twelfth, because of this, it may seem to some that there is no doubt in Doctor Soto's conclusion that he who gives for exchange in Spain a *ducat*, which is only worth 11 *reales*, so that he gets paid back in Rome another worth 12 or 13 *carlines*—which are equal to our *reales*, or are worth more than 11—commits usury because he wants to take more than what he gives and gain an extra amount. Neither this conclusion, however, nor the ones that follow from it, can be inferred from our deductions. Nor do we believe they are indisputable. They do not follow from the above because the three deductions refer to the one who lends money and to the loan that in Latin is called *mutuum*, whose very nature is gratuitous. By virtue of it, nothing more than what was loaned should be taken, as we said in another commentary. Soto's conclusion talks about the one who gives in an exchange that is not gratuitous in nature, and that is why it cannot be inferred from them; they each refer to different things. This is not a true doctrine because every day the opposite is done from Medina to Lisbon and Flanders and from there to Medina, the practice of which is licit whether by way of real purchase or by way of barter or other innominate contracts, as we go on to prove below.

16. Tomás de Mercado: *Manual of Deals and Contracts* (1569)[1]

There are two points to be investigated and clarified in this chapter. The first is that modern exchange transactions are founded on the diversity in the estimation of money. It is understood that this estimation is to be universal throughout the whole of a kingdom, not peculiar to two or three or five needy persons in a town. Thus we see that in all Flanders and in all Rome money is more highly esteemed than in all Seville, and in Seville more than in the Indies, and in the Indies more than in New Spain, and in New Spain more than in Peru.

What I have said will be clear when we come to examine this sort of commerce. Nowhere is so large an increment charged as in places where it is evident that money is greatly esteemed. The most profitable exchange transactions are those of Flanders and Rome on Spain, where money is clearly worth more than elsewhere. This is good proof that money changers take this diversity of estimation into account.

The second point is that from Seville or Medina, Lisbon, and any other place, the thing that causes a rise or fall in the market is the abundance or scarcity of silver. If it is abundant the rate is low and, if scarce, high. Clearly, then, abundance or scarcity causes money to be little or greatly esteemed. Hence, if in Seville at the present moment money is esteemed more highly than it will be in a month's time, this is simply because in some way the market will have been altered and freshly supplied and, since money will be more abundant, its estimation will fall. Estimation is and always will be the basis of such transactions.

Indeed, these two considerations seem to me to be evident and effective, and I think that they clearly show how important for this type of business is the fact that money is more highly esteemed in one place than in another. In practice we see that when a money changer knows that money is going to be very scarce in some province he tries to send large sums there in good time.

Our opinion is rendered very probable and even true by the proof which we have given earlier in this treatise that the profit gained in an exchange transaction does not arise because of any variation in the fineness of the two moneys, or because one is present and the other absent, or as a salary for transporting the money, as many people have thought. It follows that the rate can be founded on no other reason (if it is to have a foundation at all) but the diverse estimation in which money is held from city to city. Thus we see that the money changers make use of all their shrewdness and ingenuity in arranging to place large sums where money is highly esteemed either always or for a few days; and we also understand the reason for the fluctuations in the rate.

---

[1] Translated by Marjorie Grice-Hutchinson.

17. Sir Thomas Smith: *A Discourse of the Commonweal of this Realm of England* (1581)

THE THIRD DIALOUGUE

After we had well refreshed oure selves at supper, I thought longe till I had knowen the iudgement of maister Doctor, aboute the remidies of these thinges aboue remembred, howe he thought they might be best redressed, and with lest daunger or alteration of thinges; and therfore I saide to him thus: Sins yowe haue declared vnto vs (goode maister Doctor) oure deseases, and also the occasions therof, we praie youe leave vs not destitute of convenient remidies for the same; ye haue perswaded vs fully, and we perceaue that oure selves, that we are not now in so good state as we haue bene in times past; and ye haue shewed vs proveable occasions that hath brought vs to that case; therfore now we praie youe, shew vs what might remedie these oure greifes.

DOCTOR: When a mane dothe perceaue his greife, and the occasion also of the same, he is in a goode waie of amendment; for knowinge the occasion of the greife, a man may soune avoyde the same occasion; and that beinge avoided, the greife is also taken awaye; for as the Philosopher [Aristotle] saithe: Sublata causa tollitur effectus [Upon removal of the cause, the effect is removed]. But let vs breifly recounte them, and then the occasions thearof, and thirdly, goe to the inquisition of the remides for the same. First, this general and vniversal dearth is the cheifest greife that all men complaine most on. Secondly, the exhausinge of the treasure of this Realme. Thirdly, inclosures and turninge arrable grounde to pasture. Fourthely, decayinge of townes, towneshippes and villages; and last, devision and diversitie of opinions in religion. The occasions of these, althoughe I haue diversly declared after the diversitie of mens myndes and opinions, yet here I will take to be the same, but only such as I thincke veryly to be the very iust occasions in dede. For, as I shewed youe before, divers men diversly iudgethe this or that to be the cause or occasion of this or that greife; because there maie be divers causes of one thinge, and yet be one principall cause, that bringeth fourth these thinges to passe. Let vs seke oute that cause, omittinge all the meane causes, which are driven forward by the first originall cause; as in a presse, goinge in at a streight, the formost is driven by him that is next him, and the next by him that folowes him, and the thirde by some violent and stronge thinge that drives him forward; which is the first and principall cause of puttinge forward the rest before; yf he weare kept backe and staied, all they that goe forewarde would staie with all. To make this more plaine vnto youe; as in a clocke theare be many wheles, yet the first whele beinge stirred it drives the next, and that the third, till the last that moves the Instrumentes that strikes the clocke. So in makinge of a howse, theare is the maister that would haue the howse made, theare is the carpenter, theare is the stuffe to make the howse with all. The stuffe never stirres till the workeman set it foreward. The workeman never travailes, but as the maister provokes him with goode wages; and so he is the principall cause of this howse makinge. And this cause is of clerkes called efficient, as that that bringes the thinge principally to effecte; perswade this man to let his buyldinge alone, and the howse shall never come to passe; yet the howse can not be made with oute stuffe and workemen; and therfore they be called of some, Causa sine quibus non, and of other some, Materiales, and formales; but all comethe to one purpose; that is the efficient cause the efficient cause and principall cause, with oute removeinge of which cause the thinge can not be remedied. And because it was grafted in everie mans Judgement, that the cause of anie thinge beinge taken awaie the effecte is taken awaie with all, therfore men toke the causes of these thinges that be talked of withoute iudgement, not by descerninge the principall cause from the meane causes, but by takinge awaie of these causes that be but secondarie as it weare, and so they weare never the nearer to remedie the thinge they went aboute. Much like the wife of Aiax, that lost hir housband in the shippe called Argos, wished that those firre beames had never bene felled in Peleius woode, wheare the saide shippe was made; when that was not the efficient cause of the losinge of hir howsbande, but the wildefier cast in the said shippe did set it one fiere. Suche causes as they be, be called Remotae, as it weare to farre of; so they be also idle, and of no operation of them selves, with oute some other to set them on worke. And percase I, while I degresse so farre from my matter, shalbe thought to goe as farre from my purpose, yet to come to oure matter and to applie this that I haue saide to the same. Some thincke this dearthe beginnes by the tenaunte, in sellinge his ware so deare; some other, by the Lord in raisinge his land so highe; and some, by those Inclosures; and some other, by raisinge of oure coyne and alteration of the same. Therfore some, by takinge some one of these thinges awaie, (as theire opinion served them to be the principall cause of this dearthe,) thought to remedie this; but as the triall of thinges shewed, they towched not the cause efficient or principall, and therfore theire devise toke no place. And yf they had, the thinge had bene remedied fourthe with; for that is proper to the principall cause, that as soune as it is taken awaie, the effect is removed also. Yet I confesse that all these thinges risethe together with this dearthe, that everie of theim shoulde seme to be the cause of it. Neverthelesse, it is no goode proofe that they shoulde be the causes of it; no more then was the steple made at Dover the cause of the decaye of the haven at Dover, because the haven beganne to decay the same time that the steple beganne to be buylded. Nor yet, thoughe some of these be cause of the other, yet in dede they be not all the efficient causes of this dearthe. But as I haue saide before, of men thrustinge one an nother in a thronge, one drivinge an other, and but one first of all, that was the cheife cause of that force; so in this mattier that we talke of, theire is some one thinge that is the originall cause of these causes, that be as it weare secondary, and makes them to be the causes of other. As I take, the raisinge of the prices of all vittailes at the husbaudmans hand is the cause of the raysinge of the rent of his Landes; and that gentlemen fall so muche to take farmes into theire owne handes, Lest they be driven to by theire provision so deare; and that is a greate cause againe that inclosures is more vsed. For gentlemen, havinge muche landes in theire handes, and not beinge able to welde all, and to se it manured in husbandrie, (which requirethe the industrie, Labor and governaunce of a greate many of persons,) dothe convert most of that Lande to pastures; whearin is required bothe lesse charges of persons, and of the which neverthelesse comethe more cleare gaynes. Thus one thinge hanges vppon an other, and settes forwarde one a nother; but one, first of all, is the cheife cause of all this circuler motion and impulsion. I shewed a while eare, that the cheife cause was not in howsbandeman, nor yet in the gentleman. Let vs se whether it be in the marchaunt. It appeares, by reason that all wares bought of him are dearer now farre then they weare wount to be once, the husbandman is driven to sell his commodities dearer. Nowe that the mattier is brought to youe, maister marchaunt, howe can youe avoyde the cause from beinge in yow?

MERCHAUNTE: Sir, easilie enowghe; for as we nowe sell dearer all thinges then we weare wounte to doe, So we bie dearer all thinges of straungers. And therfore let them put the mattier from theim theare, for we disburden oure selves of this faulte.

DOCTOR: And they be not heare to make answere; yf they weare, I would aske theim why they sell theire wares dearer nowe then thei were wount to doe?

MERCHAUNTE: Marye, and to that I hard manie of theim answere ere this, when they weare asked that question, ij maner ways. One was, they sold no dearer than they weare wount to doe; sayinge, for proufe therof, that they woulde take for theire commodities as much and no more of oure commodities then they weare wounte to doe; as for oure todde of woll, they will geue as muche wine, spice or silke as they weare wonte to geue for so muche; yea, for an ounce of oure silver or golde as much stuffe as ever was gyuen for the same. And theire other answer was, that yf we did recken that they did sell theire wares dearer, because they demaunded more peces of oure coyne then they weare wonte to doe, that was no other faulte, they saide, but oures, that made oure peces lesse, or lesse worthe, then they weare in times past; therfore they demaunded the more peces of theim for their wares, sayinge they cared not what names we would giue oure coynes, they woulde consider the quantitie and right valew of it that they weare estemed at everie wheare throughe out the worlde.

KNIGHT: Then I would haue answered him after this sorte. Yf they came hither but for oure commodities, what lo made it mattier to theim what valew or quantitie our coyne weare of, so they might haue as muche of oure commodities for the same as they weare wonte to haue? If they came agayne for oure siluer and golde, it was nether lawfull nor expedient they should haue anye from vs. Whearfore I would thinke that was no cause whie they shoulde sell theire wares dearer then they weare wonte to doe.

DOCTOR: Then he might haue answered againe, that it chaunced not alwayes together, that when they had wares which we wanted, we had agayne all those wares that they looked for. And they, havinge (percase) more wares necessarie for vs then we had of suche wares as they looked for, woulde be glade to receiue of vs suche stuffe, currant in most places, as might bie that they looked for els wheare at theire pleasure; and they will saye was not oure coyne suche. And as for oure lawes of not transportinge over sea anie gold or siluer, they passed not therof, so they might haue the same once conveyed theim; as they haue many wayes to haue it so, which I haue before remembred. Finally, he might saye that we had not in dede oure coyne in that estate oure selves, that by the name they pretended, but estemed bothe in valew and quantitie of the stuffe it was made of; for yf they had brought to vs halte an oz of silver, we would not take it for an oz; nor yf thei brought vs brasse mingled with siluer, we would not take it for pure silver; and yf we would not take it so at theire handes, whie should they take it otherwise at oures? Then they sawe no man heare but would rather haue a cuppe of siluer then a cuppe of brasse; no, not the maisters of oure mintes, thoughe they would otherwise perswade the one to be as goode as the other. Wherfore, seinge vs esteme the one in dede better then the other, as all the worlde dothe beside, whie should not they esteme oure coyne after the quantitie and valew of the substance therof, bothe after the rate it was estemed amonge vs and also everie other wheare? And so, as in moe peces theare is but the valew that was in fewe peces before, therfore they demaunde greater number of peces, but yet the like valew in substaunce, that they weare wonte to demaunde for theire wares. Now let vs se whether goeth the cause of this mattier frome the stranger. For me thinckes he hath reasonably excused him selfe, and put it from him.

KNIGHT: By youre tale it must be in the coyne, and consequently in the kinges highenes, by whose commaundment the same was altered.

DOCTOR: Yet percase it goes further yet; yea, vnto suche as weare the firste counsellers of that dede, pretending it shoulde be to his highnes greate and notable commoditie; which, yf his grace maie now perceaue to be but a small proffitte and continuall losse, bothe to his highnes and also to his whole realme, may be sooner revoked agayne by his grace. And as a man that intendithe to heale a nother by a medicine that he thinckes goode, thoughe it proue otherwise, is not muche to be blamed; no more is the Kinges maiestie in no wise, in whose time this was not doonne, nor his highnes father, which is not to be supposed to haue intended therby no losse, but rather commoditie to him selfe and his subiectes, to be here in reprehended, albeit the thinge succeded beside purpose.

KNIGHT: Then ye thincke plainly that this alteration of the coyne is the cheifest and principall cause of this vniversall dearthe?

DOCTOR: Yea, no doubte, and of many of the said greifes that we haue talked of, by meanes it beinge the originall of all. And that, beside the reason of the thinge, (being plaine Inowhge of it selfe,) also experience and proufe dothe make more plaine; for even with the alteration of the coyne beganne this dearthe; and as the coine appered, so rose the price of thinges with all. And this to be true, the few peces of old coyne yet remaininge testefiethe; for ye shall haue, for anie of the sayde coine, as muche of anie ware either inwarde or outwarde as muche as ever was wounte to be had for the same; and so as the measure is made lesse, theare goethe the more some to make vp the tale. And because this risethe not together at all mens handes, therfore some hathe greate losse, and some other greate gaynes therby, and that makes suche a generall gruge for the thinge. And thus, to conclude, I thinke this alteration of the coyne to be the first originall cause that straungers first selles theire wares dearer to vs; and that makes all fermors and tennauntes, that rerethe any commoditie, agayne to sell the same dearer; the dearthe therof makes the gentlemen to rayse theire rentes, and to take farmes into their handes for the better provision, and consequently to inclose more groundes.

KNIGHT: Now what remedie for all these thinges?

DOCTOR: Ye se nowe the meane youre selfe, yf this be the efficient cause, as I doe thinke it is; and I knowe no meane to amende anie thinge that is amisse, but eyther by an other president that is well, or by arte. And yf we take the first waie, we may take either oure common welthe, when it was well, for a president, or an other common welthe that we se well ordered, to whose example we might conforme oure thinges. Yf the other way doe like vs better, to doe it by arte, we must then seke oute the right causes of these effectes, and by takinge the cheife and efficient causes, these effectes be taken away that proceade, as I haue oft said.

KNIGHT: I praye youe, tell playnly youre devise; what causes are these that ye would haue taken away, and howe these thinges may be remedied.

DOCTOR: I will, vnder protestation, that if ye like it not, ye doe tell youre fantasies to it, and doe reiect it; if ye like it, or anie parte thearof, vse it at youre pleasure. I meane (quod he) that all the coyne nowe curraunte shoulde be after a certayne daye not curraunte, but as men list to take theim, after the estimation of the stuffe; and the old coyne or new, after like value and quantitie and names, to be only from thence curraunt; and so the coyne throughly restored to the old rate and goodnes.

KNIGHT: All the treasure in this Realme is not able to doe that by and by at once, except it might be amended by a litle and a litle, some this yeare and some the next yeare.

DOCTOR: Howe meane you that?

KNIGHT: I meane thus, to amend the grote by one halpeny this yeare, and so the next yeare an other.

DOCTOR: God forebid that youe should advise the Kinge to doe so, for that shoulde be a meane as it hathe bene alredie to put the King to charge and the mattier never a whitt the better amended.

KNIGHT: Howe so?

DOCTOR: Marie, I will shewe youe yf youe meane one waye, thus. If this coyne that we haue, beinge curraunt, the Kinge would mend his newe coine that he makes from henceforthe a porcion, as a qu or a ob., in a pece, youe will graunte when that coine comethe abroade, the same shalbe in iust valew better by a penny or ob. then the other that we haue nowe.

KNIGHT: Yea, no doubte.

DOCTOR: Then shall not the other coine be as curraunt as it abroade?

KNIGHT: Yes.

DOCTOR: Well then, when goldsmithes, marchauntes, and other skilled persons in mettall doe perceaue that the one grote is better then the other, and yet that he shall haue as muche for the worse grote as for the better, will not he lay vp the better grote alwayes, and turne it to some other vse, and put forthe the worse, beinge like curraunte abroade? Yea, no doubt, even as they haue donne of Late with the new golde; for they, apperceavinge the new coyne of gold to be better then the new coine of siluer that was made to countervalew it, piked out all the gold, as fast as it came forthe of the minte, and layde that aside for other vses; so that nowe ye haue but a litle more then the old curraunt. And so bothe the Kinges highnes is deceaved of his treasure, and the thinge intended never the more brought to passe; and all is because theare is no dew proportion kept betewne the coines, while the one is better then the other in his degre. And as I ment to shew youe an other waie; that is, yf the Kinges highnes should call in sodenly all his now curraunt monie, and set forthe a new coyne somewhat better, but yet not all so pure as the olde; I take the like deceipte shall growe vnto the Kinge by his minters; for while the mettalles be confounded together, and can not be iustly proporcioned, with oute resolvinge agayne everie one to his owne kinde, the minters may doe what deceipt they lust, andvse that incertantie for theire owne lucre. And If in a ounce or tow they should be found faultie, then might they saie, We melted together a greate quantitie, and that lackes of oure standerd in this porcion is supplied in an other. And so they can never be burdened to doe theire dewties, left to theire owne conscience; which I feare me will be Large inoughe. And yet this waye weare but a patchinge of the thinge; and as muche as it mended one thinge one waye, it should paie an other waie.

KNIGHT: What, and the kinge would make the grote lesse, and all other his coines beside?

DOCTOR: All should then come to one mattier; for I had as leve haue xli of brasse as one oz of silver. And it is not in the power of any prince to make the oz of silver worthe two of it, of gold nor of anie other mettall. And I had as leve haue a halpenny called a halpenny, as a halpennie that should be called a penny. Well, a man may chaunge the name of thinges, but the valew in anie wise ye can not, to indure for anie space; except we weare in suche a countrie as Eutopia was imagined to be, that had no traffique with anie other outwarde countrie. And therfore I would haue the iust and dwe proportion kepte in this poincte, not only in quallitie but also in quantitie; for yf yow should admitt alteration, either in one or in the other, ye must bringe in with all manie absurdities; for albeit the prince might strike coines of other quantities and of other names then they weare of before time, thoughe they weare never so pure, yet, because thaccomptes of mens Lyvinges, rentes, stipendes, debtes and dewties vsethe the names of coines hearetofore accustomed, as poundes, markes, nobles, Rialles, and shillinges, and all writinges made by these names, ye can not alter anie of the same, but ye must bringe much alteration with all in everie manes revennwes, debtes, and duties; as it appeareth well, by the alteration of the goodnes of the coine, it hathe bene donne; which the Kinges highenes cheifely, and next his grace the noble men and gentlemen of this Realme, maye well finde at theire accomptes, yf they consider the mattier well.

KNIGHT: That I fele to be true in my selfe, thoughe I knowe not the reason whie; for albeit I may spend now more then I could xvj yeares agoe, yet I ame not able to kepe the like howse I did then.

DOCTOR: No mervaile it should be. Ye remember, I trowe, that I sayd to day morninge vnto youe, that the coine in Aristotle is called a common measure of all thinges. Then, put case ye had no rent in monie, but paid youe in suche necessaries as youe must nedes occupie, as in so many bushelles of corne and so many yeardes of clothe; the yarde and the bushell also being at the measure they be nowe at when ye did set forthe youre Landes. Yf the bushell and the yearde shoulde be made lesse by one halfe, and then, if ye weare paid but of so many busshels of corne and so many yardes of clothe as ye haue before in numbere, and yet after that measure that was after made lesse, might ye thenfede so manie persons and clothetheimas ye did before?

KNIGHT: Not by one halfe; for so muche is taken awaie of the stuffe that I should doe it with all, by youre reckeninge. But is the coine a common measure, accompted as youe saye, that may take suche diminution or abridgement as other measures may?

DOCTOR: It is not my sayinge only, but Aristotles, the sharpest philosopher of witt that ever was, as I saide before.

KNIGHT: Marie, yf that be true, the Kinge him selfe is most loser, and then his nobles and gentlemen, which is his cheife strengthe in time of nede, and all other that be paid by this measure, beinge of old appoynted to a certeyne numbre of poundes, marckes, or shillinges. And I perceaue that they that paye by this newe measure, and yet but after the old number, must nedes be great gayners.

DOCTOR: I perceaue youe feele the matter youre selfe?

KNIGHT: Yea, no doubt it must be thus. But one thinge more I must aske, how they doe in fraunce and flaunders, where they haue both brasse coyne, mixte coyne, pure siluer, pure gold, curraunt together?

DOCTOR: I warrant youe by kepinge of dew proportion everie mettall towardes other, as of brasse it towardes siluer a hundred to one, of siluer towardes gold xij to one. For the proportion of siluer towardes gold, I thinke, can not be altered by the auctoritie of anie prince.

18. Francisco García: *A Very General and Useful Treatise on Contracts* (1583)[1]

OF THE JUST PRICE, WHAT IT IS, AND HOW IT MAY BE KNOWN

Now that we come to treat of the just price, what it is, and how it may be known, we must first of all consider in what the value of things consists, since their value is the rule and measure by which we come to know their just price, in so far as value and price ought to correspond.

The value of things is very differently judged by the Moral Philosopher and by the Politician. When the Philosopher estimates the value of a thing he considers its nature: but the Politician looks only to its use and to the utility it brings, and to the service it can render us for the satisfaction of our needs and our human wants. Ask a philosopher which is better and nobler, a mouse or a measure of corn, and he will answer, the mouse, for it is a substance that has life, and the corn has none. But put the same question to a politician, and he will say that the corn is better and more valuable than the mouse, since it is necessary for preservation of human life, and the mouse has no such utility. For this reason does St Augustine say that he would rather have his house full of corn than of mice.

This utility, which causes us to esteem things and hold them dear, is of many kinds. A thing may be used in a way that is necessary for the preservation of life, as in eating, drinking, clothing ourselves, and remedying pain and human ailments. Or we may use it for our pleasures and human pastimes, such as when we read a book, contemplate the nature of things, or ride a horse. Or it may serve for the adornment of mankind or to delight our curiosity; and for this use gold and silver, precious stones, silk, brocade, tapestry, and many other such things are particularly appropriate. There are other uses that serve the infinite demands of mankind, which beyond a certain number cannot be comprehended.

Now, there are three ways in which a thing is said to be of greater or less value, bearing in mind its utility. Firstly, one thing may have many uses and serve for more purposes than another. Thus we say that a certain slave is better than his fellows if he has a wider range of skills and can perform more services. We judge between two horses in the same way and say that one is worth more than the other, all else being equal, because he can be used for riding in town or country, drawing a carriage, ploughing, and bearing burdens, whereas the other serves only for riding in town or drawing a carriage. Secondly, one thing may render a greater service than another. Corn is more valuable than stone, because the former serves to sustain life and the latter only to build houses. Thirdly, a service may be better performed by one thing than by another. Corn is worth more than fruit because it is more useful for human nourishment.

---

[1]   Translated by Marjorie Grice-Hutchinson.

All these comparisons must be understood as being true only if all other things remain equal, and not otherwise. For we must now explain that there are reasons for which prices rise and fall, and these, uniting together, may cause the value and estimation of things to decrease or increase quite apart from their utility. For example, we have said that bread is more valuable than meat because it is more necessary for the preservation of human life. But there may come a time when bread is so abundant and meat so scarce that bread is cheaper than meat.

There are four or five other reasons why the value and estimation of things should increase or decrease. The first is the abundance or scarcity of goods. The second is whether buyers and sellers are few or many.

The third is whether money is scarce or plentiful: this applies to places where the dealing is on a cash and not a credit basis. The fourth is whether vendors are eager to sell their goods, and buyers much sought after and importuned... The fifth, according to some authors, is the urgency of the vendor's need to sell and the purchaser's to buy, but this reason is not admitted by Dr Soto, who very truly remarks that the reason which moves a particular individual to buy or sell does not affect the value of the thing sold.

OF THE VALUE OF MONEY

[Money has two values.] The first of these is the natural value, which will here be called *value* absolutely; the second is the accidental value, which we shall call *estimation*.

Now, it happens with money as with other goods, that at one time or place they may be more highly esteemed and valued than at another, although their quality and nature may not have varied. Thus we see that in the Indies, where gold and silver is very plentiful, ducats and *reales* are not as highly esteemed as in Spain, where there is less gold and silver, and for this reason people there would not hesitate to pay an escudo for something that would not fetch two *reales* here. This is because an escudo is as little esteemed there as two *reales* here, even though the natural value of money is exactly the same there as here.

Also, money may be more or less esteemed at different times. Just as in the case of a private individual, so it may be with the whole republic. If a man is very rich and has plenty of money, he esteems a *real* as little as a poor man a *dinero*, and an escudo as little as a poor man a *real*, or as little as he himself esteemed a *real* at some other time, when he himself was poor. In just the same way, when the republic is rich and money is plentiful, so is the latter less esteemed; and when the republic is poor and money is scarce, so is it much more highly valued.

This greater or lesser degree of estimation usually proceeds from three causes. The first and most important is whether money is scarce or abundant, just as merchandise is little esteemed when it is plentiful, and highly valued and esteemed when it is scarce...

The second cause is whether there are many or few who wish to give or take money in exchange, just as in the sale or purchase of goods the price of the merchandise rises or falls according to whether there are many or few buyers and sellers. The third cause is whether the money is in a place where it is subject to risk or in one where it is safe. Thus, if in Flanders a city is in danger of being sacked (as Antwerp was sacked a few years ago), then money would be worth less in that city, quite apart from other considerations.

SUMMARY

Abundance or scarcity of money may be general or particular. It will be general if it is common to a whole city or kingdom, or even to all the merchants and money changers. It will be particular if it is confined to a few individuals. Money may be more abundant in one city than in another, and yet it may be scarce among merchants. In such a case the exchanges will reflect the relative abundance or scarcity of money in the two mercantile colonies, irrespective of conditions in the rest of the city. This is why, when money is sent between Seville and Medina, the exchanges turn sometimes in favour of Seville and sometimes in favour of Medina. If they depended entirely on general abundance they would always be in favour of Medina, since money is always scarcer there than in Seville. The same principles apply to the price of bills.

The rate of exchange depends partly on the conditions of supply and demand, partly on whether the money is present or absent. If a merchant pays out money in exchange at Medina at the rate of 360 *maravedis* to the ducat, he will make a profit of 50 *maravedis* on each ducat when he is repaid in Flanders. But if he pays out the same number of ducats in Flanders for repayment in Medina, he will make a profit of 75 *maravedis*. The same thing happens between Seville and Rome. From Seville to Rome a profit of 8 or 10 per cent is made, and from Rome to Seville a profit of 18 or 20 per cent, and yet the transaction is just and lawful. The explanation is this: part of the profit arises from the fact that money present is exchanged for money absent in both cases, and the former is more valuable than the latter, and part from the relative abundance and scarcity of money in the different places.

19. Bernardo Davanzati: *A Discourse upon Coins* (1588)[1]

1. The Sun and Internal Heat do Separate, as it were by Distillation, the best juices and Substances in the Bowels of the Earth; which being percolated into proper Veins and Mines, and there congeal'd, grown solid, and ripen'd, they are in time made Metals: whereof the most rare and perfect are Gold and Silver, resembling the two great Luminaries of the World in Splendor and Colour. Fire nor Rust will not consume them; they are not subject to be destroy'd by Moths, Worms, or Rottenness; nor do they waste much by Use. They may in Wire or Leaves be extended to an incredible Fineness, and have something in 'em that is Divine; at least certain Indian People think so, who fast when they are digging for Gold, and forbid themselves the Company of Women, with all other Pleasures, out of an old Superstition.

2. Now, Gold and Silver contribute very little in their own nature to our Lives, for which all Earthly Things seem to have been created. Yet Men, as if they would make Nature asham'd of this, have agreed to make those Metals of equal value to all other things, to make 'em the Price and Measure of all, and the Instruments of changing and exchanging whatever can be found good in this World. We may therefore call 'em the second Causes of a happy Life, seeing that by their means we enjoy all those Benefits which render it so. This is likewise the Reason why many have made 'em their Gods, seeing 'em perform almost impossibilities. There is not a Rock so hard, said a wise and warlike King, but an Ass loadn'd with Gold may force it. The known Fable of Jupiter's descending into Danae's Lap in a shower of Gold signifies nothing else, but the Miracles which Gold can work. We may conclude as much of the Sotry of Gyges a Lydian Shepherd, who walking in a Cave is said to have taken a Gold Ring from the Finger of a dead Man he found there, and putting it upon one of his own, he presently becomes invisible, goes into the Kings' Bed Chamber, enjoys the Queen, by whose Assistance he next murders her Husband, and seizes the Kingdom to himself.

3. Considering therefore the mighty Power and Importance of Gold in Human Affairs; and since Socrates, leaving Divine and Natural Things to the Care of the Gods, taught that Morality and Matters of Practice did only belong to us, I esteem it not a mean Subject, nor unseasonable, nor out of my Province (most courteous Academicks) to discourse now before you of Gold, of Silver, and other Coins. But it shall be with much brevity after our Florentine manner, especially because I come hither to day under a great Infirmity, my old and hereditary Distemper, which has not only render'd me feeble and uneasy, but likewise for many Years a Stranger to Books and Study. I must therefore beg your Attention, because I naturally am, and shall this day be purposely sparing of my words.

---

[1] Translated by John Toland.

4. Our Mortal Body being design'd a Habitation for the Divine and Immortal Soul, was fram'd, as became the Servant of so great a Lady, of a most noble, delicate, and tender Constitution; but withal naked and expos'd to the Injuries of Seasons, and Animals. It could not therefore but stand in need of several things, which no body can procure by himself alone; and this is the reason why we live together in Cities, to help one another by various Occupations, Offices, and Degrees. But no Person is born fit for all sorts of Business, some having a Genius for one thing, and some for another; nor can any Climate indifferently produce all the Fruits of Earth, being in a very different Situation with respect to the Sun and Stars. Hence it is that one Man labours and toils not for himself alone, but also for others, and they reciprocally for him. So one City helps another, and one Country parts with its Superfluities to another, in lieu whereof it is from thence again suppli'd with what it wants. And thus all the good things of Nature and Art are communicated and enjoy'd by the means of Human Commerce or Traffick, which at first was but simple Barter, or changing of one Commodity for another, as it still continues in the unciviliz'd parts of the World.

5. Now it was a difficult thing to know who stood in need of what you could spare, or who had an overplus of what you wanted; and so to transport, preserve, or divide them, as that both Parties might be accommodated. But Necessity, the Mother of Inventions, taught Men to pitch upon a certain place, where many meeting from different Parts with their Commodities, might the more easily supply one another; and this was the Origin of Faires and Markets. Their Eyes were open'd by this Convenience to discover a greater, that as they had chosen a particular place, so they might appoint some one thing that should bear an equivalent value to all others; and that every thing might be given or receiv'd for a certain quantity thereof, as if it had been the Medium or Fountain of the universal Value of things, their separate Substance, or Idea.

6. The first Money that the Antients wrought was Copper, and was by common Consent preferr'd to this high Office. So whatever superabounded to any Person, he gave it for as much Copper as was compar'd with, or judg'd equal to it; this Copper he afterwards gave for other things wanting to him, or otherwise he kept it by him in his Coffer, as a Security for the Supply of his future Necessities. And this was the Original of selling and buying, which we Tuscans still call comparing, in our Language comperare. Afterwards the greater Excellency of Gold and Silver did set them off, and occasion'd them to be made Money. They were at the beginning us'd in unwrought Pieces as they came to hand; but, as Additions are easily made to Inventions, they were next weigh'd, then stamp'd, and so became Money.

7. When, where, and by whom Money was first coin'd is not agreed upon by Writers. Herodotus says in Lydia, others in Naxos, Strabo in Aegina; some in Lycia by King Erichthonius; Lucan says in Thessaly by King Ionus. I cannot learn that there was any Money in use before the Flood: but the Scriptures speak plainly of it afterwards. Abraham purchas'd a Field from Ephron the Hittite for four hundred Shekals of Silver, currant Money with the Merchant. Joseph was sold by his Brethren for twenty pieces of Silver. And Moses laid upon the Israelites by Poll half a Sheckel, that is, four Drachms of Silver. Theseus, who reign'd in Attica about the time of the Judges in Isreal, coin'd Silver-Money with the Stamp of an Ox upon it, to invite those to manure and till the Ground, who till then liv'd at random in the Woods. When Janus King of Latium receiv'd Saturn fled by Sea from his Son Jupiter, who drove him from his Throne, (that was in the so well govern'd, and so much celebrated Golden Age) Janus, I say, did in the Memory of this Favour coin Copper Money, which had stamp'd upon it the Prow of a Ship. The first Money among the Romans was a piece of Copper, without any coining,

or a Pound Weight, call'd by them Aes gravis, As Assis, and Pondo. Servius Tullius stamp'd a Sheep upon it, as one of his Domestick Animals; the Riches of the Antients consisting then in their Flocks, by them call'd Peculium or Pecunia, whence Money was so nam'd. In the Year of Rome 383, Silver was there coin'd, and Gold sixty two Years after. When the Florentines defeated the Forces of Sienna at Mount Alcino in the Year 1252, they coin'd a Dram of fine Gold into a Florin, which was so well receiv'd in the World, that all People would coin such Pieces, and call them Florins too.

8. The Latin names of Money are Moneta, Pecunia, Nummus: The Greek names are [Greek words omitted]; And ours Pecunia, Danari, Danaio, 'tis call'd Moneta because the Stamp of it does admonish us of its name, Value, and Fineness. The Denomination of Money is generally deriv'd from the Stamp, as some old Coins were call'd Bigati, from the Figure of a Cart drawn by two Horses; Philippi, from the Head of King Philip; Sagittarii, from an Archer; and Armati, from the Impress of an arm'd Man. A Judg having receiv'd a thousand of the latter for passing an unjust Sentence, did in his own excuse roguishly play upon the words, saying, that he could not resist a thousand arm'd Men. The Mark or Letter X gave a Denomination to the Roman Denarius, which was worth ten Asses. Our Florin was so call'd from the Flower-de-Luce, which by Allusion shews it to be Florentine, as a Rose does Rhodian Money. The Stamp denotes oftentimes some Matters of Fact, as the Prow of a Ship the abovementioned Humanity of Janus: and a Yacht sunk, with this Motto Quare dubit asti, declar'd the vanquish'd Fortunes of Clement the VIIth. Pecunia is deriv'd, as we said before, from Pecus; and Nummus from the Greek word [Greek word omitted], which signifies a Statute, or somewhat appointed by Law, such as Money is, being made the Queen of all things. It was call'd [Greek word omitted] for its Usefulness and Goodness, seeing that by it we receive all that is good and beneficial, call'd in Greek [Greek word omitted]. Lastly, it was called [Greek word omitted], which betokens the small Money that runs amongst the common People. We of Florence make use of the Latin words; and from Denarius, which amongst the Romans was a particular Piece, we call Money in general Danari or Danato.

9. Thus far have we discours'd of the Time, Place, Invention, Authors, Names, and Advantages of Money. 'Tis now time to give its Essential Definition. Money therefore is Gold, Silver, or Copper coin'd by publick Authority at pleasure, and by the Consent of Nations made the Price and Measure of things, to contract them the more easily. I said Gold, Silver or Copper, because People have chosen those three Mettals to make Money of. If the Prince (by which word is understood whoever governs and protects the State, be it one or many, few or all) I say, if the Prince makes Money of Iron, Lead, Wood, Cork, Leather, Paper, Salt, or the like, (as it has sometimes happen'd) it will not be receiv'd out of his Dominions, as not being coin'd of the Matter generally agreed upon. It could not then be universal Money, but a particular Tally, Countermark, Note or Bill from the Prince, obliging him to pay so much good Money when he is able. And this has been frequently practis'd for want of Money, when the Publick Good requir'd it. The Romans, call'd the Masters of their Mint the Triumvirs, appointed to oversee the fining and coining of Copper, Silver, and Gold. Ulpianus, Pomponius, and others learned in the Civil Law, expressly affirm that no Money is good, but what is of Gold, of Silver, or Copper, wherefore Mark Antony was reproach'd amongst his other Crimes, for coining of base Silver mixt with Iron.

10. I said in the Definition coin'd by publick Authority, because few Metals are found altogether pure. To make Money therefore of equal Value, it is necessary to reduce the Metal

to a certain degree of Fineness, to cut it into pieces of equal Weight, and to put a known Stamp upon it as a Mark of its being good Money, that every one may not be oblig'd upon all occasions to try or essay it. This notwithstanding must not be done by private Men, who may be suspected of Fraud, but by the Prince, who is the Father of all. Wherefore no Person may coin his own Metal, be it never so good, without incurring the Penalty due to Counterfeiters and Forgers. But he is to carry it to the publick Mint, where it is receiv'd, weigh'd, essay'd mark'd, melted, allay'd, beaten, made into equal Pieces, adjusted, coin'd, and render'd every way according to Law.

11. It was likewise said in the Definition at Pleasure: For tho the Law requires Money to be coin'd, yet whether this or that way, that is, round or square, broad or narrow, more or less pure, with this or that Stamp, under one Denomination or another, these are all Accidents, and left entirely to the Magistrate's Descretion. It suffices that he touch not the Substance of it, which he has no Power to do: that is, he may coin no Money but of the three known Metals, nor set a false Price upon the Pieces, as it must needs happen, if, after trying of 'em, they should be found not to consist of fine Metal enough answerable to their Names. Should the People be thus cheated under the publick Faith that ought to protect them, they might say as the Wolf did once to the Shepherd who devour'd the Sheep. If I had done this, good Mr Shepherd, you would cry, help, help, and raise the Country to pursue me.

12. It was said in the Definition, By the Consent of Nations made the Price and measure of things, because men have agreed to fix that Value upon those Metals, for they have no such Privileges from Nature. A Natural Calf is far more noble than a Golden one, yet how much inferior in Price? An Egg that was bought for half a Grain of Gold, kept Count Ugolino alive in the Castle for ten days, which all the Treasure in the Universe could not do. What does more nearly concern our Lives than Corn? nevertheless ten thousand Grains thereof are sold for one of Gold.

13. But how comes it that things so valuable in themselves are worth so little Gold? From what root springs it, that one thing is worth just so much of another, rather than so much; worth this rather than that quantity of Gold? Let us examine whether this be the Effect of Chance or not. All Men labour to become happy, and they think to find this Happiness in the Satisfaction of all their Wants and Desires, to answer which all Earthly Things were created very good. Now all these by the Consent of Nations are worth all the Gold (comprehending also the Silver and Copper) that is wrought in the World. All Men then do passionately covet all the Gold, to buy all things for the Satisfaction of all their Wants and Desires, and so to become happy. The Parts follow the nature of the whole. How much therefore of the Happiness of a Man, City, or Country, is caus'd or occasion'd by any thing, just so much it is worth of their Gold or Labour: But it causes as much Happiness as it answers of their Desires or Wants, as Drink it pleasing proportionable to the degree of Thirst. The Will takes its measure from the Appetites and Pleasure; and Want takes its measure from the Nature, Season, Climate, and Place; from the excellency, rarity, or abundance of any thing, with perpetual Variation.

14. To be always acquainted with the Rule and Arithmetical Proportion which things bear among themselves and with Gold, it were necessary to look down from Heaven, or some exalted Prospect upon all the things that exist, or are done upon the Earth; or rather to count their Images reflected in the Heavens as in a true Mirror. Then we might cast up the Sum and say, there is on Earth just so much Gold, so many Things, so many Men, so many Desires: As many of those Desires as any thing can satisfy, so much it is worth of another thing, so much

Gold it is worth. But here below we can scarce discover those few things that are round about us, and we prize 'em according as we see 'em more or less desir'd at any time, or in any place; whereof the Merchants do carefully inform themselves, and for that reason they know the Prices of things better than all others.

15. It will not be amiss to illustrate what we have here said by some Examples. Water is excellent, said Pindar and we could not well live without it: But because every one may have enough of it for nothing, Jeremy had reason to lament that it could not be procur'd without Price. A Mole is a vile and despicable Animal, but in the Siege of Cassilino the Famine was so great, that one was sold for 200 Florins; and yet it was not dear, for he that parted with it dy'd of Hunger, and he that bought it out-liv'd the Siege. So Esau threw away his Birth-right, and Esop's Cock contemn'd the Jewel. On the contrary, Apitius, who Pliny calls a bottomless Gulf, spent two Millions and a half of Gold upon his Gut; and, finding but the fourth part of a Million in his Coffers, he poison'd himself for fear, as he said, of starving: And that, says Martial, was the daintiest bit that ever he swallow'd. Aristotle knew how to spend his Money better; for he gave for some few Books of Speusippus the Philosopher, a little after he was dead, 20250 Ducats of the Sun: So I reduce the antient Talents, after Budaeus, to our modern Money, that I maybe the better understood. Alexander the Great gave Aristotle himself forty eight thousand for writing the History of Animals. And Virgil receiv'd ten Sesterces a piece for the twenty Lines in the sixth of his Aeneids, wherein he laments the Death of Marcellus; this makes of our Money 4250 Florins. The Vanity of Mankind has set excessive Rates upon Vessels, precious Stones, Statues, Pictures, and other trifling Curiosities; because they find as much Satisfaction in these, as in the quantity of Gold they give for them. Thus the Inhabitants of Peru did at first barter Ingots of Gold for Looking glasses, Needles, little Bells, and the like; because they put a high Esteem upon those things then new to them, and drew more Satisfaction from 'em, than from the Gold and Silver wherewith they abounded. And when all the Gold in those Countries shall be transported into ours, (which must quickly happen, if we continue those rich Navigations begun Anno 1534, and then returning with less than a Million of Gold, the Spoils of Cucco and K. Atabalipa, but now bring from 16 to 18 Millions at a time, which has rais'd the Price of things one third, a sign that we have more Gold) I say, that when all the Gold in the Indies is brought into Europe, because then it will become a Drug, we must either find out something more rare to make Money of, or else return to the old way of bartering. And let so much suffice concerning the Essence of Money.

16. Some maintain that Money was a very ill Invention, for this reason, viz. That the Desire of other things could not be so great, nor the cause of so many Evils as is the Thrist of Gold; because so much of those could not be laid up and preserv'd, as there may be treasur'd of this. I answer with Epictetus, that every thing has two Handles, and may be well or ill taken and us'd; as Reason, Physick, and Law are often abus'd to the Destruction of Mankind; but are they for all this prohibited in the Common-wealth? Have all the Philosophers pluck'd out their Eyes like Democritus, because the fight of many things takes off the Mind from Contemplation? All Steel, as they say, makes its own Rust, and we must learn how to scour it. Money was an excellent invention, and an Instrument of doing infinite good; if any makes an ill use of it, 'tis not the Thing but the Person that is to be blam'd and punish'd.

17. Some grave and famous Authors have call'd Money the Sinews of War and Government; but, in my Opinion, it may be more properly stil'd the Second Blood thereof. For as Blood, which is the Juice and Substance of Meat in the natural Body, does, by circulating out of the

greater into the lesser Vessels, moisten all the Flesh, which drinks it up as parch'd Ground soaks Rain Water; so it nourishes and restores as much of it as was dri'd up and evaporated by the natural Heat: In like manner, Money, which we said before was the best Juice and Substance of the Earth, does, by circulating out of the richer Purses into the poorer, furnish all the Nation, being laid out upon those things whereof there is a continual Consumption for the Necessities of Life. From the poorer it returns again into the richer Purses; and thus circulating without Intermission, it preserves alive the Civil Body of the Common-wealth. Hence it may be easily conceiv'd that every State must have a quantity of Money, as every Body a quantity of Blood to circulate therein. But as the Blood stopping in the Head or the larger Vessels puts the Body naturally into a Consumption, Dropsy, or Apoplexy, etc. so should all the Money be only in a few Hands, as in those of the rich for Example, the State falls unavoidably into Convulsions, and other dangerous Distempers. Thus it was very near happening at Rome, when by reason of the multitude of accus'd Persons, of Condemnations, Slaughters, and Confiscations, all the Money was like to come into the Exchequer, had not Tiberius distributed two Millions and a half of Gold into the Banks, when it was to be lent to Debtors upon double Security for three Years, without any Expence or Interest. We ought therefore to set a high Value upon the living Member of the Common-wealth, and to preserve it from those Mischiefs which usually befal it, when not carefully look'd after; such as Counterfeiting, Monopolizing, Simony, Usury, and the like, already decri'd, and known everywhere. But, passing by these, I shall now confine my Discourse only to one, not so much taken notice of, and indeed neglected from the beginning; I mean debasing of Coin, which increases more and more every day. I design to shew the Causes, the Damage, the Scandal, the Remedy of this Evil, and so to conclude.

18. The Root of this, as of all other Evils, is Covetousness, which has found out many occasions and pretences for debasing of Money. But this is the chief, that Money, being once out of the Mint, does in time, by too much handling, and frequently counting, grow lighter; or that a Grain, for Example, is taken off it by some illegal Practice; the People in the mean while either take no notice of so small a matter, or care not, and so the Money passes: Hereupon the dishonest Coiner says to his Lord, Since your Money, Sir, is one Grain lighter, 'tis fitter you should get by it, than the others clip it; and so a Grain is taken off it. The neighbouring States seeing this, diminish theirs likewise. Some time after they fall to it again, and take off another Grain, and then another, and so on. Thus for sixty Years past this Worm has consum'd above the third part of the Silver of Europe; and it must at last (if this Practice continue) be brought, to nothing, or to those Nail-heads, which, perhaps, was the Iron-Money that Lycurgus gave the Spartans.

19. The Damage is manifest, because by how much Money is debas'd whether in Allay or Weight, by so much are lessen'd the publick Revenues, and the Credit and Estates of private Men, who so far receive less Gold or Silver. And he that has but little Money, can buy but a few things, which are the only true Riches: for no sooner is Money debas'd but all things grow dear: And there is Reason for it, because (as Carasulla, who was no Fool, delivers the Etymology of the word) vendo to sell comes from venio to come, and do to give; for things are given in sale, because you expect there should come to you in Exchange so much Metal as is wont, or is believ'd to be in the Money; and not so many Stamps, or Denominations, or Pieces. If that same quantity of Silver be at present in one hundred and nine pieces, which us'd before to be in a hundred only, must not one hundred and nine be now paid for that which formerly cost but a hundred?

20. Therefore Years ago our Florin was worth seven Livers, now 'tis exchang'd for ten: So that at present seven Livers, cannot purchase a whole Florin, but only seven parts in ten. The other three parts are vanish'd, and by so much are lessen'd the publick Revenues, with the Estates of private Men. Now here may be perceiv'd how great an Injury Princes do to themselves; for tho they gain once by robbing the poor People of what is taken from the Money, yet they lose by it ever after, being forc'd to receive their Revenues in the same Coin. Hence spring Disorders, and Confusions; because the People do, by the Novelty of the Coins and Prices which measure things, become, in a manner, Strangers in their own Country; and not less confounded than if the Weights and publick Measures were alter'd, with which they were wont to contract for Corn, Liquor, Cloth, etc. But what worse thing can be done to the Common-wealth than every day to change the Laws, Coins, Offices, Customs, and, as it were, to renew the Members of it? To make muddy, or rather to poison the common Fountain of the City?

21. More Confusions still follow upon debasing of Money; for when Silver is debas'd, the Price of Gold must consequently rise, as it was said before of our Florin rais'd from seven to ten Livres: Otherwise the common Proportion between Silver and Gold, which at this time is that of one to twelve or thirteen, could not hold; for all the Gold would be brought up, and carried where it was worth more Silver. Great Difficulties therefore, and Quarrels would happen about the payment of Legacies, Taxes, Rents, Profits, and of all Debts contracted when the Money was good. A Debtor of a Gold Florin of seven Livres would say to his Creditor, Sir, here are seven Livres which I ow'd you. The Creditor answers, you must pay me ten Livres; for a Gold Florin, which you promis'd to pay me, is now worth so much: and if this pleases you not, pay me a Gold Florin, flower-deluc'd, and stamp'd, as when we bargain'd. The Debtor replies, If I give you a Florin of seven Livres, as the Proclamation sings, I do enough: If the Prince has debas'd the Money, it is a common Storm, and we are all in the same Ship: Complain not of me, but of the Prince. And truly the People have reason to complain of him, being involv'd in such cruel Difficulties and Tumults, as even the wise know not how to be deliver'd from: for some of 'em are for maintaining the Law in this case, others the Intention of it; some are for the Rigor, and others for the Equity of it.

22. But how shall the Prince help debasing the Money? Suppose it be made bad by his Neighbours, by Time, or evil Practices; that all the good be spirited or exported, and after vanishing a while, it appears again made worse; must the City be fill'd with foreign, base, and clipt Money, and the People be plagu'd with it, as if they were to feed upon mouldy Bread? I answer, that so such Money is to be suffer'd by any means: That every one may be secure from being cheated, let it be quickly remov'd, but by just and discreet Methods. Let there be certain Persons appointed to receive it, and to pay the just value thereof, without making any Gain or Profit by it. So every one will bring it to be chang'd, and obey most readily, when the perceive they are to suffer none, or a very inconsiderable Loss. Thus a great Master in Politicks ordain'd in the 5th Book of his Laws, that the Government should not take the bad Money from those who brought it from Abroad, but might justly pay it after the manner of the Country.

23. There can be no danger, that your Money, for doing too good, should be exported and recoin'd: for I presume it is not bestow'd upon him that carries it Abroad; but paying for it after the rate of good Money, he leaves (as we say) his Skin behind him; and if it be made bad, if passes and is exchang'd only for bad Money. A hundred Livres of Florence go for a hundred and fix of those of Lucca: he that takes by Exchange an hundred Livres in Florence, does but

labour in vain. We don't find therefore that Lucca, nor any other City are emptying Florence of its Money to re-coin it, since the Exchange has every way levell'd and made it equal.

24. It is not fit then, that because others debase their Money, you do so too. Rather let what has been once receiv'd, always pass, because so the People are in no danger of losing, of being cheated, or offended. The Egyptians cut off both their Hands who falsified the publick Weights and Measures. But what greater falsifying can there be than diminishing the Money, that is, basely to pilfer People of their Goods? Rome being strain'd by Hannibal, and drain'd of Money, they coin'd their Assis of one Ounce, that weigh'd twelve before. But this was done by publick Advice in that Extremity, which being over, all matters were settl'd as formerly. However, had it continu'd, does it not follow, that as Money was brought down from twelve to one, so the Prices of things would be rais'd from one to twelve? The old Country-woman that us'd to sell her dozen of Eggs for an Assis of twelve Ounces, seeing it look now so deform'd, and reduc'd to one Ounce, would have said, Gentlemen, either give an Assis of twelve Ounces, or twelve of those paultry ones that weigh but one Ounce; or I'll give you an Egg apiece for your Asses; chuse which you will.

25. Remove then all the thoughts of debasing the Coin, and pluck up the Seeds of this Mischief. Let not the Mint gain by any means; for truly 'tis a most scandalous business to lessen other Peoples Metal that is sent thither to be coin'd. Greediness is a Crime that was punish'd by God with the Death of Eli the Priest in Shilo, and with that of his two Sons Hophni and Phineas his Ministers, who cut off, for their own Tables, the best of every Offering brought them to sacrifice. The Gentiles did better, who eat all the Victim except the Fat that run out of it, as if the Gods would have the Soul only for their share, so Strabo and Catullus say:

> Gnarus ut accepto veneretur carmine Divos;
> Omentum in Flamma pingue liquefaciens.

26. Now to take away all Temptations of Gain, to wash off all the Marks of it, and to make this Matter creditable, plain, and safe, command that Money pass according to its intrinsick Value, that is, for as much Gold or Silver as there is in it; and that Money of the same Allay be worth as much in Bar as when it is coin'd: so that the Metal, like an amphibious Animal, may without any Expence indifferently pass from Bullion into Coin, and from Coin into Bullion. In a word, let the Mint deliver out the same Metal in Money that it receiv'd in to coin. Would you have then, some will say, the Mint to bear all the Expence? Yes, certainly; many eminent Civil Lawyers content that the Publick must be at the Charge of maintaining this Blood in the Common-wealth, as they pay the Souldiers, and the Salaries of Magistrates for the Preservation of Liberty and Justice. Others think it equitable that Money should pay its own Minting, by being made somewhat worse, and yet of more Value than so much Bullion, like Vessels, Furniture, or other things whereupon any Labour is bestow'd. So, very often the Workmanship is of greater Value than the Materials, as those two Beakers of Silver wrought by mentor, which Lucius Crassus the Orator bought for 2500 Florins of Gold, yet never drunk out of them afterwards. And the Husbands of our time can tell whether the Embroideries and other little Trangums of the Women, cost 'em more than the Clothes they are to set off.

26. After all, the old Custom of Money's paying its own Coinage, (the People looking on and suffering it) pleads Prescription, and the Prince is in Possession of it. I shall not dispute with my Masters; but I may say that if the Mint ought not to bear this Charge, yet it should be made as easy as possible, and the Stamps be rather less beautiful. But why should not we

return (as some desire it) to the old way of casting Money? For it has all the Advantages that can be wish'd. Two Stamps of Steel can mark both sides of a Piece in two Molds of Copper, so that two Men without any more Expences than Waste, Boiling and Coals, may in one day coin any great Sum in pieces of equal Weight and Fineness, and for that reason more apt to discover clipping or counterfeiting. For Money that is made of false Metal, if it be of any ordinary Body, cannot escape being found out by its Weight in the Scales; and if it be broader or narrower, thicker or thinner than it should be, it cannot impose upon the Eyes. Nor had it been more than Justice, if Officers were appointed to see it melted, allay'd, and cast before the People within those Iron Grates, ordain'd for that purpose by our good and wise old citizens, after the Example of the Romans, who religiously perform'd all this nice business of Money in the Temple of Juno, the Doors being set wide open, that the People might freely see what so nearly concern'd them.

27. Who does not perceive that by such means as these we might eradicate those pernicious Weeds of Expence, Fraud, and Gain; which being only lopt, never fail to grow again, and to debase the Coin? Lastly, I shall add as a Corollary, that Traffick has so much trouble and difficulty in it upon the account of this blessed Money, that it would be better perhaps to do without it, and to pass our Gold and Silver by Weight and Size, as they did in the Primitive Times, and is still us'd in China, where they always carry about them their Shears and Scales, and have nothing to fear but the Allay, which by Use and the Touchstone is easily discover'd.

Concerning the Generation of Metals; the Excellency of Gold and Silver; the Origin of buying and selling, with that of Money; when, why, and by whom Money was first invented and us'd; of the Names, of the Essence, and the Importance thereof; of its debasing, and the Causes of it, with the Damages and Scandals that are the Consequences of it, and their proper Remedies; let it suffice, most patient Auditors, to have discours'd those few things, by me thought convenient for this time and place; not for you Instruction, Gentlemen, but for your Entertainment.

20. Luís de Molina: *A Treatise on Money* (1597)[1]

In the three preceding arguments we have examined one of the rulings or reasons for which it may be licit to charge an increment over the principal for the exchange carried out from one place to another. Before examining two other reasons for which this type of exchange may be licitly practiced we must explain the issue before us.

The same amount of money may have more value in one place than in another in two ways: first, because according to the law or accepted custom it has, in comparison to other coins, a different value in places that are also different. Thus, for example, a *ducat* is worth 400 *reais* in Portugal and 375 *maravedis* in Castile; and a silver *real* is worth 34 *maravedis* in Castile and today it is worth 40 in Portugal. And in the kingdom of Valencia the *real* is worth fewer *dines* than in Catalonia. The *dines* are the smallest common copper coins in those kingdoms. In other places, the *real* has different values. Consequently, 11 silver *reales* are worth 374 *maravedis* in Castile, and in Portugal they are worth today 440 *reais*, disregarding other places for the time being. The gold *escudo*, which in the past was worth in Castile 10 silver *reales* and 10 *maravedis*, that is, 350 *maravedis*, was worth in Rome 11½ *julios* (the *julio* is equivalent to the silver *real*), and in France and in other places it had different values. Today, in Castile, its value has increased to 400 *maravedis*.

There is another way money may have more value in one place than in another, namely, when it is more abundant. In equal circumstances, the more abundant money is in one place, so much less is its value to buy things or to acquire things that are not money. Just as the abundance of merchandise reduces their price when the amount of money and quantity of merchants remains invariable, so too the abundance of money makes prices rise when the amount of merchandise and number of merchants remain invariable, to the point where the same money loses purchasing power. So we see that, in the present day, money is worth in the Spanish territories much less than what it was worth eighty years ago, due to the abundance of it. What was bought before for two today is bought for five, or for six, or maybe for more. The price of salaries has risen in the same proportion, as well as dowries and the value of real estate, revenues, benefices, and all other things. That is exactly why we see that money is worth much less in the New World, especially in Peru, than in the Spanish territories, due to its abundance. And wherever money is less abundant than in the Spanish territories, it is worth more. Neither is it worth the same in all parts because of this reason, yet it varies according to its abundance and all other circumstances. This value does not remain unaltered as if it were indivisible but fluctuates within the limits defined by the people's estimation, the same as happens with merchandise not appraised by law. This money's value is not the same in all parts of the Spanish territories, but different, as ordinarily it is worth less in Seville—where

---

[1]   Translated by Jeannine Emery.

the ships arrive from the New World and where for that reason there is usually an abundance of it—than in other places of the same Spanish territories.

In addition to this, the greater the need for money there is in one place—for example, to buy merchandise, war expenses, the royal court's expenditures, or for any other reason—the more it is worth there than in other places. What is more, these same reasons make money worth more at some times than in others in one and the same place. Money that in one place is exchanged for money in another place functions as merchandise not appraised by law, whose value rises at some times and falls at others, depending on whether there is more or less need of it. That is why the abundance of one type of merchandise, the greater or lesser need of it and the greater or lesser number of merchants who want it, make its value rise or fall in a particular place. This is exactly what happens with money: its greater or lesser abundance in one place, the need there is of it, the greater or lesser number of those who want to exchange it for diverse places and of those who can and want to accept those exchanges, are the reasons for which money at a certain time is worth more in one place than in another, or at different times. And even in the same fair and in one and the same place, it shall be worth more or less according to whether at the beginning, middle, or end of the fair there are more or fewer people who need money and want to take it in exchange for other places, and more or fewer people who want to hand it over.

When in the kingdoms and republics the value of larger coins is appraised in relation to the smaller ones, such a rate applies only to the exchange of some coins for others in the same place and in the purchase of goods in that place. The kingdoms and republics have never wanted to appraise the coins as far as the value we are referring to now, that is, to exchange them for coins in other places, as this value is not constant, even if the other type of value is appraised by law. And because it is a just value even after the legal appraisal, appraising the coins in order to exchange them for coins from other places would be to the disadvantage of kingdoms and republics, whose merchandise would start going scarce due to this appraisal. That is why the custom has always rightfully, and notwithstanding the appraised price, respected the fact that coins had this other variable value when exchanging them for coins in other places. And in his bull, Pius V approved this type of exchange with an increment.

I explained that the money from one place that is exchanged for money in another functions as a merchandise not appraised by law, because concerning the place where it is, it always retains the value appraised by law or accepted by custom. For even in Medina or in any other place where exchanges are usually taken, the value of money varies because the exchange is given more expensively for one place than for another, and even in one and the same place the exchange is given more expensively to some people than to others due to the fact that it is not indivisible and during the same fair it may vary according to the circumstances. However, in comparison to Medina itself and to the merchandise bought there at different times or to pay debts, it always maintains the price appraised by law—and according to that price merchandise is bought and debts are paid—even if that other value of the coin increases or diminishes. What is more, in all the places where the exchange has to be compensated, the amount of money to be paid according to the contract is always estimated according to the value appraised by the law for the money in that place.

21. Leonard Lessius: *On Buying and Selling* (1605)[1]

A *price* consists of money, which was invented to be the measure and price of all things that come under human contracts, as Aristotle teaches. Money can neither be a commodity in itself, nor can it be sold as a commodity, except on the basis of its material or a circumstance extrinsic to its nature. Thus, money can be sold because it is old or beautiful, or convenient to transfer, or absent, or difficult to be claimed back, etc. Before money was introduced, sale-purchase as such did not exist, but merely barter. Money was invented, however, because barter was inconvenient.

...

The *just price* is considered to be that price which is determined either by the public authorities in consideration of the common good, or by the common estimation of people. A price, then, is imposed in one of two ways.

In the first case, the prince or magistrate fixes the price at which a particular good is to be sold by considering all the circumstances on which the estimation of goods depends, lest the buyers be deceived or forced to give in to the sellers' whims. The doctors call this price the legal price, as though it were laid down by law. It is obvious that this price is to be considered just (except maybe for the case in which the price certainly came about through the hope of obtaining favors, discrimination against the sellers, or gross ignorance). For whatever the public authorities decide by virtue of their office cannot be called into question by the subjects, which is exactly the case with the legal price. Just as in other circumstances it is the responsibility of the public authorities to promote the common good, likewise in business they should prevent fraud and the exploitation of the poor. In addition, superiors are better informed about all the circumstances causing the estimation of the goods to rise or to fall.

Some circumstances to be considered in determining the just price relate to the commodities themselves: their scarcity or abundance, the common need for them, and their subjective utility. Next, there are circumstances pertaining to the seller: his labor, the expenses, the risks, and the damages he incurs in obtaining, transporting, and storing the goods. Furthermore, the mode of selling plays a role, namely whether the commodities are offered spontaneously or sold on demand. A final factor concerns the buyers, whether they are few or many, and whether there is a lack or an abundance of money.

In the second case, the price is imposed by the common estimation of knowledgeable people. Hence, some call it the common price. Others speak about the natural price, as though it were constituted by natural prudence. It applies to those goods that have not received a price by the public authorities. From Digest 35.2.63 it is obvious that this price is just. There it is

---

[1]   Translated by Wim Decock, Nicholas De Sutter, and Bernard W. Dempsey.

stated that "the prices of goods are defined neither by affection nor by private advantage, but rather in common." The reason thereof is that private judgment is fallible and easily perverted by love of gain, whereas a common judgment is less subject to error. Since this rule is the most reliable guideline available, we should observe it. The common estimation is realized by taking into account all the circumstances mentioned above.

...

Because of an abundance of buyers and money but a shortage of goods, prices are higher than under opposite circumstances, namely, when there is a shortage of buyers and money but an abundance of goods. The reason thereof is that these factors make the common estimation of goods rise. For a thing will be dear when it is asked for by many buyers and can barely be obtained or can be obtained only in small amounts. Conversely, a thing will be cheap if it is abundantly available and few people ask for it. This is the reason why it may suddenly happen that prices skyrocket when plenty of rich and avid buyers arrive on the market, whereas prices may collapse just as quickly when these people all move away, as, for example, when all of a sudden a prince accompanied by his court visits a city, or the Indian fleet moors, as is correctly explained by Luís de Molina.

...

A good that must be delivered to the buyer after a few months is worth less than a good that must be delivered to him immediately. For a present good and the immediate ownership over it offer many opportunities that a future good does not. So if he buys and gives the money at once, he is allowed to pay less than he should have paid at the time of delivery.

...

First, as is evident from experience, when such bonds are offered for sale as merchandise, they are estimated to be worth less than ready money by the common judgment of people. For ready money offers many opportunities that bonds do not. Consequently, they may be bought at a lower price. This inference is right because the just price of any saleable good is the price settled by the common estimation. Why not apply the common estimation to the case of bills of debt, if in all other cases the just price is considered to be the price based on that estimation?

You might object that in this case the common estimation is based on the need of those who want more ready money, and that as a consequence the estimation is not prudent and inapplicable. Otherwise, it would be licit to demand twice as much from a person prepared to give that sum because of his need.

Yet, the inference made in the objection is not valid. For the estimation of nearly all goods depends on the common need to which people are subjected. If this common need were absent, nearly all goods would be considered worthless, such as medicine, for instance, or food and shelter. Moreover, it is not required that this need is felt by everyone. It suffices that many or most people are in need of that good in order for the common estimation to be valid. In this particular case, those bonds are needed less than ready money and do not offer the same potential of benefits and opportunities to make a profit. Therefore, they are prudently estimated to be worth less.

It does not matter that you in particular do not prefer ready money to such bonds. That is just an accidental fact because their price does not depend on your estimation but rather on the common estimation. Likewise, you could sell medicine at the common price even though you yourself are never in need of it.

...

The Bourse (Bursa) or Peristyle of Antwerp is where the merchants gather every day and take account of the abundance or shortage of money, of the number of exchanges, of the amount of merchandise, and all other sources of gain in which there is need of present money. Then either by themselves or their agents they establish the price for the privation of money. Merchants who lend may demand this price for the reason that they are deprived of their money for such and such a time and may not call it back before the time agreed. This price is sometimes 6 percent per year and sometimes 7, 8, 9, 10, 11, or 12 percent; more than 12 percent they are forbidden to demand by the Constitutions of Charles V, given at Brussels on the 4th of October, page 767... Moreover, any merchant seems to be able to demand this price in that same place even though there is no gain of his that stops because of his loan. This is the just price for the privation of money among merchants; for the just price of an article or obligation in any community is that which is put upon it by that community in good faith for the sake of the common good in view of all the circumstances. This price is put in that way; therefore it is a just price. When a price is put upon some article or obligation for just causes which are commonly present, I may demand that price for the reason that the object is commonly so evaluated, even though for me such an obligation is no burden, even though it is actually an advantage. Therefore, even if through the privation of money for a year there is no gain of mine that stops and no risk of capital, because such a price for just causes has been put upon this privation, I may demand it just as the rest do.

22. Juan de Mariana: *A Treatise on the Alteration of Money* (1609)[1]

ARGUMENT

At the time that there was a great shortage of money in Spain and the treasury was completely exhausted by long and drawn-out wars in many places and by many other problems, many ways to make up for this shortage were thought out and tried. Among others, consideration was given to the debasing of money, and that in two ways. First, by doubling the value of existing money, the king gained a good deal: half of the entire sum, which was huge—a great profit in the situation! Second, new money was minted from pure copper with no addition of silver, as was customary. Rather, its weight was diminished by half. In this way, the king profited by more than two-thirds. Men's plans are not provident. Seduced by present abundance, they gave no consideration to the plan's inherent evils into which they were rushing. There were, however, those who were more cautious because of their knowledge of history and past evils, and they criticized this approach within their own circles and even in writing. Very soon, events proved that they were not foolish prophets. Things got worse. Some convenient reason was being sought for destroying or recalling that money. Some consultants recommended the debasement of silver money to make up, with that profit, for the loss that they saw was necessarily coming because of the old copper money. The cure was more deadly than the disease. It has been rejected until the present. Rather, there was a recent decree recalling a large part of the new money and for compensating the owners from the royal revenues. Such was the occasion for a new effort to publish this treatise, which we began earlier. It aims at letting other generations learn from our misfortunes that money is hardly ever debased without calamity to the state: Profit for the moment is intimately connected with manifold ruin along with rather great disadvantages.

PREFACE

May the immortal God and all his saints grant that my labors may benefit the public, as I have always prayed. The only reward that I seek and wish is that our king, his advisers, and other royal ministers entrusted with the administration of affairs may carefully read this pamphlet. Here I have clearly, if not elegantly, attempted to illustrate certain excesses and abuses, which, I think, must be strenuously avoided. The point at issue is that copper money, as minted in the province today, is of inferior quality to earlier coins.

---

[1]   Translated by Patrick T. Brannan.

Indeed, this practice inspired me to begin and complete this slight, but not insignificant, endeavor without consideration of men's judgment. Doubtless, some will indict me for boldness and others for rash confidence. However, reckless of danger, I do not hesitate to condemn and revile things that men of greater prudence and experience considered a cure for ills. Nonetheless, my sincere desire to help will deliver me in part from such accusations and faults, and the fact of the matter is that nothing expressed in this controversy is original with me. When the entire nation, old and young, rich and poor, educated and uneducated is shouting and groaning under this burden, it should not seem remarkable that from this multitude someone dares to put in writing something that is censured with some emotion in public and in secret gatherings; in squares and the streets. If nothing else, I shall fulfill the rightful duty that a well-read man should exercise in the state because he is not unaware of what has happened in the history of the world.

The famous city of Corinth, as Lucian tells us, knew from reports and rumors that Philip of Macedon was hastening against it in arms. The citizens, in fear, acted swiftly: Some prepared arms, others fortified the walls, and others prepared provisions and instruments of war. Diogenes the Cynic was living in that city, and when he saw that he was not invited to have any part in the work and preparation and was considered useless by everyone, he came out of the barrel in which he used to live and began to roll it quite eagerly up and down. The citizens, indignant inasmuch as he seemed to make fun of the common calamity, asked him what he was doing. He answered, "It is not right for me alone to be at leisure when everyone else is busy." At Athens again, as Plutarch tells us, when there was civil unrest and all parties were bent on revolution, Solon, no longer able to help the fatherland because of his age, took his stand in arms before the doors of his house, to show that he wished to help despite his lack of physical strength. Ezekiel says that even the trumpeter does his duty if, at the appointed times, he blows into his instrument and his blast sounds—now attack, now retreat—at the leader's command, even though the soldiers may not follow the commands.

At a time when some are restrained by fear, others held, as it were, in bondage by ambition, and a few are losing their tongues and stopping their mouths because of gold and gifts, this pamphlet will achieve at least one goal: All will understand that there is someone among the people who defends the truth in his retirement and points out the public threat of dangers and evils if they are not confronted with dispatch. Finally, like Diogenes, I will appear in public, I will rattle my barrel; I will openly assert what I think—whatever the final outcome. Perhaps my earnest activity will be of some use, since everyone desires the truth and is eager to help. May my readers be open to this instruction. It was undertaken with a sincere heart. To this end, I pray to our Heavenly Majesty and to our earthly majesty who is his vicar and to all the citizens of heaven as well. Furthermore, I earnestly entreat men of every condition and dignity not to condemn my undertaking, or pass negative judgment on it, before they have read this pamphlet carefully and assiduously examined the question at issue. In my opinion, it is the most serious of issues to arise in Spain in many years.

CHAPTER 1: DOES THE KING OWN HIS SUBJECTS' GOODS?

Many enhance kingly power beyond reasonable and just limits—some to gain the prince's favor and some to amass private wealth. These most pestilent of men are not concerned with honesty and are commonly found in the courts of princes. Others reason to the conviction that an increase in royal majesty enhances the protection of public welfare. However, they are mistaken. As in the case of other virtues, power has definite limits, and when it goes beyond limits, power does not become stronger but rather becomes completely debilitated and breaks down. As the experts say, power is not like money. The more gold that one amasses, the richer and happier one is. Power, rather, is like nourishment; the stomach groans equally if it lacks food or is burdened with too much food. It is bothered in either case.

Royal power increased beyond its limits is proven to degenerate into tyranny, a form of government that is not only base but also weak and short-lived. No power and no arms can withstand the fury of their offended subjects and enemies. Surely, the very nature of royal power—if it is legitimate and just, arising from the state—makes clear that the king is not the owner of his subjects' private possessions. He has not been given the power to fall upon their houses and lands and to seize and set aside what he will. According to Aristotle, the first thing that brought kings to eminence was their protection of citizens from the impending enemy storms when their people were mustered around their standards. Thereafter, in time of peace, they were given the power to punish the guilty and the authority to settle all litigation among their people. To protect this authority in a dignified manner, the people established fixed revenue by which the kings could support their original lifestyle, and they decided how this money was to be paid. This process establishes the king's right of ownership over those revenues that the state conferred, as well as of those possessions that he acquired as a private citizen or that he received from the people after becoming king. However, he does not exercise dominion over those things that the citizens have kept either publicly or privately to themselves, for neither the power conferred upon the leader in time of war nor the authority to govern subjects grants the authorization to take possession of the goods of individuals. Thus, in the chapter of the *Novellas constitutiones*, beginning "Regalia," which treats of all aspects of the royal office, such dominion is not found.

Indeed, if the possessions of all subjects were under the king's will, the actions of Jezebel, as she appropriated Naboth's vineyard, would not have been censured so severely. If she had been just pursuing her own rights, or those of her husband who was certainly king, she would have been claiming what was her own. Had this been true, Naboth would have been accused of contumacy for unjustly refusing to pay his debt. Therefore, it is the common opinion of legal experts (as they explain in the last law of the chapter, "Si contra ius vel utilitatem publicam" and, as Panormitanus presents it, in ch. 4, *De iureiurando*) that kings cannot ratify any law that would harm their subjects without the consent of their people. Specifically, it is criminal for kings to strip their people of their goods, or part of their goods, and to claim these goods as their own. Indeed, it would not be legal to initiate a suit against the prince and to set a day for trial if everything were under his power and law. The response would be automatic: If he has stripped anyone of anything, he did not do it unjustly but of his own right. He would not purchase private homes or land when he needed them but would seize them as his own. It is useless to develop this obvious point further: Lies cannot destroy it; no flattery can present darkness as full day. On the one hand, it is the essence of a tyrant to set no limits to his power, to consider that he is master of all. A king, on the other hand, puts a limit to his authority, reins in his desires, makes decisions justly and equitably, and does not transgress. A king maintains that the goods of others are entrusted to him and under his protection and that he does not strip his people of their possessions except, perhaps, according to the prescripts and formalities of law.

CHAPTER 2: CAN THE KING DEMAND TRIBUTE FROM HIS SUBJECTS WITHOUT THEIR CONSENT?

Some people deem it a serious matter and not in keeping with majesty to make the prince's treasury depend upon the will of the people so that he cannot demand new tribute from them without their consent. That is to say, it is a serious matter when the people, and not the king, become the judge and moderator of affairs. They go on to maintain that if the king summons a parliament in the kingdom when new taxes are imposed, this fact should be attributed to his modesty. He is able to levy taxes of his own volition, without even consulting his subjects, as affairs and fiscal necessity might demand. These pleasant words are dear to kingly ears, and they have sometimes led neighboring kings into error—witness the French kings.

In his biography of Louis XI, Philippus Comineus, who lived during the aforementioned king's lifetime, writes that Louis XI's father was the first to follow this approach. Louis XI's father was none other than Charles VII. Financial problems were especially pressing in the large part of the country occupied by the English. Charles VII placated the nobles with annual pensions, but he chose to oppress the rest of the people with new taxes. Since then, as the saying goes, the French kings came into their own but stopped protecting their people. After many years, the veritable wound that they received by offending the people has not healed; it is bloody even to this day. I might add that the recent French civil wars, waged so violently for so many years, arose from no other source. For this, oppressed people—most without home or fortune and with possessions lost—agreed to take up arms. They are destined either to destroy or be destroyed, choosing to end their misery by death, or, as conquerors, to plunder riches and power. To help achieve this goal, they cloaked their obstinacy with a veil of religion and their perversity with rectitude. Countless evils have ensued.

There is certainly little benefit in summoning procurators of the states to parliaments in Castile. Most of them are poorly equipped to manage affairs. They are men who are led by chance—insignificant men of venal disposition who keep nothing in view but their desire to gain the prince's favor and to benefit from public disaster. The temptations and threats of the courtiers, mixed with prayers and promises, would uproot and fell the cedars of Lebanon. It is beyond doubt and, as things now stand, sufficiently obvious that these men will never oppose the prince's wish that he should be in total command. It would be better if these parliaments were never held. They are an excuse for useless expenditures and widespread corruption. Be that as it may, here we are not discussing what is happening but rather what right reason demands. New taxes should not be imposed on subjects without their free consent—not by force, curses, or threats.

As Comineus also advises, the people should show themselves amenable and not resist the prince's wishes. Rather, as need arises, they should manfully come to the aid of the depleted treasury; but the prince should also afford a patient ear, listen to the people, and diligently consider whether their substance and means are up to bearing the new burden, or whether there may not be other solutions to the problem. The prince may have to be exhorted to moderate and responsible spending. This, I understand, was occasionally attempted at earlier parliaments within the kingdom. The established principle, therefore, is that the prince is never permitted to oppress his subjects with new burdens without the consent of those concerned, at least of the leaders of the people and state.

What I said above confirms this point: The private goods of citizens are not at the disposal of the king. Thus, he must not take all or part of them without the approval of those who have the right to them. This is the pronouncement of legal experts: The king does not have the power to make a decision that results in loss of private goods unless the owners agree, nor may he seize any part of their property by planning and imposing a new tax. Why? Because the office of leader or director does not give him this power. Rather, because the king has the power from the state to receive specific income to maintain his original lifestyle, if he wishes these taxes to be increased, he would fulfill his duties by approaching those who originally decide on that specific income. It is their job to grant or deny what he seeks, as seems good to them, under the circumstances. Other countries may do things in different ways. In our country, this method is forbidden by the 1329 law that Alfonso XI, king of Castile, granted to the people in the parliament of Madrid in response to petition 68: "Let no tax be imposed on the nation against the will of the people." Here is the law:

> In addition, because the petitioners have requested that no extraordinary tax be imposed, either publicly or privately, unless the people have been previously summoned into parliament and the tax has been approved by all of the procurators of the states. We reply to this request: We are pleased with it. We decree that it is to be done.

In the previously cited place, Philippus Comineus repeats these words in French—twice: "Therefore, to pursue my point, no king or prince on earth can demand, except by way of violence and tyranny, even one *maravedi* from his nation, if those designated to pay it are unwilling." A little later, in addition to the claim of tyranny, Comineus adds that a prince who would act contrary to this law would incur the penalty of excommunication. His source may be the sixth chapter of the *Bulla in Coena Domini* that excommunicates anyone who imposes new taxes in his realm. At this point, some documents read: "Unless authorization has been granted for this purpose." Others read: "Except where it has been granted by right and law." Let others judge whether kings who do otherwise are exempt from this excommunication. How can they be? Neither do they have the power to tax, nor has the additional right been given to them. Yet, because Comineus was a literary man, and not in sacred orders, what he affirmed in such a statement depended upon the authority of the theologians of that time who were agreed on this point.

I personally add that not only any prince who acts this way in regard to taxes is guilty of this crime and punishment but also any prince who would fraudulently establish a monopoly without the consent of the people. It is equally fraudulent under another name, as is stealing the possessions of one's subjects to sell things for a higher price than is fair without authorization. In fact, for some years the prince has established some monopolies on lotteries, corrosive sublimate, and salt. I do not call these monopolies into question. Rather, I consider them prudently established and concerning the uprightness and the fidelity of the prince, one must believe that he has done nothing that goes beyond right reason and the laws. However, the point is, that as monopolies do not differ from taxes, caution in establishing them legally and in demanding popular consent should be no less. An example will make the point clearer. In Castile, there has frequently been talk of publicly imposing a tax on flour. Until now, the people have resisted it with difficulty, but if it were permissible for the king to buy up all the grain in the land to monopolize it and to sell it at a higher price, then it would be superfluous and meaningless to have the imposition of taxes depend upon the will of the people. In such a case, the king has the freedom to gain whatever he wishes through a monopoly that yields the same or even greater advantages than taxes. From what has been said, the point is firmly established that, if a king is not permitted to demand new taxes, he cannot even set up monopolies for merchandise without the consultation and approval of the people concerned.

CHAPTER 3: CAN THE KING DEBASE MONEY BY CHANGING ITS WEIGHT OR QUALITY WITHOUT CONSULTING THE PEOPLE?

Two things are clear. First, the king may change at will the form and engraving of money— provided that he does not diminish its value. That is the way I interpret the legal experts who grant the king the power to change money. The king owns the mints and administers them, and under the heading of "Regalia" in the *Novellas constitutiones*, money is listed among the other royal prerogatives. Therefore, without any loss to his subjects, he determines the method for minting money as he pleases. Second, we grant the king the authority to debase money without the people's consent in the pressing circumstances of war or siege—provided that the debasement is not extended beyond the time of need and that when peace has been restored he faithfully makes satisfaction to those who suffered loss.

In a very harsh winter, Frederick Augustus II was holding Faenza under siege. Those under siege were powerless. The siege was protracted, and money was lacking for salaries. He ordered money struck from leather, with his image on one side and the imperial eagle on the other, and each coin had the value of a gold coin. He did this on his own, without consultation with the people of the empire. The salvific plan brought about the conclusion of the affair. With his forces reassured by this device, he took over the city. When the war was over, he replaced the leather money with just as many golden coins. Collenucius relates this occurrence in the fourth book of his *History of Naples*. In France as well, money was struck on occasion from leather and decorated with a small silver key. Budelius, in the first book of his *On Money* (ch. 1, no. 34), recalls that money was made from paper when Leiden in Holland was under siege in 1574. These facts are undisputed.

However, the question is this: Can a prince in every case solve his fiscal problems on his own authority and debase his kingdom's money by diminishing its weight or its quality? Certainly the common opinion of legal experts agrees with that of Hostiensius, expressed in his *De censibus* in the paragraph *Ex quibus*. Among these experts are Innocent and Panormitanus who, in the fourth chapter of *De iureiurando*, maintains that a prince may not do this without the consent of his subjects.

One concludes, therefore, that if the king is the director—not the master—of the private possessions of his subjects, he will not be able to take away arbitrarily any part of their possessions for this or any other reason or any ploy. Such seizure occurs whenever money is debased: For what is declared to be more is worth less. Thus, if a prince is not empowered to levy taxes on unwilling subjects and cannot set up monopolies for merchandise, he is not empowered to make fresh profit from debased money. These strategies aim at the same thing: cleaning out the pockets of the people and piling up money in the provincial treasury. Do not be taken in by the smoke and mirrors by which metal is given a greater value than it has by nature and in common estimation. Of course this does not happen without common injury. When blood is let by whatever device or strategy, the body will certainly be debilitated and wasted. In the same way, a prince cannot profit without the suffering and groans of his subjects. As Plato maintained, one man's profit is another's loss. No one can abrogate by any means these fundamental laws of nature. In chapter 5 of *De iureiurando*, I find that Innocent III judges to be invalid the oath by which James the Conqueror, King of Aragón, bound himself for a considerable time to preserve the debased money that his father, Peter II, had minted. Among other reasons for this opinion is the fact that the consent of the people was lacking. Both Innocent and Panormitanus support this view. They confirm that a prince cannot establish anything that would cause injury to the people. We call it an injury when anything is taken from a person's fortune.

Indeed, I do not know how those who do these things can avoid the excommunication and censure pronounced for all ages by the *Bulla in Coena Domini*, because it applies to monopolies. All such schemes, under any pretense, aim at the same thing: to weigh the people down with new burdens and to amass money. This is not permissible, for if anyone maintains that our kings were granted this power long ago by the people's carelessness and indulgence, I find no trace of this custom or permission. Rather, I find that the laws concerning money of both the Catholic King and Philip, his great-grandson, were always passed in the nation's parliaments.

CHAPTER 4: THE TWOFOLD VALUE OF MONEY

Money has a twofold value. One is intrinsic and natural and comes from its type of metal and its weight, to which may be added the cost for labor and equipment in minting. The other is called the legal value and is extrinsic, inasmuch as it is established by the law of the prince, who has the right to prescribe the worth of money as well as of other goods. In a well-constituted republic, it should be the care of those who are in control of such matters to see that these two values are equal and do not differ, for just as in the case of other goods, it would be unjust for something to be appraised at 10 when it is worth 5 in itself and in common estimation, so the same thing holds for money if the legal value goes astray. This point is treated by Budelius in the first book of his *On Money* (ch. 1, no. 7), among other scholars, and they commonly consider anyone who thinks otherwise ridiculous and childish. If it is permissible to separate these values, let them mint money from leather, from paper, from lead, as we know was done in strained circumstances. The reckoning would be the same, and the cost for manufacturing less than if money were made of bronze.

I do not think that a king should produce money at his own expense, but I think it fair that some value be added to the worth of the metal in consideration of the labor of minting and of the overall monetary ministry. It would not be out of place if some small profit accrued to a prince from this function as a sign of his sovereignty and his prerogative. This opinion was ratified in the law, promulgated in Madrid in 1566, concerning the making of silver coins (*cuartillos*). In the fifth chapter of his *De iureiurando*, Innocent III implies this practice even if he does not mention it explicitly. I, however, maintain that these two values must be diligently and accurately kept equal. This same conviction may be gathered from Aristotle's *Politics* (bk. 1, ch. 6) where he says that it was originally taken for granted that men would exchange one thing for another. By common opinion, it seemed best to exchange merchandise for iron and silver, to avoid expense, and to ease the aggravation of transporting long distances wares that were heavy and cumbersome for both parties. Thus, a sheep was exchanged for so many pounds of brass, a horse for so many pounds of gold. It was difficult to weigh metal consistently. Public authority undertook to see to it that parts of the metal were marked with their weight to expedite commerce. This was the first and legitimate use of money, though time and evil produced other devices and deceptions that are certainly at odds with ancient and wholesome usage.

As our own laws tell us, our countrymen clearly decided that the two values be kept equal. Indeed, gold and silver are clear instances of this equality. Sixty-seven silver coins are made from 8 ounces of silver, called a *mark*, while the same weight of natural silver is exchanged for 65 silver coins, both in accordance with the prescripts of law. Thus, only 2 silver coins are added for the work involved in minting. Each silver coin is equivalent to 34 *maravedis*, while the same weight of natural silver is valued at about 33 *maravedis*. What about gold? Sixty-eight gold coins, called *coronas*, are struck from 8 ounces of gold. Natural gold is worth about the same amount. Copper money is valued in the same way, but in this case it seems more difficult to reconcile the legal value with the natural value.

According to the law promulgated in Medina del Campo in 1497, the Catholic Kings ordained that 8 ounces of copper, mixed with 7 grains of silver (about the weight of 1½ silver coins), would make 96 *maravedis*. The silver was worth more than 51 *maravedis*. The 8 ounces of copper and the cost of labor approximate the other 44 *maravedis* in value. In this way, the legal value is easily reconciled with the value of the metal and the labor.

Then in 1566, Philip II, King of Spain, abrogated the previous law and established that 4 grains of silver—the weight of 1 silver coin—were to be mixed with 8 ounces of copper. From this mixture, 110 *maravedis* were to be minted. In so doing, he took away more than half of the silver from the quality of the metal, and added 14 *maravedis* to the old value. He was, I think, considering the expense of minting, which doubtless had doubled with time, as well as made a profit from his supervision. Led on by this modest and slender hope, many men—after they had been authorized by the king to produce this money—made an immense profit. Consequently, as in past years, this business was considered especially lucrative. Yet the two values of money were not unreconciled in this approach, because the value of silver was mixed in with the 8 ounces of copper, and one must include both the price of copper and of production, both of which were estimated by at least two other silver coins. Moreover, debased money, which we call *blancas*, valued at half a *maravedi*, was being frequently minted and was a source of much greater vexation and nuisance.

At this time, no silver was mixed with copper in copper money, and 8 ounces of copper yielded 280 *maravedis*. The entire cost for stamping did not exceed a silver coin. Copper was selling at 46 *maravedis*. The cost of stamping and the value of the metal thus came to 80 *maravedis*. The profit was therefore 200 *maravedis* on each *mark* because the legal value of this money exceeded the intrinsic and natural value of the metal. The great danger that this fact presents to the state needs explanation. First, as indicated above, it is inconsistent with the nature and original concept of money. How, then, can anyone be stopped from debasing money in like circumstances, when enticed by the hope of gigantic profit? Finally, these values will adjust in business, as people are reluctant to give and take money that is worth more than its natural value. Fictions and frauds, once discovered, quickly collapse, and a prince who opposes the people will accomplish nothing. Would he be able to insist that rough sackcloth be sold for the cost of silken velvet, or that woolen clothing be sold for cloth of gold? Clearly, he could not. Try as he might, he could not justly make such a practice legal.

The French kings frequently devalued the *solidus*, and our silver coins were immediately valued higher than before. What was previously worth 4 *solidi*, when we were dwelling in

France, became worth 7 or 8 *solidi*. If the legal value of debased money does not decrease, surely all merchandise will sell at a higher price, in proportion to the debasement of the quality or the weight of the money. The process is inevitable. As a result, the price of goods adjusts and money is less valuable than it previously and properly was.

CHAPTER 5: THE FOUNDATIONS OF COMMERCE: MONEY, WEIGHTS, AND MEASURES

Weights, measures, and money are, of course, the foundations of commerce upon which rests the entire structure of trade. Most things are sold by weight and measure—but everything is sold by money. Everyone wants the foundations of buildings to remain firm and secure, and the same holds true for weights, measures, and money. They cannot be changed without danger and harm to commerce.

The ancients understood this. One of their major concerns was to preserve a specimen of all these things in their holy temples so that no one might rashly falsify them. Fannius bears witness to this fact in his *De ponderibus et mensuris*, and a law of Justinian Augustus concerning this tradition is extant (*Authent. De collatoribus* coll. 9). In Leviticus (27:25) we read: "Every valuation shall be according to the *shekel* of the sanctuary." Some conclude that the Jews were accustomed to keep a *shekel* weighing 4 *drachmas* of silver in the sanctuary to ensure easy recourse to a legitimate *shekel*, so that no one would dare to falsify it by tampering with its quality and weight. It was so important to maintain standards that no amount of care was considered superfluous. Even Thomas Aquinas warns (*De regim. Principum*, bk. 2, ch. 14) that money should not be altered rashly or at the whim of a prince. The recent change in the liquid measure in Castile, by which new tribute was exacted on wine and oil—not without protest—is reprehensible. In addition to other inconveniences, there is a problem adjusting the old measure to the new, and further confusion in our dealings with others. Those who are in power seem less educated than the people because they pay no attention to the disturbances and evils frequently caused by their decisions, both in our nation and beyond. Obviously, debasing money will profit the king, and we have proof that the ancients were frequently led into fraud by that hope and that these same men soon became aware of the disadvantages of their decisions. To remedy these ills, new and greater ills were needed: The situation is like giving a drink at the wrong time to a sick man. At first it refreshes him but later aggravates the causes of his illness and increases his fever. The clear fact is that great care was once taken that these foundations of human existence be not disturbed. In my *De ponderibus et mensuris* (ch. 8), I explained that the Roman ounce remained unchanged for many centuries and that it is the same as ours. The same should be true of the other weights. Our weights should not differ from those of the ancients.

CHAPTER 6: MONEY HAS FREQUENTLY BEEN ALTERED

A widespread opinion among the Jews was that the money, measures, and weights of the sanctuary were twice as great as the common ones: the *bathum*, *gomor*, *shekel*, and all the rest. They thought this way because their special effort to preserve the weights and measures in the sanctuary could not prevent the people from diminishing the common ones and, under some conditions, making them less than half. Thus, different passages in ancient writers that vary in specifics or are at odds with sacred letters may be reconciled.

We know—and Pliny (bk. 33, ch. 3) testifies to this fact—that in ancient Rome, the *as* (a copper coin with the value of 4 of our current *maravedis*), under the pressure of the First Punic War, was debased to 2 ounces, which they called a sextantarian *as*, which weighed about one-sixth of a pound—then 12 ounces, like the Italian and French *pound* today. Thereafter, under pressure during the war with Hannibal, the Romans reduced the *as* to an ounce, one-twelfth of the previous *asses*, and finally the reduction in weight reached half an ounce. The *denarius*, with a value of 40 *maravedis*, was initially minted from pure silver. Then under Drusus, the Tribune of the Plebs was mixed with an eighth part of copper and its previous purity was changed, as Pliny indicates in the same passage. In subsequent years, more copper was added. Actually, not a few *denarii* are being unearthed in our time that contain much less silver and are of less purity because of the greater weight of copper added—more than a third. Likewise, gold money of outstanding purity and weighing 2 *drachmas* was minted during the reigns of the first emperors. At that time they were minted from 6 ounces of gold and were called *solidi*. They weighed about the same as our *castellano*. A law of Emperor Justinian concerning *solidi* can be found under the heading *De susceptoribus, praepositis et arcariis*, and begins with "Quotiescumque." Commenting on the freedom to innovate in one of his prologues, the ancient poet, Plautus, seems to suggest the Roman view of debasing money when he says, "Those who use old wine I consider wise. For the new comedies produced these days are much worse than the new coins."

Money still in existence today indicates how frequently the Romans changed the value of their money. The same thing has taken place in all countries within recent memory. Princes, with or without their subjects' consent, have frequently debased coins in quality or by subtracting from their weight. The search for examples in other countries is superfluous when domestic ones are at hand in abundance.

The history of Alfonso XI, the king of Castile (ch. 14), affirmed that money was altered by King Ferdinand the Holy and by his son Alfonso the Wise, as well as by Sancho the Brave, by his son Ferdinand, and by his grandson Alfonso XI. Therefore, during the reign of these five kings, which was sufficiently long, money enjoyed no stability; it was constantly changed and debased. Remarkably, Peter, the king of Castile and the son of the last Alfonso does not seem to have debased the currency. I suspect that, rather inhibited by the inconveniences caused by the adulteration of money when his father was in power, he did not follow Alfonso's example and was careful to mint proper money. This is attested by the money minted under his name. His brother Henry II, ridden by debt that he owed to his companions and assistants in exchange for winning the kingdom and burdened with larger illegal debts for the future, had recourse to the same remedy. He minted two types of money: *reales* (silver coins) worth 3 *maravedis*, and *cruzados* worth 1 *maravedi*, as the chronicles (ch. 10) for the fourth year of his reign testify.

Serious inconveniences arose from this contrivance, but his successors were not afraid to follow his example. To pay Alencastre, the duke of a rival kingdom, the money agreed upon in a peace treaty, John I devised a new coin by the name of *blanca*, worth 1 *maravedi*, and shortly thereafter he decreed that the *blanca*, almost halved in value, be evaluated at only 6 *dineros* called *novenes*. This took place in the parliaments of Burgos in 1387. The right to devalue money by diminishing quality and increasing value continued into the reign of Henry IV. These were the most unsettled of times and, although the historians of the period do not say so, this fact is patently clear from the fluctuations in the value of silver, for when Alfonso XI was king of Castile, 8 ounces of silver were worth 125 *maravedis*. During the reign of Henry II, a silver *real* was worth 3 *maravedis* and, consequently, a *mark* was worth 400 *maravedis*. Under John I, Henry's son, it went up to 250 *maravedis*; a silver coin was worth 4 *maravedis*; a gold coin was worth 50 *maravedis* or 12 silver coins. Such is found in the 1388 parliament of Burgos (Law 1). Under Henry III, his successor, the value reached 480 or even 500 *maravedis*. Indeed, at the end of his reign and the beginning of John II's, the value increased to 1,000 *maravedis*. Finally, in the reign of Henry IV, it was valued at 2,000 and at 2,500 *maravedis*. All of these variations and increases in value did not come from variation in the metal; it was always composed of 8 ounces of silver with a small addition of copper, but the frequent debasement of *maravedis* and of other coins caused the value of silver money of the same weight to seem to be greater by comparison. Indeed, all the variations in the value of silver are taken, for the most part, from Antonio Nebrissensi's *Repetitionibus*. In fact, the extant coins of these kings are all rough and are indications of the tendency to debase money during these years.

The Catholic rulers, Ferdinand and Isabella, stabilized this volatility by a law that set the price for 8 ounces of natural silver at 2,210 *maravedis*, but when minted at 2,278. This is the price, even today. Philip II diminished the quality and weight of the *maravedi*, but since it was by a slight amount, there was no change in the value of silver in relation to the *maravedis*. I think that the recent change in copper money will alter its value and make 8 ounces of silver the equivalent of more than 4,000 *maravedis*, as presently minted. Am I wrong?

CHAPTER 7: ADVANTAGES DERIVED FROM ALTERATION OF COPPER MONEY

A careful examination and investigation of the advantages and disadvantages that result from altering copper money are in order so that the wise and prudent reader may consider calmly and without prejudice which issues are of greater weight and importance. This is the way to the truth that we seek.

First, when such a change is made, we are freed from an expenditure of silver. Lessening the quality of silver provides this advantage. For years, a great weight and many talents of silver used to be mixed with copper to no profit. Because the money weighs less, it is easier for the merchants to transport and use in trade (the cost of transport used to be high). The increased money supply expands commerce in the nation, while the desire of eager outsiders to get their greedy hands on gold and silver money is curtailed. Those who have it will share it willingly with others; thus, debts will be liquidated, farms will be cultivated in the hope of greater profit, and workshops (frequently idle for lack of money) will be busy. In short, there will be a greater abundance of flocks, fruit, and merchandise, of linen, wool, silk cloth, and of other commercial items. No doubt, abundance will produce affordable prices (whereas in the past only a few could find those who would lend them money for such goods—and then at great interest). In these circumstances, we will be content with our lot and plenty and have less need for outside merchandise. Importing goods diminishes our silver and gold and infects our people with foreign customs. Men born for war and arms are physically weakened by the softness of merchandise, and their warlike vigor of spirits is extinguished. Also, foreigners will not come to us as often as they used to, both because of our abundance of native merchandise and because of our money, which they will refuse to take back to their native land at no profit after it has been exchanged for their goods. In general, with the money received for their merchandise, they will purchase other items in our country, as convenient, and will transport them to their native land.

It is not insignificant that a good deal of money will flow into the king's treasury, for payment of his creditors to whom he has mortgaged his tax revenues—a major disaster—and this can be accomplished without injury to or complaint from anyone just by changing the value of money. The king will certainly profit greatly.

Thus, Pliny, in the passage cited above, confirms that the Romans by diminishing the weight of the *as* escaped from extreme straits and paid debts that weighed them down. The history of Alfonso XI, king of Castile (ch. 98), reports the same phenomenon and those of Henry II for the fifth year (ch. 10) report that he was relieved, after ridding himself by this means of most oppressive war debts. A great deal of money had been promised to others but especially to Bertrando Klaquino and to foreigners by whose aid he had stripped his brother of the kingdom.

The ancient Romans, and other nations in our time, used copper money exclusively with no admixture of silver or other precious metal. Indeed, this usage seems to have once been more usual and common with other monies because the Romans commonly called their money "copper." Perhaps this custom has influenced us to explain by *maravedis* the size of someone's property or yearly taxable income. The Spaniards once used gold *maravedis*, but, at a time when they had to make great changes, they removed all gold from the *maravedis*. Thus, we should not be astonished if silver is now removed from our money. It is of no use and never was of any advantage to anyone.

These advantages are important and should be considered. We will pass over the disadvantages that a diligent observer may claim to result from the recent intervention. Nothing in this life is entirely simple and free from all harm and blame. Therefore, it is the wise man's job to choose what affords the greater and less blameworthy advantages, especially since human nature is perverse in such circumstances and is used to criticizing changes and new ways. We hold firmly to traditions, as if nothing could be corrected in, or added to the practices of the ancients.

CHAPTER 8: DIFFERENT *MARAVEDIS* OF VARYING VALUES IN CASTILE

Before I explain the disadvantages necessarily involved in the new plan for devaluing copper money, it is worth explaining the different kinds of *maravedis* and their values as used in Castile at various times. The understanding of these coins is involved and complicated but is worth having if we are to reach the truth that has been shrouded in darkness.

The gold coins in frequent use at the time of the Goths have first place. Indeed, the Romans in the later Empire struck coins of less weight than the old ones: They used to mint 6 coins from an ounce of gold, 48 from 8 ounces or a *mark*. These coins were a little bigger than our *castellano*. They called these gold coins *solidi*, and the value of each was 12 *denarii*. However, if the value of a Roman *denarius* was 40 *quadrantes* or *maravedis*, the value of a *solidus* came to 480—a little more than our *castellano*. Thus, in subsequent time, the *solidus*, although struck from silver and finally made for the greater part from copper, still always kept the value of 12 *denarii*—even when the latter were no longer made from gold but from copper. Certainly in France and among the people of Aragon, where the name *solidus* is still found, each *solidus* is worth 12 *denarii*. When the Goths invaded with the sword, the Roman Empire was still flourishing in Spain, as were Roman money, laws, and customs. When government in Rome changed, the victors introduced some of their own customs and adopted some customs from the conquered. In particular, the Goths began to use Roman money. Then, when the new government was established, they devised and struck new coins that they called *maravedis*. There is no need to go into the meaning of the word, but each *maravedi* was valued at 10 *denarii*, or 400 *quadrantes*, as much as our current gold coin, that is, 400 *maravedis* or *quadrantes*. It was established that the *maravedis*, although first made of silver and then of copper, would still be valued at 10 *denarii*.

The norm for the *maravedi* was that it would contain 2 *blancas*, 6 *coronados*, 10 *denarii*, 60 *meajas*. This was their relationship to the *maravedi*, although they completely disappeared because they were worthless. The Roman *solidus* and the Gothic gold *maravedi* differed little in value. Consequently, for the number of *solidi* imposed as punishment by the courts under Roman law, the Goths substituted a like number of gold *maravedis*. Many coins of the Goths are now being unearthed in Spain that are not made from good gold. We have evidence that their worth is debased by half: They are half-*maravedis*, coins called *semises*, or rather *tremisses*, weighing one-third of the Goths' *maravedi*. We will consider this matter later.

Tumultuous times followed. Everything, money included, was in a state of frightful confusion. After Spain was defeated by the weapons of the Moors, a new race of kings sprang up, given by God for the salvation of a nation that was oppressed by every evil. We will not talk about the money of the Moors, but there were three kinds of *maravedis* under the government of the kings of Leon and Castile. There were the gold ones, which were also called *good, old, standard,* and *usual*. We must first speak about these *usual* ones and explain their value and quality because our understanding of the other types depends upon an explanation of the *usual* ones.

The value of the *usual* ones was not constant but changed with the times. It is difficult to define this variation: The only legitimate source for a guess is by reference to the value of a silver *mark*. These *maravedis* must be compared to our *maravedis* in the exact proportion as the *mark* of that age is compared to the value of the *mark* of our age. At this time, a bullion *mark* is worth 2,210 *maravedis*, but, once minted and made into coins—2,278 *maravedis*. Moreover, the quality of the silver does not enter into consideration: It has always been more or less of the same purity as today, as the chalices, and other sacred vessels and instruments, preserved in our Church treasuries, bear witness. Then the silver *mark*, in relation to the varying value of the *maravedi*, was always worth 5 gold coins (popularly called *doblas*) or a little more, and equal to 12 silver coins—not 14, as some say. Likewise, the *mark* used to be worth 60 or 65 silver coins, as we can see from the laws of King John I of Castile, but debate rushes in from another source.

The oldest known value of the *mark* is 125 *maravedis*. This was certainly the value of the *mark* in the age of King Alfonso XI, as witnessed in the history of his accomplishments (ch. 98). Thus, a silver coin was just 2 *maravedis*; now it is 34. Therefore, a *maravedi* at that time was worth as much as 17 and a bit more of ours, and there was no doubt about the quality of the silver that its value declared. In the reign of Henry II, a silver coin was worth 3 *maravedis*, as the history of his fourth year (ch. 2) declares. Therefore, the *mark*, at this time, increased to 200 *maravedis*, each one equal to 11 of ours. Henry was succeeded by his son John I, and the *mark* increased under him to 250 *maravedis* or *quadrantes*, when a silver coin was valued at 4 *maravedis* and a gold one at 50 (see the first law he enacted in the parliament of the kingdom of Burgos in 1388). Thus, the *maravedi* of that time was equal in value to 9 or 10 of ours. Even more clear is a previous law promulgated in Burgos that punishes abuse of parents by a fine of 600 *maravedis*. During the reign of Ferdinand and Isabella, that law was introduced into the *Ordinamentum* (bk. 8, title 9). It stated that the 600 *maravedis* mentioned in that law are good money and equal 6,000 *maravedis* in that time, which is also our own; for, since that time, there has been no change in the value of the *mark* or *maravedi*.

Let us look at the reigns of other kings. According to old documents, under Henry III the *mark* reached to 480 and even 500 *maravedis*. Therefore, a silver coin was worth about 8 *maravedis*, and the *maravedi* was equal to about 4 or 5 of ours. Under John II, Henry's son, the *mark* was worth 1,000 *maravedis*, especially at the end of his life. Thus, his *maravedi* was worth 2½ of ours—a remarkable variation in value! However, this fluctuation was not confined to his reign. Among many other serious ills, under Henry IV, the silver *mark* reached 2,000 *maravedis* and then 2,500, according to Antonio Nebrissensi's *Repetitionibus*. His *maravedi* was worth what ours is, and there has not been great change in the value of the *maravedi* since that time. This stability must be attributed to the care of Ferdinand and Isabella and their successors. With these facts established from laws and chronicles, let us evaluate the other *maravedis*.

The gold *maravedi* was equal to 6 of the *maravedis* current in the time of Alfonso the Wise. Law 114 of the *Lex stili* states that after this king looked into the matter, he found that a gold *maravedi* was equal to 6 of the *maravedis* of his day. This is not, as some claim, that the *maravedis* of King Alfonso were made of gold. Rather, the value was discovered by weighing *maravedis* of both kinds, and from establishing their proportions of gold to silver—12 to 1. Moreover, the law of Alfonso XI in the parliament of Leon of 1387 stated that 100 *maravedis* of good money, namely, of gold, were worth 600 of those of that age. Two important things may be gathered from these facts. First, that from the time of King Alfonso the Wise (also known as the Tenth) up until Alfonso XI, his great-grandson, there was absolutely no change in the value of the *mark* and *maravedi*, inasmuch as under both kings the gold *maravedi* equaled 6 *usual* ones. Second, inasmuch as the *maravedis* then in use equaled 17 of ours (or even a little more, as mentioned above), those who said that the gold *maravedi* was equal to 36 or 60 of ours are necessarily mistaken. Rather, they were worth as much as 300 silver ones or more. This is my opinion, and it is founded on firm arguments. I am also of the opinion that the gold *maravedis* were the *tremisses* of the Goths. The first kings of Castile used them. They did not mint new ones. Their value agrees with the known one of a little more than 3 silver coins. These coins of the Goths turn up here and there, but no gold coins struck with the crest and name of the kings of Castile have been found at all. It would be incredible if all of them have disappeared without a trace. So much for the gold *maravedi*.

Most people say that each of the old *maravedis* was worth 1½ of ours. The pronouncements of those who have a greater understanding of our law will carry more weight on this issue. Perhaps there was agreement among the legal experts that, whenever the old *maravedi* occurs in our law, 1½ of ours may be substituted, just as the gold *maravedi* found in those laws is popularly evaluated at 36 or 60 of the *usual*.

However, strictly speaking, the old *maravedis* did not have one value but varying and complex values. Whenever the quality of money was diminished, as frequently happened to avoid abolishing the old money, the kings decreed that it should coexist with the new one and be called "old." Thus, it will be easy for some of the usual *maravedis* and those of the older kind to be compared with one another and with ours. If, for example, the *maravedi* of Alfonso XI is compared with the *maravedis* minted by his son, Henry II, it will be worth 1½ of the latter and, if compared with ours, it will be worth 17. Thus, the old *maravedis* were sometimes the usual *maravedis*. Therefore, from the value of the usual *maravedis*, as we have explained, one ought to establish the value of the old ones, and from those that are called "new," one ought to establish their value when compared with ours. These are subtle and thorny considerations, but we are hurrying to end this discussion. We add that, under our law, the *maravedis*, which are current today and were current in the time of the Catholic King Ferdinand, are commonly called "new." At this time, the laws of earlier kings were gathered together in a few volumes. The *maravedis* of the earlier kings were called "old" *maravedis*.

Therefore, from the value of the *maravedi* in use under the individual kings, a decision may be made about the old *maravedi*. The *maravedi* of Alfonso XI was worth 17 of ours; that of Henry II, 11; that of John I, 10; that of Henry III, 5; that of John II, 2½. Careful consideration must be given to the times, and determinations must be made accordingly concerning the value of an old *maravedi* in any law, and the value of a new one, both among themselves and in comparison with our own *maravedis*. It should not be overlooked that the old *maravedi* was sometimes called "good," as in the above mentioned law (*Ordinamentum*, bk. 8, title 9) by which John I prescribed the punishment of 600 *maravedis* for the abuse of parents. The experts who incorporated this law in that book added on their own that the *maravedis* were good coins, equal to 6,000 of the *usual* ones. This means that the law was not referring to gold *maravedis* but to old ones that were in use under that king and that each was worth as much as 10 of ours. Remember that from the time of Ferdinand the Catholic the value of the *maravedi* remained unchanged.

Moreover, by a law passed by John II in Caraccas in 1409 (the first law in *Ordinamentum*, bk. 8, title 5) something is forbidden under punishment of excommunication of 30 days and a fine of 100 good *maravedis*, which make 600 of the old ones. However, if the obstinacy continues for 6 months, the fine increases to 1,000 good *maravedis*, which equal 6,000 of the old ones. In this citation, the good *maravedis* are gold; the old ones are those that were current under the Kings Alfonso the Wise and Alfonso XI. Only at that time, as stated above, did each gold *maravedi* equal 6 current ones. If the punishment seems very harsh—it is equivalent to 3,000 of our silver ones, since each gold *maravedi* equals as much as 3 silver ones—even more serious punishments are inflicted today. When someone is suspected of heresy, he will not escape the bond of excommunication for a full year.

CHAPTER 9: DISADVANTAGES DERIVED FROM THIS ALTERATION OF COPPER MONEY

In serious issues, it is not fair to advance subtle and speculative arguments from our own heads and thoughts. They are frequently deceptive. It is better to do battle with data from our own time and from our ancestors. This is the safest approach and the assured way to the truth because the present is certainly similar to the past. What has happened will happen. Previous events are very influential: They convince us that what sets out on the same path will reach the same conclusion.

Some disadvantages appear to be great but, in reality, are not. We could put up with them to avoid the greater disadvantages that derive from the alteration of money. First, some critics claim that this practice has never been used in our country and that, because of its novelty, every innovation triggers fear and is risky. However, this argument is proved untrue by what has already been said. Obviously, this process has frequently been tried in our country. With what success is not yet the issue! They also argue that there has been less cultivation of the land and farms, and that citizens are discouraged from working when wages are paid in debased money. This is true. Among other advantages of alteration and multiplication of copper coins, however, is the fact that with this money on hand and available to everyone, the fruits of the earth and the products of handicraft will be more easily produced. In the past, they were frequently neglected for lack of money. Therefore, this argument proves inconclusive and because it can be used by either side, it is not convincing for either.

These critics then assert that commerce will be hindered, especially with those who come from outside Spain with the sole hope of exchanging their goods for our silver. Facts speak for themselves, they say, and debased coinage will create great havoc with commerce with the Indies because most things sent to that region are imported into Spain from outside nations. The answer to this objection is not difficult either. One may argue that it is no disadvantage for Spain to obey its own laws, as it is strictly forbidden to export silver to other nations. Moreover, how is it advantageous to despoil the country of its silver? Rather, it would seem beneficial if the copper money of commerce deterred outsiders from coming into Spain. Certainly, they will exchange their goods for our goods when the hope of carrying off our wealth has been removed. This is and should be the common desire of a nation. Further, there is no danger of harming trade with the Indies because it involves goods that are native to us: wine, oil, wool, and silk cloth. If there is need for commerce with outsiders, silver will arrive from the Indies now and then and allow our merchants to buy such things as linen cloth, paper, books, trifles, and so forth. Nor does copper money prevent us from minting this foreign silver, as we have done before. There is a ready response to the next objection that denies that the king has the authority to borrow money from outsiders to meet the necessary expenses of the fleet and the salaries of the soldiers. We might rather say that there would be a greater supply of money for the king if his debts to his countrymen were paid in copper money. He could pay his foreign debts in the silver that is offered to him every year. Nor is copper money so wicked or barren that silver will completely disappear, as if chased away by a wicked and magical incantation.

It is true, we must admit, that when there is a great supply of copper, silver disappears among the citizens. This fact should be numbered among the principal disadvantages of copper money. Silver flows into the royal treasury because the king orders that taxes are to be paid in that money. It does not return to circulation because he pays whatever he owes his subjects with copper money. Thus, there will be a superabundance of copper money while he exports the silver. Moreover, the silver that remains in our citizens' hands disappears because all first spend the copper money and hide the silver, unless forced to produce it.

Some argue that the great supply of debased money would bring about this disadvantage, but the reasons for their position are not satisfactory. They advance two reasons for their position: The first is that royal money cannot be distinguished from counterfeit money once the silver, which used to be mixed with the copper, has been completely removed; the second is that the hope of profit will tempt many. This profit is three times larger than before because, while the actual value of the money has changed little, the legal value has changed much. I will not dispute these arguments. How could I? The latter one, based on the hope of profit, is quite valid, as 200 gold coins become 700 because of debased money. This fact will certainly tempt many to expose themselves and their possessions to any risk for profit. Who would bridle his inflamed desire suddenly to escape indigence in this way? However, the previous argument is not based on facts. It rests on the belief that silver was mixed with copper to prevent adulteration of copper money. In fact, the silver remains from the early quality of the *maravedi*, which was once solid silver but was later defiled with many additions. Nonetheless, some silver was always found in it. The first Catholic Kings did not ordain this, but they determined by law how much silver was to be mixed with copper, lest the debasing of that money proceed further by an ever greater amount of copper. It would not be bad if no silver were mixed into copper money. As a matter of fact, the expense of silver would be avoided.

If my argument is in any way valid, I would like the stamp on coins to be more refined, as it is on coins from the mints in Segovia. Moreover, the silver *real* would be exchanged for more copper coins, as happens in France. There, 12 *dineros* are given for a silver *solidus*, which is almost a *cuartillo*, and each *dinero* is worth 3 *liardi*. At Naples, a *carlino*, less than our silver coin, worth not more than 28 *maravedis*, is exchanged for 60 *caballi*, each with the weight and mass of 2 earlier *maravedis*, before they were constantly adulterated. All these facts confirm that the value of a silver coin is equal to the metal and the cost of minting, and this means accommodating the legal value to the natural value. Few people would undertake to debase that money because of less profit; nor would it be easy for ordinary people—and such, for the most part, are those who make counterfeit money—to maintain mints to coin similar money. If anyone does mold coins from melted copper, they will be readily distinguishable from struck money.

As a matter of fact, silver is minted in these mills at a great loss; coins of equal weight cannot be produced because of the variations in the silver ingots placed on the press. This disadvantage does not exist with copper because it is a base metal. I pass over the other proposed disadvantages—they are more apparent than true—to address greater disadvantages, which arise not from empty speculation but are proven by the experience of former times and the memory of antiquity. Critics add that with the multiplication of copper money and its currency, no fortunes would be piled up by the rich for use in pious works. Surely, so many people spend piles of money in harmful and ludicrous things that it would not seem to be a great loss if fortunes were not amassed. Copper money does not stand in the way of quantities of silver yearly arriving from the Indies. Who will prevent the owners from hoarding as much of the silver as they want? Others find fault with the cost of transportation: They do not wish the merchants to have to transport purchased goods from afar at that cost. However, those same merchants, after reckoning the cost of shipping to the end of the country (from Toledo to Murcia), claim that the expense is only 1 percent. Then, some say, it is very laborious to count this copper money and keeping it is particularly bothersome.

Others say that these troubles are sufficiently compensated for by the advantages that this money entails. Critics also find fault with the expense of copper because of the great amount minted, and they cite the difficulty of forging it at home. As a result, outsiders, who have a great deal of this metal, will grow rich at our expense. A few years ago, a hundred weight of copper sold for 18 *francs* in France. Thus, 8 ounces (what we call the weight of a *mark*) was fixed at 13 *maravedis*; in Germany, it was even cheaper. Currently, the same weight is fixed, nonetheless, at 46 *maravedis* in Castile. Therefore, the price of minting copper money endlessly increases out of necessity or, rather, out of cupidity. This is a real, not fictitious disadvantage, but there are other much greater ones in comparison with which, this one—whatever damage it causes—could seem ridiculous and relatively unimportant.

CHAPTER 10: MAJOR DISADVANTAGES DERIVED FROM THIS ALTERATION OF MONEY

First of all, the current large supply of copper money is against our Spanish laws. There is no limitation on gold and silver money in the 1497 decree of the Catholic Kings. An individual was allowed to mint as much of these metals as he had. They decreed, however, in the third law, that no more than 10 million *maravedis* were to be struck, with the responsibility for this minting divided according to a determined ratio among 7 mints. Then Philip II, king of Spain, decreed in a 1566 law that it was not advantageous to manufacture more copper money than would be enough for common use and commerce. He therefore commanded that such money was not to be minted without royal authorization.

Moreover, copper money should be commonly employed only in small purchases, and gold or silver was to be used in greater monetary exchanges. Anything beyond these limits would involve public damage and upheaval, for money was invented to facilitate trade, and money that better and more opportunely accomplishes its end is more acceptable, as Aristotle remarks in his Politics (bk. 1, ch. 6). However, abundance of copper money brings about the opposite. Counting it is a great burden: A man can hardly count 1,000 gold pieces in copper coins in a day. As for transporting coins, it is laborious and expensive to carry them to distant places to buy goods. For these reasons, an inundation of this money is opposed by our laws. Of course, I would not approve of minting just silver money as, for example, in England under the recently deceased Queen Elizabeth and in some German states. I realize that it can be divided into tiny parts. It is said that Renato, the Duke of Anjou, made 1,000 coins out of an ounce of silver (I would prefer a pound). With these coins, however, one could not buy tiny and cheap trinkets and give alms to the needy. Much greater harms result if the abuse is in the other direction—if the land is inundated with copper money like rivers flooded with winter storms. So much for the first disadvantage.

A second disadvantage is not only that it is against the laws of the land—that could be overlooked—but it is also against right reason and the natural law itself—it is a sin to change them. To prove my point, one must remember what was established above: The king is not free to seize his subjects' goods and thus strip them from their lawful owners. May a prince break into granaries and take half of the grain stored there, and then compensate for the damage by authorizing the owners to sell the remainder at the same price as the original whole? No one would be so perverse as to condone such an act but such was the case with the old copper coin. The king unjustly appropriated one-half of all the money, merely by doubling the value of each coin, so that what was worth 2 *maravedis* was thereafter worth 4. Would it be right for a king to triple by law the price for woolen and silk cloth at its present supply, while the proprietor keeps one-third for himself and turns over the rest only to the king? Who would approve of that? The same thing is happening with the copper money that has recently been minted. Less than a third of it is given to the owner. The king uses the rest for his own advantage.

Such things, of course, do not take place in other forms of commerce. They do, however, happen in the arena of money because the king has more power over money than over other things. He appoints all the ministers of the mint and changes them at will; he controls the dies and types of money, has complete authority to change them and to substitute debased coins for purer ones, and vice versa. Whether this is done rightly or wrongly is a controversial point. However, Menochius (*Consilium*, no. 48) deems it a new kind of crime to repay, with debased money, debts incurred at a time when money was sound. He proves with many arguments that what was paid out in sound money is not rightly repaid in debased money.

We come to the third disadvantage: The cost of trade will be in proportion to the debasing of money. This is not simply a private judgment. Rather, such were the evils our ancestors experienced when our money was debased. In the history of the reign of Alfonso the Wise (ch. 1), reference is made to alteration of money at the beginning of his reign: Less sound *burgaleses* were substituted for the usual sound money, *pepiones* (gold coins). Ninety copper *burgaleses* were equal in value to a *maravedi*. This money change resulted in a general inflation. To remedy this situation, as chapter 5 recalls, the king taxed all sales. His remedy, however, caused the ailment to break out again. The merchants refused to sell things at that price. Necessarily, things came to a halt lest he arouse the hatred of the nation or especially (as we believe) the arms of his nobles, who, after he was driven out, transferred affairs to his younger son, Sancho. Not content with his previous fraudulent mistake, he substituted the recalled *burgaleses* with bad money with the value of 15 *maravedis* in the sixth year of his reign. Thus, he remained obstinate in evil—a man deceitful by nature with a shattered genius that was ultimately evil.

The history of King Alfonso XI of Castile (ch. 98) informs us that he minted *novenes* and *coronados* of the same quality and stamp as his father, King Ferdinand. To avoid inflation with the change of money—doubtless it was not sound—great care was taken to keep the price of silver from rising. Eight ounces of silver were valued at 125 *maravedis*—no more than before. This concern was feckless. There ensued scarcity of goods, and the price of silver increased. Here we should consider the fact that inflation is not the immediate and necessary consequence of changing money. As a matter of fact, a silver coin is now worth 34 of these debased *maravedis*—its previous worth—and 8 ounces of silver (which we call a *mark*) sells for 65 silver coins as it actually did before. Our account has made it clear that this condition cannot continue longer without disturbance. John I, in order to pay his rival, the Duke of Alencastre, a great sum of money, which had been agreed upon, minted unsound money, which he called "good." Shortly thereafter, to avoid a scarcity of goods, he approved its payment at almost less than half, as he testified in the 1387 parliament of Burgos.

Then, there is Henry II, the father of John. As head of the kingdom, he had almost exhausted his treasury in wars against his brother Peter. Finally, reduced to dire financial straits, he minted two kinds of money: *regales*, worth 3 *maravedis*, and *cruzados*, worth 1 *maravedi*. As a result, prices and other things increased. The gold coin, known as the *dobla*, rose to 300 *maravedis*; a *caballo* was selling at 60,000 *maravedis*. This fact is found in his chronicles (the fourth year, ch. 10). Indeed in the sixth year, chapter 8, the *caballo* rose to 80,000 *maravedis*. Inflation soared. Under this pressure, this prince decreed devaluation of each coin by two-thirds. Indeed the gold coin was previously worth 30 *maravedis*, as Antonio Nebrissensi states in his *Repetitionibus* and as may be deduced from the value of silver, of which 8 ounces, or a *mark*, were valued at 125 *maravedis* or certainly a little less (see ch. 8 of this treatise for an explanation of gold and silver's increase in value at that time). As a result of the alteration in coinage, the value of gold suddenly increased almost more than tenfold. I am convinced that there is never an alteration in coinage without subsequent inflation. To illustrate, let us suppose that the value of silver is doubled: What was worth 34 *maravedis* is now worth 68.

Some believe and maintain that if the value of silver were increased, the state would benefit to a greater or lesser degree. If this is true, one must ask: If someone wishes to buy 8 ounces of debased silver for 65 silver coins as its value is set by law, would the seller comply? Of course not! He will not sell it for less than 130 new silver coins, which is almost the weight of the silver itself. However, if the value of silver is doubled because the value of coins is doubled or if the coins increase to sixfold or fourfold, the same thing will happen with the value of natural silver. We see the same thing happen with the current copper coins; they are changed in some places into silver coins at the rate of 100 percent interest; in other places at 50 percent. Doubtless, what we have shown to occur in the case of silver will happen to other commodities as well: Their price will increase to the degree that the coins have been debased or the value of the coins increased, for that is exactly the way it is.

There is no doubt that it leads to new money. Each of these developments will contribute to commercial inflation. Abundance of money makes it worth less. As in other commercial enterprises, supply leads to low prices. Next, the baseness of coins will cause those who have this money to want to get rid of it immediately. Merchants will not wish to exchange their goods for that money, except with a great increase in price. All this leads to the fourth disadvantage: There will be trade difficulties, and trade is the foundation for public and private wealth. This problem always arises with debasement of money. Taxation of goods and sales to increase prices is a rather deadly solution to the problem. This approach is burdensome for merchants, and they will refuse to sell at that price. Once trade is destroyed and commercial inflation is in place, all the people will be reduced to want, and that will lead to disturbances. Thus, as experience has frequently taught us, the new money is either completely recalled or is certainly devalued; for example, by half or two-thirds. Then, suddenly and as in a dream, someone who had 300 gold pieces in this money now has 100 or 150, and the same proportion applies to everything else.

King Henry II, according to his chronicles (sixth year, ch. 8), faced this situation and of necessity devalued the *real* from its previous worth of 3 *maravedis* to 1 and reduced the *cruzado* to 2 *coronados*, a third of its previous value. Henry's son, John I, devalued his good money to 6 *dineros*, almost half of its previous value. The resulting inflation continued, as the king admits in the 1388 parliament at Burgos. There is no need to recount how much trouble occurred in the regions. The facts speak for themselves. At the end of chapter 8, we noted occurrences of this type under John II. Eduardius Nunnius recalls in his *Chronicles of Portugal* that, under King Ferdinand, a great inflation resulted in Portugal because of the devaluing of money and that a large amount of this counterfeit money was brought in by foreigners. He also says that the younger people, of necessity, viewed this money with a singular severity because many people were reduced to helplessness. Nonetheless, he says that, in our time, the same error was imprudently committed. During the reign of Sebastian, they minted copper money, called *batacones*, with the same evil results and the need to institute the same remedies.

Let us pass over the old examples, although what happened in Portugal is not that old. Sanderus, in his first book, *De schismate Anglicano*, affirms that, as he left the Church, Henry VIII rushed into evils, and one of them was the fact that there was such a great devaluation of money. Consequently, whereas previously only a one-eleventh part of copper was mixed with silver coins, he gradually caused the coins to have no more than one-sixth part silver to five parts copper. Then he ordered the old coins gathered into the treasury, and exchanged with an equal number of the new coins. A great injustice! After his death, the citizens approached his son Edward for a cure for these evils. The only solution was to devalue the new money by half. Elizabeth, Edward's sister, succeeded him, and devalued the new money by another half. Thus, someone who had 400 coins in that money quickly found them reduced to no more than 100. Therefore, the cheating continued. When the problems connected with this money did not slacken, a new decree had all that money remitted to the mints in the hope of compensation. Such compensation was never made. An infamous highway robbery! A most disgraceful peculation!

A prudent reader should notice whether we are getting on the same road; whether that historical moment is a portrait of the tragedy certainly threatening us. The fifth disadvantage, the king's subsequent poverty, may not be greater than the ones already mentioned, but it is certainly inevitable. A king receives no income from his ruined subjects and cannot prosper when the country is sick. Both these reasons are closely connected. If the citizens are crushed with penury and if trade is in turmoil, then who will pay the king his customary revenue? The tax collectors will collect much less royal tribute. Are these statements dreams? Are they not verified by much history?

When Alfonso XI, king of Castile, was still a minor, his guardians were forced to render an account for all the royal revenues. It was discovered that all together they did not exceed 1,600,000 *maravedis*, as found in his history (ch. 14). Those *maravedis* were, of course, worth more than ours: Each one was worth 17 of our current ones. Nevertheless, it was a remarkably paltry income and seemed incredible. The historian ascribes two reasons for so great a disaster: the first, the greediness of the nobles who possessed many towns and strongholds of the kingdom; the other that, from the time of Ferdinand, five kings had altered money either by debasing it or increasing its value. In this way, with trade hampered and the nation reduced to penury, the nation's common disadvantage reached the king.

We conclude with the final disadvantage, the greatest of them all: The general hatred that will be stirred up for the prince. As a certain historian says, everyone takes responsibility for prosperity, the head is responsible for adversity. How was the victory lost? Obviously, the supreme commander was imprudent in organizing his battle lines, or he did not pay the soldiers the salary owed them. About 1300 AD, Philip the Fair, king of France, was the first-known French king to debase money. As a result, Dante, a celebrated poet of the time, called him "a forger of money." Robertus Gaguinus reports in his life of the king that Philip, at his death, repented his deed and told his son, Louis Hutin, that he had to put up with his people's hatred because he had debased the coinage and that Louis Hutin, therefore, was to correct his father's mistakes and hearken back to old reckonings. This concern proved useless. Before the people's hatred was defused, the one responsible for the monetary disaster, Enguerrano Marinio, was publicly freed at the command of King Hutin, with the encouragement of some nobles and the approval of the whole land. This was a clear-cut crime, but it did not prevent the future kings from following in the same footsteps. French history makes clear that Charles the Fair, the brother of Hutin, caused a lot of trouble for his people. There is a law extant against him, the *De crimine falsi* of John XXII, the Supreme Pontiff, and of Philip of Valois, cousin and successor to both of these kings. Because of well-remembered misfortunes, the people of Aragon, in their dedication to, and interest in holding onto their freedom, demand from the king at his coronation an oath that he will never alter money. Petrus Belluga mentions this point when he presents the two privileges granted to the people of Valencia by their kings in 1265 and 1336 (*Speculo Principum*, rubric 36, no. 5). This is, doubtless, a healthy and prudent precaution. Greed causes blindness; financial straits create pressure; we forget the past. In this way, the cycle of evils returns. Personally, I wonder if those in charge of affairs are ignorant of these things. If they do know them, I wonder why they so rashly, despite their prudent knowledge, wish to rush headlong into these perils.

CHAPTER 11: SHOULD SILVER MONEY BE ALTERED?

All the disadvantages that we have explained as coming from adulteration of copper money are found more forcefully in the case of silver money because of its quality and abundance. Gold money is always less used, and if the government is prudently administered, there will not be a great supply of copper money. Actually, silver is the backbone of commerce because it is conveniently exchanged for all other goods and used to liquidate contracted debts. Some, however, are not affected by the disadvantages derived from the debasing of copper coinage. They maintain that debasing silver coins would greatly benefit the state. I have therefore decided to explain now whether such a move would correct the damage experienced or cause all affairs of state to be subverted, everything going topsy-turvy. I personally believe that the latter will happen. Would that I were a false prophet!

This approach, they say, is the way to safety and peace. Outsiders will not be enticed by its quality to lay their greedy hands on our silver and seek profit by diverting it to other nations. Meanwhile, our legal provisions are rendered powerless through fraud and ambition. It is a fact that Spanish silver money is better than that of its neighbors by at least a one-eighth part. Although they do not go into it, silver would be a greater means of curing the king's financial needs, for, if from the exchange of base copper money of little value they bring into the treasury over 600,000 gold pieces, can we imagine what would happen if silver were debased? It is in great supply in Spain, and each year—incredibly—a greater amount is imported from the Indies. There is the further advantage—that we have no need to get this metal from outsiders, as we do, at great expense, with copper. When they exchange their copper for our silver and gold, they gain a greater benefit—one is reminded of Glaucus and Diomedes.

Certainly, we could make a huge profit if the silver were debased by a third or a fourth. Consider, for example, that silver could be devalued in three different ways. First, its value can be increased while the coin remains intact. Then, a silver coin, now worth 34 *maravedis*, would by law increase to 40, 50, or 60. Second, the weight could be diminished. We currently strike 67 silver pieces from 8 ounces of silver. In this situation, we would strike 80 or even 100, and each coin would continue to have its earlier value of 34 *maravedis*. On examination, this approach differs little from the previous one because in either case the weight of silver is lessened and the value increased.

The third way involves change by adding more copper, and this is the direction that the tricksters are going. Today 20 grains of copper are mixed with 8 ounces of silver; then they go further: Another 20 or 30 grains are mixed in. In this way, a profit of as much as 6 silver pieces on 8 ounces of silver is made because each grain equals in value about 8 *maravedis*. Now if the yearly shipments from the Indies bring in 1 million silver *marks*, at least 500,000 gold coins would be added to the treasury annually by means of this debasing. Furthermore, this income, if sold at 20 percent interest, would annually collect revenue in gold, and the profit from this sale would increase to 10 million gold pieces, or, according to the Romans, 4,000 *sesterces*. Once this type of fraud is introduced if more copper is added—as seems likely—profit will increase in direct proportion to the corruption of the metal.

We must recall that silver in Spain for some time has been stamped with the standard of purity of 11 karats (minters call them *dineros*, a standard of silver with 24 grains) and 4 grains, namely, with the admixture of no more than 20 grains of copper. This is established by law for the minters of the kingdom. Silversmiths follow the same rule in regard to bullion and unworked silver. This is the same silver that they work with in their shops and make into different vessels. The same has been true for many centuries for the old silver in our churches. There is also a law of John II, king of Castile, as promulgated in the 1435 parliament of Madrid (petition 31)—the first law in *novae recopilationis* (bk. 5, title 22). Under these circumstances, I wish to ask these men who want to debase silver: Would their decree apply only to mints, or would it extend also to the workshops of the silversmiths? If they answer, "both places," confusion will certainly reign. The silver already worked will not remain at its previous price. It will also vary in relation to the time when it was made.

Moreover, experts in this field say that silver, debased with more copper, will not be fit for elegant craftsmanship because of its crudity. Should people wish to resist corruption in money and not extend it to silversmiths, they should always bear in mind that silver, both as bullion and as minted, must be of the same quality. Furthermore, silver, as bullion, will always necessarily be worth more than debased money, to the degree that the money has been debased. The complicated process has been going on for a great many years and only the destruction of the robbers and of the entire land will bring it to an end, as Tacitus maintains in a similar instance (*Annals*, bk. 20).

What, then, is to be done about silver already minted? Is it to be worth the same as new debased money? That would be unjust because the old is better and will contain more silver. Everyone will prefer it to the new, given the choice. However, will it be worth more? That would be fair but also confusing: With the same weight and stamp, some silver coins would be worth more and others worth less. However, if we wish to go back to an earlier state, and to exchange them for just as many new ones, as we indicated was formerly done in England, that transaction will be just as profitable for the king, as it was in the case of copper money. One must consider, however, if this is a new speculation: to exchange good money for bad. It is not profitable to try people's patience. Patience can become exasperated and wear out and can destroy everything else, as well as be self-destructive.

Now, what will become of gold money? That must be considered too. This issue will certainly confound the highest with the lowest, and turn upside down things better left undisturbed. Once again, the same problems will arise. If gold is not debased, it certainly follows that a gold piece (which we call a *corona*) will not be valued at 12 silver coins but, rather, at 14 or 15, in proportion to the debasing of silver. As silver is debased, commodities always become more expensive. Then foreigners and natives as well, conscious of the situation, will say, "Twelve new silver pieces contain no more silver than 10 of the previous ones; I will subtract the same proportion from the goods I used to give as well." We explained above what will happen if controls are imposed. Furthermore, not all prices can be controlled. Commerce, when interfered with, is like milk that is so delicate that it is spoiled by the most gentle breeze. As a matter of fact, money—especially silver money, because of its quality—is the ultimate foundation of commerce. When it is altered, everything else resting upon it will necessarily collapse. The stability of silver explains why the disadvantages from the alteration of copper money are not completely obvious. It acts as a restraint on copper money, because, as before, a silver piece is still exchanged for 34 *maravedis* of this new and debased coinage. Without this restraint, commerce would all but fail; everything would cost much more than before.

Moreover, suppose that our only money is copper and that silver is not being transported from the Indies. All the evils described in the previous chapter would suddenly come upon us in one fell swoop. Silver wards off these evils because it is honorable and there is a good supply of it in the country. If this last reason seems weak, then a new and valid argument appears. All monetary income will be diminished to the degree that silver is changed. Someone who has an annuity of 1,000 gold pieces will suddenly receive only 800 or fewer, depending on the degree of debasing of silver. Certainly, when payment is necessarily made in new money, 1,000 gold pieces of new money will not have more silver and will not be more useful for living than 800 previous ones. Therefore, people scarcely coping with previous taxes will be oppressed by a new and very heavy one. Among those affected will be churches, monasteries, hospitals, gentlemen, and orphans—no one will be spared. Earlier, the point was clearly made that a new tax cannot be imposed without the people's consent. We still have to respond to the arguments advanced for the other side. The king gains nothing by profiting at the expense of his subjects, nor may he seize the citizens' possessions by either sheer force, cunning, or deceit. One man's loss is another man's gain. There is no way around that fact.

However, the previous argument asserted that silver was exported because of its excellence. I deny this statement outright, and point out that, although French gold pieces are somewhat better than ours and more valuable, ours are nonetheless found in that country in abundance. Two particular reasons explain this. First, Spaniards import the foreign goods they need and because they cannot exchange an equal amount of their own goods for the imports they have to pay money for the excess. Linen cloth, paper, books, metals, leather goods, trifles, different objects, and, sometimes, grain are imported. Foreigners are under no obligation to give these goods free of charge but they do so for other goods they need and exchange them for money. Second, the king's yearly expenses and payments to foreigners reach 3,000 *sesterces*, 7 million a year. Unless this sum were paid out to bankers with the authority to postpone payment, when the king needs it, it would not be at hand. Someone, however, may tenaciously insist that the excellence of silver serves the same purpose. I do not disagree, provided my adversary understands that there is no way to keep foreigners from constantly making their money inferior to ours. In this way, they get their hands on our silver, which they certainly need more than life.

Is there, then, a way to correct the disadvantages that arise from the debasement and abundance of copper money? I have never believed that a concrete disadvantage may be corrected by a greater disadvantage, or a sin by a sin. Some cures are worse than the sickness. Furthermore, I am not aware of any cure for this illness, except the one that our ancestors constantly used in similar straits, namely: The value of the new money is reduced by half or by two-thirds. If that approach is not enough to heal the wound, the bad money is to be completely recalled and good money put in its place. It is, of course, only just that either solution makes the one who profited from the general disaster pay. Because I see this approach is not common—indeed never employed—it is preferable for those who are in possession of the money to suffer a loss. Otherwise, by continuing longer in error, we aggravate the causes of a stubborn illness. On the other hand, we can have recourse to devaluing money. This would involve general disaster for all. It is clear that the pivots on which this entire issue turns are those two values of money that were explained in chapter 4. They must be mutually adjusted if we want things to be sound. That means that money should be legal, but if the values are separated (which, it seems, will happen if silver is debased), every possible evil will come upon the state.

We end with this point: In 1368, when a great part of France was under the English kings, the Prince of Wales, who was running affairs in France for his father, the king, levied a new tax on his vassals. He did this because his treasury was exhausted by the wars he was waging on behalf of Peter, the king of Castile. Very many refused to accept this new burden; others like those in Poitiers, Limoges, and La Rochelle agreed, on condition that the prince would not alter money for the next 7 years. Jean Froissart, the French historian, relates this in his *Annals* (vol. 1). This account makes it clear that princes have debased money but that the citizenry have always disapproved of and rejected it as they could. It would be beneficial if our people would learn from this example and agree to financial subsidies when the king requests them, on condition that the prince promises that money would be stable for as long as they could demand.

CHAPTER 12: CONCERNING GOLD MONEY

Gold money varies greatly. I am not talking about the still extant money of the first Roman emperors—gold coins minted from the most pure gold with their names inscribed on them. On the other hand, when the Goths were in control in Spain, impure and base gold was coined— gold of 12 or 13 karats—because of many additions. Nonetheless, some of their kings' coins of better gold have been discovered. We have, moreover, seen one coin that was 22 karats. We need not go into the monetary arrangements of the kings of León and Castile when Spain was coming into power: We do not happen to see gold from that period, and it would be very laborious to delay on it.

I will deal only with those changes that were made in gold from the time of King Ferdinand and Queen Isabella. At the beginning of their reign, these rulers minted coins from very pure gold of 23¾ karats, which they called *castellanos*: 50 from 8 ounces of gold, with each coin worth 485 *maravedis*. Thus, the 8 ounces, once minted, were worth 24,250 *maravedis*. However, as bullion of the same quality, the *mark* was worth only 250 *maravedis* less. This difference, after the gold was minted, used to be divided equally among the officers of the mint and the owner of the gold. At the same time, 8 ounces of 22 karat gold bullion was worth 22,000 *maravedis*, and the bullion weight of a *castellano* was worth 440 *maravedis* because gold of that sort was not being minted at that time. Only goldsmiths employed it in their craft. Neighboring nations used gold minted in accordance with our quality and price. This fact created no difficulties.

Then, a little while later, to the glory and prosperity of our nation, the western passage to the Indies was opened and a large amount of gold was imported every year. In their desire for our gold, some of our neighbors debased the quality of their own and others increased the price of ours. Conscious of these ploys, our people did not debase the quality of their gold at that time; they just increased its price. Therefore, in the 1497 parliament of Medina, the same rulers decreed by law that no more *castellanos* were to be minted, but, in their place, *ducats* were to be minted, which they called "excellent." From the previous 8 ounces of gold of the same purity, 65⅓ such coins were to be minted, each valued at 375 *maravedis*. Therefore, minted gold advanced to 24,500 *maravedis*; gold bullion or jewelry of the same weight was worth

24,250 *maravedis*. At the same time, 8 ounces or a *mark* of 22 karat gold was worth 22,500 *maravedis*, and the value of a *castellano* was 450 *maravedis*. This rate continued for several years until it was noticed that the neighbors were further debasing gold.

Thus, in the 1537 parliament of Valladolid, Charles Augustus changed things completely and decreed by law that gold of precisely 22 karats was to be minted. Sixty-eight coins were to be minted from 8 ounces and, called *coronas*, each was worth 350 *maravedis*. As a result, 8 ounces of this money was worth 22,800 *maravedis*. There was no legislation concerning gold bullion or gold, either coined or as jewelry. It was bought and sold by agreement like merchandise. The *novae recopilationis* (bk. 5, pt. 1, law 4, title 24) decrees that goldsmiths were to work no other gold but the purest, or 22 karat, or at least 20 karat. Therefore, unlike silver, gold bullion did not always parallel minted gold and was not governed by the law for minted gold. Nonetheless, for the most part, 22 karat gold was minted and was common with goldsmiths. Because of its lower price in Castile, foreigners kept exporting gold, which had been exchanged for crafts and goods. This fact compelled Philip II, king of Spain, to increase the price of gold in each *corona* by 50 *maravedis* in the parliament of Madrid. Consequently, what used to be valued at 350 *maravedis* went up to 400 *maravedis*. With this law, 8 ounces of minted gold reached 27,200 *maravedis*. The *castellano* was worth 16 silver coins or *reales*.

At this point, we may consider the possibility of debasing gold coins. Just as the quality of copper coins was diminished, and just as they are thinking about doing the same with silver coins—as rumor has it—would the state benefit if the same thing were done with gold coins? They would have less quality and be increased in value. The issue is the same. I personally believe that every alteration in money is very dangerous. It is never expedient to mint unlawful money and thus increase by law the cost of something that is commonly considered to be worth less. Nor can our neighbors be prevented from further debasing their money because of our example. We have learned by experience from the four changes made in gold since the time of the rulers, Ferdinand and Isabella, that it is impossible to prevent the gold from being carried off.

If gold coins are greatly debased, perhaps foreigners would scorn it. Certainly, it would lose much of its value. I doubt that such a situation would befit the majesty of Spain. In my opinion, however, it would not cause serious harm if gold were altered by taking away part of its quality and increasing its price. This is especially true because such a change in the past, when repeated frequently within a few years, did not bring serious disadvantages. The supply of gold is always small in comparison to silver, and its use as money is less common and usual. Therefore, I have not been accustomed to believe that it would be very disadvantageous if an alteration were to occur. In any event, I have always been convinced that I would wish things to hold to their course and not be concerned with money. Nor does the opposite approach benefit in any way, except to provide income for the prince. Income should not always be our goal, especially by this means, that is, debasing money. As a matter of fact, provided that the original quality and reckoning of copper and silver money remain intact, I would not be too concerned about what happens to gold in either way. Two things are important: One, that it be done with the consent of the subjects concerned; the other, that the money always be legitimate or legal and not otherwise. To achieve this end for copper money, both values must be equal: The value of the metal, whether mixed with silver or not, must be computed, as well as the cost of minting. Thus, if 8 ounces, or a *mark*, of copper along with the expenses of minting cost only 80 *maravedis*, it is unreasonable to permit its value to be increased by law to 280 *maravedis*, as is now done. It is unlawful to do so to the degree that legal value deviates from real value. To preserve parity in the case of gold and silver, their proportional relationship must be considered. If they are of equal purity, gold is compared to silver by a ratio of 12 to 1, as Budaeus says in *De asse* (bk. 3). I say of each, "purity or quality," because just as the purity of gold is commonly divided into 24 grades, which the goldsmiths call "karats," so the purity of silver is divided into 12 *dineros*. Thus, silver of 11 *dineros* ably corresponds to 22 karat gold. This proportion generally holds between these two metals. Of course, the ratio would change because of the scarcity or plenitude of one or the other metal. They are like other goods: An ample supply lowers the price, and scarcity raises it. As a result, we should not be surprised that the ancient authors do not agree on how gold and silver were related to one another in value. Therefore, gold and silver money of the same purity and weight should be carefully exchanged at the rate of 12 silver coins for 1 gold coin, as now happens. For that is lawful. If that value is exceeded or lessened, the whole transaction smacks of fraud. For example, if a gold *corona* is exchanged for 16 or 18 silver ones (*reales*), this transaction is a clear-cut violation of monetary justice, unless, of course, the purity of the gold is increased or the purity of the silver lessened. When such is the case, what seemed to be unjust is lawful and in keeping with equity. Finally, it is of the utmost importance that princes do not profit from debased money. Were that permitted, it would be impossible to curb the greed of foreigners and countrymen who, in the hope of great profit, would force upon us counterfeit and adulterated money of the same kind.

CHAPTER 13: IS THERE SOME WAY TO ASSIST THE PRINCE IN HIS NEED?

The popular proverb is quite true: "Necessity knows no law." Another one says: "The stomach has no ears," which is to say that it is a harsh demander; it does not give way to arguments. However, that problem is easily handled. The stomach settles down after eating. Certainly, such needs and wants arise in the state that it is not surprising that those in charge of administration dream up some uncommon and inept remedies. One such remedy is clearly the recently adopted debasement of money. We have explained this point in the arguments of this disputation, but if this remedy is not satisfactory, we will have to find a more suitable way to fill up the treasury.

I do not intend to treat so great an issue. My purpose has been to condemn the alteration of money as a base crime that is full of great disadvantages. It would be pleasant to address some other ways and means—perhaps more suitable and ultimately more fruitful—of enriching the prince. One might add that there are ways and means that involve no injury to, or groaning of, the nation; they will, rather, meet with the greatest approval. First, somehow, court expenditures could be lessened, for reasonable and prudent moderation is more splendid and manifests more majesty than unnecessary and unseasonable consumption.

In an account of royal taxes and expenses, receipts, and outlays of John II, king of Castile, for the year 1429, we find that the annual expenses of the court, including the ministers' salaries, gifts, and the royal table, amounted to hardly 30,000 gold pieces. Someone might say that these accounts are very old; everything has changed; prices are much more expensive; kings are more powerful, and, therefore, greater pomp and majesty are found at court. I do not deny these facts, but, really, all of these do not adequately explain the difference between the 30,000 of those days and the 120,000 that are spent at this time for the support of the court. Moreover, a more recent account of royal taxes, with the expenses for 1564 for the court of Philip II king of Spain, for the support of prince Charles his son, and for John of Austria, reports that annually they amounted to no more than 40,000 gold pieces.

How, you ask, can court expenses be curtailed? I do not know. Prudent men who are involved in the court should make that determination. Common opinion has it that whatever the purveyor hands over to the stewards is stored in the pantry and paid for automatically. Second, royal gifts would perhaps be smaller if a large tax were added to them. I do not believe that a king should have a reputation for being cheap, or not be sufficiently generous in response to his people's good works and services. I believe that two things have to be taken into consideration. There is, of course, no nation in the world with more and greater public rewards available: commissions, offices, pensions, benefices, military towns, and gifts. Were these distributed reasonably and deliberately, one could dispense with extraordinary gifts from the royal treasury and other income. In addition, we should remember that excessive gifts do not make men more disposed for service, or even well disposed to the giver. It is human to be led on more by the hope of a future reward than by the memory of a favor received. This is so true that those who have prospered much at court constantly think of retirement and the peaceful life.

No king of Castile lived more magnificently than did Henry IV, and in no other time was the unrest as great. As a result, after Henry's abdication, the nobles made his brother, Alfonso, king. After his death, they offered the kingdom to Isabella, who was the sister of both of them. Tacitus makes a telling comment at the end of book 19: "Vitellius, inasmuch as he wished to have friends because of the greatness of his gifts rather than because of the constancy of his morals, bought more friends than he had." Robert of Sorbonne, his confessor and archdeacon of Tornai, tells us in his life of Saint Louis, king of France, that when he wanted to establish a college in Paris that still bears his name, the Sorbonne—no other college in the world may be compared with it for learning—he asked the king for a contribution. The king answered that he would willingly comply with his request if only chosen theologians, after examining public expenses and income, would determine how he might lawfully contribute to this work. He was a great king and a real saint. If he did not lavish money on this holy work without discernment and examination, would he squander it on fattening up the courtiers on the vain pleasures of gardens and unnecessary buildings? The reality is that a king has income from the nation to support public works. When he has taken care of them, he may direct it to other things—but not before. If I were to send a commissioner to Rome to foster my affairs, would he be permitted to divert the money that I gave him for necessary expenses to other uses?

A king is not permitted to apply money given to him by his subjects as freely as he may apply income from lands held as a private citizen. Furthermore, he should exempt himself from unnecessary expenditures and from wars. Parts that cannot be cured should be timely cut off from the rest of the body. Philip II, king of Spain, wisely separated the Belgians from the rest of his empire. Mapheius indicates in *Indicarum historiarum* (bk. 6) that the Chinese nation—an empire once much bigger than it is now—as if in a bloodletting and correction of excess, gave up many lands that it could not conveniently govern. Emperor Hadrian did the same thing when he destroyed the bridge that Trajan had built over the Danube. He wished the Danube on the north and the Euphrates in the east to be the limits of the Roman empire, which was already struggling under its own weight.

The fourth rule should be that, first of all, court ministers must be accountable and after them the magistrates of the provinces and all others who play any role in the state. We are in a dangerous situation where hardly anyone is safe. The way that people think is pitiful. They believe that merit now has nothing to do with gaining anything in our land: office, commission, benefice, and even a bishopric. Everything is for sale, and nothing is conferred without its price. Although it may not be true and is exaggerated, it is pernicious to have such a thing stated.

In general, royal ministers and penniless nobodies enter upon public commissions and almost instantly become blessed and reckon their annuities in thousands of gold pieces. All these things come from the blood of the poor, from the very marrow of litigants and office seekers. Moreover, such transformations have led me to think that the state would benefit if it adopted the ways of the Church. Before they assume office, bishops must present a witnessed account of all their possessions. Then, at death, they may leave these things, and nothing else, to those whom they wish. The chosen ministers of court, or magistrates, or other commissioners should have to do what bishops do. Through periodic investigations, they will be forced to render an account of their newly acquired wealth and will be stripped of that wealth whose definite sources and causes they fail to identify. The treasury would greatly profit from money recovered should this inquiry and investigation be instituted.

Public opinion often condemns those in charge of royal taxes because, by agreement with tax collectors, they usurp a sizable part of the gain and money that the collectors gather. Worse yet, in every city, leaders make money by selling the local or royal laws every year to those who refuse to obey them. They openly grant public privileges to those from whom they secretly receive money. We cannot ignore the different forms of corruption and ways of cheating the provincials. When King Philip II recently decreed that the value of *coronados* rise by an eighth, a favorite of the king with knowledge of this decision was proven to have scraped together all the gold brought across the Atlantic each year and to have made a huge profit.

A certain Jewish chief treasurer asked one of the earlier kings of Castile—John II or his father Henry, I believe—why he did not play dice with his courtiers to pass the time. The king answered, "How can I do that since I do not own a hundred gold pieces?" The treasurer let that pass at the time. Later, at an opportune moment, he said, "O King, your statement to me the other day sorely disturbed me. So much so, that I thought I was being indirectly rebuked. If you agree, I will make you wealthy and happy instead of poor." The king went with his proposal. Then, the treasurer said, "I want control of three secluded castles." There he intended to keep money and the prisoners proved guilty of crimes in the use of royal money. Then, questioning minor treasurers, he kept finding the royal name on forged documents and other bequests of the prince, paid with a third or a fourth subtracted for those who handled the royal promissory notes. Then he asked those who had been defrauded if they would be content with half of what they had lost and if they would give the rest to the king. They agreed, considering the offer a gain, since until then they had no hope of future compensation. When these arrangements had been made, he put the treasurer and his bailsmen into chains, where they remained until payment of all the money. In this way, he enriched the treasury.

It would be nice if such could occur now. It would save a large amount of money. Nowadays, this new corruption is an indication of the perverted government—treasurers purchase their positions at a large price and have to sell the office and profit from the misery of others. They invest the royal money in commerce and do not meet royal debts for a year or two. Most conveniently, after 4 or 8 months they pay the debt, even with some expense deducted, namely, an ounce or 2 ounces from the entire sum as they agreed with the creditor. Such corruption could be eradicated if individuals were investigated as we mentioned above. Truly or falsely, the claim is commonly made that every one of these treasurers has supporters in the court among the magistrates. Part of the explanation for this is, of course, the hope for peculation, and this misfortune is no less deadly than the earlier ones. Above all, the royal taxes and income should be taken care of diligently and faithfully. Under current practice, scarcely half of the taxes and income is turned to royal use. Money, transferred through many ministers, is like a liquid. It always leaves a residue in the container. Our *Annals* (bk. 19, ch. 14) testify that the king of Castile, Henry III, by exercising such care, escaped the shameless poverty once found in his court. He used to have to buy ram's meat for dinner and finally wound up very wealthy. He left his son, John II, huge treasures without any complaints from the provincials. His only warning to him and to his brother Ferdinand was not to let the ministers get their greedy hands on public money.

Finally, strange and luxurious merchandise—which softens people and that we can do without and suffer no harm—should be sold at a high tariff, for such an approach will discourage their import, which is something very desirable. On the other hand, if they are imported, the treasury will be bolstered by the tariff levied upon delicacies of foreign people: gold brocade, tapestries, all sorts of perfumes, sugar, and delicacies. Alexander Severus did this once in Rome and was endlessly praised. We have discussed this point rather fully in our *De rege et regis institutione* (bk. 3, ch. 7), and there is no need to dwell on it here. I add only this point: The ways to provide for the royal needs discussed here, indeed any one of them, would provide more than the 200,000 gold pieces annually, which is the same amount the first authors promised the king in their paper on debasing copper money. Moreover, this will happen without any censure from the people. Rather, the poor will enthusiastically support the measure.

There might be an objection that we should not be surprised to find a means—that is, debasing coinage—being employed that different kings used in the past. We readily reply. Times have changed much since the past: The king's income was much less then; there was no sales tax; there was no gold from the Indies; there was no tax on wine and oil; there were no monopolies, no Church tithes, no crusade subsidies; and kings were not grand masters of military orders. Every year, all of these provide abundant income. The problems were greater at that time: The Moors were at the gates, there were wars with neighboring kings, the nobles were frequently in revolt, and internal rebellion resulted. Now, on the other hand, by the grace of God there is internal peace throughout all of Spain. I will say absolutely nothing about foreign affairs. In 1540, Francis I, king of France, debased the *solidus*—the nation's common coin—and his son Henry mixed in even more copper. Charles IX, following the example of his grandfather and his father, reduced its quality and weight even further. Great difficulties were certainly impending, but the monetary troubles were so great that there was no need to lament the other evils. The afflicted people were in tumult: Ancient religious convictions were changed at random and very many, driven by want, changed their countries and lived at the mercy of others.

The account in our *Annals* (bk. 29, ch. 12) deserves mention here. Because of Philip of Austria's death and the weakness of his bereaved wife, Maximilian Augustus and Ferdinand the Catholic were long at odds over the administration of Castile and were considering some means of reaching peace. Among other things, Augustus was demanding the payment of 100,000 gold pieces from the income of Castile. The Catholic King was not able to grant the request and pleaded as an excuse that the public debt had increased to 500,000 gold pieces. Clearly, this is a remarkable response. Taxes were much less than they are now, wars were more serious than ever, and corresponding hopes were aroused. Portugal was conquered and driven out of our territory; Atlantic trade was open; the kingdom of Granada was subjugated; the coasts of Africa, the Basques, and Neapolitans were defeated; moreover, there was peace in the kingdom, and the Italian wars in which the kingdom always played a major role were abating. Nevertheless, the kingdom was oppressed by a burden that was indeed light if compared with the debts of our day. It makes sense. A prince of outstanding prudence kept account of income and outlays and did not wish to be pressed further. That is great wisdom. It is not reasonable to blame the times. That incident took place in 1509 when a good deal of gold was being brought into the treasury every year. I do not believe that times have changed since then, but men, abilities, morals, and pleasures have changed. The weight of these evils will dash this empire to the ground if God does not support it with his favor and saving hand.

Such are my thoughts on the subjects discussed in this disputation and particularly on the subject of altering and debasing copper money. If such is done, without consulting the people, it is unjust; if done with their consent, it is in many ways fatal. If my arguments have been true and reasonable, I thank God. If, however, I have been mistaken, I certainly deserve to be pardoned because of my sincere desire to help. My knowledge of past evils makes me afraid that we will fall into misfortunes from which it will be difficult to extricate ourselves, but if my statements in this disputation have irritated anyone, he should recall that salubrious remedies are frequently bitter and stinging. Moreover, when a subject is a common concern, everyone is free to express his opinion on it, whether he speaks the truth or is mistaken. Finally, I beg God to shed his light upon the eyes and minds of those who are responsible for these things so that they may peacefully agree to embrace and put into action wholesome advice once it is known.

23. Hugo Grotius: *The Rights of War and Peace* (1625)[1]

The most natural Measure of the Value of any Thing, is the Want of it, as *Aristotle* rightly observes, and this is what the least civilized People are altogether guided by; yet this is not the only Measure; for the Will of Men, which governs every Thing, covets many Things more than are necessary. *Luxury*, says *Pliny*, *gave the Price to Pearls*. And *Cicero*, in his Oration against *Verres*, *In Proportion to our Passion for such Sort of Things, is our Value for them*. And so on the contrary, it happens that Things which are the most necessary, are, on the Account of their Plenty, abundantly cheaper; which *Seneca* illustrates by several Instances, *De Benefic*. Lib. 6. Cap. 15. where he also subjoins this, *The Price of every Thing is according to the Markets; when you have commended them ever so much, they are worth no more than they can be sold for*. And *Paulus*, the Lawyer, *The Prices of Things do not depend on this or that Man's Humour or Interest, but on the common Estimation*; that is, as he explains it elsewhere, *on the Value that all the World puts on them*. Hence is it, that a Thing is only valued at so much as is usual and customary to be offered and given for it, which can scarce be so settled as not to admit a Demand of more or less, except it be where the Law has fixed a certain Rate, precisely, and to a Point, as *Aristotle* expresses it.

And now in that common and current Price of Things, we usually have a Regard to the Pains and Expences the Merchants and Traders have been at; and it often rises and falls all on a Sudden, according as there are more or fewer Chapmen, and according to the Plenty or Scarcity of Money or Commodities. Besides, there may possibly some such Circumstances intervene, as may very justly raise or lessen the ordinary Market Price; as, the Loss we sustain, the Profit we lose, a particular Fancy for certain Things, the Favour we do one in buying or selling what we should not otherwise have bought or sold; all which Circumstances the Person we deal with ought to be acquainted with. And we may also have Regard to the Loss or Gain that arises from the Delay or the Promptness of Payment.

As to Buying and Selling, we must observe, that the Bargain and Sale is good, from the very Moment of the Contract; and tho' the Thing be not actually delivered, yet may the Property be transferred, and this is the most simple Way of Dealing: So *Seneca* says, *Selling is the alienating of a Thing that belongs to us, and the translating of it, and the Right we have in it, to some other*: For it is so in an Exchange. But if it be agreed, that the Property shall not pass immediately, then the Seller shall be obliged to transfer his Property at such a Time, and in the mean While, both the Profits and Hazards shall be the Seller's. And therefore, that a Contract of Sale consists in the Seller's engaging himself to deliver the Thing sold, and that the Buyer should not be molested in the Possession of it, or should be indemnified, in Case of such Molestation;

---

[1] Translated by A.C. Campbell.

that the Buyer must run all Risques, and that the Profits shall belong to him before the Property be actually transferred, are Maxims of the Civil Law, which are not in all Places observed. Nay, on the contrary, most Law-Makers have thought fit to enact, that till the Delivery of them the Seller shall have the Advantage, and stand to the Hazard of the Goods, as *Theophrastus* has remarked, in a Passage of *Stobaeus*, where you may also find many other Customs touching the Formalities of Selling, about giving Earnest, about retracting, very different from the *Roman* Laws; and *Dion Prusaeensis* too has observed, that among the *Rhodians*, a Sale was not compleated, nor other Contracts finished, till they were publickly registred.

And we must know too, that if one and the same Thing be twice sold, of the two Sales, that shall stand good which had the Property immediately transferred, either by Delivery or otherwise; for by this the moral Power of the Things goes from the Seller, which it does not by a bare Promise.

All Monopolies are not repugnant to the Law of Nature, for they may sometimes be permitted by the Sovereign upon a just Cause, and at a certain Rate; as may appear from the Example of *Joseph*, when he was Governor of *Aegypt*: So also under the *Romans*, the *Alexandrians* had the Monopoly, as *Strabo* tells us, of all Commodities brought from the *Indies* and *Aethiopia*. The like may be done by private Persons, provided they are contented with a reasonable Profit. But they, who, as the Oylmen in the *Velabrum*, do purposely combine to advance the Value of their Wares above the highest Degree of the current Price, and those also who use Force or Fraud to prevent the Importation of any greater Quantity, or else agree to buy up all, in Order to sell them again, at a Rate very exorbitant, considering the Season, commit an Injustice, and are obliged to make Amends and a Reparation for it. If indeed they do by any other Means hinder the bringing in of Goods, or ingross them to themselves, to vend them dearer, tho' at a Price not unreasonable for the Season, they act against the Rules of Charity, as St *Ambrose* proves by several Arguments, in his third Book of Offices, but properly speaking, they violate no Man's Right.

Now as for Money, we must observe, that it naturally derives its Currency, or Equivalence, not from the Matter only, nor from this or that particular Denomination and Form, but from a more general Capacity of being compared with, or answering the Value of all other Things, at least such as are more immediately Necessary. And its Value, if it be not otherwise agreed, must be according to the Rate it bears at the Time, and in the Place of Payment; thus *Michael Ephesius*, Nicom. *Money itself varies, as our Necessities do; for as we have not always the same Occasion for Things that belong to another, so Money is not always of the same Value, but sometimes is more, and sometimes less worth; but yet the Value of Money is what lasts longest, and therefore we use it as the Standard and Measure of all Things in Trade.* The Meaning of which is this, That which is the Measure or Standard to other Things, ought in itself to be constant, and such are Gold, Silver, and Copper, in Things susceptible of Price, for they are in themselves of the same Value, almost always, and in all Places. But as other Things which are useful or necessary, are either scarce, or in abundance, so the same Money, made of the same Metal, and of the same Weight, is sometimes worth more, sometimes less.

Letting and Hiring, as *Caius* well observes, very much resembles Buying and Selling, and is guided by the same Rules. That which answers to the Price is the Rent or Hire; and that which answers the Property, is the possessing and enjoying the Benefit of it. Wherefore, as when a Thing perishes, the Owner bears the Loss; so when a Thing rented or hired proves barren, or by any other Accident unprofitable, the Loss is to the Tenant, nor has the Person who lets it any

Thing the less Right to the Money agreed for, because when he delivered the Thing to his Use, it was then worth as much as was contracted for, tho' this may be altered either by the Laws, or particular Agreements. But if the Landlord, upon the first Tenant's not being able to make Use of it, shall let it to another, whatsoever he shall get thereby, he shall repay to him who first took it, that he may not enrich himself by another Man's Due.

And what we have before said concerning Selling, that the Price may be more or less, if what would otherwise not be bought or sold at all, be bought or sold to gratify another, the same may be understood of any Thing or Work, let or hired. But if a Man, by the same Pains, can serve several Persons, as by carrying them from Place to Place, if the Undertaker shall oblige himself entirely to every one of them, he may demand the same Reward from each of them, as from any one of them, if the Law does not oppose it; because a second Person's receiving Benefit by my Labour does no Ways prejudice the Agreement made with the first.

24. Samuel Pufendorf: *The Elements of Universal Jurisprudence* (1660)[1]

The most natural foundation of worth in things is their ability to exhibit some use in communal life. Hence things which are utterly useless we are accustomed commonly to call worthless. Now the use of a certain thing is defined not merely from the circumstance that it truly helps to preserve or to make pleasurable our existence, but in addition that it contributes some pleasure or ornament, even though this be in the sole opinion of certain men. Upon such things the luxury and the lustfulness of men have generally placed an inordinate worth. Now in comparing things with one another according to their worth, various considerations are commonly regarded. For here to such a degree does the necessity of a thing, or the nobility of its application, fail always to have chief consideration, that, by a singular provision of nature, those things which our life cannot do without are rather accorded the less worth, because nature presents a bounteous supply of them. Therefore it is rarity which is principally effective here, and this is held in an esteem none too slight when there are brought from far distant places things to which frequently the desires of men are violently drawn. For most men value chiefly those things which are to be had in common with a few; and, on the contrary, that thing is held cheap, whatever it may be, which is seen among the household goods of any and everybody.

Determinately, moreover, worth is commonly recognized from usage or custom, that is, a thing is commonly estimated at as much as is very generally offered or given for it. This is scarcely so that it does not have some range within which more or less can be demanded, except when the law has fixed the worth of a thing at a definite point. Now in common worth the labours and expenses which merchants undergo are customarily taken into account. There may also be certain estimable accidents of a thing because of which it may be legitimately bought or sold above or below the common price, for example, because of a loss which is to follow, deferred profit, peculiar affection, or if it be bought or sold as a favour to another, when otherwise it was not to be bought or sold. These same accidents are customarily pointed out to the man with whom a bargain is being made about a thing, and can properly be imputed. That deferred or increased gain also which arises from delayed or anticipated payment of the worth can be computed. For the day of payment is a part of the price, and it means more to give something immediately than after a time; since, forsooth, in the meantime profit might have been secured therefrom. Also there is not a little in the consideration of the place where the merchandise is produced or the worth paid. For the same thing is valued differently in different places, and the value of money, or the interest, is not the same everywhere, and the rates of exchange for forwarding money are different in different places. Moreover, it very frequently happens that the worth of a thing changes, that is, goes either up or down, this change being

---

[1]   Translated by William Abbott Oldfather.

due to the large or small supply of buyers, of money, of merchandise, or because of impending peace or war, and similar chance happenings.

Now not merely corporeal things have their own worth, but also incorporeal things and the very actions of men, in so far as they can bring to others some utility or delectation. About these, however, it must be noted that, by the laws of God and of man, some of them have been placed outside of human bartering, to such a degree that man ought not to fix a price for them, and ought not in turn to supply or perform these actions for a price. Of this kind are those sacred actions to which a certain supernatural effect has been assigned by divine will and institution, for example, the remission, through priestly absolution, of sins and of punishment due sins, the application of spiritual benefactions through the exhibition of the sacraments, and the like, in regard to which, if a man supplies them to another for a price, he is said to be committing simony. Thus the judge cannot rightly sell for a price the justice which he ought to administer gratis. Thus the plyer of the dagger, or the poisoner, does not rightly for a price sell his services in murdering a man, or the harlot sell her favours, or the man who disseminates lies to the injury of others, his stilus, or the man who sets out to help unjust causes, or to overthrow just ones by the perjuries of others, his honour; and so others of this ilk. Furthermore, the worth of useful or delectable actions is commonly estimated in proportion to the necessity, utility, difficulty, or delicacy of the action, or the multitude or scarcity of the artisans or workmen, the large or small number of contractors available, and the abundance or scantiness of their means.

In incorporeal things utility and splendour are principally regarded. And in all things corporeal as well as incorporeal, worth is determined in particular cases by law or custom, or by an understanding between the parties to the agreement.

Now worth can be divided into *common* and *eminent*. The former is that which inheres, from the foundations already mentioned, in all sorts of things which enter into exchange. Before the use of money was introduced, men knew no other worth besides that, and even yet some barbarians do not know of any. Hence business intercourse on the part of such men consisted merely in the simple exchange of things, and they were not able to let or to hire one another's services except in return for a thing. Now, indeed, that was a highly inconvenient method of fulfilling contracts between men, since it is not easy for anyone whatsoever to possess things of that kind for which another is willing to give his own in exchange, or which have the exact value of the other's property; and in states where citizens are distinguished by different statuses, it is necessary that there be several classes of men which cannot at all maintain life with that kind of exchange, or else are able to do so with extreme difficulty. Hence civil life was rude and simple as long as that was the sole method which obtained of exchanging goods; and those who use it today are far removed from the customs of the more civilized nations. Having considered, therefore, the inconveniences of exchange, most nations agreed with one another to set a certain eminent worth, as it were, upon a definite thing, according to which as a standard the worth of other things should be exacted, and in which that same worth should be, as it were, eminently contained; and all that to such a degree that this thing could be used in exchange for any thing at all, and could be conveniently employed for conducting business and fulfilling all kinds of contracts. For this end the nobler metals, gold, silver, and bronze, were judged to be the most suitable, forasmuch as their substance is not too common, is durable, and is not clumsy because of its bulk; although a state might destine other substances also for this use, which would have to be employed by citizens in the place of money. These metals, in quantities of a definite weight, and marked with definite figures, are called coins, upon which the administrators of states, or the mutual agreement of the users, set a fixed value. Nevertheless, that increase or decrease of worth which other things undergo because of scarcity or abundance, money also itself does not entirely escape, as a coin made of the same material and with the same weight is worth now more and now less; although that variation is not as sudden or as frequent as the variations of value among other things. From what has been said in passing can be explained also the controversy among the ancient Roman jurisconsults regarding worth. Sabinus and Cassius, of their number, affirmed that other things besides money had worth, and therefore they included exchange under purchase and sale. Both of these positions were denied by Proculus and Nerva, because otherwise it could not be made clear, when things had been exchanged, just which would appear to have been sold and which to have been given under the name of price. For it seemed to them to be absurd that both things had been sold and both given under the name of price. Now, in truth, both views can stand in a certain way. The first can stand, indeed, if we say that the purchase was made at common or eminent worth; and that the price in exchange appears to be the thing which is given by the one who started the business transaction. For he appears to be the purchaser who asks that something be given him in exchange for some property of his own. And the latter opinion can stand if only that in which eminent worth appears is called purchase.

25. Samuel Pufendorf: *The Whole Duty of Man* (1673)[1]

After *Property* was introduced into the World, all Things not being of the same *Nature*, nor affording the same *Help* to Human Necessities; and every Man not being sufficiently provided with such Things as were necessary for his Use and Service, it was early brought into Practice among Men to make *mutual Exchanges* of one Thing for another. But because it very often happened, that Things of a *different Nature* and *Use* were to be transferred; lest either Party should be a Loser by such *Exchanging*, it was necessary, by a common Agreement or Consent among themselves, to assign to Things a certain *Quantity* or *Standard*, by which those *Things* might be compar'd and reduced to a Balance between each other. The same also obtained as to *Actions*, which it was not thought good should be done *gratis* by one Man for another. And this *Quantity* or *Standard* is that which we call *Price* or *Value*.

This *Price* is divided into *Common* and *Eminent*; the *First* is in *Things* or *Actions* which come within the compass of *ordinary Commerce*, according as they afford either Usefulness or Delight to Mankind. But the other is in *Money*, as it virtually contains the Value of all Things and Works, and is understood to give them their common Estimate.

The natural Ground of the *Common Value*, is that *Fitness* which any Thing or Action has for supplying, either mediately or immediately, the *Necessities* of Human Life, and rendring the same more *easie* or more *comfortable*. Hence it is we call those Things which are not of any *Use* to us, *Things of no Value*. There are nevertheless some *Things most useful* to Human Life, which are not understood to fall under any *determinate Price* or *Value*; either because they are or ought to be exempted from Dominion and Property, or because they are not capable of being exchanged, and therefore cannot be traded for; or else, because in Commerce they are not otherwise regarded than as Appendages to be supposed of course to belong to another Thing. Besides also, when the Law of God or Man places some Actions above the Reach of Commerce, or forbids that they should be done for a Reward, it is to be understood that the same Laws have set them without the Bounds of Price or Valuation. Thus the Upper Regions of the *Air*, the *Sky*, and the *Heavenly Bodies*, and even the vast *Ocean* are exempt from Human Property, so that no Rate or Value can be put upon them. So there is no Rate or Price to be set upon a *Freeman*, because Freemen come not within the Compass of Commerce. Thus, the Lying open to the Sun, a clear and wholesome Air, a pleasant Prospect to the Eye, the Winds, Shades, and the like, consider'd separately in themselves, bear no Price, because they cannot be enjoy'd and purchas'd separately from the Lands they belong to; but yet of what Moment they are in raising the Value of Lands and Tenements to be purchas'd, no Man is ignorant. So likewise 'tis unlawful to set any Rate or Price on *Sacred Actions*, to which any moral Effect

---

[1] Translated by Andrew Tooke.

is assign'd by *Divine Institution*; which Crime is call'd *Simony*. And it is great Wickedness in a *Judge* to expose *Justice* to Sale.

Now there are various Reasons, why the Price of one and the same Thing should be *increas'd* or *diminish'd*, and why one Thing should be preferr'd before another, though it may seem to be of *equal* or *greater Use* to Human Life. For here the *Necessity* of the Thing, or its extraordinary *Usefulness*, is not always regarded; but, on the contrary, we see those Things are of the least Account or Value, without which Human Life is least able to subsist; and therefore, not without the singular Providence of Almighty God, *Nature* has been very *bountiful* in providing *plentiful* Store of those Things. But the *Rarity* or *Scarceness* of Things conduces chiefly to the inhansing their Value; which is the more look'd upon, when they are brought from remote Countries. And hence the wanton Luxury of Mankind has set *extravagant Rates* upon many Things which Human Life might very well be without; for Instance, upon *Pearls* and *Jewels*. But the Prices of Things, which are of *daily Use*, are then chiefly rais'd when the *Scarcity* is join'd with the *Necessity* or *Want* of them. The Prices of *Artificial Things*, besides their *Scarceness*, are for the most Part inhans'd by the ingenious *Contrivance* and Curiosity of *Art*, that is seen in them, and sometimes by the Fame and Renown of the Artificer, the Difficulty of the Work, the Want of Artists in that Way, and the like. The Prices of *Works* and *Actions* are rais'd by their Difficulty, Neatness, Usefulness, Necessity, by the Scarcity, Dignity, and Ingenuity of the *Authors* of them; and lastly, by the Esteem and Reputation which that Art has gotten in the World. The *Contrary* to these are wont to *diminish* the Price of Things. Sometimes again, there may be some certain Thing, which is not *generally* much esteem'd, but only by some *particular Persons*, out of a peculiar Inclination; for Example, because he, from whom we had it, is mightily *belov'd* by us, and that it was given as a *Token* of his particular Affection to us; or because we have been *accustom'd* thereto, or because it is a *Remembrancer* of some remarkable Accident, or because by the Help thereof, we have escap'd any extraordinary *Danger*, or because the Thing was made by *Our selves*. And this is called *The Estimate of singular Affection*.

But there are other Circumstances likewise to be consider'd in *stating* the Rates and Prices of *particular Things*. And among those indeed, who live in a Natural Independance on any other, the Prices of particular Things are determin'd no otherwise, than by the *Will* of the *Persons contracting*; since they are intirely at their own Liberty to make over or to purchase what they please, nor can they be controlled in their Dealings by any superior Authority. But in States and Governments the *Prices of Things* are determin'd two several Ways: The *First* is by an *Order* from the *Magistrate*, or some *particular Law*; the *Second* is by the common *Estimate* and *Judgment* of Men, or according as the *Market* goes, together with the *Consent* and *Agreement* of those who contract among themselves. The former of these by some is call'd the *Legal*, the other the *Vulgar Price*. Where the *Legal Rate* is fix'd for the sake of the *Buyers*, as it is for the most part, there it is not lawful for the *Sellers* to exact *more*; though they are not forbidden, if they will, to take *less*. So where the Rate of any *Labour* or *Work* is tax'd by the Publick Magistrate for the sake of those who have Occasion to hire, it is not lawful for the Workman to demand *more*, though he be not prohibited to take *less*.

But the *Vulgar* Price, which is not fix'd by the Laws, admits of a certain *Latitude*, within the Compass whereof more or less may be, and often is, either taken or given, according to the *Agreement* of the Persons *dealing*; which yet for the most part, goes according to the Custom of the *Market*. Where commonly there is Regard had to the Trouble and Charges which the

Tradesmen generally are at, in the bringing home and managing their Commodities, and also after what manner they are bought or sold, whether by Wholesale or Retail. Sometimes also on a sudden the Common Price is alter'd by reason of the *Plenty* or *Scarcity* of *Buyers*, *Money*, or the *Commodity*. For the *Scarcity* of Buyers and of Money, (which on any particular Account may happen) and the Plenty of the Commodity, may be a Means of *diminishing* the Price thereof. On the other hand, the Plenty of Buyers and of Money, and the Scarcity of the Commodity, *inhanses* the same. Thus as the Value of a Commodity is lessen'd, if it *wants* a Buyer, so the Price is augmented when the Possessor is solicited to sell what otherwise he would not have parted with. Lastly, it is likewise to be regarded, whether the Person offers *ready Money*, or desires *Time* for Payment; for Allowance of *Time* is Part of the *Price*.

But after Mankind degenerated from their primitive Simplicity, and introduced into the World several, it was not easie for every one to become Master of That which another would be willing to take in Exchange, or which might be of equal Value to the kinds of Gaining, it was easily discern'd, that that *Common* and *Vulgar* Price was not sufficient for the dispatching the Business of Men, and for the carrying on of Commerce, which then daily increas'd. For at first all Kind of Trading consisted only in *Exchanging* and *Bartering*, and the Labours of others could no otherwise be valued than by Work for Work, or some Thing given in Hand for Recompence. But after Men began to desire so many several Things for *Convenience* or *Pleasure*, it was not easie for every one to become Master of That which another would be willing to take in Exchange, or which might be of equal Value to the Things he wanted from him. And in civiliz'd States or Societies, where the Inhabitants are distinguish' into *several Stations*, there is an absolute Necessity there should be different Degrees and Sorts of Men, which, if that simple and plain Way of *bartering* of *Things* and *Works* had been still in Use, could not, or at least, not without great Difficulty, support themselves. Hence most Nations, which were pleased with a more sumptuous Way of Living, thought fit, by Publick Consent, to set an *Eminent Price* or *Value* upon some Certain Thing, whereby the *Common* and *Vulgar* Prices of other Things should be measured, and wherein the same should be virtually contain'd. So that by Means of this *Thing*, any one may purchase to himself whatsoever is to be sold, and easily manage and carry on any Kind of Traffick and Bargain.

For this purpose, most Nations chose to make use of the nobler Kind of *Metals*, and such as were not very Common; because these being of a very compacted Substance, they cannot easily be *worn out*, and admit of being *divided* into many minute Parts; nor are they less proper to be *kept* and *handled*; and for the *Rarity* of 'em are equivalent to many other Things. Altho' sometimes for Necessity, and by some Nations for Want of *Metals*, other *Things* have been made Use of instead of *Money*.

Moreover, in Communities, it is only in the Power of the Chief Magistrates to assign the *Value* of *Money*; and thence *Publick Stamps* are wont to be put upon them. Nevertheless, in the assigning thereof, respect is to be had to the Common Estimate of the *Neighbouring Nations*, or of those with whom we have any *Traffick* or *Commerce*. For otherwise, if the State should set *too high a Value* on their Money, or if they should not give it a *just* and *true Alloy*, all Commerce with Foreign Nations, which could not be carried on by *Exchange* or *Barter* alone, would be at a Stand. And for this very Reason, the Value of Money is not rashly to be *alter'd*, unless a very great Necessity of State require it. Tho' as Gold and Silver grow more plentiful, the *Value* of *Money*, in Comparison to the Price of Land, and Things thereon depending, is wont, as it were insensibly and of its self, to grow lower.

26. John Locke: *Some Considerations of the Consequences of the Lowering of Interest, and Raising the Value of Money* (1691)

Sir,

I have so little concern in paying or receiving of 'interest', that were I in no more danger to be misled by inability and ignorance, than I am to be biassed by interest and inclination, I might hope to give you a very perfect and clear account of the consequences of a law to reduce interest to 4 per cent. But, since you are pleased to ask my opinion, I shall endeavour fairly to state this matter of use, with the best of my skill.

The first thing to be considered is, 'Whether the price of the hire of money can be regulated by law?' And to that I think, generally speaking, one may say, it is manifest it cannot. For since it is impossible to make a law, that shall hinder a man from giving away his money or estate to whom he pleases, it will be impossible, by any contrivance of law, to hinder men, skilled in the power they have over their own goods, and the ways of conveying them to others, to purchase money to be lent them, at what rate soever their occasions shall make it necessary for them to have it; for it is to be remembered, that no man borrows money, or pays use, out of mere pleasure: it is the want of money drives men to that trouble and charge of borrowing; and proportionably to this want, so will every one have it, whatever price it cost him. Wherein the skilful, I say, will always so manage it, as to avoid the prohibition of your law, and keep out of its penalty, do what you can. What then will be the unavoidable consequences of such a law?

1. It will make the difficulty of borrowing and lending much greater, whereby trade (the foundation of riches) will be obstructed.
2. It will be a prejudice to none, but those who most need assistance and help; I mean widows and orphans, and others uninstructed in the arts and management of more skilful men, whose estates lying in money, they will be sure, especially orphans, to have no more profit of their money, than what interest the law barely allows.
3. It will mightily increase the advantage of bankers and scriveners, and other such expert brokers, who, skilled in the arts of putting out money, according to the true and natural value, which the present state of trade, money, and debts, shall always raise interest to, they will infallibly get what the true value of interest shall be above the legal; for men, finding the convenience of lodging their money in hands, where they can be sure of it, at short warning, the ignorant and lazy will be forwardest to put it into these men's hands, who are known willingly to receive it, and where they can, readily have the whole, or part, upon any sudden occasion, that may call for it.
4. I fear I may reckon it as one of the probable consequences of such a law, that it is likely to cause great perjury in the nation; a crime, than which nothing is more carefully to be pre-

vented by law-makers, not only by penalties, that shall attend apparent and proved perjury, but by avoiding and lessening, as much as may be, the temptations to it; for where those are strong (as they are, where men shall swear for their own advantage) there the fear of penalties to follow will have little restraint, especially if the crime be hard to be proved; all which, I suppose, will happen in this case, where ways will be found out to receive money upon other pretences than for use, to evade the rule and rigour of the law: and there will be secret trusts and collusions amongst men, that though they may be suspected, can never be proved, without their own confession.

...

But that law cannot keep men from taking more use than you set (the want of money being that alone which regulates its price) will perhaps appear, if we consider how hard it is to set a price upon wine, or silks, or other unnecessary commodities: but how impossible it is to set a rate upon victuals, in a time of famine; for money being a universal commodity, and as necessary to trade as food is to life, every body must have it, at what rate they can get it; and unavoidably pay dear, when it is scarce; and debts, no less than trade, have made borrowing in fashion. The bankers are a clear instance of this: for some years since, the scarcity of money having made it in England worth really more than 6 per cent, most of those that had not the skill to let it for more than 6 per cent, and secure themselves from the penalty of the law, put it in the bankers' hands, where it was ready at their call, when they had an opportunity of greater improvement; so that the rate you set, profits not the lenders; and very few of the borrowers, who are fain to pay the price for money, that commodity would bear, were it left free; and the gain is only to the banker: and should you lessen the use to 4 per cent, the merchant or tradesman that borrows would not have it one jot cheaper than he has now; but probably these two ill effects would follow: first, that he would pay dearer; and, second, that there would be less money left in the country to drive the trade: for the bankers, paying at most but 4 per cent and receiving from 6–10 per cent or more, at that low rate could be content to have more money lie dead by them, than now, when it is higher; by which means there would be less money stirring in trade, and a greater scarcity, which would raise it upon the borrower by this monopoly; and what a part of our treasure their skill and management, joined with others' laziness, or want of skill, is apt to draw into their hands, is to be known by those vast sums of money they were found to owe, at shutting up of the Exchequer: and though it be very true, yet it is almost beyond belief, that one private goldsmith of London should have credit, upon his single security (being usually nothing but a note, under one of his servants' hands) for above eleven hundred thousand pounds at once. The same reasons, I suppose, will still keep on the same trade; and when you have taken it down by law to that rate, nobody will think of having more than 4 per cent of the banker; though those who have need of money, to employ it in trade, will not then, any more than now, get it under 5 or 6, or as some pay, 7 or 8. And if they had then, when the law permitted men to make more profit of their money, so large a proportion of the cash of the nation in their hands, who can think but that, by this law, it should be more driven into Lombard-street now? There being many now, who lend them at 4 or 5 per cent who would not lend to others at 6. It would therefore, perhaps, bring down the rate of money to the borrower, and certainly distribute it better to the advantage of trade in the country, if the legal use were kept pretty near to the natural; (by natural use, I mean that rate of money, which the present scarcity of it makes it naturally at, upon an equal distribution of it) for then men, being licensed by the law to take near the full natural use, will not be forward to carry it to London, to put it into the banker's hands; but will lend it to their neighbours in the country, where it is convenient for trade it should be. But, if you lessen the rate of use, the lender, whose interest it is to keep up the rate of money, will rather lend it to the banker, at the legal interest, than to the tradesman, or gentleman, who, when the law is broken, shall be sure to pay the full natural interest, or more; because of the engrossing by the banker, as well as the risque in transgressing the law: whereas, were the natural use, suppose 7 per cent and the legal 6; first, the owner would not venture the penalty of the law, for the gaining 1 in 7, that being the utmost his money would yield: nor would the banker venture to borrow, where his gains would be but 1 per cent, nor the moneyed man lend him what he could make better profit of legally at home. All the danger lies in this; that your trade should suffer, if your being-behind hand has made the natural use so high, that your tradesman cannot live upon his labour, but that your rich neighbours will so undersell you, that the return you make will not amount to pay the use, and afford a livelihood. There is no way to recover from this, but by a general frugality and industry; or by being masters of the trade of some commodity, which the world must have from you at your rate, because it cannot be otherwhere supplied.

Now, I think, the natural interest of money is raised two ways: first, when the money of a country is but little, in proportion to the debts of the inhabitants, one amongst another. For, suppose ten thousand pounds were sufficient to manage the trade of Bermudas, and that the ten first planters carried over twenty thousand pounds, which they lent to the several tradesmen and inhabitants of the country, who living above their gains, had spent ten thousand pounds of this money, and it were gone out of the island; it is evident, that, should all the creditors at once call in their money, there would be a great scarcity of money, when that, employed in trade, must be taken out of the tradesmen's hands to pay debts; or else the debtors want money, and be exposed to their creditors, and so interest will be high. But this seldom happening, that all, or the greatest part, of the creditors do at once call for their money, unless it be in some great and general danger, is less and seldomer felt than the following, unless where the debts of the people are grown to a greater proportion; for that, constantly causing more borrowers than there can be lenders, will make money scarce, and consequently interest high. Second, that, which constantly raises the natural interest of money, is, when money is little, in proportion to the trade of a country. For in trade every body calls for money, according as he wants it, and this disproportion is always felt. For, if Englishmen owed in all but one million, and there were millions of money in England, the money would be well enough proportioned to the debts: but, if two millions were necessary to carry on the trade, there would be a million wanting, and the price of money would be raised, as it is of any other commodity in a market, where the merchandize will not serve half the customers, and there are two buyers for one seller.

It is in vain, therefore, to go about effectually to reduce the price of interest by a law; and you may as rationally hope to set a fixed rate upon the hire of houses, or ships, as of money. He that wants a vessel, rather than lose his market, will not stick to have it at the market-rate, and find ways to do it with security to the owner, though the rate were limited by law: and he that wants money, rather than lose his voyage, or his trade, will pay the natural interest for it; and submit to such ways of conveyance, as shall keep the lender out of the reach of the law. So that your act, at best, will serve only to increase the arts of lending, but not at all lessen the charge of the borrower: he, it is likely, shall, with more trouble, and going farther about, pay also the more for his money; unless you intend to break in only upon mortgages and contracts already made, and (which is not to be supposed) by law, *post factum*, void bargains lawfully made, and give to Richard what is Peter's due, for no other reason, but because one was borrower, and the other lender.

But, supposing the law reached the intention of the promoters of it; and that this act be so contrived, that it fixed the natural price of money, and hindered its being, by any body, lent at a higher use than 4 per cent, which is plain it cannot: let us, in the next place, see what will be the consequences of it.

1. It will be a loss to widows, orphans, and all those who have their estates in money, one-third of their estates; which will be a very hard case upon a great number of people: and it is warily to be considered, by the wisdom of the nation, whether they will thus, at one blow, fine and impoverish a great and innocent part of the people, who having their estates in money, have as much right to make as much of the money as it is worth (for more they cannot) as the landlord has to let his land for as much as it will yield. To fine men one-third of their estates, without any crime, or offence committed, seems very hard.
2. As it will be a considerable loss and injury to the moneyed man, so it will be no advantage at all to the kingdom. For, so trade be not cramped, and exportation of our native commodities and manufactures not hindered, it will be no matter to the kingdom, who amongst ourselves gets or loses: only common charity teaches, that those should be most taken care of by the law, who are least capable of taking care for themselves.
3. It will be a gain to the borrowing merchant. For if he borrow at 4 per cent, and his returns be 12 per cent, he will have 8 per cent, and the lender 4; whereas now they divide the profit equally at 6 per cent. But this neither gets, nor loses, to the kingdom, in your trade, supposing the merchant and lender to be both Englishmen; only it will, as I have said, transfer a third part of the moneyed man's estate, who had nothing else to live on, into the merchant's pocket; and that without any merit in the one, or transgression in the other. Private men's interests ought not thus to be neglected, nor sacrificed to any thing, but the manifest advantage of the public. But, in this case, it will be quite the contrary. This loss to the moneyed men will be a prejudice to trade: since it will discourage lending at such a disproportion of profit to risque; as we shall see more by and by, when we come to consider of what consequence it is to encourage lending, that so none of the money of the nation may lie dead, and thereby prejudice trade.
4. It will hinder trade. For, there being a certain proportion of money necessary for driving such a proportion of trade, so much money of this as lies still, lessens so much of the trade. Now it cannot be rationally expected, but that, where the venture is great and the gains small, (as it is in lending in England, upon low interest) many will choose rather to hoard up their money, than venture it abroad, on such terms. This will be a loss to the kingdom, and such a loss, as, here in England, ought chiefly to be looked after: for, we having no mines, nor any other way of getting, or keeping of riches amongst us, but by trade; so much of our trade as is lost, so much of our riches must necessarily go with it; and the over-balancing of trade, between us and our neighbours, must inevitably carry away our money, and quickly leave us poor and exposed. Gold and silver, though they serve for few, yet they command all the conveniencies of life, and therefore in a plenty of them consist riches.

...

In a country not furnished with mines, there are but two ways of growing rich, either conquest or commerce. By the first the Romans made themselves masters of the riches of the world; but I think that, in our present circumstances, nobody is vain enough to entertain a thought of our reaping the profits of the world with our swords, and making the spoil and tribute of vanquished nations the fund for the supply of the charges of the government, with an overplus for the wants, and equally craving luxury, and fashionable vanity of the people.

Commerce, therefore, is the only way left to us, either for riches, or subsistence: for this the advantages of our situation as well as the industry and inclination of our people, bold and skillful at sea, do naturally fit us: by this the nation of England has been hitherto supported, and trade left almost to itself, and assisted only by the natural advantages above-mentioned, brought us in plenty of riches, and always set this kingdom in a rank equal, if not superior to any of its neighbours; and would no doubt, without any difficulty, have continued it so, if the more enlarged and better understood interest of trade, since the improvement of navigation, had not raised us many rivals; and the amazing politics of some late reigns let in other competitors with us for the sea, who will be sure to seize to themselves whatever parts of trade our mismanagement, or want of money, shall let slip out of our hands: and when it is once lost, it will be too late to hope, by a mistimed care, easily to retrieve it again. For the currents of trade, like those of waters, make themselves channels, out of which they are afterwards as hard to be diverted, as rivers that have worn themselves deep within their banks.

Trade, then, is necessary to the producing of riches, and money necessary to the carrying on of trade. This is principally to be looked after, and taken care of. For if this be neglected, we shall in vain by contrivances amongst ourselves, and shuffling the little money we have, from one another's hands, endeavour to prevent our wants: decay of trade will quickly waste all the remainder; and then the landed-man, who thinks, perhaps, by the fall of interest to raise the value of his land, will find himself cruelly mistaken; when the money being gone, (as it will be, if our trade be not kept up) he can get neither farmer to rent, nor purchaser to buy his land. Whatsoever, therefore, hinders the lending of money, injures trade; and so the reducing of money to 4 per cent, which will discourage men from lending, will be a loss to the kingdom, in stopping so much of the current money, which turns the wheels of trade. But all this upon a supposition, that the lender and borrower are both Englishmen.

...

The necessity of a certain proportion of money to trade (I conceive) lies in this, that money, in its circulation, driving the several wheels of trade, whilst it keeps in that channel (for some of it will unavoidably be drained into standing pools) is all shared between the landholder, whose land affords the materials; the labourer, who works them; the broker, that is, the merchant and shopkeeper, who distributes them to those that want them; and the consumer who spends them. Now money is necessary to all these sorts of men, as serving both for counters and for pledges and so carrying with it even reckoning, and security, that he that receives it shall have the same value for it again, of other things that he wants, whenever he pleases. The one of these it does by its stamp and denomination; the other by its intrinsic value, which is its quantity. For mankind, having consented to put an imaginary value upon gold and silver, by reason of their durableness, scarcity, and not being very liable to be counterfeited, have made them, by general consent, the common pledges, whereby men are assured, in exchange for them, to receive equally valuable things, to those they parted with, for any quantity of these metals; by which means it comes to pass, that the intrinsic value, regarded in these metals, made the common barter, is nothing but the quantity which men give or receive of them; for they having, as money, no other value, but as pledges to procure what one wants or desires, and they procuring what we want or desire only by their quantity, it is evident that the intrinsic value of silver and gold, used in commerce, is nothing but their quantity.

...

To return to the business in hand, and show the necessity of a proportion of money to trade. Every man must have at least so much money, or so timely recruits, as may in hand, or in a short distance of time, satisfy his creditor who supplies him with the necessaries of life, or of his trade. For nobody has any longer these necessary supplies than he has money, or credit, which is nothing else but an assurance of money, in some short time. So that it is requisite to trade, that there should be so much money as to keep up the landholder's, labourer's, and broker's, credit: and therefore ready money must be constantly exchanged for wares and labour, or follow within a short time after.

This shows the necessity of some proportion of money to trade: but what proportion that is, is hard to determine; because it depends not barely on the quantity of money, but the quickness of its circulation. The very same shilling may, at one time, pay twenty men in twenty days: at another, rest in the same hands one hundred days together. This makes it impossible exactly to estimate the quantity of money needful in trade; but, to make some probable guess, we are to consider how much money it is necessary to suppose must rest constantly in each man's hands, as requisite to the carrying on of trade.

There is another seeming consequence of the reducing of money to a low price, which at first sight has such an appearance of truth in it, that I have known it to impose upon very able men, and I guess it has no small influence, at this time, in promoting this alteration; and that is, that the lowering of interest will raise the value of all other things in proportion. For money being the counter-balance to all other things purchaseable by it, and lying, as it were, in the opposite scale of commerce, it looks like a natural consequence, that as much as you take off from the value of money, so much you add to the price of other things which are exchanged for it; the raising of the price of any thing being no more but the addition to its value in respect of money, or, which is all one, lessening the value of money. For example: should the value of gold be brought down to that of silver, one hundred guineas would purchase little more corn, wool, or land, than one hundred shillings; and so, the value of money being brought lower, say they, the price of other things will rise, and the falling of interest from six pounds to four pounds per cent is taking away so much of the price of money, and so consequently lessening its value.

The mistake of this plausible way of reasoning will be easily discovered, when we consider that the measure of the value of money, in proportion to any thing purchaseable by it, is the quantity of the ready money we have in comparison with the quantity of that thing, and its vent; or, which amounts to the same thing, the price of any commodity rises or falls, by the proportion of the number of buyers and sellers: this rule holds universally in all things that are to be bought and sold, bating now and then an extravagant fancy of some particular person, which never amounts to so considerable a part of trade, as to make any thing in the account worthy to be thought an exception to this rule.

The vent of any thing depends upon its necessity or usefulness; as convenience, or opinion, guided by fancy, or fashion, shall determine.

The vent of any commodity comes to be increased, or decreased, as a greater part of the running cash of the nation is designed to be laid out, by several people at the same time, rather in that than another; as we see in the change of fashions.

I shall begin first with the necessaries, or conveniencies of life, and the consumable commodities subservient thereunto; and show, that the value of money, in respect of those, depends only on the plenty or scarcity of money, in proportion to the plenty and scarcity of those things; and not on what interest shall, by necessity, law, or contract, be at that time laid on the borrowing of money; and then afterwards I shall show that the same holds in land.

There is nothing more confirmed, by daily experience, than that men give any portion of money, for whatsoever is absolutely necessary, rather than go without it. And in such things, the scarcity of them alone makes their prices. As for example: let us suppose half an ounce of silver, or half a crown now in England, is worth a bushel of wheat: but should there be next year a great scarcity of wheat in England, and a proportionable want of all other food, five ounces of silver would, perhaps, in exchange purchase but one bushel of wheat: so that money would be then nine-tenths less worth in respect of food, though at the same value it was before, in respect of other things, that kept their former proportion, in their quantity and consumption.

...

The fall, therefore, or rise of interest, making immediately, by its change, neither more nor less land, money, or any sort of commodity in England, than there was before, alters not at all the value of money, in reference to commodities. Because the measure of that is only the quantity and vent, which are not immediately changed by the change of interest. So far as the change of interest conduces, in trade, to the bringing in, or carrying out money, or commodities, and so in time to varying their proportions here in England, from what it was before; so far the change of interest, as all other things that promote or hinder trade, may alter the value of money, in reference to commodities. But that is not in this place to be considered.

2. Money has a value, as it is capable, by exchange, to procure us the necessaries or conveniencies of life, and in this it has the nature of a commodity; only with this difference, that it serves us commonly by its exchange, never almost by its consumption. But though the use men make of money be not in its consumption, it has not at all a more standing, settled value, in exchange with any other thing, than any other commodity has; but a more known one, and better fixed by name, number, and weight, to enable us to reckon what the proportion of scarcity and vent of one commodity is to another. For supposing, as before, that half an ounce of silver would last year exchange for one bushel of wheat, or for 15 lb weight of lead; if this year wheat be ten times scarcer, and lead in the same quantity to its vent as it was, is it not evident, that half an ounce of silver will still exchange for 15 lb of lead, though it will exchange but for one-tenth of a bushel of wheat? And he that has use of lead will as soon take 15 lb weight of lead as half an ounce of silver, for one-tenth of a bushel of wheat, and no more. So that if you say, that money now is nine-tenths less worth than it was the former year, you must say so of lead too, and all other things, that keep the same proportion to money which they had before. The variation, indeed, is first and most taken notice of in money: because that is the universal measure by which people reckon, and used by every body in the valuing of all things. For calling that half an ounce of silver half a crown, they speak properly, and are readily understood, when they say, half a crown, or two shillings and six-pence, will now buy one-tenth of a bushel of wheat, but do not say, that 15 lb of lead will now buy one-tenth of a bushel of wheat, because it is not generally used to this sort of reckoning; nor do they say, lead is less

worth than it was, though, in respect of wheat, lead be nine-tenths worse than it was, as well as silver; only by the tale of shillings we are better enabled to judge of it: because these are measures, whose ideas by constant use are settled in every Englishman's mind.

This, I suppose, is the true value of money, when it passes from one to another, in buying and selling; where it runs the same changes of higher, or lower, as any other commodity doth: for one equal quantity whereof you shall receive in exchange more or less of another commodity, at one time, than you do at another. For a farmer that carries a bushel of wheat to market, and a labourer that carries half a crown, shall find that the money of one, as well as corn of the other, shall at some times purchase him more or less leather, or salt, according as they are in greater plenty, and scarcity, one to another. So that in exchanging coined silver for any other commodity, (which is buying and selling) the same measure governs the proportion you receive, as if you exchanged lead, or wheat, or any other commodity. That which regulates the price, that is, the quantity given for money (which is called buying and selling) for another commodity (which is called bartering) is nothing else but their quantity in proportion to their vent. If then lowering of use makes not your silver more in specie, or your wheat or other commodities less, it will not have any influence at all to make it exchange for less of wheat or any other commodity, than it will have on lead, to make it exchange for less wheat, or any other commodity.

…

He that will justly estimate the value of any thing, must consider its quantity in proportion to its vent, for this alone regulates the price. The value of any thing, compared with itself or with a standing measure, is greater, as its quantity is less in proportion to its vent: but, in comparing it, or exchanging it with any other thing, the quantity and vent of that thing too must be allowed for, in the computation of their value. But, because the desire of money is constantly almost everywhere the same, its vent varies very little, but as its greater scarcity enhances its price, and increases the scramble: there being nothing else that does easily supply the want of it: the lessening its quantity, therefore, always increases its price, and makes an equal portion of it exchange for a greater of any other thing. Thus it comes to pass, that there is no manner of settled proportion between the value of an ounce of silver and any other commodity: for, either varying its quantity in that country, or the commodity changing its quantity in proportion to its vent, their respective values change, that is, less of one will barter for more of the other: though, in the ordinary way of speaking, it is only said, that the price of the commodity, not of the money, is changed. For example, half an ounce of silver in England will exchange sometimes for a whole bushel of wheat, sometimes for half, sometimes but a quarter, and this it does equally, whether by use it be apt to bring in to the owner six in the hundred of its own weight per annum, or nothing at all: it being only the change of the quantity of wheat to its vent, supposing we have still the same sum of money in the kingdom; or else the change of the quantity of our money in the kingdom, supposing the quantity of wheat, in respect to its vent, be the same too, that makes the change in the price of wheat. For if you alter the quantity, or vent, on either side, you presently alter the price, but no other way in the world.

…

I have met with patrons of 4 per cent who (amongst many other fine things they tell us of) affirm, 'That if interest were reduced to 4 per cent then some men would borrow money at this low rate, and pay their debts; others would borrow more than they now do, and improve their land; others would borrow more, and employ it in trade and manufacture'. Gilded words indeed, were there any thing substantial in them! These men talk as if they meant to show us not only the wisdom, but the riches of Solomon, and would make gold and silver as common as stones in the street: but at last, I fear, it will be but wit without money, and I wish it amount to that. It is without question, that could the countryman and the tradesman take up money cheaper than now they do, every man would be forward to borrow, and desire that he might have other men's money to employ to his advantage. I confess, those who contend for 4 per cent have found out a way to set men's mouths a watering for money at that rate, and to increase the number of borrowers in England, if any body can imagine it would be an advantage to increase them. But to answer all their fine projects, I have but this one short question to ask them: Will 4 per cent increase the number of the lenders? If it will not, as any man at the very first hearing will shrewdly suspect it will not, then all the plenty of money, these conjurers bestow upon us, for improvement of land, paying of debts, and advancement of trade, is but like the gold and silver which old women believe other conjurers bestow sometimes, by whole lapfuls, on poor credulous girls, which, when they bring to the light, is found to be nothing but withered leaves; and the possessors of it are still as much in want of money as ever.

Indeed, I grant it would be well for England, and I wish it were so, that the plenty of money were so great amongst us, that every man could borrow as much as he could use in trade for 4 per cent; nay, that men could borrow as much as they could employ for 6 per cent. But even at that rate, the borrowers already are far more than the lenders. Why else doth the merchant, upon occasion, pay 6 per cent and often above that rate, for brokerage? And why doth the country gentleman of 1000*l.* per annum find it so difficult, with all the security he can bring, to take up 1000? All which proceeds from the scarcity of money and bad security; two causes which will not be less powerful to hinder borrowing, after the lowering of interest; and I do not see how any one can imagine that reducing use to 4 per cent should abate their force, or how lessening the reward of the lender, without diminishing his risk, should make him more forward and ready to lend. So that these men, whilst they talk that at 4 per cent men would take up and employ more money to the public advantage, do but pretend to multiply the number of borrowers among us, of which it is certain we have too many already. While they thus set men a longing for the golden days of 4 per cent, methinks they use the poor indigent debtor, and needy tradesman, as I have seen prating jackdaws do sometimes their young, who, kawing and fluttering about the nest, set all their young ones a gaping, but, having nothing in their empty mouths but noise and air, leave them as hungry as before.

It is true these men have found out by a cunning project how, by the restraint of a law, to make the price of money one-third cheaper, and then they tell John a Nokes that he shall have 10,000*l.* of it to employ in merchandize, or clothing; and John a Stiles shall have 20,000*l.* more to pay his debts; and so distribute this money as freely as Diego did his legacies, which they are to have, even where they can get them. But till these men can instruct the forward borrowers where they shall be furnished, they have perhaps done something to increase men's desire, but not made money one jot easier to come by; and, till they do that, all this sweet jingling of money, in their discourses, goes just to the tune of 'If all the world were oatmeal'. Methinks these undertakers, whilst they have put men in hopes of borrowing more plentifully, at easier rates, for the supply of their wants and trades, had done better to have bethought themselves of a way how men need not borrow upon use at all: for this would be much more advantageous, and altogether as feasible. It is as easy to distribute twenty pair of shoes amongst thirty men, if they pay nothing for them at all, as if they paid 4*s.* a pair; ten of them (notwithstanding the statute-rate should be reduced from 6*s*. to 4*s*. a pair) will be necessitated to sit still barefoot, as much as if they were to pay nothing for shoes at all. Just so it is in a country that wants money in proportion to trade. It is as easy to contrive how every man shall be supplied with what money he needs (i.e. can employ in improvement of land, paying his debts, and returns of his trade) for nothing, as for 4 per cent. Either we have already more money than the owners will lend, or we have not. If part of the money, which is now in England, will not be let at the rate interest is at present at, will men be more ready to lend, and borrowers be furnished for all those brave purposes more plentifully, when money is brought to 4 per cent? If people do already lend all the money they have, above their own occasions, whence are those who will borrow more at 4 per cent to be supplied? Or is there such plenty of money, and scarcity of borrowers, that there needs the reducing of interest to 4 per cent to bring men to take it?

...

OF RAISING OUR COIN

Being now upon the consideration of interest and money, give me leave to say one word more on this occasion, which may not be wholly unseasonable at this time. I hear a talk up and down of raising our money, as a means to retain our wealth, and keep our money from being carried away. I wish those that use the phrase of raising our money had some clear notion annexed to it; and that then they would examine, 'Whether, that being true, it would at all serve to those ends for which it is proposed?'

The raising of money, then, signifies one of these two things; either raising the value of our money, or raising the denomination of our coin.

The raising the value of money, or any thing else, is nothing but the making a less quantity of it exchange for any other thing than would have been taken for it before; for example, If 5*s*. will exchange for, or (as we call it) buy a bushel of wheat; if you can make 4*s*. buy another bushel of the same wheat, it is plain the value of your money is raised, in respect of wheat, one-fifth. But thus nothing can raise or fall the value of your money, but the proportion of its plenty, or scarcity, in proportion to the plenty, scarcity, or vent of any other commodity with which you compare it, or for which you would exchange it. And thus silver, which makes the intrinsic value of money, compared with itself, under any stamp or denomination of the same or different countries, cannot be raised. For an ounce of silver, whether in pence, groats, or crown-pieces, stivers, or ducatoons, or in bullion, is, and always eternally will be, of equal value to any other ounce of silver, under what stamp or denomination soever; unless it can be shown that any stamp can add any new or better qualities to one parcel of silver, which another parcel of silver wants. Silver, therefore, being always of equal value to silver, the value of coin, compared with coin, is greater, less, or equal, only as it has more, less, or equal silver in it: and in this respect, you can by no manner of way raise or fall your money...

All then that can be done in this great mystery of raising money, is only to alter the denomination, and call that a crown now, which before, by the law, was but a part of a crown. For example: supposing, according to the standard of our law, 5*s*. or a crown, were to weigh an ounce (as it does now, wanting about 16 grains) whereof one-twelfth were copper, and eleven-twelfths silver (for thereabouts it is) it is plain here, it is the quantity of silver gives the value to it. For let another piece be coined of the same weight, wherein half the silver is taken out, and copper, or other alloy, put into the place, every one knows it will be worth but half as much. For the value of the alloy is so inconsiderable as not to be reckoned. This crown now must be raised, and from henceforth our crown-pieces coined one-twentieth lighter; which is nothing but changing the denomination, calling that a crown now, which yesterday was but a part, namely nineteen-twentieths of a crown; whereby you have only raised 19 parts to the denomination formerly given to 20. For I think nobody can be so senseless as to imagine that 19 grains or ounces of silver can be raised to the value of 20; or that 19 grains or ounces of silver shall at the same time exchange for, or buy as much corn, oil, or wine, as 20; which is to raise it to the value of 20. For if 19 ounces of silver can be worth 20 ounces of silver, or pay for as much of any other commodity, then 18, 10, or 1 ounce may do the same. For if the abating one-twentieth of the quantity of the silver of any coin, does not lessen its value, the abating nineteen-twentieths of the quantity of the silver of any coin will not abate its value. And so a single three pence, or a single penny, being called a crown, will buy as much spice, or silk, or any other commodity, as a crownpiece, which contains 20 or 60 times as much silver; which is an absurdity so great, that I think nobody will want eyes to see, and sense to disown.

Now this raising your money, or giving a less quantity of silver the stamp and denomination of a greater, may be done in two ways.

1. By raising one species of your money.
2. By raising all your silver coin, at once proportionably; which is the thing, I suppose, now proposed.

1. The raising of one species of your coin, beyond its intrinsic value, is done by coining any one species (which in account bears such a proportion to the other species of your coin) with less silver in it than is required by that value it bears in your money.

For example: a crown with us goes for 60 pence, a shilling for 12 pence, a tester for 6 pence, and a groat for 4 pence; and accordingly, the proportion of silver in each of them, ought to be as 60, 12, 6, and 4. Now, if in the mint there should be coined groats, or testers, that, being of the same alloy with our other money, had but two-thirds of the weight that those species are coined at now; or else, being of the same weight, were so alloyed, as to have one-third of the silver, required by the present standard, changed into copper, and should thus, by law, be made current; (the rest of your silver money being kept to the present standard in weight and fineness) it is plain, those species would be raised one-third part; that passing for 6*d.* which had but the silver of 4*d.* in it; and would be all one, as if a groat should by law be made current for 6*d.* and every 6*d.* in payment pass for 9*d.* This is truly raising these species: but is no more in effect, than if the mint should coin clipped money; and has, besides the cheat that is put by such base, or light money, on every particular man that receives it, that he wants one-third of that real value, which the public ought to secure him, in the money it obliges him to receive, as lawful and current. It has, I say, this great and unavoidable inconvenience to the public, that, besides the opportunity it gives to domestic coiners to cheat you with lawful money, it puts it into the hands of foreigners to fetch away your money, without any commodities for it. For if they find that two-penny weight of silver, marked with a certain impression, shall here in England be equivalent to 3*d.* weight, marked with another impression, they will not fail to stamp pieces of that fashion; and so importing that base and low coin, will here in England, receive 3*d.* for 2*d.* and quickly carry away your silver in exchange for copper, or barely the charge of coinage.

...

The quantity of silver, that is in each piece, or species of coin, being that which makes its real and intrinsic value, the due proportions of silver ought to be kept in each species, according to the respective rate, set on each of them by law. And, when this is ever varied from, it is but a trick to serve some present occasion; but is always with loss to the country where the trick is played.

2. The other way of raising money is by raising all your silver coin at once, the proportion of a crown, a shilling, and a penny, in reference to one another, being still kept (namely that a shilling shall weigh one-fifth of a crown-piece, and a penny-weight one-twelfth of a shilling, in standard silver) but out of every one of these you abate one-twentieth of the silver they were wont to have in them. If all the species of money be, as it is called, raised, by making each of them to have one-twentieth less of silver in them than formerly, and so your whole money be lighter than it was; these following will be some of the consequences of it.

1. It will rob all creditors of one-twentieth (or 5 per cent) of their debts, and all landlords one-twentieth of their quit-rents for ever; and in all other rents, as far as their former contracts reach, (of 5 per cent) of their yearly income; and this without any advantage to the debtor, or farmer. For he, receiving no more pounds sterling for his land, or commodities, in this new lighter coin, than he should have done of your old and weightier money, gets nothing by it. If you say, yes, he will receive more crown, half-crown, and shilling pieces, for what he now sells for new money, than he should have done, if the money of the old standard had continued; you confess your money is not raised in value, but in denomination: since what your new pieces want in weight must now be made up in their number. But, which way soever this falls, it is certain the public (which most men think ought to be the only reason of changing a settled law, and disturbing the common current course of things) receives not the least profit by it. Nay, as we shall see by and by, it will be a great charge and loss to the kingdom. But this, at first sight, is visible. That in all payments to be received upon precedent contracts, if your money be in effect raised, the receiver will lose 5 per cent. For money having been lent, and leases and other bargains made, when money was of the same weight and fineness that it is now, upon confidence that under the same names of pounds, shillings, and pence, they should receive the same value, that is, the same quantity of silver, by giving the denomination now to less quantities of silver by one-twentieth, you take from them 5 per cent of their due.

When men go to market, to buy any other commodities with their new, but lighter money, they will find 20*s.* of their new money will buy no more of any commodity than 19 would before. For it not being the denomination, but the quantity of silver, that gives the value to any coin, 19 grains, or parts, of silver, however denominated or marked, will no more be worth, or pass for, or buy so much of any other commodity, as 20 grains of silver will, than 19*s.* will pass for 20*s.* If any one thinks a shilling, or a crown in name, has its value from the denomination, and not from the quantity of silver in it, let it be tried; and hereafter let a penny be called a shilling, or a shilling be called a crown. I believe nobody would be content to receive his debts or rents in such money: which, though the law should raise thus, he foresees he should lose eleven-twelfths by the one, and by the other four-fifths of the value he received; and would find his new shilling, which had no more silver in it than one-twelfth of what a shilling had before, would buy him of corn, cloth, or wine, but one-twelfth of what an old shilling would. This is as plainly so in the raising, as you call it, your crown to 5*s.* and 3*d.* or (which is the same thing) making your crown one-twentieth lighter in silver. The only difference is, that the loss is so great (it being eleven-twelfths) that every body sees, and abhors it at first proposal;

but, in the other (it being but one-twentieth, and covered with the deceitful name of raising our money) people do not readily observe it. If it be good to raise the crown-piece this way one-twentieth this week, I suppose it will be as good and profitable to raise it as much again the next week. For there is no reason, why it will not be as good, to raise it again, another one-twentieth, the next week, and so on; wherein, if you proceed but ten weeks successively, you will, by new-year's day next, have every half-crown raised to a crown, to the loss of one-half of people's debts and rents, and the king's revenue, besides the confusion of all your affairs: and, if you please to go on in this beneficial way of raising your money, you may, by the same art, bring a penny-weight of silver to be a crown.

Silver, that is, the quantity of pure silver, separable from the alloy, makes the real value of money. If it does not, coin copper with the same stamp and denomination, and see whether it will be of the same value. I suspect your stamp will make it of no more worth than the copper money of Ireland is, which is its weight in copper, and no more. That money lost so much to Ireland as it passed for above the rate of copper. But yet I think nobody suffered so much by it as he by whose authority it was made current.

If silver give the value, you will say, what need is there then of the charge of coinage? May not men exchange silver by weight for other things; make their bargains and keep their accounts in silver by weight? This might be done, but it has these inconveniencies:

1. The weighing of silver to every one we had occasion to pay it to would be very troublesome, for every one most carry about scales in his pocket.

2. Scales would not do the business; for, in the next place, every one cannot distinguish between fine and mixed silver: so that though he received the full weight, he was not sure he received the full weight of silver, since there might be a mixture of some of the baser metals, which he was not able to discern. Those who have had the care and government of politic societies introduced coinage, as a remedy to those two inconveniencies. The stamp was a warranty of the public, that, under such a denomination, they should receive a piece of such a weight, and such a fineness; that is, they should receive so much silver. And this is the reason why counterfeiting the stamp is made the highest crime, and has the weight of treason laid upon it: because the stamp is the public voucher of the intrinsic value. The royal authority gives the stamp, the law allows and confirms the denomination, and both together give, as it were, the public faith, as a security, that sums of money contracted for under such denominations shall be of such a value, that is, shall have in them so much silver; for it is silver, and not names, that pays debts, and purchases commodities. If therefore I have contracted for twenty crowns, and the law then has required that each of those crowns should have an ounce of silver; it is certain my bargain is not made good; I am defrauded (and whether the public faith be not broken with me, I leave to be considered) if, paying me twenty crowns, the law allots them to be such as have but nineteen-twentieths of the silver they ought to have, and really had in them, when I made my contract.

3. It diminishes all the king's revenue 5 per cent. For though the same number of pounds, shillings, and pence are paid into the exchequer as were wont, yet these names being given to coin that have each of them one-twentieth less of silver in them; and that being not a secret concealed from strangers, no more than from his own subjects; they will sell the king no more pitch, tar, or hemp, for 20s., after the raising your money, than they would before for 19; or, to speak in the ordinary phrase, they will raise their commodities 5 per cent as you have raised your money 5 per cent. And it is well if they stop there. For usually in such change, an outcry

being made of you, lessening your coin, those, who have to deal with your taking the advantage, of the alarm, to secure themselves from any loss by your new trick, raise their price even beyond the par of your lessening your coin.

...

It will possibly be here objected to me, that we see 100*l.* of clipped money, above 5 per cent lighter than the standard, will buy as much corn, cloth, or wine, as 100*l.* in milled money, which is above one-twentieth heavier: whereby it is evident that my rule fails, and that it is not the quantity of silver that gives the value to money, but its stamp and denomination. To which I answer, that men make their estimate and contracts according to the standard, upon supposition they shall receive good and lawful money, which is that of full weight: and so in effect they do, whilst they receive the current money of the country. For since 100*l.* of clipped money will pay a debt of 100*l.* as well as the weightiest milled money; and a new crown out of the mint will pay for no more flesh, fruit, or cloth, than five clipped shillings; it is evident that they are equivalent as to the purchase of any thing here at home, whilst nobody scruples to take five clipped shillings in exchange for a weighty milled crown. But this will be quite otherwise as soon as you change your coin, and (to raise it as you call it) make your money one-twentieth lighter in the mint; for then nobody will any more give an old crown of the former standard for one of the new, than he will now give you 5*s.* and 3*d.* for a crown: for so much then his old crown will yield him at the mint.

Clipped and unclipped money will always buy an equal quantity of any thing else, as long as they will without scruple change one for another. And this makes that the foreign merchant, who comes to sell his goods to you, always counts upon the value of your money, by the silver that is in it, and estimates the quantity of silver by the standard of your mint; though perhaps by reason of clipped or worn money amongst it, any sum that is ordinarily received is much lighter than the standard, and so has less silver in it than what is in a like sum, new coined in the mint. But whilst clipped and weighty money will equally change one for another, it is all one to him, whether he receives his money in clipped money or no, so it be but current. For if he buy other commodities here with his money, whatever sum he contracts for, clipped as well as weighty money equally pays for it. If he would carry away the price of his commodity in ready cash, it is easily changed into weighty money: and then he has not only the sum in tale that he contracted for, but the quantity of silver he expected, for his commodities, according to the standard of our mint. If the quantity of your clipped money be once grown so great, that the foreign merchant cannot (if he has a mind to it) easily get weighty money for it, but having sold his merchandize, and received clipped money, finds a difficulty to procure what is weight for it; he will, in selling his goods, either contract to be paid in weighty money, or else raise the price of his commodity, according to the diminished quantity of silver in your current coin.

...

By this example, in a neighbour country, we may see how our new milled money goes away. When foreign trade imports more than our commodities will pay for, it is certain we must contract debts beyond sea, and those must be paid with money, when either we cannot furnish, or they will not take our goods to discharge them. To have money beyond sea to pay our debts, when our commodities do not raise it, there is no other way but to send it thither. And since a weighty crown costs no more here than a light one, and our coin beyond sea is valued no otherwise than according to the quantity of silver it has in it, whether we send it in specie, or whether we melt it down here to send it in bullion (which is the safest way, as not being prohibited) the weightiest is sure to go. But when so great a quantity of your money is clipped, or so great a part of your weighty money is carried away, that the foreign merchant, or his factor here, cannot have his price paid in weighty money, or such as will easily be changed into it, then every one will see (when men will no longer take five clipped shillings for a milled or weighty crown) that it is the quantity of silver that buys commodities and pays debts, and not the stamp and denomination which is put upon it. And then too it will be seen what a robbery is committed on the public by clipping. Every grain diminished from the just weight of our money is so much loss to the nation, which will one time or other be sensibly felt; and which, if it be not taken care of, and speedily stopped, will, in that enormous course it is now in, quickly, I fear, break out into open ill effects, and at one blow deprive us of a great part (perhaps near one-fourth) of our money. For that will be really the case, when the increase of clipped money makes it hard to get weighty: when men begin to put a difference of value between that which is weighty and light money; and will not sell their commodities, but for money that is weight, and will make their bargains accordingly.

...

Hitherto we have only considered the raising of silver coin, and that has been only by coining it with less silver in it, under the same denomination. There is another way yet of raising money, which has something more of reality, though as little good in it as the former. This too, now that we are upon the chapter of raising money, it may not be unseasonable to open a little. The raising I mean is, when either of the two richer metals (which money is usually made of) is by law raised above its natural value, in respect of the other. Gold and silver have, in almost all ages and parts of the world (where money was used) generally been thought the fittest materials to make it of. But there being a great disproportion in the plenty of these metals in the world, one has always been valued much higher than the other; so that one ounce of gold has exchanged for several ounces of silver.

...

The effect indeed, and ill consequence of raising either of these two metals, in respect of the other, is more easily observed, and sooner found in raising gold than silver coin: because your accounts being kept, and your reckonings all made in pounds, shillings, and pence, which are denominations of silver coins, or numbers of them; if gold be made current at a rate above the free and market value of those two metals, every one will easily perceive the inconvenience. But there being a law for it, you cannot refuse the gold in payment for so much. And all the money, or bullion, people will carry beyond sea from you, will be in silver; and the money, or bullion, brought in, will be in gold. And just the same will happen, when your silver is raised and gold debased, in respect of one another, beyond their true and natural proportion (natural proportion or value I call that respective rate they find, any where, without the prescription of law). For then silver will be that which is brought in, and gold will be carried out; and that still with loss to the kingdom, answerable to the over-value set by the law. Only as soon as the mischief is felt, people will (do what you can) raise the gold to its natural value. For your accounts and bargains being made in the denomination of silver money, if, when gold is raised above its proportion, by the law, you cannot refuse it in payment (as if the law should make a guinea current at 22*s.* 6*d.*) you are bound to take it at that rate in payment. But if the law should make guineas current at 20*s.*, he that has them is not bound to pay them away at that rate, but may keep them, if he pleases, or get more for them, if he can; yet, from such a law, one of these things will follow. Either, first, the law forces them to go at 20*s.* and then being found passing at that rate, foreigners make their advantage of it; Or, second, people keep them up, and will not part with them at the legal rate, understanding them really to be worth more, and then all your gold lies dead, and is of no more use to trade than if it were all gone out of the kingdom; Or, third, it passes for more than the law allows, and then your law signifies nothing, and had been better let alone. Which way soever it succeeds, it proves either prejudicial or ineffectual. If the design of your law takes place, the kingdom loses by it: if the inconvenience be felt and avoided, your law is eluded.

Money is the measure of commerce, and of the rate of every thing, and therefore ought to be kept (as all other measures) as steady and invariable as may be. But this cannot be, if your money be made of two metals, whose proportion, and, consequently, whose price, constantly varies in respect to one another. Silver, for many reasons, is the fittest of all metals to be this measure; and therefore generally made use of for money. But then it is very unfit and inconvenient that gold, or any other metal, should be made current, legal money, at a standing, settled rate. This is to set a rate upon the varying value of things by law, which justly cannot be done; and is, as I have showed, as far as it prevails, a constant damage and prejudice to the country, where it is practised.

…

What then! (Will you be ready to say) would you have gold kept out of England? Or, being here, would you have it useless to trade; and must there be no money made of it? I answer, quite the contrary. It is fit the kingdom should make use of the treasure it has. It is necessary your gold should be coined, and have the king's stamp upon it, to secure men in receiving it, that there is so much gold in each piece. But it is not necessary that it should have a fixed value set on it by public authority: it is not convenient that it should in its varying proportion, have a settled price. Let gold, as other commodities, find its own rate. And when, by the king's image and inscription, it carries with it a public assurance of its weight and fineness; the gold money, so coined, will never fail to pass at the known market rates, as readily as any other species of your money. Twenty guineas, though designed at first for 20*l.*, go now as current for 21*l.* 10*s.* as any other money, and sometimes for more, as the rate varies. The value, or price, of any thing, being only the respective estimate it bears to some other, which it comes in competition with, can only be known by the quantity of the one which will exchange for a certain quantity of the other. There being no two things in nature whose proportion and use does not vary, it is impossible to set a standing, regular price between them. The growing plenty, or scarcity, of either in the market (whereby I mean the ordinary place where they are to be had in traffic) or the real use, or changing fashion of the place, bringing either of them more into demand than formerly, presently varies the respective value of any two things. You will as fruitlessly endeavour to keep two different things steadily at the same price one with another, as to keep two things in an equilibrium, where their varying weights depend on different causes. Put a piece of sponge in one scale, and an exact counterpoise of silver in the other; you will be mightily mistaken if you imagine, that because they are to-day equal, they shall always remain so. The weight of the sponge varying with every change of moisture in the air, the silver, in the opposite scale, will sometimes rise and sometimes fall. This is just the state of silver and gold, in regard of their mutual value. Their proportion, or use, may, nay constantly does vary, and with it their price. For, being estimated one in reference to the other, they are, as it were, put in opposite scales; and as the one rises the other falls, and so on the contrary.

Farthings, made of a baser metal, may on this account too deserve your consideration. For whatsoever coin you make current, above the intrinsic value, will always be damage to the public, whoever get by it. But of this I shall not, at present, enter into a more particular inquiry; only this I will confidently affirm, that it is the interest of every country, that all the current money of it should be of one and the same metal; that the several species should be of the same alloy, and none of a baser mixture: and that the standard, once thus settled, should be inviolably and immutably kept to perpetuity. For whenever that is altered, upon what pretence soever, the public will lose by it.

27. Dudley North: *Discourses upon Trade* (1691)

A DISCOURSE CONCERNING THE ABATEMENT OF INTEREST

Arguments for Abatement of Interest are many, viz.

I.   When Interest is less, Trade is incourag'd, and the Merchant can be a Gainer; whereas, when it is great, the Usurer, or Money-owner takes all.
II. The *Dutch*, with whom Interest is low, Trade cheaper, and under-sell us.
III. Land falls in value, as Interest riseth.

With divers others, whereof the Facts may be true, but proceed from another Cause, and conduce nothing to the purpose for which they are alledg'd.

I shall not formally apply myself to answer all the Arguments and Discourses, that commonly are found in Pamphlets, and Conversation upon this Subject; as if I were to Advocate the Cause of Interest: But give my thoughts impartially in the whole matter, with regard to the Profit of the whole Nation, and to no particular Persons project: Wherein I hope to propose, that which may resolve any doubt that can be raised, and leave every one to apply it, as they think fit.

The Question to be considered is, Whether the Government have reason by a Law, to prohibit the taking more than 4 *l. per Cent* Interest for Money lent, or to leave the Borrower and Lender to make their own Bargains.

In the Disquisition of this, many things are to be considered, and particularly such as relate to Trade, of which a true Notion will set right a World of Mistakes, wherefore that now shall be chiefly treated of.

Trade is nothing else but a Commutation of Superfluities; for instance: I give of mine, what I can spare, for somewhat of yours, which I want, and you can spare.

Thus Trade, whilst it is restrained within the limits of a Town, Country, or Nation, signifieth only the Peoples supplying each other with Conveniences, out of what that Town, Country, or Nation affords.

And in this, he who is most diligent, and raiseth most Fruits, or maketh most of Manufactory, will abound most in what others make, or raise; and consequently be free from Want, and enjoy most Conveniences, which is truly to be Rich, altho' there were no such thing as Gold, Silver, or the like amongst them.

Mettals are very necessary for many Uses, and are to be reckon'd among the Fruits and Manufactories of the World. And of these, Gold and Silver being by nature very fine, and more scarce than others, are higher prized; and a little of them is very reasonably esteem'd equal in value with a great quantity of other Mettals, &c. For which reason, and moreover that they are imperishable, as well as convenient for easie stowage and removal, and not from any Laws, they are made a Standard, or common Measure to deal with; and all Mankind concur in it, as every one knows, therefore I need not inlarge further in this matter.

Now it is to be consider'd, that Mankind being fallen into a way of commuting in this manner, to serve their occasions, some are more provident, others more profuse; some by their Industry and Judgment raise more Fruits from the Earth, than they consume in supplying their own occasions; and then the surplus remains with them, and is Property or Riches.

And Wealth thus contracted, is either commuted for other Mens Land (supposing all Men to have had some) or massed up in heaps of Goods; be the same of Mettals, or anything valuable. And those are the Rich, who transmit what they have to their Posterity; whereby particular Families become rich; and of such are compounded Cities, Countries, Nations, &c.

And it will be found, that as some particular Men in a Town grow richer, and thrive better than others; so also do Nations, who by Trade serving the occasions of their Neighbours, supply themselves with what they have occasion for from abroad; which done, the rest is laid up, and is Silver, Gold, &c. for as I said, these being commutable for everything, and of small bulk, are still preferr'd to be laid up, till occasion shall call them out to supply other Necessaries wanted.

Now Industry and Ingenuity having thus distinguisht Men into Rich and Poor; What is the consequence? One rich Man hath Lands, not only more than he can manage, but so much, that letting them out to others, he is supplied with a large over-plus, so needs no farther care.

Another rich Man hath Goods; that is, Mettals, Manufactures, &c. in great quantity, with these he serves his own occasions, and then commutes the rest in Trade; that is, supplies others with what they want, and takes in exchange what they had of, beyond their own occasions, whereby managing cunningly, he must always advance.

Now as there are more Men to Till the Ground than have Land to Till, so also there will be many who want Stock to manage; and also (when a Nation is grown rich) there will be Stock for Trade in many hands, who either have not the skill, or care not for the trouble of managing it in Trade.

But as the Landed Man letts his Land, so these still lett their Stock; this latter is call'd Interest, but is only Rent for Stock, as the other is for Land. And in several Languages, hiring of Money, and Lands, are Terms of common use; and it is so also in some Countries in England.

Thus to be a Landlord, or a Stock-lord is the same thing; the Landlord hath the advantage only in this: That his Tenant cannot carry away the Land, as the Tenant of the other may the Stock; and therefore Land ought to yield less profit than Stock, which is let out at the greater hazard.

These things consider'd, it will be found, that as plenty makes cheapness in other things, as Corn, Wool, &c. when they come to Market in greater Quantities than there are Buyers to deal for, the Price will fall; so if there be more Lenders than Borrowers, Interest will also fall; wherefore it is not low Interest makes Trade, but Trade increasing, the Stock of the Nation makes Interest low.

It is said, that in Holland Interest is lower than in England. I answer, It is; because their Stock is greater than ours. I cannot hear that they ever made a Law to restrain Interest, but am certainly informed, that at this day, the Currant Interest between Merchant and Merchant, when they disburse Money for each others Account, is 6 *per Cent* and the Law justifies it.

I allow Money is many times lent at 3, and 4 *per Cent* but it is upon Mortgages, out of which the State hath a Duty, and by the course of Titles there, such dealing is perfectly safe; and this is still by private consent and agreement, and not by co-ersion and order of Law. The like often happens here, when poor Widows and Orphans purchase, the Security of their Livelihoods, and punctual Payment, by lending at small Interest, to such as need not the Money.

It might not be amiss in this place, to say somewhat of the Publick Banks that are in Forreign Parts, as Amsterdam, Venice, &c. but that is a Subject I have not time to dilate upon: I shall only say, that it is a cunning way of supplying the Government once with a great Sum; and as long as the Government stands, it is no loss to them that have the Credit, nor no great Inconveniency; for all Bills of Exchange are made by Law payable in Bank, and not otherwise; for Dealers in Exchanges it is best that way, and such as want their Money, find no difficulty in selling their Credits, the price of which riseth and falleth according to Demanders, as of other things.

I do not understand that true, two Banks pay any Interest; it is true there are several Funds, viz. The Mint in Venice, and the Chamber in Amsterdam, with several others in those and other Cities, where Money is put out at Interest for Lives, and several other ways, and at different Rates, more or less, according to the Credit these Funds have, which are the Security; and these may, by mistake, be called the Banks, which they are not, being only such as the Chamber of London, East-India-House, &c. were.

I do not believe, but the Usurer, according to the saying, will take half a Loaf, rather than no bread: But I avert, that high Interest will bring Money out from Hoards, Plate, &c. into Trade, when low Interest will keep it back.

Many Men of great Estates, keep by them for State and Honour, great Quantities of Plate, Jewels, &c. which certainly they will be more inclin'd to do, when Interest is very low, than when it is high.

Such as have nothing to subsist by, but the Interest of Money, must either let it out, or Trade with it themselves, and be contented with what they can get; but that hinders not, but very many other Men, who are rich, and not so prest, may, if Interest be very low, choose to make use of their Stocks in Jewels, Plate, &c. rather than run the hazards, and be at the trouble of dealing with necessitous and knavish Men, such as many Borrowers are, for inconsiderable gains.

So that it cannot be denied, but the lowering of Interest may, and probably will keep some Money from coming abroad into Trade; whereas on the contrary, high Interest certainly brings it out.

Next is to be considered, that Dealings between Borrowers and Lenders are of two kinds: 1. Upon Mortgage, or Pawn. 2. Upon Personal Security, and that either by single Bond, or with Sureties; all which, as they differ in goodness, so ought in reason to bear different Prizes. Shall any Man be bound to lend a single Person, upon the same Terms, as others lend upon Mortgages, or Joynt Obligations?

Then again it is to be considered, that the Moneys imployed at Interest in this Nation, are not near the Tenth part, disposed to Trading People, wherewith to manage their Trades; but are for the most part lent for the supplying of Luxury, and to support the Expence of Persons, who though great Owners of Lands, yet spend faster than their Lands bring in; and being loath to sell, choose rather to mortgage their Estates.

So that in truth an Ease to Interest, will rather be a Support to Luxury, than to Trade; the poor Trading Man, who hath but a narrow Stock, or none at all, supplies himself by buying Goods of rich Men at time, and thereby pays Interest, not at the rate of 5, 6, or 8, but 10, 12, and more *per Cent*. And this is not in the Power of any Legislature to prevent, or remedy.

It may be said, let him take Money at Interest, and not buy at Time. But then Men must be found, that will lend; the Legislative must provide a Fund to borrow upon.

The Trade of setting out Ships, runs very much upon this course, wherein it is usual to Bum'em (as they call it) at 36 *per Cent*. And this cannot be remedied; and if it were, it would be a stop, as well to the Building, as the setting out of many Ships; whereby, after all, not only the publick, but the private Persons concern'd are Gainers for the most part.

Thus when all things are considered, it will be found best for the Nation to leave the Borrowers and the Lender to make their own Bargains, according to the Circumstances they lie under; and in so doing you will follow the course of the wise Hollanders, so often quoted on this account: and the consequences will be, that when the Nation thrives, and grows rich, Money will be to be had upon good terms, but the clean contrary will fall out, when the Nation grows poorer and poorer.

Let any one Answer me, why do not the Legislators in those poor Countries, where Interest is at 10, & 12 *per Cent*, make such Laws to restrain Interest, and reduce it for the good of the People? If they should attempt it, it wou'd soon appear, that such Laws would not be effectual to do it. For when there are more Borrowers than Lenders, as in poor Countries, where if a rich Man hath 100 *l.* to dispose, and there are four, five or more Men striving for it; the Law would be evaded by underhand Bargains, making Loans in Goods, drawing Bills, and a thousand Ways beside; which cannot be prevented.

It is probable that when Laws restrain Interest of Money, below the Price, which the Reason of Trade settles, and Traders cannot (as we will suppose) evade the Law, or not without great difficulty, or hazard, and have not Credit to borrow at Legal Interest, to make, or increase their Stock; so much of Trade is lopt off; and there cannot be well a greater obstruction to diminish Trade then that would be. The consideration of all these Matters, makes out an universal Maxime, That as more Buyers than Sellers raiseth the price of a Commodity, so more Borrowers than Lenders, will raise Interest.

And the State may with as much Justice make a Law that Lands which heretofore have been Lett for 10 *s. per* Acre, shall not now be Lett for above 8 *s. per* Acre, as that Money, or Stock, from 5 *per Cent*, shall be Lett for 4 *per Cent*, the Property being as good, and as much the Substance of the Kingdom in the one, as in the other.

I will not say any thing to the Theological Arguments against Interest of Moneys; by those 3 *per Cent* is no more lawful, than 4, or 12. But this I shall maintain Politically, that if you take away Interest, you take away Borrowing and Lending. And in consequence the Gentry, who are behind hand, be it for what cause soever, must sell, and cannot Mortgage; which will bring down the Price of Land. And the Trader whatever his skill is, if he hath no Stock, must either sit still, or buy at Time, which is Interest under another Name. And they who are poor, will always be so, and we should soon relapse into the state of One Thousand Years ago.

And whereas the Stock of the Nation is now reckon'd great, let it be fairly valued, and it will be found much less than it seems to be; for all the Monies that are owing Land Securities, must be struck off, and not estimated; or else you will have a wrong Account; for if a Gentleman of

500 *l. per Anum*, owes 8000 *l.* and you value his Land, and the Lender's Stock both, you make an account of the same thing twice.

And whereas we make great Accounts of Moneyed Men in the Nation, in truth there are but few; for suppose all that have lent upon Mortgage, had Land for their Moneys, as indeed in strictness of Law they have, there wou'd be but few Money'd Men in the Nation left. The borrowing of Money of one, to pay another, call'd, Robbing of Peter to pay Paul, so much practis'd now-a-days, makes us think the Nation far richer than it is.

A DISCOURSE OF COYNED MONEY

In the former Discourse, it hath already made appear, that Gold and Silver for their scarcity, have obtained in small quantities, to equal in value far greater quantities of other Metals, &c. And farther, from their easie Removal, and convenient Custody, have also obtained to be the common Measure in the World between Man and Man in their dealings, as well for Land, Houses, &c., as for Goods and other Necessaries.

For the greater Improvement of this Convenience, and to remove some Difficulties, which would be very troublesome, about knowing quantities and qualities in common and ordinary dealing: Princes and States have made it a matter of Publick concern, to ascertain the Allay, and to determine the Weights, viz. the quantities of certain Pieces, which we call Coyn, or Money; and such being distinguish'd by Stamps, and Inscriptions, it is made difficult, and highly Penal to Counterfeit them.

By this means the Trade of the World is made easie, and all the numerous species of several Commodities have a common Measure. Besides the Gold and Silver being thus coyned into Money, and so become more useful for Commerce than in the Log or Block, hath in all places, except in England since the free Coynage, reasonably obtained a greater value than it had before: And that not only above the real charge of making it so, but is become a State-Revenue (except as before) tho' not very great. Whereas if Silver coyned and uncoyned bore the same rate, as it doth with us in England, where it is coyned at the Charge of the Publick, it will be lyable frequently to be melted down, as I shall shew anon.

Money being thus the Common Measure of Buying and Selling, every body who hath any thing to sell, and cannot procure Chapmen for it, is presently apt to think, that want of Money in the Kingdom, or Country is the cause why his Goods do not go off; and so, want of Money, is the common Cry; which is a great mistake, as shall be shewn. I grant all stop in Trade proceeds from some cause; but it is not from the want of specifick Money, there being other Reasons for it; as will appear by the following Discourse.

No Man is richer for having his Estate all in Money, Plate, &c. lying by him, but on the contrary, he is for that reason the poorer. That man is richest, whose Estate is in a growing condition, either in Land at Farm, Money at Interest, or Goods in Trade: If any man, out of an humour, should turn all his Estate into Money, and keep it dead, he would soon be sensible of Poverty growing upon him, whilst he is eating out of the quick stock.

But to examine the matter closer, what do these People want, who cry out for Money? I will begin with the Beggar; he wants, and importunes for Money: What would he do with it if he had it? buy Bread, &c. Then in truth it is not Money, but Bread, and other Necessaries for Life that he wants. Well then, the Farmer complains, for the want of Money; surely it is not for the Beggar's Reason, to sustain Life, or pay Debts; but he thinks that were more Money in the Country, he should have a Price for his Goods. Then it seems Money is not his want, but a Price for his Corn, and Cartel, which he would sell, but cannot. If it be askt, if the want of Money be not, what then is the reason, why he cannot get a price? I answer, it must proceed from one of these three Causes.

1. Either there is too much Corn and Cartel in the Country, so that most who come to Market have need of selling, as he hath, and few of buying: Or, 2. There wants the usual vent abroad, by Transportation, as in time of War, when Trade is unsafe, or not permitted. Or, 3. The Consumption fails, as when men by reason of Poverty, do not spend so much in their Houses as formerly they did; wherefore it is not the increase of specifick Money, which would at all advance the Farmers Goods, but the removal of any of these three Causes, which do truly keep down the Market.

The Merchant and Shop-keeper want Money in the same manner, that is, they want a Vent for the Goods they deal in, by reason that the Markets fail, as they will always upon any cause, like what I have hinted. Now to consider what is the true source of Riches, or in the common Phrase, plenty of Money, we must look a little back, into the nature and steps of Trade.

Commerce and Trade, as hath been said, first springs from the Labour of Man, but as the Stock increases, it dilates more and more. If you suppose a Country to have nothing in it but the Land it self, and the Inhabitants; it is plain that at first, the People have only the Fruits of the Earth, and Metals raised from the Bowels of it, to Trade withal, either by carrying out into Foreign Parts, or by selling to such as will come to buy of them, whereby they may be supplyed with the Goods of other Countries wanted there.

In process of time, if the People apply themselves industriously, they will not only be supplied, but advance to a great overplus of Forreign Goods, which improv'd, will enlarge their Trade. Thus the English Nation will sell unto the French, Spaniards, Turk, &c. not only the product of their own Country, as Cloath, Tin, Lead, &c. but also what they purchase of others, as Sugar, Pepper, Callicoes, &c. still buying where Goods are produc'd, and cheap, and transporting them to Places where they are wanted, making great advantage thereby.

In this course of Trade, Gold and Silver are in no sort different from other Commodities, but are taken from them who have Plenty, and carried to them who want, or desire them, with as good profit as other Merchandizes. So that an active prudent Nation groweth rich, and the sluggish Drones grow poor; and there cannot be any Policy other than this, which being introduc'd and practis'd, shall avail to increase Trade and Riches.

But this Proposition, as single and plain as it is, is seldom so well understood, as to pass with the generality of Mankind; but they think by force of Laws, to retain in their Country all the Gold and Silver which Trade brings in; and thereby expect to grow rich immediately: All which is a profound Fallacy, and hath been a Remora, whereby the growing Wealth of many Countries have been obstructed.

The Case will more plainly appear, if it be put of a single Merchant, or if you please to come nearer the point, of a City or County only.

Let a Law be made, and what is more, be observ'd, that no Man whatsoever shall carry any Money out of a particular Town, County, or Division, with liberty to carry Goods of any sort: so that all the Money which everyone brings with him, must be left behind, and none be carried out.

The consequence of this would be, that such Town, or County were cut off from the rest of the Nation; and no Man would dare to come to Market with his Money there; because he must buy, whether he likes, or not: and on the other side, the People of that place could not go to other Markets as Buyers, but only as Sellers, being not permitted to carry any Money out with them.

Now would not such a Constitution as this, soon bring a Town or County to a miserable Condition, with respect to their Neighbours, who have free Commerce, whereby the Industrious gain from the slothful and luxurious part of Mankind? The Case is the same, if you extend your thought from a particular Nation, and the several Divisions, and Cities, with the Inhabitants in them, to the whole World, and the several Nations, and Governments in it. And a Nation restrained in its Trade, of which Gold and Silver is a principal, if not an essential Branch, would suffer, and grow poor, as a particular place within a Country, as I have discoursed. A Nation in the World, as to Trade, is in all respects like a City in a Kingdom, or Family in a City.

Now since the Increase of Trade is to be esteem'd the only cause that Wealth and Money increase, I will add some farther Considerations upon that subject.

The main spur to Trade, or rather to Industry and Ingenuity, is the exorbitant Appetites of Men, which they will take pains to gratifie, and so be disposed to work, when nothing else will incline them to it; for did Men content themselves with bare Necessaries, we should have a poor World.

The Glutton works hard to purchase Delicacies, wherewith to gorge himself; the Gamester, for Money to venture at Flay; the Miser, to hoard; and so others. Now in their pursuit of those Appetites, other Men less exorbitant are benefitted; and tho' it may be thought few profit by the Miser, yet it will be found otherwise, if we consider, that besides the humour of every Generation, to dissipate what another had collected, there is benefit from the very Person of a covetous Man; for if he labours with his own hands, his Labour is very beneficial to them who imploy him; if he doth not work, but profit by the Work of others, then those he sets on work have benefit by their being employed.

Countries which have sumptuary Laws, are generally poor; for when Men by those Laws are confin'd to narrower Expence than otherwise they would be, they are at the same time discouraged from the Industry and Ingenuity which they would have imployed in obtaining wherewithal to support them, in the full latitude of Expence they desire.

It is possible Families may be supported by such means, but then the growth of Wealth in the Nation is hindered; for that never thrives better, then when Riches are tost from hand to hand.

The meaner sort seeing their Fellows become rich, and great, are spurr'd up to imitate their Industry. A Tradesman sees his Neighbour keep a Coach, presently all his Endeavors is at work to do the like, and many times is beggared by it; however the extraordinary Application he made, to support his Vanity, was beneficial to the Publiek, tho' not enough to answer his false Measures as to himself.

It will be objected, That the Home Trade signifies nothing to the enriching a Nation, and that the increase of Wealth comes out of Forreign Trade.

I answer, That what is commonly understood by Wealth, viz. Plenty, Bravery, Gallantry, &c. cannot be maintained without Forreign Trade. Nor in truth, can Forreign Trade subsist without the Home Trade, both being connected together.

I have toucht upon these matters concerning Trade, and Riches in general, because I conceive a true Notion of them, will correct many common Errors, and more especially conduce to the Proposition I chiefly aim to prove; which is, that Gold and Silver, and, out of them, Money are nothing but the Weights and Measures, by which Traffick is more conveniently carried on, then could be done without them: and also a proper Fund for a surplusage of Stock to be deposited in.

In confirmation of this, we may take Notice, That Nations which are very poor, have scarce any Money, and in the beginnings of Trade have often made use of something else; as Sueden hath used Copper, and the Plantations, Sugar and Tobacco, but not without great Inconveniences; and still as Wealth hath increas'd, Gold and Silver hath been introduc'd, and drove out the others, as now almost in the Plantations it hath done.

It is not necessary absolutely to have a Mint for the making Money plenty, tho' it be very expedient; and a just benefit is lost by the want of it, where there is none; for it hath been observed, that where no Mints were, Trade hath not wanted a full supply of Money; because if it be wanted, the Coyn of other Princes will become currant, as in Ireland, and the Plantations; so also in Turky, where the Money of the Country is so minute, that it is inconvenient for great Payments; and therefore the Turkish Dominions are supplied by almost all the Coyns of Christendom, the same being currant there.

But a Country which useth Forreign Coyns, hath great disadvantage from it; because they pay strangers, for what, had they a Mint of their own, they might make themselves. For Coyned Money, as was said, is more worth than Uncoyned Silver of the same weight and allay; that is, you may buy more Uncoyned Silver, of the same fineness with the Money, than the Money weighs; which advantage the Stranger hath for the Coynage.

If it be said, That the contrary sometimes happens, and coyned Money shall be current for less than Bullion shall sell for. I answer, That where-ever this happens, the Coyned Money being undervalued, shall be melted down into Bullion, for the immediate Gain that is had from it.

Thus it appears, that if you have no Mint whereby to increase your Money, yet if you are a rich People, and have Trade, you cannot want Specifick Coyn, to serve your occasions in dealing.

The next thing to be shewed is, That if your Trade pours in never so much Money upon you, you have no more advantage by the being of it Money, then you should have were it in Logs, or Blocks; save only that Money is much better for Transportation than Logs are.

For when Money grows up to a greater quantity than Commerce requires, it comes to be of no greater value, than uncoyned Silver, and will occasionally be melted down again.

Then let not the care of Specifick Money torment us so much; for a People that are rich cannot want it, and if they make none, they will be supplied with the Coyn of other Nations; and if never so much be brought from abroad, or never so much coyned at home, all that is more than what the Commerce of the Nation requires, is but Bullion, and will be treated as such; and coyned Money, like wrought is Plate at Second hand, shall sell but for the Intrinsick.

I call to witness the vast Sums that have been coyned in England, since the free Coynage was set up; What is to become of it all? no body believes it to be in the Nation, and it cannot well be all transported, the Penalties for so doing being so great. The case is plain, it being exported, as I verily believe little of it is, the Melting-Pot devours all.

The rather, because that Practice is so easie, profitable, and safe from all possibility of being detected, as every one knows it is. And I know no intelligent Man who doubts, but the New Money goes this way.

Silver and Gold, like other Commodities, have their ebbings and flowings: Upon the arrival of Quantities from Spain, the Mint commonly gives the best price; that is, coyned Silver, for uncoyned Silver, weight for weight. Wherefore is it carried into the Tower, and coyned? not long after there will come a demand for Bullion, to be Exported again: If there is none, but all happens to be in Coyn, What then? Melt it down again; there's no loss in it, for the Coyning cost the Owners nothing.

Thus the Nation hath been abused, and made to pay for the twisting of straw, for Asses to eat. If the Merchant were made to pay the price of the Coynage, he would not have sent his Silver to the Tower without Consideration; and coyned Money would always keep a value above uncoyned Silver: which is now so far from being the case, that many times it is considerably under, and generally the King of Spain's Coyn here is worth One penny per Ounce more than our New Money.

This Nation, for many Years last past, hath groaned, and still groans under the abuse of clipt Money, which with respect to their Wisdom, is a great mistake; and the Irish whom we ridicule so much, when in Peace, would not be so gulled, but weighed their (Pieces of Eight) Cobbs, as they call them, Piece by Piece; this Errour springs from the same Source with the rest, and needs no other Cure then will soon result from Non-currency. Whereof I shall set down my thoughts.

There is great fear, that if clipt Money be not taken, there will be no Money at all. I am certain, that so long as clipt Money is taken, there will be little other: And is it not strange, that scarce any Nation, or People in the whole World, take diminisht Money by Tale, but the English?

What is the reason that a New Half-crown-piece, if it hath the least snip taken from the edge, will not pass; whereas an Old Half-crown clipt to the very quick, and not intrinsically worth Eighteen Pence, shall be currant?

I know no reason, why a Man should take the one, more than the other; I am sure, that if New Money should pass clipt, there would soon be enough served so. And I do not in the least doubt, unless the currency of clipt Money be stopt, it will not be very long before every individual piece of the Old Coynes be clipt.

And if this be not remedied, for fear of the Evil now, how will it be born hereafter, when it will be worse? surely at length it will become insupportable, and remedy itself as Groats have done; but let them look out, in whose time it shall happen; we are all shoving the Evil-Day as far off as may be, but it will certainly come at last.

I do not think the great Evil is so hard to be remedied, nor so chargeable as some have judged; but if rightly managed, it may be done with no intolerable loss, some there will be, and considerable; but when I reflect where it will fall, I cannot think it grievous.

The general Opinion is, That it cannot be done otherwise, then by calling in of all the Old Money, and changing of it, for doing which the whole Nation must contribute by a general Tax; but I do not approve of this way, for several Reasons.

For it will be a matter of great trouble, and will require many hands to execute, who will expect, and deserve good pay; which will add to the Evil, and increase the Charge of the Work; and the Trust of it, is also very great, and may be vastly abused.

Now before I give any Opinion for the doing this thing, let some estimate be made of the loss, wherein I will not undertake to compute the Total, but only how the same may fall out in One Hundred Pound: There may be found in it Ten Pound of good New Money, then rests

Ninety Pound; and of that I will suppose half to be clipt Money, and half good; so there will be but Five and Forty, in One Hundred Pounds, whereupon there will be any loss; and that will not surely be above a Third part: so I allow 15 *l. per Cent* for the loss by clipt Money, which is with the most, and in such Computes, it is safest to err on that side.

Now in case it should be thought fit, that the King should in all the Receipts of the Publick Revenue, forbid the taking of clipt Coyn, unless the Subject were content to pay it by weight at 5 *s.* 2 *d. per* Ounce, every Piece being cut in Two, (which must be especially and effectually secured to be done) I grant it would be a great surprize, but no great cause of Complaint when nothing is required, but that the Publick Revenue may be paid in lawful English Money.

And those who are to make Payments, must either find good Money, or clip in two their cropt Money, and part with it on such terms; by this Example it would likewise be found, that in a short time, all Men would refuse clipt Money in common Payment.

Now let us consider, where the loss would light, which I have estimated to be about 15 *per Cent*.

We are apt to make Over-estimates of the Quantities of current Money; for we see it often, and know it not again; and are not willing to consider how very a little time it stays in a place; and altho' every one desires to have it, yet none, or very few care for keeping it, but they are forthwith contriving to dispose it; knowing that from all the Money that lies dead, no benefit is to be expected, but it is a certain loss.

The Merchant and Gentleman keep their Money for the most part, with Goldsmiths, and Scriveners; and they, instead of having Ten Thousand Pounds in Cash by them, as their Accounts shew they should have, of other Mens ready Money, to be paid at sight, have seldom One Thousand in Specie; but depend upon a course of Trade, whereby Money comes in as fast as it is taken out: Wherefore I conclude, that the Specifick Money of this Nation is far less than the common Opinion makes.

Now suppose all the loss by clipt Money should happen and fall where the Cash is, it would be severe in very few Places. It could do no great harm to Hoards of Money; because those who intend to keep Money, will be sure to lay up that which is good. It would not signifie much to the poor Man, for he many times hath none; and for the most part, if he hath any, it is very little, seldome Five Shillings at a time. The Farmer is supposed to pay his Landlord, as fast as he gets Money; so it is not likely he should be catcht with much: Wherefore it will light chiefly upon Trading Men, who may sometimes be found with Hundreds by them; and frequently not with many Pounds. Those who happen to have such great Cashes at such time would sustain loss.

In short, clipt Money is an Evil, that the longer it is born with, the harder will the Cure be. And if the Loss therein be lain on the Publick, (as the Common Project is) the Inconveniences are (as hath been shewed) very great; but in the other way of Cure it is not such a terrible Grievance, as most Men have imagined it would be.

So to conclude, when these Reasons, which have been hastily and confusedly set down, are duly considered, I doubt not but we shall joyn in one uniform Sentiment: That Laws to hamper Trade, whether Forreign, or Domestick, relating to Money, or other Merchandizes, are not Ingredients to make a People Rich, and abounding in Money, and Stock. But if Peace be procured, easie Justice maintained, the Navigation not clogg'd, the Industrious encouraged, by indulging them in the participation of Honours, and Imployments in the Government, according to their Wealth and Characters, the Stock of the Nation will increase, and consequently Gold and Silver abound, Interest be easie, and Money cannot be wanting.

POSTSCRIPT

When a Nation is grown Rich, Gold, Silver, Jewels, and every thing useful, or desirable, (as I have already said) will be plentiful; and the Fruits of the Earth will purchase more of them, than before, when People were poorer: As a fat Oxe in former Ages, was not sold for more Shillings, than now Pounds. The like takes place in Labourers Wages, and every thing whatever; which confirms the Universal Maxim I have built upon, viz. That Plenty of any thing makes it cheap.

Therefore Gold and Silver being now plentiful, a Man hath much more of it for his labour, for his Corn, for his Cattle, &c. then could be had Five Hundred Years ago, when, as must be owned, there was not near so much by many parts as now.

Notwithstanding this, I find many, who seem willing to allow, that this Nation at present, abounds with Gold and Silver, in Plate and Bullion; but are yet of Opinion, That coyned Money is wanted to carry on the Trade, and that were there more Specifick Money, Trade would increase, and we should have better Markets for every thing.

That this is a great Error, I think the foregoing Papers makes out: but to clear it a little farther, let it be considered, that Money is a Manufacture of Bullion wrought in the Mint. Now if the Materials are ready, and the Workmen also, 'tis absurd to say, the Manufacture is wanted.

For instance: Have you Corn, and do you want Meal? Carry the Corn to the Mill, and grind it. Yes; but I want Meal, because others will not carry their Corn; and I have none: say you so; then buy Corn of them, and carry it to the Mill your self. This is exactly the Case of Money. A very rich Man hath much Plate, for Honour and Show; whereupon a poorer Man thinks, if it were coyned into Money, the Publick, and his self among the rest, would be the better for it; but he is utterly mistaken; unless at the same time you oblige the rich Man to squander his new coyn'd Money away.

For if he lays it up, I am sure the matter is not mended: if he commutes it for Diamonds, Pearl, &c. the Case is still the same; it is but changed from one hand to another: and it may be the Money is dispatcht to the Indies to pay for those Jewels: then if he buys Land, it is no more than changing the hand, and regarding all Persons, except the Dealers only, the Case is still the same. Money will always have an Owner, and never goeth a Beggar for Entertainment, but must be purchast for valuable consideration in *solido*.

If the use of Plate were prohibited, then it were a sumptuary Law, and, as such, would be a vast hindrance to the Riches and Trade of the Nation: for now seeing every Man hath Plate in his House, the Nation is possest of a solid Fund, consisting in those Mettals, which all the World desire, and would willingly draw from us; and this in far greater measure than would be, if Men were not allowed that liberty. For the poor Tradesman, out of an ambition to have a Piece of Plate upon his Cupboard, works harder to purchase it, than he would do if that humour were restrain'd as I have said elsewhere.

There is required for carrying on the Trade of the Nation, a determinate Sum of Specifick Money, which varies, and is sometimes more, sometimes less, as the Circumstances we are in requires. War time calls for more Money than time of Peace, because every one desires to keep some by him, to use upon Emergiences; not thinking it prudent to rely upon Moneys currant in dealing, as they do in times of Peace, when Payments are more certain.

This ebbing and flowing of Money, supplies and accommodates itself, without any aid of Politicians. For when Money grows scarce, and begins to be hoarded, then forthwith the Mint works, till the occasion be filled up again. And on the other side, when Peace brings out the Hoards, and Money abounds, the Mint not only ceaseth, but the overplus of Money will be presently melted down, either to supply the Home Trade, or for Transportation.

Thus the Buckets work alternately, when Money is scarce, Bullion is coyn'd; when Bullion is scarce, Money is melted. I do not allow that both should be scarce at one and the same time; for that is a state of Poverty, and will not be, till we are exhausted, which is besides my subject.

Some have fancied, that if by a Law the Ounce of Silver were restrained to 5 *s.* value, in all dealings, and at the Tower the same were coyned into 5 *s.* 4 *d.* or 5 *s.* 6 *d. per* Ounce, all the Plate in England would soon be coyned. The answer to this, in short, is: That the Principle they build upon is impossible. How can any Law hinder me from giving another Man, what I please for his Goods? The Law may be evaded a thousand ways. As be it so: I must not give, nor he receive above 5 *s. per O*unce for Silver; I may pay him 5 *s.* and present him with 4 *d.* or 6 *d.* more; I may give him Goods in barter, at such, or greater profit; and so by other contrivances, *ad Infinitum.*

But put case it took effect, and by that means all the Silver in England were coyned into Money; What then? would any one spend more in Cloaths, Equipages, Housekeeping, &c. then is done? I believe not; but rather the contrary: For the Gentry and Commonalty being nipt in their delight of seeing Plate, &c. in their Houses, would in all probability be dampt in all other Expences: Wherefore if this could be done, as I affirm it cannot, yet instead of procuring the desired effect, it would bring on all the Mischiefs of a sumptuary Law.

Whenever the Money is made lighter, or baser in allay, (which is the same thing) the effect is, that immediately the price of Bullion answers. So that in reality you change the Name, but not the thing: and whatever the difference is, the Tenant and Debtor hath it in his favor; for Rent and Debts will be paid less, by just so much as the intrinsick value is less, then what was to be paid before.

For example: One who before received for Rent or Debt, 3 *l.* 2 *s.* could with it buy twelve Ounces, or a Pound of Sterling Silver; but if the Crown-piece be worse in value than now it is, by 3 *d.* I do averr, you shall not be able to buy a Pound of such Silver under 3 *l.* 5 *s.* but either directly, or indirectly it shall cost so much.

But then it is said, we will buy an Ounce for 5 *s.* because 'tis the Price set by the Parliament, and no body shall dare to sell for more. I answer, If they cannot sell it for more, they may coyn it; And then what Fool will sell an Ounce of Silver for 5 *s.* when he may coyn it into 5 *s.* 5 *d.?*

Thus we may labour to hedge in the Cuckow, but in vain; for no People ever yet grew rich by Policies; but it is Peace, Industry, and Freedom that brings Trade and Wealth, and nothing else.

28. Isaac Gervaise: *The System or Theory of the Trade of the World* (1720)

PREFACE

Having, for a long time since, looked upon Gold and Silver, as the Design or End of Commerce; I never could reconcile myself, to that generally-received Opinion, that they increase it, and that by consequence, Credit also does the like; for how to imagine the End to be the Cause? This Contradiction induced me to seek out the Reason or first Cause, that drives Man to trade: And as for Years past, some Nations of Europe swell their Credit to such a prodigious Bulk, as though they strove to surpass one another, and as if Trade and Credit had not their Bounds: my Design, by this Tract, is to shew the ill Consequences of an unnatural Use of Credit. I extend it no farther than just what is necessary to attain that End; and I entitle it, *The System or Theory of the Trade of the World*, because it contains such Principles, as seem to me capable of answering any Event in Trade. I draw those Principles from the natural Bent of Man; and the Remarks and Conclusions I infer from them, appear to me most natural. But as this System will seem new, and contrary to the Notions hitherto generally received, and hath the ill Fate to appear at a time, when I myself could wish it false; I beg of my Readers, if possible, to reflect on it without regard to those former Notions.

I hope this Favour will be granted, together with that of excusing both the Style and Correction; my Design being easily perceived, and I expecting no private Profit or Interest, but in the Publick Welfare.

OF GOLD AND SILVER, OR REAL DENOMINATOR

All things, either necessary or useful to Mankind, have besides a proper Name to distinguish one from the other, another Name, that distinguishes or denotes what Proportion they bear to Gold and Silver; and that Proportion is call'd Value.

The Value or Proportion of all things useful, or necessary, is to Gold and Silver, in proportion to the Quantity of Gold and Silver that is in the World; so that the more Gold and Silver is in the World, the greater the Value of things will be.

As Gold and Silver not only express the Value of things; but also carry with them a Right, or Demand at will, on all things necessary: all Men have, one with the other, an equal desire to draw them to themselves; which can be done, but by Labour only: And as Man naturally loves his Ease, the Possession of a part of them lessens his Desires, and causes him to labour less; which gives him that hath little or no Possession (and consequently preserves his Desire intire) an opportunity by his Labour to slip into his place.

This Desire may be look'd upon as the great Spring that forces Movement or Labour; and the Love of Ease, as the small Spring or Pendulum, that keeps Men in a continual Equilibral Vibration of Rich and Poor: so that the one always ballances the other, in such manner, as keeps Labour or Movement continually going, in a certain equal proportion.

All things in the World belong to all Mankind, the Rich and Poor taken together, half of them to half Mankind, a quarter to a quarter, and so on in proportion to the Quantity of Men; by reason all that is necessary or useful to Men, is the Produce of their Labour: And as all Men work all the Labour of the World, one half of them can work but one half of it, and so in proportion to the quantity of Men.

The Nations of the World, with respect to Commerce, are but certain quantities of Men, which by reason of an advantageous Disposition or Situation, for transporting their Labour, inhabit one place of the World preferably to another.

The mutual Exchange that Nations make of their Labour, is call'd Trade or Commerce.

The Design or End of Commerce, is the drawing to one's self Gold and Silver; which I call the grand real Measure or Denominator of the real Value of all things.

A Nation can naturally draw and keep unto itself, but such a proportion of the real Denominator of the World, as is proportion'd to the quantity of its Inhabitants, because the Denominator can be attracted but by Labour only; and as the whole World tend to the same End, the Labour of each Nation is continually opposed, by all the Labour of the rest of the World.

Whenever I mention the quantity of Inhabitants, I always suppose, that regard which ought to be had, to the Situation, and Disposition, of the different Countries of the World; the same quantity of inhabitants, not producing the same Effect, in all Countries, according as their Dispositions differ: which I shall shew hereafter.

OF ACCIDENT THAT CHANGE THE PROPORTION OF PARTICULAR DENOMINATORS OF NATIONS AND THEIR EFFECTS

War and Mortality, Etc. may alter the Proportion of private Denominators; as when several Nations are at war together, it may happen, that other Nations may reap the benefit thereof: Because War disturbs and lessens the Labour of those Nations that are at war, by taking off their Poor from their usual Labour, and imploying them in the Defence of the State; so that those Nations not furnishing unto the World their Proportion of Labour, cannot retain their former Proportion of the grand Denominator of the World; and those nations which are at peace, and keep at work their whole Proportion of Poor, draw from those that are at war, besides their own Proportion, such a part of the grand Denominator, as is proportion'd to the number of Men imployed in the War.

When a Nation has attracted a greater Proportion of the grand Denominator of the World, than its proper share; and the Cause of that Attraction ceases, that Nation cannot retain the Overplus of its proper Proportion of the grand Denominator, because in that case, the Proportion of Poor and Rich of that Nation is broken; that is to say, the number of Rich is too great, in proportion to the Poor, so as that Nation cannot furnish unto the World that share of Labour which is proportion'd to that part of the grand Denominator it possesses: in which case all the Labour of the Poor will not ballance the Expence of the Rich. So that there enters in that

Nation, more Labour than goes out of it, to balance its want of Poor: And as the End of Trade is the attracting Gold and Silver, all that difference of Labour is paid in Gold and Silver, until the Denominator be lessen'd, in proportion to other Nations; which also, and at the same time, proportions the number of Poor to that of Rich.

Thus as Labour draws the Denominator of the World, also the Denominator draws Labour from the World; so that if the particular Denominator of any Nation, be greater than its just Proportion, it will draw from the other Nations a Portion of Labour, proportion'd to its Excess; and if its Denominator be less than its just Proportion, it will draw a Portion of Gold and Silver, proportion'd to what it wants of its just Proportion.

Rich Gold and Silver Mines, that belong to certain Nations, and increase their Revenues beyond their natural Proportion, act on those Nations, as if they had drawn unto themselves by their Labour, a too great Portion of the Denominator of the World; and the Effects thereof, will last as long as the Mines, and act more or less in proportion as they are rich.

OF CREDIT, AND ITS EFFECTS ON TRADE

Man, generally speaking, being eager and greedy of Gain, is impatient in Trade; so that when he cannot have the Value of things, as soon as he would, he chuses rather to allow unto the Buyer, more or less time, at once to force the Vent, and to prevent any other's supplanting him.

That Time which is allow'd in Trade, is call'd Credit; and as it proceeds from Fear and Desire, and as all Men one with the other, are equally subject to the same Passions, the several Denominators of all the different Nations of the World, are all equally increased by Credit, in proportion to their quantity of Inhabitants.

Credit is to the Denominator, much as the Cypher is to Arithmetick; which of itself is of no Value, unless accompanied or mixed with Numbers, and loses that Value, as those Numbers vanish; in like manner, Credit, the Cypher of the grand Denominator, losing its Value, as Gold and Silver vanish: And as in Arithmetick, Cyphers increase the Value of Numbers; in like manner Credit increases the Denominator, and adds unto all things, an Increase of Denomination of Value, proportion'd to the Increase of the Denominator by Credit. And as that Addition, or Credit, proceeds from the Nature of Man; I call the real Denominator, mixed with a natural Portion of Credit, the grand Natural Measure or Denominator of the World: and that Denomination which proceeds from it, the Natural Value of things.

If a Nation adds to its Denominator, such a Portion of Credit, as increases it beyond that Proportion which by Trade naturally belongs to it, that Increase of Credit will act on that Nation, as if it had drawn an equal Sum from a Gold or Silver Mine, and will preserve but its Proportion of that Increase; so that the rest thereof will in time be drawn off by the Labour of other Nations, in Gold or Silver. That Nation in that case being unable to furnish unto the rest of the World, the same quantity of Labour it furnish'd when its Denominator was Natural, and proportion'd to the Numbers of its Inhabitants, the Rich in that case being either richer than they were, or in greater number, consume more Labour than before; so that less Labour is exported from that Nation than was, before the Excess of its Denominator: And the contrary happens, when a Nation retrenches from its Denominator, such a Portion of Credit, as loosens it beyond its natural Proportion; that Diminution breaking the Proportion, between that and the other Nations, will cause it in time, to draw Gold and Silver proportionally from other Nations, until its Denominator recovers its natural Proportion.

OF THE BALLANCE OF TRADE

When a Nation exports more or less Labour, than is imported into it, that difference between Exports and Imports of Labour, is called Ballance of Trade.

When the Ballance of Trade proceeds from the natural Excess, or Diminution of the Denominator by Trade only, it neither is very great, nor lasts long; because as a Denominator, under its Proportion, draws part of all the other Denominators, till it hath attain'd its Proportion; also a Denominator above its Proportion, draws the Labour from other Nations, till it be lessen'd to its Proportion: so that Trade causes a Vibration, or continual Ebbing and Flowing; which may be called the natural Ballance of Trade.

Besides this natural Ballance, another is sometimes felt, which may be called the lasting Ballance, and happens when the Denominator, or yearly Revenues, exceed unnaturally.

To give an Idea of the manner by which this lasting Ballance is formed, I shall suppose a Nation composed of four Millions of Souls, and that with a natural Denominator, the Produce of the annual Labour of that Nation, amounts to ten Pounds Sterling a Head, one with the other; which in all makes forty Millions a Year. I suppose also, that this Nation, in this natural State, will draw from the rest of the World, for its Necessities, Conveniences, or Superfluities, ten Millions of Labour, or foreign Goods; and as I suppose its Denominator exactly natural, it will export such an equal quantity of Labour, as will ballance the ten Millions of Imports: but if to the natural Denominator of this Nation, there be added a Portion of Credit; for example, twenty Millions, bearing an annual Income unto the Proprietors thereof, after the rate of five per Cent, there will be an unnatural annual Million added to the Rich of that Nation, which amounts to two and a half per Cent, of all the Labour of that Nation; so that the Labour thereof must extend itself in Denomination of Value, so as to answer the extraordinary Demand of the Rich. And as I suppose the Trade of that Nation to amount to ten Millions of Imports, it's easy to conceive, that after this Excess of Denomination, the ten Millions of Exports will not ballance the ten Millions of Imports; so that the Ballance will run two and a half per Cent, against this Nation: consequently there will be 250 Thousand Pounds exported in Coin or Bullion, preferably to any other Store of Labour, that being not only the End of Trade, but also the only Store of Labour, that retains a real Denomination, by the Strength of Law that fixes Coin, while all other Labour receives an Addition of negative Denomination. And thus in proportion to a greater Excess, even with respect to the Store, or Capital; for example, I suppose that to the whole Value of the Lands, and other Store of natural and real Labour, there be a sudden, unnatural, and imaginary Addition of 500 Millions, it's easy to conceive, that the Proprietors of these 500 Millions, will draw a Portion of annual Labour, proportioned to their Portion of the whole Capital; and there being no Augmentation of Poor, Labour must extend itself, in proportion to the additional Stock: So that if I suppose the Denomination of all the Capital, or natural and real Store of Labour of that Nation to amount to 1000 Millions, this unnatural and imaginary Denomination, will raise Labour to fifty per Cent of negative or imaginary Denomination, and cause the Ballance to run against that Nation, in like Proportion, and so annually, or thereabouts, until its whole Denomination return, into the proportional Equilibrium of the rest of the World.

What precedes, supposes the real Part of the Denominator, of such a Bulk, as if the Ballance of Trade had reduced the Denominator to its natural Proportion, there should still remain such a Part, as could support that unnatural Portion of Credit, which had been added to the

Denominator of that Nation: But if the real Part of the Denominator, is found to be so small, that being wholly taken off, the Denominator would still exceed the natural Proportion; in that case, when the Ballance had reduced the real part of the Denominator, so as to be just sufficient to support the remaining Excess of the Denominator, that Nation would then be obliged to live on its Store or Capital of exportable Labour. After which, Credit would in time be forc'd to yield, in proportion to the remaining Excess of the Denominator. Thus would the Denominator take its natural Proportion, after which all things in time would enter into their natural Proportions, and Denominations; so that all the Profit a Nation gains, by unnaturally swelling its Denominator, consists only in the Inhabitants living for a time in proportion to that swelling, so as to make a greater Figure than the rest of the World, but always at the cost of their Coin, or of their Store of real and exportable Labour. For as the whole Creation is in a perpetual Motion, and as God made Man for Labour, so no thing in this World is of any solid or durable Worth, but what is the Produce of Labour; and whatever else bears a Denomination of Value, is only a Shadow without Substance, which must either be wrought for, or vanish to its primitive Nothing, the greatest Power on Earth not being able to create any thing out of nothing. It may substitute the Shadow instead of the Substance, to the full proportion of Substance that belongs to that Power; but then that Substance should be drawn off, or will in time disappear or slip away of itself. For all Men have a natural Right to their Proportion of what is in the World; so that if we see private Men enjoy above their Proportions, it's either by a greater Government of Passions, or a superior Strength, Genius, or some other Accident. But as Nations are composed of all sorts of Men, they all move in the same equally mix'd manner, and attain to the same End, each in proportion to its number. Thus do Nations attract their Proportions of what is in the World, by the force of the natural Right of their Inhabitants; consequently a Nation cannot retain more than its natural Proportion of what is in the World, and the Ballance of Trade must run against it.

OF EXCHANGE, AND ITS EFFECTS

The Excess of the Denominator, with respect to the Indies, or other far distant Countries, between whom is no Exchange, and where the Ballance is always exported in Species or Bullion, is never sensible, but when the real part of the Denominator is so far reduced, as not to be able to support the remaining Excess of the Denominator. But in Europe, where Exchanges are made use of, the Excess is felt by their difference, which always follows the Excess of the Denominator, and is greater or lesser between one Nation and the rest, as the Proportion of their several private Denominators differ. For as there happens an Overplus or Difference, which cannot be paid in Labour; those Foreigners that will not run the hazard of transporting Coin, and that cannot or will not stay till the Ballance return in its Equilibrium, allow to those that are willing to stay, or run those risks, a certain Consideration great or small, in proportion to the Balance of Trade, or according as they can agree.

When by the excess of the Denominator, the Difference of Exchange is considerably increas'd against a Nation, and Coin become scarce; Foreigners finding a great Loss by way of Exchange, become more impatient of having their own transmitted to them, and chuse rather to imploy it in Goods or Labour, to be transported for their Account, to those Countries it will yield most, in hopes by that means to prevent part of that Loss they would be obliged to bear by way of Exchange. This forces the Labour of that Nation to rise and extend itself in Denomination of Value, so as to answer that Increase of Demand: But as that Increase is forced by the negative part of the Denominator, proceeding from its Excess, or from those Debts that compose it, all that Increase is imaginary or negative. So that when Merchants go about to convert elsewhere, the Labor of that Nation into Gold or Silver, they find themselves in that case obliged to retrench all that forc'd Increase; because that Labour of the rest of the World which interferes with it, being charged but with a natural Denomination, will force its Vent preferably to that which is charged with a greater Denomination. Thus Foreigners finding also their Account short this way, cease to credit this Nation, by importing into it no more Labour than they are sure to export out of it. Thus will that Nation, after having lived on its Coin, be obliged to live on its Store of exportable Labour, until Credit yields; and in the mean while, foreign Manufacturers, whoso Labour is not risen, and consequently having more Demand for it than before, find themselves in a condition to imploy that Nation's Produce, or Materials, perceiving they can, by the great Difference of Exchange, allow a great Price for them: this forces those Materials to rise in Denomination of Value, even beyond the Proportion of Exchange, and consequently beyond the Proportion of Manufactures. After which, the Manufacturer finding neither the same Demand, nor Profit as before, is obliged to lessen the Number of his Workmen. Thus by degrees the Workmen are obliged to quit their usual Labour, and betake themselves to other, being forced out of the natural Proportion, to fill up that, which hath regard to the Excess of the Denominator.

From what hath been said hitherto, may be drawn the following Conclusions.

1. That Credit is of pernicious consequence to that Nation, that uses or encourages it beyond Nature, by reason it exists but at the cost or exclusion of Coin, which composes the real part of the Denominator.
2. That what is properly call'd Value of things, in a Nation whose Denominator exceeds not its natural Proportion, is a mix'd Denomination, composed of the Real Part, and of the Natural Portion of Credit of the Denominator.
3. That what is call'd Value, in a Nation whose Denominator exceeds the natural Proportion, is not only a mix'd Denomination compos'd of the Real Part, and Natural Portion of Credit but also of the Excess of the Denominator; and that that Excess of Value is negative, and acts positively against that Nation: so that instead of gaining by Trade, it loses proportionably to that Excess of Denomination of Value.
4. That the Denominator of the World being unlimited, and indefinite, by reason of that indefinite Variation, or Increase, it continually bears, by a continual Addition of Gold and Silver, which is daily drawn from the several Mines of the World; it follows, that the private Denominators of private Nation, are also indefinite.
5. That although the natural Denominator of a Nation be indefinitely moving, it is however a certain Point, to which a Nation can naturally attain to, by Trade.
6. That that Point is ever proportioned to the bulk of the general Denominator of the World, and to its number of Inhabitants.
7. That as Labour is the Foundation of Trade, that Point cannot be attained to, but by that Portion of Labour, which is proportioned to the number of Inhabitants that compose a Nation; nor maintained, when attained to, but by that same Labour.
8. That when the Ballance of Trade runs, and continues generally running, against a Nation, we may conclude its Denominator exceeds its natural Proportion.

9. That if Trade was not curbed by Laws, or disturbed by those Accidents that happen in long Wars, etc. which break the natural Proportion, either of People, or of private Denominators; Time would bring all trading Nations of the World into that Equilibrium, which is proportioned, and belongs to the number of their Inhabitants.

10. That the Riches or Strength of a Nation consists in the Number of its Inhabitants.

11. Lastly, That as one State may be defended by another, by means of Gold and Silver, as was experienced in the last Wars; Trade is absolutely necessary, being the only means by which a Nation can attain to its Proportion of Riches.

OF MANUFACTURES

The Manufactures of the World may be reduced to two sorts; that is, the Necessary, which consist in all that is wrought for Man's Necessities or Conveniences; and the Superfluous, which consist in all that is wrought, and serves to gratify his Vanity or Pleasures.

While the private Denominator of a Nation is, and lasts in its natural Proportion, all Manufactures are also in their natural Proportions, and fly from that Proportion, as it moves from it: So that if the Denominator be under its Proportion, necessary Manufactures flourish, and gain from the superfluous in like Proportion; and when it is above its Proportion, the superfluous flourish, and gain also from the necessary in like Proportion.

National Profit happens only, when necessary Manufactures are in their full Proportions, or beyond it; and national Loss, when the superfluous exceed their Proportion.

Manufactures of private Nations may be considered three Ways. That is, the Natural in a bare Proportion, which are those which are naturally just sufficient to answer the entire Demand of the Inhabitants. The Natural in great Proportion, which are those, which besides the Demand of the Inhabitants, furnish an Overplus which is transported to the rest of the World. And the Natural in small Proportion, which are those that cannot naturally be sufficient to answer the Inhabitants Wants, without Help from the rest of the World.

Every Nation naturally possesses a Mixture of these three sorts of Manufactures; but in such a manner, as the Natural in great Proportion, exceed as much, or more, the Demand of the Inhabitants, as those in small Proportion, are short of that Demand; so that they ballance one another by Trade. Neighbouring Nations have, generally speaking, a certain natural Portion, either great or small, of the same Produce and Manufactures, according to their Number of Inhabitants, and as they are disposed and situated.

No Nation can encourage or enlarge its Proportion of any private and natural Manufacture, without discouraging the rest; because whether an Allowance be given, either to the Manufacturer, or Transporter, that Allowance serves, and is employed to attract the Workmen from those other Manufactures, which have some Likeness to the encouraged Manufacture: So that what is transported of the encouraged Manufacture, beyond nature, only ballances the Diminution of the others.

When the natural Proportion of one, or more Manufactures, although necessary, is not large enough to answer the entire Demand of the Inhabitants, the best and safest Way is freely to suffer their Importation from the rest of the World; Taxes on Imports being no more than a Degree of Prohibition, and Prohibition only forcing those Manufactures to extend themselves beyond their natural Proportions, to the prejudice of those, which are, according to the Disposition of the Country, natural beyond the entire Demand of the Inhabitants; which lessens or hinders their Exportation, in proportion to the prejudice they receive by the Increase of those Manufactures, which are but in part natural, and whereof the Importation is prohibited.

This considered we may conclude, that Trade is never in a better condition, than when it's natural and free; the forcing it either by Laws, or Taxes, being always dangerous: because though the intended Benefit or Advantage be perceived, it is difficult to perceive its Countrecoup; which ever is at least in full proportion to the intended Benefit: Nature not yielding at once, sharpens those Countrecoups, and commonly causes a greater Evil, than the intended Benefit can ballance. Moreover, Trade being a tacit and natural Agreement, to give or furnish a Proportion of certain Denominations of Labour, to be drawn back in like Proportion, in such other Denominations, as best suits Necessity or Fancy; Man naturally seeks, and finds, the most easy and natural Means of attaining his Ends, and cannot be diverted from those Means, but by Force, and against his Will.

OF THE SITUATION AND DISPOSITION OF COUNTRIES, WITH THEIR PROPORTIONS OF DENOMINATOR

The best Situations are those near the Sea, where the Labour of the World may be imported and exported with least Charges; and whose Dispositions are such, as by means of Rivers or Canals, the Labour of the Inhabitants may be easily transported from one end of the Country to the other, at small Charge; The Inhabitants of such a Situation, and Disposition, bearing a greater Denominator, than an inferior Situation and Disposition could, though occupy'd by an equal number of Inhabitants; because all the Charge in transporting Labour, from the Extremitys to the Sea-Ports, is properly a Waste, or Loss, of the Inhabitants Labour: so that there will be more Days work required, to attract one from the Sea-Ports, according to the Distance or Disposition. For example, I suppose the Charges of Transportation of Labour from the Extremitys to the Ports, increase it one half every hundred Miles, and reciprocally from the Ports to the Extremitys; that is, supposing one with another a Day's work at two hundred Miles from the Port, is worth or will produce Eight-pence, that this same Day's Work transported within a hundred Miles of the Port, will produce Twelve-pence by reason of the Charge of Transportation, and that for the same reason it yields Eighteen-Pence at the Port, it is plain one Day's Labour of the most distant Inhabitants can produce one at the Port, but after Ten-Pence or five Quarters of a Day's Charges, so that they must furnish nine Quarters of a Day's Work, for one at the Port; and reciprocally a Day's Work transported from the Port to them, will produce but four Ninths of a Day's Work, the Charges of Transportation abated. So that those Inhabitants neither furnishing, nor attracting, the Labour of the World, but after the rate of two Days and a quarter for one, they can neither attract, nor retain, the Denominator, but in like proportion; and nine Inhabitants will be required at the Extremitys, to support such a Denominator, as four Inhabitants could at the Port: and in like manner, it will require three Inhabitants at a hundred miles from the Port, to support such a Denominator, as two could support at the Port. And thus in proportion to a greater Distance, or a worse Disposition than the Supposition; such as mountainous Countries, which are inaccessible to Carriages, and of such a Disposition, as cannot receive Inhabitants but here and there, in certain Corners, which are capable of Productions, but so far and dispers'd from one another, that those Inhabitants may be look'd upon as out of the World, and are of use to a Country only when they quit their Habitations, either to work elsewhere in Harvest-time, or to defend the State.

OF COMPANIES

Companies, generally speaking, can be of no advantage to the State, excepting only when private People are not able to attain the intended Ends; such as the bettering the Disposition of the Country, either in making Rivers navigable, or adding Canals in order to quicken the Communication, and render the Disposition capable of bearing a greater number of Inhabitants.

My Reasons are, First, They deprive Man of his natural Right to make the best of his Industry, according to his Genius, or Inclination. Secondly, They encourage Foreigners to live on the Labour of the State. Thirdly, It's exceeding hard to find a number of Men as careful and laborious, as is necessary in buying and selling, and at the same time so generous and disinterested, as not to turn things to their own private advantage, when occasion serves. So that considering the natural Bent of Man, I conceive private Persons will trade to better advantage for the State, than Companies can; besides the danger of their extending their Credit beyond their Proportions to the prejudice and exclusion of Coin, and dividing annually more than they gain by Trade or Labour, to the prejudice of the Proprietors of the real annual Revenues of the Kingdom, by thrusting them out of their natural Proportions of the Whole. For if to the whole Property there be added an unnatural and negative Half, that bears an annual Revenue or Attraction of Labour, in proportion to that Half, the Possessors of the first and natural All, will not be able to attract above two Thirds of all the annual Labour. It is true, they will still attract the same Denomination of Labour they did before the Addition; but as the added Portion, in attracting its Portion of Labour, would raise it 50 per Cent in Denomination, the Proprietors of the first and natural All, having no more than their first annual Denomination, will not be able to attract any more Labour, than two Thirds of that they attracted before the Addition. Thus they are thrust out of one Third, and are in effect Proprietors but of two Thirds, instead of the Whole they were possessed of: which is properly only a Transfer of the Propriety of Labour, from the real to the negative possessors; the whole annual Labour of a Nation being always equal to all its annual Revenues, of what Denomination soever they be.

OF ALTERING THE DENOMINATION OF COIN, AND ITS EFFECTS

When by some Accident or other, the Denominator or Denomination of the Whole is larger than the State can bear, the Remedys are, either to proportion the People to the Denominator, or the Denominator to the People: But as the first is most difficult, and almost impossible, the proportioning the Denominator to the People must be prefer'd. Which may be done either by laying a Tax on the Inhabitants, to be employ'd in sinking the Debts of the Nation, or be reserved against a future Exigency of the State; or by raising the Denomination of Coin, in proportion to such a Portion as would be thought necessary to be cut off from a Nation. For example, I suppose, that by reason of the Excess of the Denominator, whether it be to draw more Coin into a Nation, or only to preserve that already in it, the Denomination of Coin be doubled; it is plain Credit then would be reduced to one half, whilst the real Part of the Denominator should still be the same, although raised to a double Denomination: because Coin, the real Part of the Denominator, still being the same Portion of the grand Denominator of the World, it can express but that selfsame Portion, and can retain but that same Strength or Value, which is proportioned to that Portion, whether its Denomination be high or low, which is different as to Credit; it being only a Denomination of a certain Number of Unities of the private Denominator of a Nation, that Denomination alters in Value in like proportion, as the Unity is altered. And as in this case the Unity would be reduced to half its former Value, Credit would also be reduced to half its former Value, and would express but one half of that Portion of the grand Denominator of the World, it did express before this Operation; and reciprocally, the lowering the Denomination of Coin, enlarge the Denominator, by enlarging Credit.

What precedes, shews what is feasible in case of extreme Necessity; but as such an Operation would be of great prejudice to the Proprietors of Land, Nations ought by all means to prevent, either the Want of such a Remedy, or Necessity of such an Unravelling, as would be the more pernicious, the longer it had been a coming; and when the Disproportion of natural Manufactures would be enlarged, in proportion to the swelling of the Denominator and Denomination: because supposing a Nation had enlarged its Denominator, and Denomination, so as to want such a Reduction; that Nation ought first to consider how long the Evil was coming, that the Remedy might be applied accordingly: for when the Evil is new and sudden, it may at once alter the natural Proportion of Rich and Poor of that Nation; but it cannot, though ever so great, alter the natural Proportion of necessary and superfluous Manufactures, but gradually, and with time. And while necessary and superfluous Labours are in their natural Proportions, the Denominator may be proportioned thereto, without exposing Trade to any sensible Convulsions: But when the Evil is of long standing, the Proportion of necessary Manufactures is then too small, by reason as the Denominator of a Nation increases, the Manufactures of Superfluities draw from the necessary Manufactures their Workmen, the Masters of the superfluous raising more Apprentices than before, and those of the necessary less in like proportion. So that if after several Years unnatural Increase of Denominator, a Nation would suddenly cure the Evil, by suddenly proportioning the Denominator to the Inhabitants, the Remedy would prove too sharp; for in that case the Wants of Superfluities would be much lessened, and those of Necessities much increased; and in such a manner as the necessary Manufactures could not at any rate answer the extraordinary Demand, until they had attracted from the superfluous, those Workmen they had lost, while the Denominator was increasing; which is a Work of time.

As I suppose that Nation I make use of for example in a natural State, I do not suppose it loaded with a foreign Debt; therefore before I make an end of this Tract, I think proper to take notice, that a Nation must look upon a foreign Debt, as part of its All; which, though negative, acts positively on that Nation, and, according to the Rules of this System, as long as both the Confidence and Fear of Strangers keep them in a ballance. But when those two Passions fly from their Equilibrium, the Debt acts beyond the Rules, in proportion to the Distance of that Equilibrium, and to the Largeness of the Debt. Thus is an indebted Nation not only obliged to keep those strange Creditors out of its own Labour, but also its Coin and Bullion are ever subject to their Passions and Occasions; they having it in their power, at will, irregularly to turn the Ballance.

As I do not pretend to know the State of Nations; I make no Application, but leave it to those, who, by their Station, are best capable of it. I shall only add, That in stating the Case of Nations, regard ought to be had, either to the Empire over, or Subjection to other Nations; that, in many cases, altering the Proportion of the Denominator. For supposing two equal Nations, and that one hath such a Power or Right over the other; as, for example, one quarter of the yearly Produce of its Labour be expended in the other: in that case the imperial Nation will support a Denominator one quarter above its natural Proportion; and its Proportion of superfluous Manufactures, will run above nature in like Proportion. But then the subjected Nation will support but three quarters of its natural Denominator; and its Proportion of necessary Manufactures will run above nature; and as fast as the other quarter is attracted from the World, it will be drawn off by the imperial one: So that these two Nations must be looked upon, one as composed of more Rich by one quarter than its natural Proportion, and the other of less Rich in like proportion. And as the Excess of Rich in the one, is supported by the Inhabitants of the other, it will keep its ground; but both taken together, will still keep but their natural Proportion. So that where a Nation is found to bear a greater Proportion of Denominator, and superfluous Manufactures, than its Number of Inhabitants seem capable of naturally supporting, it will, if looked into, appear, That that Increase is maintained by the Labour of other Nations; which, by some Accident or other, are either subjected or indebted to it.

29. Richard Cantillon: *An Essay on Economic Theory* (1730)[1]

CHAPTER 1: BARTER

In Part One, an attempt was made to prove that the real value of everything used by men is proportional to the quantity of land used for its production, and for the upkeep of those who produced it. In this Part Two, I will start by summing up the different degrees of land fertility in several countries, and the different kinds of products it can bring forth in greater abundance, according to its intrinsic quality. Then, assuming the establishment of towns and their markets to facilitate the sale of these products, it will be shown, by comparing exchanges that could be made, wine for cloth, wheat for shoes, hats, etc., and by the difficulty involved in transporting these different products or merchandises, that it was impossible to fix their respective intrinsic value. Therefore, it was absolutely necessary for men to find a substance easily transportable, not perishable, and having, by weight, a proportion or value equal to the different products and merchandises, whether needed or convenient. Hence there arose the choice of gold and silver for large business, and of copper for small transactions.

These metals are not only durable and easy to transport, but correspond to the employment of a large area of land for their production, which gives them the true value people seek in an equivalent (i.e., a medium of exchange).

Mr. Locke, who, like all the English writers on this subject, has looked only to market prices, establishes that the value of all things is proportional to their abundance or scarcity, and to the abundance or scarcity of the silver for which they are exchanged (i.e., the naïve quantity theory of money). It is generally known that the prices of products and merchandise have increased in Europe ever since a great quantity of silver has been imported from the West Indies.

However, I think we must not believe, as a general rule, that the market prices of things ought to be proportional to their quantity and to the amount of silver in circulation in a particular place, because the products and merchandise that are to be exported do not influence the prices of those which remain. If, for example, there is twice as much wheat in a market town than what is consumed there, and we compare the whole quantity of wheat to that of silver, the wheat would be more abundant, in proportion, to the silver destined for its purchase. The market price will be maintained just as if there were only half the quantity of wheat, since the other half can be, and even must be, sent into the city, and the cost of transport will be included in the city price, which is always higher than that of the town. Nevertheless, apart from the case

---

[1] Translated by Chantal Saucier and Mark Thornton.

of hoping to sell in another market, I consider that Mr. Locke's idea is correct in the sense of the following chapter, and not otherwise.

CHAPTER 2: MARKET PRICES

Let us assume that there are butchers on one side, and buyers on the other. The price of meat will be determined after some bargaining, and a pound of beef will be valued in silver (i.e., money) approximately the same as all beef offered for sale in the market (i.e., supply), is to all the silver brought there to buy beef (i.e., demand).

This proportion (or price) is settled by bargaining. The butcher sets his price according to the number of buyers he sees, while the buyers, on their side, offer less if they think the butcher will make fewer sales. The price set by some is usually followed by others. Some are cleverer in marketing their merchandise, others in discrediting them. This method of fixing market prices has no exact or geometrical foundation, since it often depends upon the eagerness or the abilities of a small number of buyers or sellers. However, it does not appear that it could be done in a more suitable way. It is clear that the quantity of products or merchandise offered for sale, proportioned to the demand or number of buyers, is the basis on which are fixed, or always assumed to be fixed, actual market prices. In general, these prices do not vary much from intrinsic value.

Let us take another case. Several hotel managers have been told at the beginning of the season to buy green peas. One owner has ordered the purchase of 10 quarts for 60 livres, another 10 quarts for 50 livres, a third 10 quarts for 40 livres, and a fourth 10 quarts for 30 livres. If these orders are to be carried out, there must be 40 quarts of green peas in the market. Suppose there are only 20. The sellers, seeing many buyers, will keep up their prices, and the buyers will come up to the prices asked, so that those who offer 60 livres for 10 quarts will be the first served. The sellers, seeing later that no one will go above 50, will let the other 10 quarts go at that price. Those who had orders not to exceed 40 and 30 livres will go away empty handed. If instead of 40 quarts there were 400, not only would the hotel managers get the green peas much below the sums laid down for them, but the sellers, in order to be preferred over the others by the few buyers, will lower their green peas almost to their intrinsic value, and in that case, many managers who had no orders will buy some.

It often happens that sellers, who are too stubborn in keeping up their price in the market, miss the opportunity of selling their products or merchandise to their advantage and are thereby losers. It also happens that by sticking to their prices, they may be able to sell more profitably another day.

Distant markets can always affect the prices of local markets: if wheat is extremely expensive in France, its price will increase in England and in other neighboring countries.

CHAPTER 3: THE CIRCULATION OF MONEY

It is the general opinion in England that a farmer must make three rents. The first is the principal and true rent that he pays to the property owner, which is assumed to be equal in value to one-third of the farm's output. A second rent goes for his maintenance and that of the men and horses he employs to operate the farm, and a third rent that he keeps for making the business profitable.

The same idea generally is the norm in other countries of Europe, though in some states, like Milan, the farmer gives up half the product instead of a third. It is also true that many landlords in all countries try to lease their farms at the highest price they can; but when it is above one-third of the product, the farmers generally are very poor. I do not doubt that the Chinese landowner extracts from his farmer more than three-quarters of the product of the land.

However, when a farmer has some capital to carry on the management of this farm, the owner who leases him the farm for one-third of the product will be sure of payment and will be better off by such a deal than if he leases his land at a higher rate to a poor farmer and faces the risk of losing all his rental income. The larger the farm, the better off the farmer will be. This is seen in England where farmers are generally more prosperous than in other countries where farms are small.

The assumption I shall make in this inquiry of the circulation of money is that farmers earn three rents and they spend the third rent to live more comfortably, instead of saving it. This is indeed the case with most farmers in all countries.

All the products in the state come directly or indirectly from the hands of the farmers, as well as all the materials from which commodities are made. The land produces everything but fish, and even then, the fishermen who catch the fish must be maintained by the products of the land.

The three rents of the farmer must therefore be considered the principal sources or, so to speak, the mainspring of circulation in the state. The first rent must be paid to the property owner in cash. For the second and third rents, cash is needed for the iron, tin, copper, salt, sugar, cloth, and generally all the products from the city that are consumed in the countryside. However, all that hardly exceeds one-sixth of the total of the three rents. As for the food and drink of the country folks, cash is not always necessary to obtain them.

The farmer may brew his beer or make his wine without spending money. He can make his bread, slaughter the oxen, sheep, pigs, etc., that are eaten in the country. He can pay most of his assistants in wheat, meat, and drink, not only laborers, but country artisans as well, by valuing products at the prices of the nearest markets, and labor at local wage rates.

The things necessary to life are food, clothing, and housing. There is no need for cash to obtain food in the country, as I have just explained. If coarse linen and cloths are made there and if houses are built there, as is often the case, the labor may be paid in barter by valuation without cash being needed.

The only cash needed in the countryside is for the rent payment to the property owner and for the goods obtained from the city, such as knives, scissors, pins, needles, cloths for some farmers or other well-to-do people, kitchen utensils, plates, and generally all that is obtained from the city for use in the countryside.

I have already noted that it has been estimated that half the inhabitants of a state live in the cities, and that consequently, those who live in the city consume more than half the production of the land. Cash is therefore necessary, not only for the rent payment to the owner, corresponding to one-third of the product of the land, but also for the city merchandise consumed in the country, which may amount to something more than one-sixth of the product of the soil. However, one-third and one-sixth amount to half the product. The cash circulating in the country must therefore be equal to at least one-half the product of the land, while the other half, or somewhat less, may be consumed in the country without need for cash.

The circulation of this money takes place when the property owners spend the rents they collected in lump sums from the farmers on retail purchases in the city. The entrepreneurs of the cities (e.g., butchers, bakers, brewers, etc.) then collect this same money, little by little, in order to buy goods from the farmers, such as cattle, wheat, barley, etc. In this way, all the large sums of money are distributed in small amounts, and all the small amounts are then collected to make payments in large amounts, directly or indirectly, to the farmers. Therefore this money serves both in wholesale and retail.

When I stated that the necessary quantity of money for circulation in the countryside is often equal to half the product of the land, this is the minimum. For the circulation in the countryside to be easily conducted, I will suppose that the cash needed is equal in value to two-thirds of the farmers' income, or two-thirds of the product of the land. It will be seen later that this assumption is not far from the truth.

Let us now imagine that the money conducting the whole circulation in a small state is equal to 10,000 ounces of silver, and that all the payments made with this money, country to city, and city to country, are made once a year. In addition, these 10,000 ounces of silver are equal in value to two of the farmers' rents, or two-thirds of the product of the land. The rents collected by the property owners will correspond to 5,000 ounces, and the whole circulation of the remaining silver between the people of the countryside and those of the city, made by annual payments, also will correspond to 5,000 ounces.

However, if the owners stipulate that their farmers make payments every six months instead of once a year, and if the other debtors also make their payments every six months, this will alter the pace of circulation. While 10,000 ounces were needed to make the annual payments, only 5,000 will now be required because 5,000 ounces paid twice over will have the same effect as 10,000 ounces paid once.

Furthermore, if the owners stipulate that their farmers make quarterly payments, or if they are satisfied to receive payments from the farmers as the four seasons enable them to sell their products, and if all other payments are made quarterly, only 2,500 ounces will be needed for the same circulation that would have required 10,000 ounces paid annually. Therefore, supposing that all payments are made quarterly in the small state in question, the proportion of the value of the money needed for the circulation is to the annual product of the soil (or the three rents), as 2,500 livres is to 15,000 livres, or 1 to 6, so that money would correspond to one-sixth of the annual production.

However, considering that each branch of the circulation (i.e., the economy) in the cities is carried out by entrepreneurs, and that the consumption of food is paid for daily, weekly, or monthly, and that clothing purchased once or twice a year by families is paid for at different times by different people; and considering also that the expenditure on beverages is usually made daily, and that payment for beer, coal, and a thousand other articles of consumption is very prompt, then it would seem that the proportion we have established for quarterly payments would be too high and that the circulation of products estimated at 15,000 ounces of silver in value could be conducted with much less than 2,500 ounces of silver coins.

However, because farmers have to make large payments to the owners at least every quarter and the taxes collected by the prince or the state upon consumption goods are accumulated by the tax collectors to make large payments to the receivers general, there must be enough cash in circulation to make these large payments without difficulty, and without hindering the circulation of currencies for the food and clothing of the people.

It will be understood from this that the proportion of the amount of money needed for circulation in a state is not incomprehensible, and that this amount may be greater or less in a state depending on the mode of living and the speed of payments. It is very difficult to lay down anything definite about this quantity in general, as the proportion may vary in different countries. Therefore, it is only conjectural when I say that generally, "the cash or money necessary to carry on the circulation and exchange in a state is roughly equal in value to one-third of all the owners' annual rents of the said state."

Whether money is scarce or plentiful in a state, this proportion will not change much, because where money is abundant, land is leased at higher rates and at lower rates where money is scarce. This rule will always be true, at all times. In states where money is scarcer, there usually is more barter by valuation, than in those where money is plentiful, and circulation is more prompt and less sluggish than in those where money is not so scarce. Thus it is always necessary, when estimating the amount of money in circulation, to take into account the speed of its circulation.

Assuming that the money in circulation is equal to one-third of all the owners' rents and that these rents equal to one-third of the annual product of the land, it follows that "the money circulating in a state is equal in value to the one-ninth of all the annual product of the land."

Sir William Petty, in a 1685 manuscript, frequently assumes that the money in circulation is equal to one-tenth of the product of the land without explaining his reasoning. I believe he formed this opinion from experience and from his practical knowledge of both the money circulating in Ireland (a country he had measured as a surveyor) and of production, which he estimated from observation. I am not far removed from his idea, however, I chose to compare the money circulating to the owners' rents, which are ordinarily paid in cash and easily ascertainable by a uniform land tax, rather than to the products of the land because of their daily price variations in the markets, and the fact that a large part of the product is consumed without ever entering the markets. In the next chapter, I shall give several reasons, supported by examples, to strengthen my conclusion. I think this rule is useful, even if it is not mathematically exact in any country. It is sufficient if it is near the truth and if it prevents governors of states from forming extravagant ideas about the amount of money in circulation. There is no branch of knowledge in which one is more subject to error than statistics when they are based on one's imagination, and none is more informative when they are based upon detailed facts.

Some cities and states, which have no land to call their own, subsist by exchanging their labor and manufactured goods for the products of other lands. For example, in Hamburg, Dantzig, several other cities of the Empire, and even part of Holland, it seems more difficult to estimate the amount of cash in circulation. However, if we could estimate the amount of foreign land used for their subsistence, the calculation would probably not differ from the one I made for the other states that chiefly subsist on their own products, and which are the subject of this essay.

As to the cash needed to carry on foreign trade, it seems that no more is required than what is in circulation in the state when the balance of foreign trade is equal, that is when the products and merchandise sent abroad are equal in value to those imported.

If France sends cloth to Holland and receives spices of equal value in return, the property owner who consumes these spices pays their value to the grocer, who pays the same amount to the cloth maker, to whom the same amount is due in Holland for the cloth he sent there. This is done using bills of exchange, which I will explain later. These two payments take place in France, unconnected to the rent of the property owner, and no money leaves France because of these transactions. All other classes of society consuming Dutch spices similarly pay the grocer. Those living on the first rent, that is the property owners, pay from this rent, and those who live on the other two rents, in the country or the city, pay the grocer, directly or indirectly, out of the money that conducts the circulation of these rents. The grocer again pays this money to the manufacturer in Holland for his bill of exchange and when the balance is equal, no increase of money is needed for circulation in the state due to foreign trade. But if it is not equal, if more merchandise is sold to Holland than is bought back, or vice versa, money is needed for the surplus that Holland must send to France or France to Holland. This will increase or diminish the amount of money circulating in France.

It may even occur that when the balance with the foreigner is equal to the trade with him, commerce with this foreigner may slow down the circulation of currencies, and consequently, a greater quantity of money is required because of this commerce.

For example, if the French ladies who wear French fabrics wish to wear Dutch velvets paid for by the cloth sent to Holland, they will buy these velvets from the merchants who imported them from Holland, and these merchants will pay the cloth manufacturers. The money thus passes through more hands than if these ladies took their money to the cloth manufacturers and contented themselves with French fabrics. When the same money passes through the hands of several entrepreneurs, the rapidity of circulation is slowed down. But it is difficult to make an exact estimate of this sort of delay, which depends upon various circumstances. Thus, in the present example, if the ladies pay the merchant for the velvet today, and the merchant pays his bill with the manufacturer in Holland tomorrow, and if the manufacturer pays the wool merchant the next day, and this last pays the farmer the day after, it is possible that the farmer will keep the money in hand more than two months to make up the quarter's rent he owes to his landlord. This money might, in two months, have circulated through the hands of a hundred entrepreneurs without slowing down the circulation needed in the state.

After all, we must consider the rent collected by the property owner as the most necessary and considerable part of the money in circulation. If the owner lives in the city and the farmer sells all his production and buys all the goods needed in the country in the same city, the money may always remain in the city. The farmer will sell products there exceeding half the output of his farm and will pay his landlord the money value of one-third of his product and the rest to merchants or entrepreneurs for goods to be consumed in the country. Even here, however, as the farmer sells his products for lump sums, which are subsequently distributed in retail purchases, and are again collected to serve for lump payments to the farmers, the circulation always has the same effect (subject to its rapidity) as if the farmer took the money received for his products to the country, and sent it back again to the city.

The circulation always consists of the large sums, received by the farmer for his products, being distributed at retail, and being brought together again to make large payments. Whether part of this money leaves the city, or remains there entirely, may be regarded as the circulation between city and country. All the circulation takes place between the inhabitants of the state, and they are all fed and maintained in any event from the product of the land and raw materials of the country.

It is true that the wool, for example, which is brought from the country, is worth four times its former value when made up into cloth in the city. However, this increase of value, which is the price of the workmen's labor and manufactures in the city, is again exchanged for the country products that serve for the laborer's maintenance.

CHAPTER 4: FURTHER REFLECTION ON THE RAPIDITY OR SLOWNESS OF THE CIRCULATION OF MONEY IN EXCHANGE

Let us assume that the farmer pays 1,300 ounces of silver every quarter to the property owner, who pays, every week, 100 ounces to the baker, butcher, etc., and that these, in turn, pay the farmer 100 ounces every week, so that the farmer collects every week as much money as the property owner spends. In this case there will be only 100 ounces in constant circulation; the other 1,200 ounces will remain held partly by the property owner and partly by the farmer.

However, it rarely happens that the property owners spend their rents in a fixed and regular proportion. In London, as soon as a property owner receives his rent, he deposits most of it with a goldsmith or banker, who lends it at interest, so that this part is in circulation. Or else the property owner spends a large part of it on the many things he needs for his household. He may even borrow money before he gets his next quarter's rent. Thus the money of the first quarter's rent will circulate in a thousand ways before it is accumulated by the farmer to make his second-quarter payment.

When it comes time to pay the second-quarter rent, the farmer will sell his products in large amounts. Those who buy his cattle, wheat, hay, etc., will already have collected the price of these goods from their retail sales. Thus, the money of the first quarter will have circulated in the retail trade for nearly three months before being collected by the retail dealers, and given to the farmer who will use it to make his second-quarter payment. It would seem from this that less money would suffice for the circulation in a state than we have assumed.

Barter does not require much cash because goods can be evaluated at the market price on the day of delivery. If a brewer supplies a tailor with beer for his family, and if the tailor in turn supplies the brewer with the clothes he needs, the only cash needed between these two traders is the amount of the difference between the two transactions.

If a merchant in a market town sends commodities to an entrepreneur in the city, and in return the entrepreneur sends the merchant products from the city to be consumed in the country, throughout the year, business between these two dealers and mutual confidence leads them to account for their commodities and merchandise at their respective market prices, and the only money needed for this commerce will be the balance that one owes to the other at the end of the year. Even then, this balance may be carried forward to the next year, without the actual payment of any money. All the entrepreneurs of a city who continually do business with each other may practice this method. Barter exchange by valuation does seem to reduce the cash in circulation, or at least to accelerate its movement by making it unnecessary when people have confidence in each other and can use this method of exchange by valuation. It is not without reason, as is commonly said, that trust in commerce makes money less scarce.

Goldsmiths and bankers, whose tickets serve as payment like coin money, also add to the speed of circulation, which would be retarded if money was required for payments where tickets now suffice. And although these goldsmiths and bankers always keep on hand a large part of the coin money they have received for their tickets, they also put into circulation a considerable amount of this effective money, as I shall explain later when dealing with public banks.

All these reflections seem to prove that the circulation in a state could be conducted with much less coin money than what I previously assumed was necessary. However, the following inductions appear to counterbalance them and to contribute to the slowing down of circulation.

I will first observe that all commodities are produced by labor that may possibly—strictly speaking—be carried on with little or no actual money, as I have often suggested. But the workers who make goods in cities or market towns must be paid in coin money. If a house has cost 100,000 ounces of silver to build, all this sum or most of it, must have been paid in small amounts on a weekly basis to the brickmaker, masons, carpenters, etc., directly or indirectly. The expenditures of small families, which are always more numerous in cities, must be made with coin money. With such small purchases, credit, barter, and tickets, like banknotes do not work. Merchants and entrepreneurs demand cash for the things they supply, and if they give credit to a family for a few days or months, they require a substantial down payment. A wagon builder, who sells a wagon for 400 ounces of silver in notes, will have to convert them into coin money to pay for all the materials and the men who have worked on the wagon if they have worked on credit. If he has paid them already, the money will be used to pay them to start working on a new one. The sale of the wagon will leave him the profit of his enterprise and he will spend this profit to maintain his family. He could not be satisfied with notes, unless he can afford to put something aside or deposit it to earn interest.

The consumption of the inhabitants of a state is, in a sense, entirely for food. Lodging, clothing, furniture, etc., correspond to the food of the men who have worked upon them, and in the cities, all beverages and food are necessarily paid for in coin money. In the families of landowners, who live in the city, food is paid for every day or every week. In their families, wine is paid for every week or every month; hats, stockings, shoes, etc., are ordinarily paid for in coin money, at least the payments correspond to cash for the men who have worked upon them. All the sums used to make large payments are divided, distributed, and spread in small payments corresponding to the maintenance of the workmen, servants, etc., and all these sums are necessarily collected and reunited by the entrepreneurs and retailers, who are employed in providing the subsistence of the inhabitants, to make large payments when they buy commodities from the farmers. An alehouse keeper collects by sols and livres the sums he pays to the brewer, who uses them to pay for all the grain and materials he buys from the country. One cannot imagine that anything could be purchased for cash in a state, like furniture, merchandise, etc., at a value that does not correspond to the maintenance of those who have produced it.

Circulation in the cities is carried out by entrepreneurs and always corresponds, directly or indirectly, to the subsistence of the servants, workmen, etc. It is inconceivable that the circulation in small retail businesses could be conducted without cash. Notes may serve as counters in large payments for a certain time, but when the large sums come to be distributed and spread into small transactions, as is always the case sooner or later in the course of circulation in a city, notes cannot serve this purpose and cash is needed.

All this presupposes that all the classes in a state who practice some economy, save and keep out of circulation small amounts of cash until they have enough to invest at interest or profit.

Many miserly and timid people will bury and hoard cash for considerable periods of time.

Many property owners, entrepreneurs, and others, always keep some cash in their pockets or safes so that they do not run out of money and to protect them against unforeseen emergencies. If a gentleman says that he never had less than 20 louis in his pocket throughout the whole year, it may be said that this pocket has kept 20 louis out of circulation for a year. No one likes to spend to their last penny or to be completely without money. People like to receive a new payment before paying debt, even if they have the money.

The funds of minors and of litigants are often deposited in cash and kept out of circulation.

Besides the large quarterly payments that pass through the hands of the farmers, there are wholesale transactions between entrepreneurs and payments from borrowers to lenders that occur at different times. All these sums are collected in the retail trade, are dispersed again, only to come back to the farmer sooner or later. However, they would seem to require a larger amount of cash for circulation than if these large payments were made at times different from those when the farmers are paid for their commodities.

In conclusion, there is such a great a variety in the organization of the inhabitants in the state, and in the corresponding circulation of coin money, that it seems impossible to lay down anything precise or exact about the proportion of money sufficient for circulation. I have produced so many examples and inductions which make it clear that I am not far from the truth in my conclusion "that the actual money necessary for the circulation of the state corresponds nearly to the value of the third of all the annual rents of the property owners." When the owners have a rent that amounts to half the production, or more than a third, a greater quantity of coin money is needed for circulation, other things being equal. When there is great confidence in the banks and in book credits, or when the speed of circulation is accelerated in any way, less money will suffice. However, I shall show later that public banks do not bring as many advantages as is usually assumed.

CHAPTER 5: ON THE INEQUALITY OF THE CIRCULATION OF MONEY IN A STATE

The city always supplies various goods to the country, and the property owners who reside in the city should always receive about one-third of the production of their land. The country thus owes to the city more than half the production of the land. This debt would always exceed one-half if all property owners lived in the city, but because most owners with less significant land holdings live in the country, I suppose that the balance or debt, which continually returns from the country to the city, is equal to half the production of the land and is paid to the city with half of the commodities transported from the countryside and sold to pay this debt.

The countryside of a state or kingdom owes a constant balance to the capital to pay rents to the great property owners who reside there, and to pay taxes to the state or crown, most of which are spent in the capital. All the provincial cities owe a constant balance to the capital, for the state's property and consumption taxes, and for the different goods that they obtain from the capital. It is also the case that several individuals and property owners, who live in the provincial cities, will spend some time in the capital for pleasure, or for the judgment of their lawsuits in final appeal, or because they send their children there for an elite education. Consequently, all these expenses incurred in the capital are drawn from the provincial cities.

It may therefore be said that all the countryside and cities of a state regularly owe an annual balance or debt to the capital. However, because such payments are made in money, it is clear that the provinces always owe considerable sums to the capital. The products and commodities that the provinces send to the capital are sold to pay for these debts and balances.

Now assume that the circulation of money in the provinces and in the capital is equal both in terms of the quantity of money and the speed of circulation. The balance will be first sent to the capital in cash and this will decrease the quantity of money in the provinces and increase it in the capital. Consequently, products and goods will be more expensive in the capital than in the provinces because of the greater abundance of money in the capital. The difference between the prices in the capital and the provinces must pay for the costs and risks of transport, otherwise cash will be sent to the capital to pay the balance and this will continue until the differences in prices between the capital and the provinces cover the costs and risks of transport. Then the merchants and entrepreneurs of the market towns will buy the products of the villages at a low price and will have them transported to the capital to be sold at a higher price. This difference in price will of necessity pay for the maintenance of the horses and employees of the entrepreneur, plus profit, or else he would cease his enterprise.

As a result, the price of farm products of equal quality will always be higher in areas that are closer to the capital than in those more distant in proportion to the costs and risks of transport. In addition, areas that are adjacent to seas and rivers flowing into the capital will get a better price for their products relative to those which are distant (other things being equal), because water transport is considerably less expensive than land transport. On the other hand, there are certain foods and goods that cannot be consumed in the capital because they are not suitable or cannot be sent there on account of their bulk, or because they would be spoiled on the way. These will be infinitely cheaper in the country and distant provinces than in the capital, because of the much smaller amount of money in circulation in the distant provinces.

Therefore fresh eggs, game, fresh butter, firewood, etc., will generally be much cheaper in the province of Poitou, while wheat, cattle, and horses will be more expensive in Paris, the difference being the cost and risk of transport, and the fees for entering the city. It would be easy to make an infinite number of inductions of the same kind to justify by experience the necessity of an inequality in the circulation of money in the different provinces of a great state or kingdom, and to show that this inequality is always relative to the balance or debt, which belongs to the capital.

If we assume that the balance owed to the capital amounts to one quarter of the production of the land of all the provinces of the state, the best use that can be made of the land would be to employ the country bordering on the capital to produce the kinds of products which could not be drawn from distant provinces without much expense or deterioration. This is in fact what always takes place. The market prices in the capital regulate how the farmers employ the land for this or that purpose. They use the closest lands, when suitable, for market gardens, pasture, etc.

Therefore, when possible, factories for cloth, linen, lace, etc., ought to be set up in remote provinces and factories to make tools of iron, tin, copper, etc., should be located in the neighborhood of coal mines or forests, which are otherwise useless because of their distance. In this way, finished manufactured goods could be sent to the capital with much lower transportation cost than by sending the raw materials to be manufactured in the capital, as well as the subsistence of the artisans who manufacture them. This would save a large quantity of horses and transport workers who could be better employed for the benefit of the state. The land could serve to maintain the nearby workmen and useful artisans and a multitude of horses could be saved that are now used for unnecessary transportation. In this way, the remote areas would yield higher rents to property owners and the inequality of circulation between the provinces and the capital would be considerably less and better proportioned.

Nevertheless, to set up manufacturing in this way requires not only much encouragement and capital funds, but also some way to ensure a regular and constant demand, either in the capital itself or in foreign countries. Exports to foreign countries serve the capital by either paying for the goods it imports, or with the money it gets in return.

When these factories are established, perfection is not attained immediately. If some other province produces the goods better or cheaper, or has an advantage in transportation costs because it is closer to the capital or can resort to river and sea transportation, the new manufactures will not succeed. All these circumstances have to be considered when setting up a factory. My intention in this essay is not to explain these issues, but only to suggest that so far as practicable, significant manufacturing should be set up in provinces far from the capital to produce a less unequal distribution of money between rural areas and the capital.

For when a distant province has no factories and produces only ordinary foodstuffs and is without water communication to the capital or the ocean, it is surprising how scarce money is compared to that which circulates in the capital, and how little revenue the prince and the property owners who reside in the capital receive from even their best lands.

The wines of Provence and Languedoc that are sent to the north, must be sent on the long and difficult route around the Straits of Gibraltar and after having passed through the hands of several entrepreneurs, yield very little to the property owners living in Paris.

However, these distant provinces must send their commodities to the capital or elsewhere (either within the state or to foreign countries), despite all the disadvantages of transport and distance, in order to pay the balance owed to the capital. If there were rural factories to pay this balance, the commodities would be mostly consumed locally and in that case, the rural population would be much larger.

When a province pays its balance only with commodities that yield little in the capital because of transport costs, it is clear that the property owners living in the capital give up the production of a large amount of land in the country to receive little in the capital. This arises from the inequality of money, and this inequality results from the constant balance owed to the capital by the province.

Currently, if a state or kingdom supplies foreign countries with goods from its own factories and does enough of this commerce to draw in a constant balance of money from abroad every year, money will be more plentiful and the circulation will become more substantial than in foreign countries, and consequently, land and labor will gradually command a higher price. It therefore follows that in all the branches of commerce, this state will exchange a smaller amount of land and labor with the foreigner for a larger amount, so long as these circumstances continue.

But if a foreigner resides in the state in question, he will be in roughly the same situation and circumstances as the citizen of Paris who owns land in distant provinces.

Beginning in 1646, factories for making cloth and other goods were built in France and it appeared to trade, at least in part, in the way I described. Since the decay of France, England has taken possession of this trade, and all states appear to flourish by it to a larger or lesser extent. The inequality of the circulation of money in the different states represents the inequality of their comparative power, other things being equal, and this inequality of circulation is always related to the balance of foreign trade.

It is easy to judge from what has been said in this chapter that the assessment of taxes by the royal tithe, as suggested by Mr. de Vauban, would be neither advantageous, nor practicable. If taxes on land were levied in money, in proportion to the rents of the property owners, it would be fairer. But I must not stray from my subject to show the inconveniences and impossibility of Mr. de Vauban's proposal.

CHAPTER 6: THE INCREASE AND DECREASE OF THE QUANTITY OF MONEY IN A STATE

If gold or silver mines were found in a state, and considerable quantities of minerals were extracted from them, the owners of these mines, the entrepreneurs, and all those who work there, will increase their expenditures in proportion to the wealth and profit they make. They will also lend the money they have over and above what they need for their expenses and earn interest.

All this money, whether lent or spent, will enter into circulation and will not fail to raise the price of commodities and goods in all the channels of circulation it enters. Increased money will bring about increased expenditure, and this will cause an increase of market prices in the good years and to a lesser degree in bad years.

Everybody agrees that the abundance of money, or an increase in its use in exchange, raises the price of everything. This truth is substantiated in experience by the quantity of money brought to Europe from America for the last two centuries.

Mr. Locke lays it down as a fundamental maxim that the quantity of goods in proportion to the quantity of money is a regulator of market prices. I have tried to elucidate his idea in the preceding chapters: he has clearly seen that the abundance of money makes everything more expensive, but he has not considered how this happens. The great difficulty of this question consists in knowing in what way and in what proportion the increase of money raises the price of things.

I have already noted that acceleration or a greater pace in the circulation of money in exchange, is equivalent to, to a certain degree, an increase of actual money. I have also noted that an increase or decrease of prices in a distant market, domestic or foreign, influences the local market prices. On the other hand, money flows through so many retail channels that it seems impossible not to lose sight of it, seeing that having been amassed to make large sums, it is distributed in small amounts in exchange, and then gradually accumulated again to make large payments. For these operations, it is necessary to constantly exchange between gold, silver, and copper money, according to the requirements of exchange. It is also usually the case that the increase or decrease of hard money in a state is not perceived because it comes into a state from foreign countries by such imperceptible means and proportions that it is impossible to know exactly the quantity which enters or leaves the state.

However, all these operations happen before our eyes and everybody takes a direct part in them. I therefore venture to offer a few observations on the subject, even though I may not be able to give an exact and precise account.

In general, an increase of hard money in a state will cause a corresponding increase in consumption and this will gradually produce increased prices.

If the increase of hard money comes from gold and silver mines within the state, the owner of these mines, the entrepreneurs, the smelters, refiners, and all the other workers will increase their expenses in proportion to their profits. Their households will consume more meat, wine, or beer than before. They will become accustomed to wearing better clothes, having finer linens, and to having more ornate houses and other desirable goods. Consequently, they will give employment to several artisans who did not have that much work before and who, for the same reason, will increase their expenditures. All this increased expenditure on meat, wine, wool, etc., necessarily reduces the share of the other inhabitants in the state who do not participate at first in the wealth of the mines in question. The bargaining process of the market, with the demand for meat, wine, wool, etc., being stronger than usual, will not fail to increase their prices. These high prices will encourage farmers to employ more land to produce the following year, and these same farmers will profit from the increased prices and will increase their expenditure on their families like the others. Those who will suffer from these higher prices and increased consumption will be, first of all, the property owners, during the term of their leases, then their domestic servants and all the workmen or fixed wage earners who support their families on a salary. They all must diminish their expenditures in proportion to the new consumption, which will compel a large number of them to emigrate and to seek a living elsewhere. The property owners will dismiss many of them, and the rest will demand a wage increase in order to live as before. It is in this manner that a considerable increase of money from mines increases consumption and, by diminishing the number of inhabitants, greater expenditures result by those who remain.

If money continues to be extracted from the mines, the abundance of money will increase all prices to such a point that not only will the property owners raise their rents considerably when the leases expire and resume their old lifestyle, increasing their servants' wages proportionally, but the artisans and workmen will increase the prices of the articles they produce so high that there will be considerable gains in buying them from foreigners who make them much cheaper. This will naturally encourage several people to import products at lower prices from foreign factories, and this will gradually ruin the artisans and manufacturers of the state who will be unable to sustain themselves by working at such low rates because of the high cost of living.

When the overabundance of money from the mines has diminished the number of inhabitants in a state, accustomed those who remain to excessive expenditures, raised the prices of farm products and the wages for labor to high levels, and ruined the manufactures of the state by the purchase of foreign products by property owners and mine workers, the money produced by the mines will necessarily go abroad to pay for the imports. This will gradually impoverish the state and make it, in a way, dependent on foreigners to whom it is obliged to send money every year as it is extracted from the mines. The great circulation of money, which was widespread in the beginning, ceases; poverty and misery follow and the exploitation of the mines appears to be only advantageous to those employed in them and to the foreigners who profit thereby.

This is approximately what has happened to Spain since the discovery of the Indies. As for the Portuguese, since the discovery of gold mines in Brazil, they have nearly always used foreign articles and manufactured goods; and it seems that they worked the mines only for the account and advantage of foreigners. All the gold and silver that these two states extract from the mines does not supply them with more precious metal in circulation than others. England and France usually have even more.

Now, if the increase of money in the state comes from a balance of foreign trade (i.e., from sending abroad articles and manufactured goods of greater value and quantity than are imported and consequently receiving the surplus in money), this annual increase of money will enrich a great number of merchants and entrepreneurs in the state, and will give employment to numerous artisans and workmen who provide the goods sent to the foreigner from whom money is drawn. This will gradually increase the consumption of these industrious inhabitants and will raise the price of land and labor. But the industrious people who are eager to acquire property will not at first increase their expenditures, they will wait until they have accumulated a large sum from which they can draw a secure interest income, independent of their occupation. Once a large number of inhabitants have acquired considerable fortunes from this money, which enters the state regularly and annually, they will not fail to increase their consumption and raise the price of everything. Although these higher prices result in greater expenditures than they at first contemplated, they will, for the most part, continue so long as their capital lasts, for nothing is easier or more pleasant than to increase the family expenditures, and nothing is more difficult or unpleasant than to decrease them.

If an annual and continuous balance has caused a considerable increase of money in a state, it will not fail to increase consumption, raise the price of everything and even diminish the number of inhabitants, unless additional products are drawn from abroad proportionate to the increased consumption. Moreover, in states that have acquired a considerable abundance of money, it is natural to import many goods from neighboring countries where money is rare and consequently everything is cheap. However, as money must be exchanged for these products, the balance of trade will become smaller. The cheapness of land and labor in foreign countries where money is rare will naturally cause the building of factories and businesses similar to those of the state, but which will not, at first, be as perfect or as highly valued.

In this situation, the state can retain its abundance of money, consume all its own products and a great deal of foreign products and, over and above all this, maintain a small balance of trade against the foreigner or at least keep the balance leveled for many years. In other words, the state will import, in exchange for its commodities and manufactured goods, as much money from these foreign countries as it sends to them for the goods or products of the land it takes from them. If the state is a maritime state, the easiness and low cost of its shipping for the transport of its commodities and manufactured goods to foreign countries may compensate, in some way, for the high cost of labor caused by the overabundance of money. Therefore, the commodities and manufactured goods of this state, expensive though they may be, will continue to sell in foreign countries, and sometimes will be cheaper than the manufactured goods of another state where labor is paid less.

The cost of transport greatly increases the prices of goods sent to distant countries. However, these costs are very moderate in maritime states, where there is regular shipping to all foreign ports and ships are nearly always found there ready to sail, taking on board all cargoes entrusted to them at a very reasonable freight.

This is not so in states where navigation does not flourish. There, it is necessary to build ships especially for the transportation of goods and this sometimes absorbs all the profit; and transportation there is always very expensive, which entirely discourages commerce.

England today consumes not only most of its own small production, but also a large amount of foreign products, such as silks, wines, fruits, linens in great quantity, etc. Meanwhile, she sends abroad the products of her mines and manufactured goods, for the most part. No matter how expensive labor is due to the abundance of money, she does not fail to sell her products to distant countries, because of her maritime advantage, at prices as reasonable as those of France, where these same products are cheaper.

The increased quantity of money in a state may also be caused, without a balance of trade, by subsidies paid to this state by foreign powers, by the expenditures of several ambassadors or travelers wanting to stay there for political reasons, curiosity, or pleasure, or by the transfer of the property and wealth of families who choose to leave their country to seek religious freedom or for other reasons, and to settle down in this state. In all these cases, the sums entering the state always cause an increase in expenditures and consumption, and consequently increase the prices of all goods in the channels of exchange where money enters.

Before the increase in the quantity of money, suppose that a quarter of the inhabitants of the state consume meat, wine, beer, etc., on a daily basis and frequently acquire clothes, linens, etc., but that after the increase, a third or half of the inhabitants consume these same things. Prices for these goods will increase and the high price of meat will convince several of those who formed the original quarter, to consume less meat than usual. A man who eats three pounds of meat daily will manage with two pounds, but he feels the reduction. Meanwhile, the other half of the inhabitants who hardly ate any meat at all will not feel the reduction. The price of bread will increase gradually because of increased consumption, as I have often suggested, but it will be proportionally less expensive than meat. The increase in the price of meat is noticeably felt because it causes a reduction in consumption on the part of a small portion of the people, but the increased price of bread is less noticeable because the decreased consumption is spread across the entire population. If 100,000 extra people move to a state with 10 million inhabitants, their extra consumption of bread will amount to only one pound in 100, which must be subtracted from the old inhabitants. But when a man consumes 99 pounds of bread for his subsistence instead of 100, he hardly feels the reduction.

When the consumption of meat increases, farmers increase the size of their pastures to produce more meat, and this diminishes cropland, and consequently the amount of wheat produced. However, what generally causes meat to become proportionally more expensive than bread is that imports of foreign wheat are usually permitted while imports of beef are absolutely forbidden, as is the case in England, or heavy import duties are imposed as in other states. This is the reason why the rents for meadows and pastures rise in England, with the abundance of money, three times more than the rents of cropland.

There is no doubt that when ambassadors, travelers, and families move to a state, the increased consumption will cause higher prices in all the markets where they spend their money.

As for the subsidies the state has received from foreign powers, they are either hoarded for state necessities or are put into circulation. If we assume they are hoarded, they do not concern my argument for I am considering only money in circulation. Hoarded money, silverware, churches' money, etc., are resources that the state turns to in emergency situations, but are of no present utility. If the state puts these funds into circulation, it can only do so by spending them and this will certainly increase consumption and raise the price of all goods. Whoever receives this money will set it in motion the principal business of life—which is the food—either for himself or someone else, since everything is connected to this, directly or indirectly.

CHAPTER 7: MORE ON THE INCREASE AND DECREASE IN THE QUANTITY OF MONEY IN A STATE

Where gold, silver, and copper are extracted from the mines, they have an intrinsic value proportional to the land and labor that enter into their production. States that have no mines have the added cost of importing the metal. The quantity of money, like that of all other commodities, determines its value against all other goods in the bargaining process of the marketplace.

If England begins for the first time to make use of gold, silver, and copper in exchanges, money will be valued according to the quantity in circulation, proportionally to its power of exchange against all other merchandise and products. The bargaining process of the market will determine this estimation of value. On the basis of this estimation, the property owners and entrepreneurs will set the wages of their domestic servants and workmen at so much a day or a year, so that they and their families may be able to live on the wages they receive.

Let us now assume that because of ambassadors and foreign travelers residing in England, as much money has been introduced into circulation as there was before (thereby doubling the quantity of money). This money will pass first into the hands of various artisans, servants, entrepreneurs, and others who have had a share in providing transportation, amusements, etc., for these foreigners. Manufacturers, farmers, and other entrepreneurs will feel the effect of the increased money, which will increase the expenditures of a great number of people, and this will in turn increase market prices. Even the children of these entrepreneurs and artisans will enter into new expenditures. With this abundance of money, their fathers will give them a little money for their petty pleasures and they will buy cakes and meat pies, etc. This new quantity of money will be distributed so that many who lived without using money before will now have some. Many exchanges, which used to be made on credit by valuation, will now be made with cash, and that will increase the pace of the circulation of money in England compared to before.

I conclude from all this that by doubling the quantity of money in a state, the prices of products and merchandise are not always doubled. The river, which runs and winds about in its bed, will not flow with double the speed when the amount of water is doubled.

The change in relative prices, introduced by the increased quantity of money in the state, will depend on how this money is directed at consumption and circulation. No matter who obtains the new money, it will naturally increase consumption. However, this consumption will be greater or less, according to circumstances. It will more or less be directed to certain kinds of commodities or merchandise, according to the judgment of those who acquire the money. Market prices will increase more for certain goods than for others, however abundant the money may be. In England, the price of meat might triple, but the price of wheat might increase less than one quarter.

In England, it is still permitted to import wheat from foreign countries, but not cattle. For this reason, however great the increase of money may be in England, the price of wheat can only be raised, above the price in other countries where money is scarce, by the cost and risks of importing wheat from these foreign countries.

It is not the same with the price of cattle, which will necessarily be proportioned to the quantity of money offered for meat, in relation to the quantity of meat and the number of cattle raised there.

An ox weighing 800 pounds sells in Poland and Hungary for two or three ounces of silver, but commonly sells in the London market for more than 40. Yet the bushel of flour does not sell in London for even double the price in Poland and Hungary.

An increase of money only increases the price of commodities and merchandise by the difference of the cost of transport, when this transport is allowed. But in many cases, transportation would cost more than the good is worth, therefore, for example, timber is useless in many places. This cost of transportation is also the reason why milk, fresh butter, lettuce, game, etc., are almost given away in the provinces distant from the capital.

I conclude that an increase of actual money in a state always causes an increase of consumption and a routine of greater expenditures. But the higher prices caused by this money do not affect all commodities and merchandise equally. Prices do not rise proportionally to the quantity of money, unless what has been added continues in the same circulation channels as before. In other words, those who offered one ounce of silver in the market would be the same and only ones to offer two ounces when the amount of money in circulation is doubled, and that is hardly ever the case. I recognize that when a large surplus of money is introduced in a state, the new money gives a new direction to consumption, and even a new speed to circulation. However, it is not possible to say exactly to what extent.

CHAPTER 8: FURTHER REFLECTIONS ON THE INCREASE AND DECREASE OF MONEY IN A STATE

We have seen that the quantity of money circulating in a state may be increased by working its mines, by subsidies from foreign powers, by the immigration of foreign families, by the residence of ambassadors and travelers, but above all, by a regular and annual balance of trade, from supplying goods to foreigners, and by receiving from them at least part of the price in gold and silver. It is by this last means that a state grows most substantially, especially when its trade is accompanied and supported by ample shipping and by a significant output of the raw materials necessary for the production of exported manufactured goods.

However, the continuation of this commerce gradually introduces a great abundance of money and, little by little, increases consumption. Foreign products must be imported to meet this demand and must be paid for by a reduction in the annual balance of trade. On the other hand, increased expenditures increase the cost of labor and the prices of manufactured goods. It often happens that some foreign countries try to set up the same kinds of factories for themselves, in which case they stop buying those of the state in question. Although these newly established factories and manufactures are not perfect at first, they reduce and even prevent the export of those goods from the neighboring state into their own country, where they can be acquired at a better price.

In this manner, the state begins to lose some branches of its profitable trade and many of its workmen and artisans who lose their jobs will leave the state to find employment in new foreign factories. In spite of this diminution in the balance of trade, the custom of importing various products will continue. If the manufactured products of a state have a great reputation and can be shipped to distant countries at low cost, the state will maintain its advantage over the new foreign manufacturers for many years and will maintain a small balance of trade, or at least keep it even. If, however, some other maritime state tries to perfect the same articles and its navigation at the same time, it will, because of the cheapness of its manufactures, take away several branches of trade from the state in question. Consequently, this state will begin to lose its balance of trade and will be forced to send a part of its money abroad every year in order to pay for its imports.

Moreover, even if the state in question could keep a balance of trade and its greater abundance of money, it is reasonable to suppose that this abundance will plunge many wealthy individuals into luxury. They will buy paintings, precious stones from abroad, they will want silks and rare objects, and they set such an example of luxury in the state that in spite of the advantage of its ordinary trade, its money will flow abroad annually to pay for this luxury. This will gradually impoverish the state and cause it to pass from great power to great weakness.

When a state has arrived at the highest point of wealth, and I always assume that the comparative wealth of states consists mainly in their respective quantities of money, it will inevitably fall back into poverty by the ordinary course of things. The too-great abundance of money, which gives power to states so long as it lasts, throws them back imperceptibly, but naturally, into poverty. Thus it would seem that when a state expands by trade, and the abundance of money raises the price of land and labor, the prince or the legislator ought to withdraw money from circulation, keep it for emergencies, and try to slow down its circulation by every means, except compulsion and bad faith, to prevent its goods from becoming too expensive and avoid the drawbacks of luxury.

However, it is not easy to perceive the opportune time for this, or to know when money has become more abundant than it ought to be for the good and preservation of the advantages of the state. Therefore, princes and heads of republics do not concern themselves much with this sort of knowledge and strive only to make use of the abundance of their state revenues, to extend their power and to insult other countries on the most frivolous pretexts. All things considered, working to perpetuate the glory of their reigns and administration and to leaving monuments of their power and wealth is perhaps the best they can do because according to the natural course of humanity, the state must collapse on its own, they only accelerate its fall a little. Nevertheless, it seems that they should try to make their power last during the time of their own administration.

Few years are needed to raise abundance to the highest point in a state, however still fewer are needed to bring it to poverty for lack of commerce and manufacturing. Without speaking of the rise and fall of the Venice Republic, Hanseatic cities, Flanders and Brabant, the Dutch Republic, etc., who have succeeded each other in profitable branches of trade, one may say that France's power has only been on the rise from 1646 (when factories were established to produce clothing which had previously been imported) to 1684 when a number of Protestant entrepreneurs and artisans were driven out of France. That kingdom has done nothing but recede since this last date.

I know no better measure than the leases and rents of property owners to judge the abundance and scarcity of money in circulation. When land is leased at high rates, it is a sign that there is plenty of money in the state; but when land has to be leased at much lower rates, it shows, other things being equal, that money is scarce. I have read in *The State of France* that acres of vineyard near Mantes—not far from the French capital—which leased for 200 livres tournois of full weight in 1660, only leased for 100 livres tournois of lighter money in 1700. However, the silver brought from the West Indies in the interval should naturally have raised the price of land in Europe.

The author [of *The State of France*] attributes this fall in rent to defective consumption. In fact, it seems that he observed a reduction in wine consumption. However, I think he has mistaken the effect for the cause. The cause was a greater rarity of money in France, and the effect of this was naturally a decrease in consumption. In this essay, I have always suggested, on the contrary, that an abundance of money naturally increases consumption and contributes above everything else to a higher valuation of the land. When abundant money raises products to honest prices, the inhabitants eagerly work to acquire them; although they do not show the same eagerness to acquire food and merchandise beyond what is needed for their maintenance.

It is clear that a state with more money in circulation than its neighbors has an advantage over them, so long as it maintains this abundance of money.

In the first place, given that the price of land and labor are calculated in terms of money, the state where money is most abundant will give up less land and labor than it receives in all areas of trade. Thus the state in question sometimes receives the product of two acres of land in exchange for that of one acre, and the work of two men for that of only one. It is because of this abundance of money in circulation in London that the work of one English embroiderer costs more than that of 10 Chinese embroiderers, though the Chinese embroiderers are much better and turn out more work in a day. In Europe, people are amazed that these people can live by working so cheap and that the wonderful fabrics they send us cost so little.

Secondly, tax revenues are more easily raised in a state where money is plentiful, and in relatively larger amounts. This gives the state, in case of war or dispute, the means to gain all sorts of advantages over its adversaries with whom money is scarce.

If there are two princes at war over the sovereignty or conquest of a state, where one has much money and the other has little money but many estates worth twice the money of his enemy, the first will be better able to attract generals and officers with gifts of money than the second will be by giving twice the value in lands and estates. Grants of land are subject to challenge and revocation and cannot be relied upon like money. With money, munitions of war and food can be bought, even from the enemies of the state. Money can be given for secret services without witnesses, but land, produce, and goods would not serve for these purposes, not even jewels or diamonds, because they are easily recognized. After all, it seems to me that the comparative power and wealth of states consist, other things being equal, in the greater or less abundance of money circulating in them *hic et nunc*.

I still have to mention two other methods of increasing the amount of money circulating in a state. The first is when entrepreneurs and private individuals borrow money from their foreign correspondents at interest, or when foreigners send their money into the state to buy shares or government stocks. This often amounts to very considerable sums on which the state must annually pay interest to these foreigners. These methods for increasing money in the state do make it more abundant and diminish the rate of interest. With this money, the entrepreneurs in the state find it possible to borrow more cheaply, to provide work, and to establish factories with the anticipation of a profit. The artisans, and all those whose hands this money passes through, consume more than they would have done if they had not been employed by means of this money. This consequently increases prices just as if the money belonged to the state and through the increased consumption or expenditures this causes, public revenues derived from taxes on consumption are increased. Money lent to the state in this manner brings many advantages with it, but in the end, it is always burdensome and harmful. The state must pay the interest to the foreigners every year and, aside from this loss, the state is at the mercy of the foreigners who can always cause trouble if they decide to withdraw their capital. Surely, they will want to withdraw their capital when the state needs it the most, as when preparing for war and defeat is feared. The interest paid to the foreigner is always much more considerable than the increase in public revenue caused by this money. One can observe these loans passing from one country to another, according to investors' confidence in the states to which they are sent. But in reality, states that have paid heavy interest on these loans for many years will often find themselves bankrupt and unable to repay the capital. When trust is shaken, shares or public stocks fall; foreign shareholders do not like to sustain losses, preferring to content themselves with collecting interest, while waiting for confidence to return. But sometimes it does not return. In declining states, the principal objective of public administrators usually is to restore confidence in order to attract foreign loans. If the ministry does not act in bad faith and keeps its obligations, the money of the subjects will circulate without interruption. In this case, money from abroad has the power of increasing the quantity of money in a state.

But the borrowing road, which holds an advantage in the present, leads to a dead end and is but a flash in the pan. To restore a poor state with a shortage of money, a constant and real balance of trade is needed on an annual basis, as is the development, through navigation, of the articles and manufactures produced cheaper and thereby suitable for exportation. Merchants are the first to make their fortunes, then the lawyers may get part of it, the prince and tax collectors get a share at the expense of all the others, and distribute their graces as they please. When money becomes too plentiful in the state, luxury will follow and the state will fall into poverty.

This is roughly the cycle that may be experienced by a large state which has both capital and industrious inhabitants. A talented public administrator is always able to begin the cycle over again. Not many years are needed to see it tried and succeed, at least in the beginning, which makes for the most interesting situation. The increased quantity of money in circulation will be brought about by several factors that my argument does not allow me to examine now.

As for states without much capital and where capital can only be increased by accidents or by particular circumstances of the times, it is difficult to find the means that would allow them to flourish by trade. No administrator can restore the republics of Venice and Holland to the brilliant situation from which they have fallen. But Italy, Spain, France, and England, however poor they may be, are still capable of attaining a high degree of power by trade alone if led by a good administration and if they operate separately. If all these states were equally well administered, they would be great only in proportion to their respective capital and to the greater or lesser industriousness of their people.

The last method I can think of to increase the quantity of money actually circulating in a state is by violence and arms, and this method is often blended with the others, since in all peace treaties one will try to maintain trading rights and other privileges one could obtain. When a state mandates contributions or makes several other states tributary to it, this is a very sure method of obtaining their money. I will not examine the methods of putting this theory into practice, but I will say that all the nations who have flourished in this manner have not failed to decline, like states that have flourished through their commerce. The ancient Romans were more powerful in this manner than all the other peoples we know of. Nevertheless, these same Romans, before losing an inch of the land of their vast states, fell into decadence through luxury and impoverished themselves by the reduction of money which circulated among them, and it was this luxury that caused their empire to pass into the hands of the eastern nations of the Orient.

So long as Romans' luxury (which did not begin until after the defeat of Antiochus, King of Asia, around AUC 564) came from the product of the land and the labor of all the vast estates of their dominion, the circulation of money only increased instead of decreasing. The public was in possession of all the gold, silver, and copper mines in the empire. They had the gold mines of Asia, Macedonia, Aquileia, and the rich mines, both gold and silver, of Spain and other countries. They had several mints where gold, silver, and copper coins were struck. In Rome, the consumption of all the goods and merchandise drawn from their vast provinces did not diminish the circulation of money, any more than the pictures, statues, and jewels themselves. Although the wealthy landlords spent excessive amounts for their feasts, and paid 15,000 ounces of silver for a single fish, all that did not diminish the quantity of money circulating in Rome, given that the provinces made tributes regularly, not to mention the money brought in by lenders and by governors with their extortions. The amounts annually extracted from the mines increased the circulation in Rome during Augustus's whole reign. However, luxury was already on a very great scale, and there was much eagerness, not only for curiosities produced in the empire, but also for jewels from India, pepper and spices, and all the rarities of Arabia. Silks, which were not made in the empire, began to be in demand there. Nevertheless, the money drawn from the mines still exceeded the sums sent out of the empire to buy all these things. However, under Tiberius, money became scarce when that emperor collected 2.7 billion sesterces in his treasury. To restore an abundant circulation, he only needed to borrow 300 million on a mortgage of his estates. After his death, Caligula spent all of Tiberius's treasure in less than one year, and it was then that the abundance of money in circulation was at its highest in Rome and the wind of luxury kept on blowing. The historian Pliny estimated that in his time the empire exported at least 100 million sesterces annually. This was more than was drawn from the mines. Under Trajan, land prices fell by one-third or more, according to the younger Pliny, and money continued to decrease until the time of the Emperor Septimus Severus. Money was then so scarce in Rome that the emperor collected enormous quantities of wheat, being unable to collect enough tax money for his enterprises. Thus the Roman Empire declined through the loss of its money before losing any of its estates. That is what luxury brought about, and what it always will bring about in similar circumstances.

CHAPTER 9: INTEREST ON MONEY AND ITS CAUSES

Just as the prices of goods are set by the bargaining process in the market and by the quantity of goods offered for sale relative to the quantity of money offered for them, or in other words, by the relative number of sellers and buyers, so in the same way the interest on loans in a state is settled by the relative number of lenders and borrowers.

Although money serves as a medium of exchange, it does not multiply itself or earn interest simply by being in circulation. It is the needs of mankind that seem to have introduced the usage of interest. A man who lends money backed by good securities or a mortgage only runs the risk of the ill will of the borrower, or of expenses, lawsuits, and losses. However, when he lends without collateral, he runs the risk of losing everything. For this reason, needy men must have begun by tempting lenders with profit as bait and this profit must have been proportionate to the needs of the borrowers and the fear and avarice of the lenders. This seems to be the origin of interest although its continued use in states seems to be based upon the profits that entrepreneurs can make from it.

Land aided by human labor naturally produces 4, 10, 20, 50, 100, 150 times the amount of wheat sown, depending on the fertility of the soil and the industry of the inhabitants. It also produces fruits and cattle. The farmer who runs the operation generally keeps two-thirds of the production, with one-third paying his expenses and upkeep and the other being the profit for his enterprise.

If the farmer has enough capital for this enterprise, such as the necessary tools, horses for plowing, cattle to increase the value of the land, etc., he will keep for himself, after paying all expenses, one-third of the farm's production. But if a competent laborer, who lives on his wages from day to day and who has no land, can find someone willing to lease land or the money to buy some, he will be able to give the lender all of the third rent, or one-third of the production of the farm over which he will become the farmer or entrepreneur. However, he will see his condition improved because he will obtain his upkeep in the second rent, and will become master instead of employee. If he can save and do without some necessities, he can gradually accumulate some capital and have less to borrow every year. Eventually, he will manage to keep all of the third rent.

If this new entrepreneur can buy wheat or cattle on credit that will be paid back long term when he sells his farm products for money, he will gladly pay more than the cash market price. This is the same thing as if he borrowed cash to buy wheat, with the interest paid being the difference between the cash price and the price payable at a future date. However, whether he borrows cash or goods, there must be enough left over for his upkeep, or he will become bankrupt. This risk is the reason why he will be required to pay 20 or 30 percent profit or interest on the amount of money or value of the goods he borrows.

In a similar manner, a master hatmaker who has capital to carry on his manufacture of hats; to rent a house, buy beaver skins, wool, dye, etc., and to pay for the subsistence of his workmen every week, should obtain his own upkeep from this enterprise and a profit similar to that of the farmer who keeps one-third of his farm's output as profit. This upkeep and the profit should come from the sale of the hats, the price of which ought to cover not only the materials, but also the upkeep of the hatter and his workmen, and also the profit in question.

A capable journeyman hatter with no capital may undertake the same business by borrowing money and materials and giving the profit to anybody who is willing to lend him the money or entrust him with the beaver, wool, etc., for which he will pay sometime later when he has sold his hats. If, when his bills are due, the lender requires his capital back, or if the wool merchant and other lenders will not grant him further credit, he must give up his business, in which case he may prefer to go bankrupt. But if he is prudent and industrious, he may be able to show his creditors that he has, in cash or in hats, about the same value that he has borrowed, and they will probably choose to continue to give him credit and be satisfied, for the time being, with their interest or profit. In this way, he will carry on and will perhaps gradually save some capital by cutting back upon his necessities. In this manner, he will have less to borrow every year, and when he has collected enough capital to conduct his business (which will always be proportional to his sales) he will keep his entire profit and grow rich if he does not increase his expenditures.

It is useful to observe that the upkeep of such a manufacturer is small compared to the sums he borrows for his business or to the value of materials entrusted to him. Therefore, the lenders run no great risk of losing their capital if the borrower is respectable and hardworking. However, as he may not be, the lenders will always require a profit or interest of 20 to 30 percent of the value of their loan. Even then, only those who have a good opinion of him will trust him. The same inductions may be made with regard to all the masters, artisans, manufacturers, and other entrepreneurs in the state, who carry on enterprises in which the capital considerably exceeds the value of their annual upkeep.

However, if a water carrier in Paris sets himself up as the entrepreneur of his own work, all the capital he needs is the price of two buckets, which he can buy for one ounce of silver, after which all his gains are profit. If he earns 50 ounces of silver a year by his labor, the amount of his capital or borrowing relative to his profit is 1 to 50. That is, he will earn 5,000 percent, while the hatter will earn only 50 percent and will also have to pay 20 or 30 percent to the lender.

Nevertheless, a moneylender will prefer to lend 1,000 ounces of silver to a hatmaker at 20 percent interest, rather than lend 1,000 ounces to 1,000 water carriers at 500 percent interest. The water carriers will quickly spend on their maintenance, not only the money they gain by their daily labor, but all that is lent to them. These amounts of capital are small compared with what they need for their maintenance; however much or little they work, they can easily spend all that they earn. Therefore, it is difficult to determine the profitability of small entrepreneurs. It may well be that a water carrier earns 5,000 percent of the value of the buckets that are the capital of his company. He could even earn 10,000 percent, if by hard work he earns 100 ounces of silver a year. However, because he could easily spend 100 ounces on himself just as easily as 50, it is only by knowing what he devotes to his upkeep that we can determine how much clear profit has been made.

It is always necessary to deduct the subsistence and maintenance of the entrepreneur before determining their profit. We have done this in the example of the farmer and of the hatmaker. However, we have shown that this is difficult to determine in the case of the smallest entrepreneurs, the majority of whom will eventually go bankrupt.

Ordinarily, brewers in London will lend a few kegs of beer to pub owners, and when they pay for the first kegs they continue to lend them more. If these pubs do a brisk business, the brewers can make an annual profit of 500 percent; and I have heard that the big brewers grow rich when no more than half the pubs go bankrupt on them in the course of the year.

All the merchants in a state are in the habit of lending merchandise or products to retailers. They proportion the amount of their profit or interest to that of their risk. The risk is always considerable when the proportion of the borrower's maintenance is high relative to the amount of the loan. If the borrower or retailer does not have a prompt flow of sales in his small business, he will quickly be ruined and will spend all he has borrowed on his own subsistence and will consequently be forced into bankruptcy.

The fish merchant, who buys fish at Billingsgate in London to sell again in other areas of the city, generally pays, under a contract made by a professional writer, one shilling per guinea or per twenty-one shillings of interest per week, which amounts to 260 percent per year. The market women in Paris, whose business is smaller, pay five sols for the week's interest on an ecu of three livres, which exceeds 430 percent per year. And yet, there are few lenders who make a fortune from such high interest.

These high rates of interest are not only tolerated but are in a way useful and necessary in a state. Those who buy fish in the streets pay for these high interest rates with an increase in the price they charge. They provide a convenience for their customers who do not consider it a loss. In the same manner, an artisan who drinks a beer and pays a price that gives the brewer his 500 percent profit, is satisfied with this convenience and does not feel the loss of this small detail.

The Casuists, who hardly seem suitable to judge the nature of interest and matters of trade, have created a concept (damnum emergens) through which they will tolerate these high interest rates. Rather than disrupt its use and suitability to business, they have agreed to allow those who lend at great risk to charge a proportionally high rate of interest. And there is no limit, for they would be at a loss to find any definite limit because in reality, this business depends on the fears of the lenders and the needs of the borrowers.

Maritime merchants are praised when they can generate a profit from their enterprise's capital, even though it is as high as 10,000 percent; and whatever profit wholesale merchants make or demand for selling products or merchandise to smaller retail merchants on long credit, I have not heard the Casuists declare it a crime. They are, or seem to be, a little more scrupulous about loans of money even though it is essentially the same thing. They even tolerate these loans by a distinction (lucrum cessans) that they invented. I understand this means that a man who usually makes a 500 percent profit in his business may demand this rate when he lends money to another. Nothing is more entertaining than the multitude of laws and rules made in every century on the subject of the interest of money—always unnecessarily—by wiseacres who hardly understand the facts of commerce.

From these examples and inductions, it seems that there are many classes and pathways of interest or profit in a state. In the lowest classes, interest is always highest in proportion to the greater risk, and it diminishes, from class to class, up to the highest which is that of rich merchants who are known to be creditworthy. The interest stipulated for this class is called the current rate of interest in the state and it differs little from the interest rate charged on land mortgages. A bill of exchange from a solvent and solid merchant is as well regarded, at least in the short run, as a mortgage on land, because the possibility of a lawsuit or a dispute involving the mortgage is equivalent to the possibility of the merchant's bankruptcy.

If entrepreneurs in a state could not make a profit on the money or goods that they borrow, the use of interest would probably be less frequent than it is. Only extravagant people and spendthrifts would contract for loans. But accustomed as everyone is to depend on entrepreneurs, there is a constant source for loans and consequently for interest. Entrepreneurs are the ones who cultivate the land and supply bread, meat, clothes, etc., to all the inhabitants of a city. Those who work on wages for these entrepreneurs, also seek to set themselves up as entrepreneurs, in emulation of each other. The multitude of entrepreneurs is much greater among the Chinese as they have a lively spirit, a genius for enterprise, and a determination to achieve their goals. There are among them many entrepreneurs whose work here is done by people on fixed wages. They even supply meals for laborers in the fields. It is perhaps this large number of small entrepreneurs and others, from the various classes, who earn a living from consumption without injuring the consumer, that keeps the rate of interest for the highest classes at 30 percent, while it hardly exceeds 5 percent in Europe. At Athens, in Solon's time, interest was at 18 percent. In the Roman Republic, it was most commonly 12 percent, but has also been known to be 48, 20, 8, 6, and its lowest was 4 percent. It was never so low in the free market as toward the end of the Republic and under Augustus after the conquest of Egypt.

The Emperor Antoninus and Alexander Severus only reduced interest to 4 percent by lending public money on the mortgage of land.

CHAPTER 10: THE CAUSES OF INCREASES AND DECREASES OF THE INTEREST RATE ON MONEY IN A STATE

It is a common idea, accepted by all those who have written on commerce, that an increased quantity of money in a state decreases the rate of interest, because when money is abundant it is easier to find some to borrow. This idea is not always true or accurate. For proof, we need only to remember that in 1720, nearly all the money in England was brought to London. In addition, the number of notes in circulation further accelerated the movement of money to an extraordinary level.

However, this abundance of money and increased circulation did not decrease the interest rate, which had been running at 5 percent or lower. It only served to raise the rate, which increased up to 50 and 60 percent. It is easy to account for this increased rate of interest by the principles and the causes of interest that I established in the previous chapter. The reason is that everyone had become an entrepreneur in the South Sea scheme and wanted to borrow money to buy shares, expecting to make an immense profit with which it would be easy to pay this high rate of interest.

If the abundance of money in the state comes from the hands of moneylenders, the increase in the number of lenders will probably lower the rate of interest. However, if the abundance comes from the hands of people who will spend it, this will have just the opposite effect and will raise the rate of interest by increasing the number of entrepreneurs who go into business as a result of this increased spending, and will need to supply their businesses by borrowing at all types of interest.

The abundance or scarcity of money in a state always raises or lowers the price of everything in markets, without any necessary connection to the rate of interest, which may very well be high in states where there is plenty of money, and low in those where money is scarcer—high where everything is expensive, and low where everything is cheap; high in London, low in Genoa.

The rate of interest rises and falls every day from mere rumors, which might decrease or increase the confidence of lenders without affecting the prices of product in markets.

The most constant source for a high rate of interest in a state is the great expenditures of nobles, property owners, and other rich people. Entrepreneurs and master craftsmen supply the great houses with all the elements of this spending and entrepreneurs almost always need to borrow money in order to supply them. When the nobles consume beyond their income and borrow money, they doubly contribute to raising the interest rate.

In contrast, when the nobles of the state live frugally and buy firsthand (without middlemen) as often as they can, they will acquire many products from their servants without dealing with entrepreneurs. This diminishes profits and the numbers of entrepreneurs in the state and it consequently reduces the number of borrowers, as well as the interest rate. Because these entrepreneurs work with their own capital, borrowing as little as they can, and content themselves with small profits, they prevent those who have no capital from starting similar enterprises with borrowed money. Such is the case today in the republics of Genoa and Holland, where interest is sometimes at 2 percent, or lower for the upper classes. Meanwhile, in Germany,

Poland, France, Spain, England, and other countries, the affluence and expenses of noblemen and property owners have kept the country's entrepreneurs and master artisans accustomed to large profits, enabling them to pay a high rate of interest, which is higher still when they import everything from abroad with the added risk for the enterprises.

When the prince or the state incurs heavy expenses, such as when making war, the rate of interest increases for two reasons. The first is that it increases the number of entrepreneurs with several new large enterprises for war supplies, and it therefore increases borrowing. The second is because of the greater risk that war always brings.

On the contrary, when the war is over, risk diminishes, the number of entrepreneurs decreases, and war-contractors who go out of business, reduce their expenditures and become lenders of the money they have gained. In this situation, if the prince, or state, offers to repay part of the public debt, it will reduce the rate of interest significantly. This will truly have an effect if part of the debt can be paid off without borrowing elsewhere, because the repayments increase the number of lenders in the highest class of interest (i.e., the prime rate), which will affect all the other classes.

When the abundance of money in the state is caused by a continuous (positive) balance of trade, this money first passes through the hands of entrepreneurs. And although it increases consumption, it does not fail to lower the rate of interest because most of the entrepreneurs will acquire enough capital to conduct their business without borrowing, and even become lenders of the amount they have gained beyond what they need to operate their business. If the state does not have a great number of nobles and rich people who spend lavishly, the abundance of money will certainly lower the interest rate, while increasing the price of goods and merchandise exchanged. This is what usually happens in republics that have neither much capital nor considerable land, and which grow rich only by foreign trade. But in states that have considerable capital and large property owners, the money brought in by foreign trade increases their rents, and enables them to spend heavily, which maintains several entrepreneurs and artisans besides those who engage in the foreign trade. This always keeps interest rates high despite the abundance of money.

When a noble or property owner ruins himself by extravagant expenditures, the lender who holds the mortgages on the property often acquires the absolute ownership to it. It may also be the case in a state that lenders provide more credit than money in circulation. In this case, they are subordinate owners of the land and its production, which have been mortgaged as security, and without which the lenders' capital would be lost by the bankruptcy of the borrowers.

In the same manner, one may consider the owners of public debt to be the subordinate owners of state revenues, which are used to pay them interest. However, if the legislature was compelled by the needs of the state to use these revenues for other purposes, the owners of public debt would lose everything, while the amount of money circulating in the state would not diminish by a single coin.

If the prince or the administrators of the state want to regulate the current interest rate by law, the regulation must be established on the basis of the current market rate in the highest class, or thereabout. Otherwise the law will be useless because entrepreneurs are obedient to the forces of competition, or the current price as settled by the proportion of lenders to borrowers, and as a result, they will resort to secret deals. This legal constraint will only hamper trade and raise the interest rate, instead of fixing it. Historically, the Romans, after passing several laws to restrict interest rates, passed one to prevent the lending of money altogether. This law had no more success than its predecessors. Justinian's law, which restrained well-to-do people from taking more than 4 percent, those of a lower order 6 percent, and traders 8 percent, was equally amusing and unjust, because it was not forbidden to make 50 and 100 percent profit in all sorts of enterprises.

If it is allowable and respectable for a property owner to lease a farm to a poor farmer at a high rent, risking the loss of the rent for a whole year, it seems that it should be permissible for a lender to lend money to a needy borrower, at the risk of not only losing his interest or profit, but also his capital, and to stipulate any interest rate that the borrower will freely consent to pay. It is true that loans of this type can make lenders worse off; they can lose both the interest and their capital because they are far less likely to recoup losses compared to the property owner who cannot lose the land he rents. Because bankruptcy laws are relatively favorable to debtors and allow them to start again, it seems that usury laws should always be adjusted to market rates, as is the case in Holland.

The current interest rate in a state seems to serve as a basis for establishing the market price of land. If the current rate is 5 percent or one-twentieth part, the price of land should be the same (i.e., twenty times the amount of interest paid per year on the mortgage of similar land). However, because ownership of land gives a certain status and rights in some states, it will be the case that when interest is 5 percent or one-twentieth part, the price of land is set at 1/24 or 1/25 (twenty-five times), although the mortgage rate on the same land hardly exceeds the current interest rate.

After all, the price of land, like all other prices, is regulated naturally by the proportion of sellers to buyers, etc. And as there will be many more buyers in London, for example, than in the provinces, and as these buyers who live in the capital will prefer to buy land in their locality rather than in distant provinces, they would rather buy land in their vicinity at 1/30 or 1/35, than distant lands at 1/25 or 1/22. There are often other acceptable reasons affecting land prices, unnecessary to mention here, since they do not invalidate our explanations of the nature of interest.

30. Jacob Vanderlint: *Money Answers All Things* (1734)

[T]he Prices of the Produce or Manufactures of every Nation will be higher or lower, according as the Quantity of Cash circulating in such Nation is greater or less, in Proportion to the Number of People inhabiting such Nation.

To illustrate this, let it be supposed that we have ten Millions of Cash, and as many People in England; it's evident they have twice as much Money amongst them, in Proportion to their Number, as they wou'd have if their Number were doubled, and the Quantity of Cash remain'd just the same. And therefore, I think, they could give but half the Price for Things in general in this Case, that they could do when they were but half the Number, with the same Quantity of Money circulating and divided amongst them. Wherefore, if the People increase, and the Cash doth not increase in like Proportion, the Prices of Things must fall; for all the People must have Necessaries, to procure which they must all have Money: This will divide the same Quantity of Cash into more Parts, that is, lessen the Parts; and then it's evident they can't pay so much for their Necessaries, as when the same Cash divided into fewer Parts, makes the Parts greater.

The Prices of all Things in this Kingdom, some Centuries ago, were vastly lower than they are now. In the Reign of King Henry the Eighth, it was enacted, that Butchers should sell their Meat by Weight; Beef at an Half-penny, and Mutton at Three-farthings per Pound: And if we look back to the Reign of King Edward the Third, we find Wheat was sold at two Shillings per Quarter, a fat Ox for a Noble, a fat Sheep for Six-pence, six Pidgeons for a Penny, a fat Goose for Two-pence, a Pig for a Penny; and other Things in Proportion. See *Baker's Chronicle*.

Now, since the great Difference of the Prices of these Things now, to what they then sold for, is undoubtedly owing solely to the great Quantity of Gold and Silver, which since that Time hath been brought into this Kingdom by Trade, which hath furnished us with so much more Money, to pay such a vast deal more as we now must, and do give for them; it follows, that the Prices of Things will certainly rise in every Nation, as the Gold and Silver increase amongst the People; and, consequently, that where the Gold and Silver decrease in any Nation, the Prices of all Things must fall proportionably to such Decrease of Money, or the People must be distress'd; unless the Number of People decrease in as great Proportion as the Cash decreaseth in any such Nation.

Banking, so far as one is paid with the Money of another, that is, where more Cash Notes are circulated, than all the Cash the Bankers are really possessed of will immediately answer and make good; I say, so long as this Credit is maintain'd, it hath the same Effect, as if there was so much more Cash really circulating and divided amongst the People; and will be attended with these Consequences, that as the Price of Things will hence be rais'd, it must and will make us the Market, to receive the Commodities of every Country whose Prices of Things are cheaper than ours. And though we should lay on Duties, or prohibit such Goods, this will not prevent the Mischief, because we shall not be able to carry our Commodities thus raised to any Nation, where Things are cheaper than ours; and because such Nations will hence be enabled to set up many of our Manufactures, &c. and by their Cheapness so interfere in our Trade at all other foreign Markets, as to turn the Balance of Trade against us, which will diminish the Cash of the Nation. The same Thing must be understood of all publick Securities whatever, that operate as Money amongst us.

The Plenty or Scarcity of any particular Thing, is the sole Cause whence any Commodity or Thing can become higher or lower in Price; or, in other Words, as the Demand is greater or less in Proportion to the Quantity of any Thing, so will such Thing, whatsoever it is, be cheaper or dearer. Nor can any Arts or Laws make this otherwise, any more than Laws or Arts can alter the Nature of Things.

31. Francis Hutcheson: *Philosophiae Moralis Institutio Compendiaria* (1747)[1]

CHAPTER 12: CONCERNING THE VALUES OR PRICES OF GOODS

I. To maintain any commerce among men in interchanging of goods or services, the values of them must be some way estimated: for no man would give away things of important and lasting use or pleasure in exchange for such as yielded little of either; nor goods which cost much labour in acquiring, for such as can easily be obtained.

The ground of all price must be some *fitness* in the things to yield some use or pleasure in life; without this, they can be of no value. But this being presupposed, the prices of things will be in a compound proportion of the *demand* for them, and the *difficulty* in acquiring them. The *demand* will be in proportion to the numbers who are wanting them, or their agreeableness or necessity to life. The *difficulty* may be occasioned many ways; if the quantities of them in the world be small; if any accidents make the quantity less than ordinary; if much toil is required in producing them, or much ingenuity, or a more elegant genius in the artists; if the persons employed about them according to the custom of the country are men in high account, and live in a more splendid manner; for the expence of this must be defrayed by the higher profits of their labours (and few can be thus maintained).

Some goods of the highest use, yet have either no price or but a small one. If there's such plenty in nature that they are acquired almost without any labour, they have no price; if they may be acquired by easy common labour, they are of small price. Such is the goodness of God to us, that the most useful and necessary things are generally very plentiful and easily acquired.

Other things of great use have no price, either because they are naturally destined for community, or cannot come into commerce but as appendages of something else, the price of which may be increased by them, tho' they cannot be separately estimated; or because some law natural or positive prohibits all buying or selling of them. Of this last sort are all religious offices, actions, or privileges; and even the salaries of religious offices, which are either deemed only what is necessary for the support of persons in such offices, or are committed to their trust as funds of liberality and charity toward the indigent. Buying and selling of such things from a well-known piece of history is called *simony*.

II. But as it may often happen that I want some goods of which my neighbour has plenty, while I have plenty of other goods beyond my own use, and yet he may have no need of any of my superfluous stores; or that the goods I am stored with beyond my occasions, may be quite superior in value to all I want from my neighbour, but my goods cannot be divided into

---

[1]   This work was translated by the author's son, also named Francis Hutcheson.

parcels without great loss: for managing of commerce there must some sort of standard goods (outstanding price) be agreed upon; something settled as the measure of value to all others; which must be so generally demanded, that every one will be willing to take it in exchange for other goods, since by it he may obtain whatever he desires. And indeed as soon as any thing is thus made the standard of all values, the demand for it will become universal (as it will serve every purpose).

The goods which are made the standard, should have these properties; first, they should be of high value, that so a small portable quantity of them may be equal in value to a great quantity of other things; again, they should not be perishable, or such as wear much in use; and lastly they should admit of all manner of divisions without loss. Now these three properties are found only in the two more rare mettals, silver and gold; which therefor have been made the standards of commerce in all civilized nations.

III. (At first they have dealt in them by weight) but to prevent the trouble of making accurate divisions of the several barrs or pieces of mettal, and to prevent frauds by mixing them with baser mettals, *coinage* has been introduced. For when the coining of money is committed under proper regulations to trusty hands, there's security given to all for the quantities of pure mettal in each piece, and any broken sums agreed upon can be exactly paid without any trouble.

But the real value of these mettals and of money too (like that of all other goods) is lessened as they are more plentiful; and increase when they grow scarcer (tho' the pieces keep the same names). The common necessaries of life have a more stable natural price, tho' there are some (not) little changes of their values according to the fruitfulness of the several seasons. Were one to settle perpetual salaries to certain offices, or secure revenues, which should support men perpetually in the same station in respect to their neighbours, these (salaries) should be constituted in certain quantities of such necessary goods as depend upon the plain inartificial labours of men, such as grain, or other necessaries in a plain simple way of living.

IV. No state which holds any commerce with its neighbours can at pleasure alter the values of their coin in proportion to that of goods. Foreigners pay regard, not to the names we give, but to the real quantities of pure metal in our coin, and therefor the rates of goods must be proportioned to these quantities. But after a legal settlement of the denominations of coins, and many contracts and obligations settled in these legal sums or denominations, a decree of state raising the nominal values of the pieces will be a fraud upon all the creditors (and do much gain to the debtors); and the lowering their nominal values will have just the contrary effects (will be a fraud upon the debtors).

The values too of these two mettals may alter their proportions to each other; if an extraordinary quantity of either of them be brought from the mines; or a great consumption made only of one of them in the ornaments of life, or great quantities of it exported. And unless the legal denominations or values of the pieces be changed in like manner, such coin as is valued with us too low in proportion to the natural value of the mettal, will be exported; and what is valued with us too high will remain, or be imported, to the great detriment of the country.

Wheresoever a coinage is made in baser mettals, the quantities in each piece must be made so much the greater; otherways the trade with foreigners must be lost. When notes or tickets pass for money, their value depends on this, that they give good security for the payment of certain sums of gold or silver.

32. Ferdinando Galiani: *On Money* (1751)[1]

The acquisition of gold and silver, of which the most precious money is made, has always been—and is now—the ultimate goal of the multitudes. At the same time, it is the source of loathing and contempt for those who arrogate to themselves the venerable name of sage. Of these contrary opinions the first is often base and sometimes poorly controlled; the second is generally unjust or not very sincere. Moreover, since those who are interested in accumulating the metals usually overvalue them, while their detractors tend to undervalue them, none value them legitimately and reasonably. Many regard the prices of the metals as purely arbitrary and imaginary. These persons believe such prices arise out of common error and are passed on to us along with our education. Describing price in derogatory terms, such people refer to it variously as folly, fraud, or madness; they regard price as unreal. Others, more discreetly, believe that the common consensus of men has caused them, for their greater convenience, to adopt the common use of money, for the first time giving the metals a value they do not intrinsically possess. Few understand that the just price and value of the metals has been fixed and firmly established by their very nature and by the disposition of human minds. Under these circumstances, the reader will have to decide for himself where the truth resides before continuing. He must bear in mind that in each step in the discussion of extrinsic value—the augmentation of the value of money, interest, exchange, and the proportions of money—reference is always made to an intrinsic, certain, and natural value.

Aristotle, a great genius and a man of wonder, has laid bare many fine considerations concerning the nature of money as, for example, in *Ethics*, Chapter Seven, Book Five where he has written as follows: "money has become by convention a sort of representative of demand; and this is why it has the name 'money' (*nomisma*)—because it exists not by nature but by law (*nomos*) and it is in our power to change it and make it useless."

This is repeated in Chapter Six, Book One of *Politics*. If this philosopher has ever been heeded in his teachings more than is appropriate, it would be in this matter, to our detriment. Following his master, Bishop Covarruvias, for example, proceeds in this manner:

> If money gets its value, from the prince but not nature, and can be rendered valueless by his reversing the law, certainly the gold or silver material itself is not valued as highly as the money itself; since, if it were valued as highly, its price would come from nature, not from the law.

Aristotelians, which include Moralists and Jurisconsults, reason in the same way. It is obvious how correct such conclusions are. Given the truth of such a principle, I should not wish any to have to demonstrate by direct experience just how fatal and productive of grief such considerations can be. These opinions cannot be contradicted without destroying their very basis.

---

[1]   Translated by Peter R. Toscano.

Hence, I do not know, or even begin to understand, how it could be possible that such writers as John Locke, Davanzati, Broggia, the authors respectively of the works *Sul commercio* and of *Dello spirito delle leggi*, among others, could have had contrary sentiments so firmly established on so false a foundation, without ever denying the first principle. They were not aware either of the weakness of the latter or the instability of the former. For this reason, I myself, more than all others, have done my utmost to show—with every study I have made—what I have long believed. Namely, that not only the metals comprising money but every other worldly thing, barring none, has its natural value derived from certain, general, and invariant principles; that neither whimsy, law, nor princes, nor anything else can violate these principles and their effects. Finally, concerning value, the Scholastics have said: passive se habent.

Any edifice built on these foundations will be durable and everlasting. I trust my readers will pardon any verbosity here, given the importance of the subject. It would be wrong to consider me responsible for so great a truth, should any be inclined to do so; the responsibility belongs instead to the infinite number of writers who have either failed to understand, or have not wished to demonstrate it.

The value of things, in general, is defined by many as the esteem which men have for such things. Perhaps, these words do not evoke an idea which is as clear or as distinct as it might be. One might say that esteem or value, as conceived by an individual, is an idea of proportion between the possession of one thing and another. If we say that ten bushels of grain are worth as much as a cask of wine, we are expressing a proportion of equality between possession of one thing and the other. It follows that because men are always most careful not to be defrauded of their own pleasures, one thing exchanges for another, and, consequently, equality involves neither loss nor fraud.

It can be seen from what I have said that the value of things varies as men's ideas and needs vary. Since some things are more generally enjoyed and demanded than others, they have a value which is called current; other things have a value only because of the desire of those who wish to have them and those who can provide them.

Value, then, is a ratio which is, in turn, composed of two other ratios expressed by the names utility and scarcity. Allow me to explain my understanding of value with some examples, in order to avoid any confusion over words. Obviously, air and water, which are the most useful things for human life, have no value at all, because they are not scarce. A small bag of sand from the shores of Japan, on the other hand, would be a rare thing, but since it has no particular utility, it would also have no value.

Some will wonder what great utility one would possibly find in many things which have very high prices. This is a natural and frequently asked question which makes men appear foolish and irrational. It also destroys the basis on which the science of money rests. It will, therefore, be necessary to explore the utility of things and its measurement in more general terms. If utility does not depend on principles which are certain, then there can be no principles on which the prices of things are based either. Where there is no certainty or any means of demonstrating it, there is no science.

Utility is the ability a thing has to provide us with happiness. Man is a mixture of passions which move him with unequal force. Pleasure consists of gratifying these passions; and happiness is the acquisition of pleasure. But, I am not an Epicurean, and do not wish to appear to be one; permit me, therefore, to elaborate, on some points in the argument introduced which must be refuted.

The gratification of a passion which stimulates and arouses another passion is not a true pleasure. Indeed, if the trouble caused by it is greater than the pleasure itself, then the pleasure should be abhorred as a true pain and an evil. If the pain is less than the pleasure, however, it is a benefit, though reduced in intensity and duration. This view, therefore, considers the pleasures of this life without reference to the other, eternal life, as though one and the other could possibly be considered with the same admiration. It is obvious to us, thanks to Providence, that after this life we shall live another, the pleasures and pains of which are closely connected with our behavior in the present life. Now, without altering anything I have just said, note that true and perfect pleasures are pleasures which produce no pain in that life. Those pleasures which produce pain in that life are always false and deceitful pleasures, since the difference between the pleasures and pains of this life and that is infinite, however large the enjoyment of this and small the pain of that might be. Had this assertion been made by all concerned, the ancient dispute between Epicureans and Stoics—that is, between delight and virtue—could not have arisen. Either the Stoics would have been totally correct in their view or it would have been clear that the differences between the two are simply verbal differences.

To return to where I left off, utility is anything which produces a true pleasure, something which gratifies the excitement of the passions. Our passions are not just the desires to eat, drink, and sleep, however, these are just the first or primary passions. Once satisfied, these give rise to others which are just as strong. For man is so constituted that once he has satisfied one desire, another springs up in its place, always exciting him with an intensity equal to the first. He is, therefore, perpetually agitated in this manner, never quite succeeding in the achievement of full gratification. For this reason, it is incorrect to say that the only things which are useful are those which are required for the primary needs of life. Nor can any limits or frontiers be found between things we need and things we do not need. It is an ultimate truth that just as a thing is attained and, consequently, as soon as one ceases to need it, a person begins to crave something else.

Once man has satisfied the passions which appear in the human mind, passions which he holds in common with beasts and which are needed for survival of the individual and of the species, then nothing moves him more vehemently or more strongly than the desire to distinguish himself from others and to be superior to them. This is prior even to self-love; it is the very source of action in us, and surpasses every other passion. Those things which are of use to, and which satisfy us, have the greatest value, superceding every other pleasure and, often, the security of life itself.

Men seek food when they have none with the same justification as they seek titles of nobility, once they have been provided with food. Life is miserable and sad when we are hungry, but it can be just as miserable and sad when we are not held in high esteem or noticed. Indeed, sometimes the latter unhappiness is so much greater that we are more disposed to die or to place ourselves in a situation in which we risk the loss of life itself, than to go on living unhappily without the respect of others.

What is more just, therefore, than to acquire something of great utility, even with great privation and labor, as long as it produces a great many pleasures? If the feeling of pleasure derived from the reverence and high esteem in which others hold us should be ridiculed, this would constitute a reproach against our nature, which has provided us with a disposition of mind which we could not otherwise have acquired for ourselves, and which—like hunger, thirst, and the need for sleep—we neither should nor can defend or explain to anyone.

Some philosophers are contemptuous of riches and of the esteem of others; such philosophers have also trampled dignity underfoot. They are not honest when they say they hold such a position because these things bring them no pleasure! They have only spoken and behaved in this manner because of the security they were already enjoying, the security of knowing that they were enthusiastically applauded and commended by the public, even after they had revealed their contempt for public acclaim.

The things which bring us respect are, therefore, deservedly valued most highly. Among those most often cited are dignity, titles, honors, nobility, and the power to command. Close behind these is a variety of things which have at all times been sought after by men because of their beauty. Those who have had the good fortune to acquire these and to adorn their persons with them have been, at the same time, admired and envied. These are: gems, rare stones, certain skins, the most beautiful metals such as gold and silver, and certain works of art embodying both a great deal of effort and great beauty. According to some, these bodies, which add dignity to the awkward appearance of people, have also come to provide the superiority which is a source of the most considerable satisfaction, as I have already indicated. Hence, the value of such things is deservedly great. Indeed, even kings owe the greater part of the veneration of their subjects to the external magnificence which always surrounds them. Deprived of these trappings, kings would retain only powers and gifts of mind which they had formerly; they have come to realize that the reverence shown them has been greatly reduced in such circumstances. Consequently, those powers which possess less true force and authority seek to regulate, with more attention to external pomp, the ideas of men among whom the august and magnificent are often nothing more than exaggerated nonentities. This is formally called, with words taken from the Scholastics and very appropriately adopted, which mean, in effect, "id quod non est, neque nehil, neque aliquid."

If the desire to make a good appearance generates in men affection for these fairest and most beautiful products of nature, then the more ardent desire to appear beautiful makes these bodies even more valuable to women and children. Women constitute half of the human race and exist only, or in large part, solely for our propagation and breeding. They do not have any other value and merit than the love they arouse in men. And because this attribute is almost entirely derived from beauty, women have no greater duty than to appear attractive in the eyes of men. How useful they are as ornaments is attested to by common consensus. Hence, if the value of women arises from their amiableness, which is, in turn, enhanced by ornaments, it is reasonable to conclude that the value of ornaments must be great indeed.

As for children, they require the most tender care of parents. Men know of no other way to show this tender love than to make the object loved more desired and charming in their view. Thus, a man will not be moved to adorn his children except by the desire to satisfy a woman.

This is how it has come about that the most beautiful metals were first collected, with great difficulty, from the sands of the rivers and, later, from the very bowels of the earth. It is still true that nations which are known to be rich in these metals, such as Mexico and Peru, hold nothing—except gems—in higher esteem than gold and silver. And insofar as they hold such trifles as glass and steel in higher esteem, what I have just said would be confirmed, not denied. For it would be the beauty that results from our toil which enchants people. Inasmuch as the beauty of glass and crystal results from art rather than from nature, their value varies only insofar as nature varies their scarcity, which because it was unknown to the Americans cannot be regarded as a contradiction of what I have demonstrated.

The greater portion of mankind reasons, as does Bernardo Davanzati, that "A natural lamb is more noble than one of gold, but how much less is it valued?" I reply to him as follows. If a natural lamb were as rare as one of gold, its price would be higher than that of the golden lamb, to the degree that its utility and the necessity for it exceeded those of the golden lamb. Such people imagine that value is derived from one principle alone, and not from many which join together to form a compound reason. I hear others say, "A pound of bread is more useful than a pound of gold." To this I reply that this is a shameful paralogism derived from not knowing that "more useful" and "less useful" are relative terms, and that they are measured according to the different conditions of different people. To a person who has neither bread nor wine, bread is surely the more useful; an examination of the facts of this case would confirm this assertion because one will not find anyone who would choose gold and forgo bread to die of hunger. Those who dig in the mines, for example, never forget to eat and sleep. Nonetheless, there is nothing more useless than bread for one who is sated. In this case it makes sense for a person to satisfy other drives. The precious metals are the handmaidens of luxury, but only when the primary needs are already satisfied. It is for this reason, Davanzati asserts, that: "an egg worth half a grain of gold would have kept Count Ugolino from starving to death, even after ten days in his tower prison. All the gold in the world would not have matched it in value."

Davanzati badly confuses the difference in value between an egg to one who is not in danger of starving to death, and the needs of Count Ugolino. On what basis does he conclude that the count would not have paid even as much as a thousand grains of gold for the real egg? Though not aware of it, Davanzati himself provided evidence of this error a little later on when he said: "Though a mouse is a most loathsome creature, one was sold for two hundred florins in the siege of Casilino. And this was not actually dear, because the seller died of hunger, while the buyer lived." Note that he was agreed, thanks to heaven, at least in this instance, that dear and cheap are relative terms.

Some find it strange that precisely the most useful things have a low value, while the less useful have a great and excessive value. Such persons should be reminded that the world is well constituted just for our welfare. What amazing good fortune! In general, utility is never matched with scarcity. Indeed, the more the basic utility of a thing increases, the greater the abundance in which it is found: hence, its value cannot be great. Those things which are needed to sustain life are profusely distributed over the entire world; they either have no value at all or have value to a very moderate degree. Many draw false conclusions, regarding my purpose, from these considerations; some unjustly regard my judgement with contempt. My desire to do good should rather evoke prayers to God, feelings of self abasement; such an intention should be blessed at every turn. But few do this.

Many philosophers may, perhaps, say to me that although the value of gems and their scarcity spring from the nature of humans, as I have already demonstrated, these concepts do not cease to seem to them as ridiculous and miserable madness. To whom I reply: I wonder whether they could ever find any other human thing which does not appear this way to them! Nothing is likely to divert them from this opinion. But I would like the good philosopher— after he has rid himself of earthly deceptions and after having virtually dehumanized himself and has so raised himself above the others that he is able to laugh at us poor mortals and amuse himself—when he has then separated himself from these ideas and returned down here to mix in society—which will, of course, force the needs of life upon him—I would like him to return as a common man and not as a philosopher. That smile, which healed his soul, while he was philosophizing, would disturb his work and also the work of others now that he must labor. It is better that these concepts remain locked in his mind. For as he understands and deplores—together with his peers—that man is not very much superior to brutes (which I concede), he will by attempting to improve them only make them worse. This is an impossible enterprise for him. If men are guided to perfect virtue by our divine religion, then our teachers are assisted by supernatural and divine power; if examples of the highest perfection are seen among us, these works come from heavenly grace and not from human nature. He who is thus armed comes to perfect us—and well he can. For philosophy is not capable of doing this! We have seen Stoics, who have wished to render men perfectly virtuous, and have instead rendered them fiercely proud; others have wished to make them silent and contemplative but have, instead, made them gluttonous; those who would see them as poor, have brutalized them; and, finally, wishing to purge them of prejudice, Diogenes has ended by establishing an infamous race of dogs. But, alas, they have finally let us live in peace. They have left to the metals and precious stones the value they have, whatever it may be.

No longer, then, can Horace proclaim: "Let us fling all our jewels and useless gold into the nearest sea if we feel true remorse for our greed."

Since we have been able to advance, without suffering, by means of these otherwise useless bodies, from a primitive life in which we literally devoured each other to a civilized state in which we live peacefully, by trade, we need not return, in the name of wisdom, to the barbarism from which we have, by the grace of God, been happily delivered. The community of man can only improve its ideas within certain limits; attempts made to exceed these limits of the order of things will destroy and corrupt man.

Leaving these considerations aside, considerations spawned out of superficial and imperfect ideas, we conclude at once that those substances which enhance the respect of men, increase the beauty of women and the amiability of children are useful and deservedly precious. The important consequence that gold and silver had value as metals, before becoming money, follows from this. I will treat this subject at greater length in the next chapter; here I have spoken of value in general and have explained what I understand utility to mean, I turn now to a discussion of scarcity.

Scarcity refers to the proportion between the quantity of a thing and the use which is made of it. Use is not so much the destruction as the employment of a thing, where its employment by one person, and the satisfaction of his desires, precludes the satisfaction of another person's desires. Assume, for example, that one hundred paintings are offered for sale. If some gentleman should buy fifty of them, the paintings would become about twice as rare, not because they are consumed, but because they have been withdrawn from the market or, as some might say, they are no longer a part of trade. It is true, however, that the destruction of a thing raises its price more than its removal from trade. This is because its destruction completely eliminates all hope, while its removal preserves its value in accordance with the probability that the thing will be used and returned again to circulation and trade. This merits more serious consideration.

Turning now to the discussion of quantity, two classes may be distinguished. For some things, quantity depends upon the different degrees of abundance with which nature provides them. For others, it depends on the different amounts of labor employed upon them. The first class is formed by a group of things which are reproduced after a short time and which are expended as they are consumed. This group consists of animals and of the fruits of the earth.

With the same work, their harvest may be as much as eight or ten times more than it was just a short time earlier, depending on differences in climate. Plenty, obviously, does not depend on human will but on the circumstances of climate and of the elements.

Another class includes certain bodies such as minerals, stones, and marble, different amounts of which are scattered throughout the world, though their total does not vary from year to year. But the amount mined does vary according to our wishes. More of this class of bodies can be extracted from the earth as more people are put to work on them; thus, in order to determine the amount produced, one needs only compute the labor, for the quantity of these things always corresponds to this labor. Of course. I really do not believe that new metals and gems are not regenerated in their great natural laboratory, but their creation is very slow compared to their destruction and it is, therefore, not necessary to take this into account.

I turn next to a discussion of labor. This alone gives things value whether they are entirely works of art, such as paintings, sculptures, carvings, *et cetera*, or such things as minerals, stones, wild fruit trees, and so on. The quantity of the material in these bodies contributes to value in no other manner except that it increases or reduces work. Thus, should one inquire why gold is worth more than sand, despite the fact that gold and sand are found mixed together on the banks of many rivers, he should be reminded that he could easily fill his sack with sand in just a quarter of an hour, but that it would take him many years to gather the very scarce grains of gold.

One must keep three things in mind in connection with the calculation of labor: the number of people, or the population; time; and the different prices of those who work. I shall discuss first the number of people.

Certainly, no one works except to live, nor can one work without sustenance. For example, the work of 50 persons is needed for the manufacture of a bale of cloth, beginning with the clipped wool and continuing on through the state in which it is displayed at a shop. The cloth will be worth more than the wool it contains. Its price is equal to the cost of food for the 50 persons, for a time equal to the period of time involved in the work. For example, if 20 men are employed for an entire day, ten for half a day, and 20 for three days, the value of the cloth produced is equal enough to feed a man for 85 days. Twenty of these days will be earned by the first, five by the second, and 60 by the third. This obviously assumes that these persons all have equal compensation. So much for population.

Time includes not only the period actually involved in the work but also the period during which a person is at rest, because he must eat even during that period. This is because the work of an individual is interrupted either by law or because of the very nature of the arts, and not simply by slothfulness of the individual. Laziness is not so general in a nation that it would have a significance equal to that of laws and customs. Similarly, feast days among those people who observe them without working make things more costly than they would otherwise be. Consider, for example, a man who works 300 days in a year and produces 100 pairs of shoes. The value of the shoes must correspond to his subsistence for an entire year. Another man producing 120 pairs while working 360 days will sell his product for one-fifth less, since it is not necessary for the latter to earn any greater wage, while producing 120 pairs of shoes, than the first man received for his 100 pairs.

There are, in addition, some types of labor which cannot, by nature, exert themselves constantly. The fine arts belong to this group, I do not believe there is a sculptor or musician who works more than 100 days a year. So much time is needed to determine where employment can be found, in order to get started, for travel, and so on. Therefore, their work is properly worth more.

Finally, I would add the diverse lengths of time it takes different men to begin to enjoy profit from their work. For this reason, those arts and studies which require a great deal of time and expense to master must be higher in price. These are no different than pine timber and some walnut trees which, because of the length of time they take to grow, are worth more than poplars and elms. So much for time.

A correct appraisal of the value of different human talents, from which various prices of labor result, is a more difficult matter. This concerns a question about which less is known. I will discuss my thoughts on it here without knowing whether others believe as I do, since I have not found any other writer who has discussed this matter. I would certainly be pleased if anyone who knows better, or simply just thinks differently, would refute any of my arguments with logic and candor.

I think the value of human talents is appraised by the same means as the value of inanimate things that is, by the same principles of scarcity and utility considered together. Different men are providentially disposed to different occupations at the time of birth. Although these are not equally scarce, they correspond to human needs with remarkable wisdom. For example, of 1,000 men, 600 are only fit for agriculture, 300 inclined to the various manufacturing arts, 50 to the richer trades, and another 50 disposed to succeed in different studies and disciplines. Granting this, the worth of a man of letters compared to a peasant would be in inverse proportion to these figures, or as 600 to 50: he will be 12 times better. Consequently, it is not utility alone which determines prices. This is why the good Lord has willed that men who practice the most useful arts be born in large numbers. Since these are the very bread and wine of mankind, their value cannot be great. Learning and wisdom, on the other hand, are like gems among talents, and these deservedly have the highest prices.

Note, here, that scarcity should not be valued according to the proportions in which talents are provided, but instead in accordance with how rapidly different talents come to maturity. Consequently, the price of a talent is greater, the greater the difficulties of bringing it to a degree in which the talent is important and worthy of such a price. Great generals such as Prince Eugene or Marshall Turenne command an unlimited price compared to a simple soldier. This is not so much because nature produces few men as able as these, as because wherever military victories are reported these same few men find themselves in the fortunate circumstance of being present, practicing their skills. Nature behaves here as it does in the case of seeds and plants. Almost anticipating a great loss between sowing the seed and harvesting the plants which finally blossom, nature provides a much greater quantity of seeds, depositing more of them into the earth than the number of plants which finally bloom. Or, a plant is worth more than the seed from which it springs.

Reflecting on these sound principles, one notes how brilliantly the wisdom of human judges gleams. Everything is valued in measure. Wealth does not fall to a person except as payment for the just value of his work, although he can give his wealth to a person who is not worthy of acquiring it. For example, no family exists, indeed, there is no man, who can boast of wealth which has not been obtained either by merit or as a gift originally obtained on the basis of merit. Such a gift is referred to simply as a gift, when it is made in life, or as an inheritance, if given after death. But in either case, if one were to examine the early history of the wealth which someone might have received undeservedly, he would observe that it was originally

acquired wholly on the basis of merit. Though it is true that, in this connection, it is often necessary to ignore scores of persons for long periods of time, reason will show that, in the end,
even these exceptions will fit this group.

Some would assert that merit, or virtue, often goes unrewarded—that it is madness to deny
the frequent existence of the most atrocious acts of injustice. But note the false reasoning here.
First, there is no need to refer to some professions as synonymous with virtue or kindness, just
because they may be scarce and acquired only with great difficulty; virtue or kindness may not
be able to produce either true utility or true pleasure for the multitudes. Prices are made by the
many, not by the few.

Second, bear in mind that since man is made up of virtues and vices taken together, there is
no way of rewarding a man's virtues without at the same time also rewarding his vices, despite
the fact that one will never find vice exalted by anyone. These defects only occasionally fail to
get in his way; barring such defects, he would surely have achieved greater success.

Third, always bear in mind that possession of skill in obtaining employment is one matter.
To know how to perform the duties of a position well is quite another. The first consists merely
of the arts of being pleasing to persons responsible for filling the position, whether the position
involved be military or civilian. On the other hand, the skills required to perform different
employments are never the same, depending on the various needs of different offices. In any
event, no one has ever acquired employment which he is not worthy of being able to secure.
It would be well if, when the science of acquiring a position is not joined with the ability of
filling it well, a person were held responsible for the consequences and regarded as undeserving of the position. Men regard as worthy only the ability to employ well the talents which one
may have. Anything else will either not be virtuous or will not require skill for the application
of any labor. Consequently, they refer to as an injustice what is not an injustice at all. But
we must not include here those who are able to acquire some high office, either as a favor
from others, which is tantamount to a gift among living persons, or because of birth, which is
a bequest from one's ancestors. I am aware that this argument extends beyond the confines of
this work, but because this has appeared to me to be a useful subject, worthy of careful reflection, I have not been able to restrain myself from dealing with it. I beg my readers' indulgence.
How pleased I would be if he should share my view. Nevertheless, I fear that few will agree
with me, so much do men prefer to protect themselves from committing an error and to accuse
others of doing so.

Enough has now been said of the principles from which value is derived. It has been seen
that since these principles are certain, invariant, universal, and based on the order and nature
of earthly matters—nothing among us is arbitrary and accidental, all is necessarily order and
harmony. Values vary from one thing to another, but not capriciously. Their very variation is
orderly, with exact and immutable rules. These values are ideal; but those ideas of ours which
are based on need and pleasure are part of man's internal makeup. They contain within them
the ideas of justice and stability.

An exception to what I have just said would appear to be required here. Sometimes fashion
affects our ideas and values. As for the sense in which the word fashion is intended, after considerable thought I have found it possible to give it only one definition. Fashion is a malady of
the cerebrum common to the nations of Europe, because of which many things are rendered of
little value simply because they are not new. This is an illness of the mind which rules over but

few things. To find some rationality in it, you would have to say that a good part of such tastes results from imitation of the customs of more dominant nations.

Having said this much about fashion, it is necessary that I define its limits, which I shall do now, in order not to have to do it in a less appropriate place.

Fashion is entirely in the realm of the beautiful; none of it is in the useful. As a result, when a thing which is more useful and convenient is in fashion, I do not think of it as fashionable but as an improvement of the arts and of the comforts of life. Beauty is divided into two classes. One is founded on certain ideas engraved on our minds at birth. The other consists, though it does not seem to, of things which only appear beautiful out of habit of mind, or custom. The power of fashion is extended only over the second class, which is greater by far than the first. It is appropriate, therefore, to say that the beauty of gems and of gold and silver is universally established on the constitution of our minds, no part of it ever having succumbed to fashion, for it could not. Hence, the prices of such things are always recognized to be great and unique. Nevertheless, none of my observations are altered by fashion which only varies the utility of things as the pleasure enjoyed by using them varies. The rest remain the same.

I will complete my remarks by discussing the value of unique things and of monopoly, that is, of those things which cannot be made by others, like the statue of *venere de' Medici* those which become unique because of the unity of sellers. I have often found that even the wisest writers describe the value of these commodities as being infinite. But of all words that come from the mouths of those who reason about mortal things so often, I can think of none that is more appropriate than infinite. These writers have, perhaps, wished to say indefinite, but even this is inappropriate, for I believe every human thing has order and limits. Indefinite is no less alien to these limits than infinite. These things, then, have limits. Their prices always correspond to the needs and desires of the buyer joined together to form a compound ratio with the esteem of the seller. Hence, at times, their value can even be equal to nothing. Moreover, it is always regulated, although it may not be everywhere the same.

It may, perhaps, seem to many that from the observations made thus far it is easy to determine the value, of all things. But to believe this is to close one's mind on the matter prematurely. It is most difficult, often impossible, for us to draw such a conclusion from principles thus established, which logicians would call *a priori*. Because, we would have to establish, for certain, that because scarcity and value depend on consumption, consumption likewise corresponds to, and varies with, value. The problem is rendered indeterminate by this relationship, as it always is, when two unknown quantities which have some relationship between them are set against each other.

That differences of consumption emerge from price is obvious, if one recalls that aside from the air we breathe and the soil we stand upon, man regards nothing else as an absolute and eternal necessity. He must feed himself, but not with any food in particular or any sooner than with any other. Air and earth are not scarce, nor do they have value of any kind. Man can abstain from the consumption of other things, more easily for some than for others; and he is willing to do so in proportion to the discomfort, work, and cost of acquisition of a thing. Those which are worth less are, therefore, taken for consumption more readily. Consumption is, therefore, regulated by price; price, in turn, arises out of scarcity.

Price, on the other hand, is regulated by the exhaustion of a commodity. Because if, for example, 50 thousand casks of wine were being consumed in a nation, at the same time that a similar quantity was being produced, and if suddenly a military contingent should appear in the nation, then the price of wine would rise, because now people would be drinking more of it.

Some find an unalterable relationship here, a vicious circle. They would be able to solve this problem if only they would reflect on what I have already said. That is, in many instances, scarcity and abundance suddenly reverse places due to external causes, without man's interference but, instead, because of seasonal changes. In such cases, prices follow scarcity and, although men possess unequal wealth, purchase of certain commodities always corresponds to a certain degree of wealth. Should these commodities fall in price, even those of less wealth would purchase them. If their prices should rise, those who formerly used them would begin to abstain from their use. This is supported by many observations. For example, in good growing seasons, in the kingdom of Naples, a total of approximately 15 million tumoli of grain are consumed annually. We know from experience that occasionally, in the most fertile years, as many as six or seven million more tumoli of grain, than usual, are harvested. Moreover, export is never more than one and a half million, nor is the amount stored for their later use greater. On the contrary, in barren years it is certain that no more than eight million have been harvested, and we have not imported more than a million from abroad. Nor has the amount stored from previous years come to two million. For this reason, in years of plenty, incomparably more grain is consumed, otherwise used up and sown, and smaller quantities in calamitous years. This is why the limits on consumption are fixed more by price than by the number of tumoli. Every year, for example, the kingdom consumes 13 million ducats worth of grain. This is always the same whether this sum purchases as many as 15 of as few as ten million tumoli.

Changes in the scarcity of goods, whose production is not subject to variation, have no other extrinsic reason but fashion. Precious metals, however (and, due to their regal beauty, gems), are not subject to such capricious changes in tastes or to such variations in production. They, therefore, have constant prices more so than any other product. Their production varies in accordance with the discovery of richer mines, as in the case of the American discoveries. This is why their value fell as their use rose. It was this increased use which prevented their value from falling as much as their abundance would have required. For it is from this relationship that the great and most useful effect of the proportional equilibrium of all things has arisen. This equilibrium, in its turn, conforms neatly with the proper abundance of both the comforts of life and worldly happiness, although not from human prudence and virtue but from the lowest stimuli of all—private gain. For, in spite of ourselves, due to His infinite love of mankind, Providence has so arranged all things that our base passions are often ordered for the benefit of all. I shall endeavor to explain how this has come about.

Let us suppose that a country which is thoroughly Mohammedan in customs and religion should adopt the religion and customs of Christianity. Few grapevines would be found in such a country, because Mohammedans are forbidden from drinking wine, and I suppose they would have been obeying this law. But now, wine would quickly be rendered dear in price because of its scarcity; and merchants would begin to import a great deal of wine from abroad. Soon, however, because all would wish to enjoy such high profits, many new vines would be planted, so much wine would be imported, that everyone would end by gaining only a just profit. Thus, things always arrange themselves at some common level, such is their intrinsic nature. Frequently, the size of a population even grows so much in this way that, though first drawn to this type of industry by the example of the first producers who entered the industry and by the earliest rumors, they impetuously turn to it, albeit so belatedly, that value falls, to a just level. But then, as each person pays the penalty of his rashness, all begin to withdraw from the industry, and the just limit of value is restored anew.

Two great consequences are drawn from this. First, one should not pay particular attention to the first movements of things, but only to permanent and fixed states. It is in the latter that order and sameness are found, just as water in a bowl finds its own level after some disturbance has caused a disoriented and irregular tossing about. Secondly, nature provides no examples of phenomena which display infinite changes. A certain moral gravity, which all things possess, always draws them from an infinite linear path and pulls them into one which, though perpetual, is circular and finite.

I have applied what I have said here to money, hundreds of times. As a result, my readers have fixed it in their minds. They have, consequently, been persuaded that the laws of commerce correspond with no less exactness to the laws of gravity and the laws of fluids. The desire for gain, or the desire to live happily, is to man what gravity is to physics. Once this is given, all physical laws of matter can be verified perfectly, by one who knows how, to the ethical principles of our lives.

33. David Hume: *Of Money* (1752)

Money is not, properly speaking, one of the subjects of commerce; but only the instrument which men have agreed upon to facilitate the exchange of one commodity for another. It is none of the wheels of trade: It is the oil which renders the motion of the wheels more smooth and easy. If we consider any one kingdom by itself, it is evident, that the greater or less plenty of money is of no consequence; since the prices of commodities are always proportioned to the plenty of money, and a crown in HARRY VII's time served the same purpose as a pound does at present. It is only the public which draws any advantage from the greater plenty of money; and that only in its wars and negociations with foreign states. And this is the reason, why all rich and trading countries from CARTHAGE to GREAT BRITAIN and HOLLAND, have employed mercenary troops, which they hired from their poorer neighbours. Were they to make use of their native subjects, they would find less advantage from their superior riches, and from their great plenty of gold and silver; since the pay of all their servants must rise in proportion to the public opulence. Our small army of 20,000 men is maintained at as great expence as a FRENCH army twice as numerous. The ENGLISH fleet, during the late war, required as much money to support it as all the ROMAN legions, which kept the whole world in subjection, during the time of the emperors.

The greater number of people and their greater industry are serviceable in all cases; at home and abroad, in private, and in public. But the greater plenty of money, is very limited in its use, and may even sometimes be a loss to a nation in its commerce with foreigners.

There seems to be a happy concurrence of causes in human affairs, which checks the growth of trade and riches, and hinders them from being confined entirely to one people; as might naturally at first be dreaded from the advantages of an established commerce. Where one nation has gotten the start of another in trade, it is very difficult for the latter to regain the ground it has lost; because of the superior industry and skill of the former, and the greater stocks, of which its merchants are possessed, and which enable them to trade on so much smaller profits. But these advantages are compensated, in some measure, by the low price of labour in every nation which has not an extensive commerce, and does not much abound in gold and silver. Manufactures, therefore gradually shift their places, leaving those countries and provinces which they have already enriched, and flying to others, whither they are allured by the cheapness of provisions and labour; till they have enriched these also, and are again banished by the same causes. And, in general, we may observe, that the dearness of every thing, from plenty of money, is a disadvantage, which attends an established commerce, and sets bounds to it in every country, by enabling the poorer states to undersell the richer in all foreign markets.

This has made me entertain a doubt concerning the benefit of banks and paper-credit, which are so generally esteemed advantageous to every nation. That provisions and labour should become dear by the encrease of trade and money, is, in many respects, an inconvenience; but an inconvenience that is unavoidable, and the effect of that public wealth and prosperity which are the end of all our wishes. It is compensated by the advantages, which we reap from the possession of these precious metals, and the weight, which they give the nation in all foreign wars and negociations. But there appears no reason for encreasing that inconvenience by a counterfeit money, which foreigners will not accept of in any payment, and which any great disorder in the state will reduce to nothing. There are, it is true, many people in every rich state, who having large sums of money, would prefer paper with good security; as being of more easy transport and more safe custody. If the public provide not a bank, private bankers will take advantage of this circumstance; as the goldsmiths formerly did in LONDON, or as the bankers do at present in DUBLIN: And therefore it is better, it may be thought, that a public company should enjoy the benefit of that paper-credit, which always will have place in every opulent kingdom. But to endeavour artificially to encrease such a credit, can never be the interest of any trading nation; but must lay them under disadvantages, by encreasing money beyond its natural proportion to labour and commodities, and thereby heightening their price to the merchant and manufacturer. And in this view, it must be allowed, that no bank could be more advantageous, than such a one as locked up all the money it received, and never augmented the circulating coin, as is usual, by returning part of its treasure into commerce. A public bank, by this expedient, might cut off much of the dealings of private bankers and money-jobbers; and though the state bore the charge of salaries to the directors and tellers of this bank (for, according to the preceding supposition, it would have no profit from its dealings), the national advantage, resulting from the low price of labour and the destruction of paper-credit, would be a sufficient compensation. Not to mention, that so large a sum, lying ready at command, would be a convenience in times of great public danger and distress; and what part of it was used might be replaced at leisure, when peace and tranquillity was restored to the nation.

But of this subject of paper-credit we shall treat more largely hereafter. And I shall finish this essay on money, by proposing and explaining two observations, which may, perhaps, serve to employ the thoughts of our speculative politicians.

It was a shrewd observation of ANACHARSIS the SCYTHIAN, who had never seen money in his own country, that gold and silver seemed to him of no use to the GREEKS, but to assist them in numeration and arithmetic. It is indeed evident, that money is nothing but the representation of labour and commodities, and serves only as a method of rating or estimating them. Where coin is in greater plenty; as a greater quantity of it is required to represent the same quantity of goods; it can have no effect, either good or bad, taking a nation within itself; any more than it would make an alteration on a merchant's books, if, instead of the ARABIAN method of notation, which requires few characters, he should make use of the ROMAN, which requires a great many. Nay, the greater quantity of money, like the ROMAN characters, is rather inconvenient, and requires greater trouble both to keep and transport it. But notwithstanding this conclusion, which must be allowed just, it is certain, that, since the discovery of the mines in AMERICA, industry has encreased in all the nations of EUROPE, except in the possessors of those mines; and this may justly be ascribed, amongst other reasons, to the encrease of gold and silver. Accordingly we find, that, in every kingdom, into which money begins to flow in greater abundance than formerly, every thing takes a new face: labour and industry gain life; the merchant becomes more enterprising, the manufacturer more diligent and skilful, and even the farmer follows his plough with greater alacrity and attention. This is not easily to be accounted for, if we consider only the influence which a greater abundance of coin has in the kingdom itself, by heightening the price of Commodities, and obliging every one to pay a greater number of these little yellow or white pieces for every thing he purchases. And as to foreign trade, it appears, that great plenty of money is rather disadvantageous, by raising the price of every kind of labour.

To account, then, for this phenomenon, we must consider, that though the high price of commodities be a necessary consequence of the encrease of gold and silver, yet it follows not immediately upon that encrease; but some time is required before the money circulates through the whole state, and makes its effect be felt on all ranks of people. At first, no alteration is perceived; by degrees the price rises, first of one commodity, then of another; till the whole at last reaches a just proportion with the new quantity of specie which is in the kingdom. In my opinion, it is only in this interval or intermediate situation, between the acquisition of money and rise of prices, that the encreasing quantity of gold and silver is favourable to industry. When any quantity of money is imported into a nation, it is not at first dispersed into many hands; but is confined to the coffers of a few persons, who immediately seek to employ it to advantage. Here are a set of manufacturers or merchants, we shall suppose, who have received returns of gold and silver for goods which they sent to CADIZ. They are thereby enabled to employ more workmen than formerly, who never dream of demanding higher wages, but are glad of employment from such good paymasters. If workmen become scarce, the manufacturer gives higher wages, but at first requires an encrease of labour; and this is willingly submitted to by the artisan, who can now eat and drink better, to compensate his additional toil and fatigue. He carries his money to market, where he, finds every thing at the same price as formerly, but returns with greater quantity and of better kinds, for the use of his family. The farmer and gardener, finding, that all their commodities are taken off, apply themselves with alacrity to the raising more; and at the same time can afford to take better and more cloths from their tradesmen, whose price is the same as formerly, and their industry only whetted by so much new gain. It is easy to trace the money in its progress through the whole commonwealth; where we shall find, that it must first quicken the diligence of every individual, before it encrease the price of labour.

And that the specie may encrease to a considerable pitch, before it have this latter effect, appears, amongst other instances, from the frequent operations of the FRENCH king on the money; where it was always found, that the augmenting of the numerary value did not produce a proportional rise of the prices, at least for some time. In the last year of LOUIS XIV, money was raised three-sevenths, but prices augmented only one. Corn in FRANCE is now sold at the same price, or for the same number of livres, it was in 1683; though silver was then at 30 livres the mark, and is now at 50. Not to mention the great addition of gold and silver, which may have come into that kingdom since the former period.

From the whole of this reasoning we may conclude, that it is of no manner of consequence, with regard to the domestic happiness of a state, whether money be in a greater or less quantity. The good policy of the magistrate consists only in keeping it, if possible, still encreasing; because, by that means, he keeps alive a spirit of industry in the nation, and encreases the stock of labour, in which consists all real power and riches. A nation, whose money decreases, is actually, at that time, weaker and more miserable than another nation, which possesses no more money, but is on the encreasing hand. This will be easily accounted for, if we consider, that the alterations in the quantity of money, either on one side or the other, are not immediately attended with proportionable alterations in the price of commodities. There is always an interval before matters be adjusted to their new situation; and this interval is as pernicious to industry, when gold and silver are diminishing, as it is advantageous when these metals are encreasing. The workman has not the same employment from the manufacturer and merchant; though he pays the same price for every thing in the market. The farmer cannot dispose of his corn and cattle; though he must pay the same rent to his landlord. The poverty, and beggary, and sloth, which must ensue, are easily foreseen.

The second observation which I proposed to make with regard to money, may be explained after the following manner. There are some kingdoms, and many provinces in EUROPE, (and all of them were once in the same condition) where money is so scarce, that the landlord can get none at all from his tenants; but is obliged to take his rent in kind, and either to consume it himself, or transport it to places where he may find a market. In those countries, the prince can levy few or no taxes, but in the same manner: And as he will receive small benefit from impositions so paid, it is evident that such a kingdom has little force even at home; and cannot maintain fleets and armies to the same extent, as if every part of it abounded in gold and silver. There is surely a greater disproportion between the force of GERMANY, at present, and what it was three centuries ago, than there is in its industry, people, and manufactures. The AUSTRIAN dominions in the empire are in general well peopled and well cultivated, and are of great extent; but have not a proportionable weight in the balance of EUROPE; proceeding, as is commonly supposed, from the scarcity of money.

How do all these facts agree with that principle of reason, that the quantity of gold and silver is in itself altogether indifferent? According to that principle wherever a sovereign has numbers of subjects, and these have plenty of commodities, he should of course be great and powerful, and they rich and happy, independent of the greater or lesser abundance of the precious metals. These admit of divisions and subdivisions to a great extent; and where the pieces might become so small as to be in danger of being lost, it is easy to mix the gold or silver with a baser metal, as is practised in some countries of EUROPE; and by that means raise the pieces to a bulk more sensible and convenient. They still serve the same purposes of exchange, whatever their number may be, or whatever colour they may be supposed to have.

To these difficulties I answer, that the effect, here supposed to flow from scarcity of money, really arises from the manners and customs of the people; and that we mistake, as is too usual, a collateral effect for a cause. The contradiction is only apparent; but it requires some thought and reflection to discover the principles, by which we can reconcile reason to experience.

It seems a maxim almost self-evident, that the prices of every thing depend on the proportion between commodities and money, and that any considerable alteration on either has the same effect, either of heightening or lowering the price. Encrease the commodities, they become cheaper; encrease the money, they rise in their value. As, on the other hand, a diminution of the former, and that of the latter, have contrary tendencies.

It is also evident, that the prices do not so much depend on the absolute quantity of commodities and that of money, which are in a nation, as on that of the commodities, which come or may come to market, and of the money which circulates. If the coin be locked up in chests, it is the same thing with regard to prices, as if it were annihilated; if the commodities be hoarded in magazines and granaries, a like effect follows. As the money and commodities, in these cases, never meet, they cannot affect each other. Were we, at any time, to form conjectures concerning the price of provisions, the corn, which the farmer must reserve for seed and for the maintenance of himself and family, ought never to enter into the estimation. It is only the overplus, compared to the demand, that determines the value.

To apply these principles, we must consider, that, in the first and more uncultivated ages of any state, ere fancy has confounded her wants with those of nature, men, content with the produce of their own fields, or with those rude improvements which they themselves can work upon them, have little occasion for exchange, at least for money, which, by agreement, is the common measure of exchange. The wool of the farmer's own flock, spun in his own family, and wrought by a neighbouring weaver, who receives his payment in corn or wool, suffices for furniture and cloathing. The carpenter, the smith, the mason, the tailor, are retained by wages of a like nature; and the landlord himself, dwelling in the neighbourhood, is content to receive his rent in the commodities raised by the farmer. The greater part of these he consumes at home, in rustic hospitality: The rest, perhaps, he disposes of for money to the neighbouring town, whence he draws the few materials of his expence and luxury.

But after men begin to refine on all these enjoyments, and live not always at home, nor are content with what can be raised in their neighbourhood, there is more exchange and commerce of all kinds, and more money enters into that exchange. The tradesmen will not be paid in corn; because they want something more than barely to eat. The farmer goes beyond his own parish for the commodities he purchases, and cannot always carry his commodities to the merchant who supplies him. The landlord lives in the capital, or in a foreign country; and demands his rent in gold and silver, which can easily be transported to him. Great undertakers, and manufacturers, and merchants, arise in every commodity; and these can conveniently deal in nothing but in specie. And consequently, in this situation of society, the coin enters into many more contracts, and by that means is much more employed than in the former.

The necessary effect is, that, provided the money encrease not in the nation, every thing must become much cheaper in times of industry and refinement, than in rude, uncultivated ages. It is the proportion between the circulating money, and the commodities in the market, which determines the prices. Goods, that are consumed at home, or exchanged with other goods in the neighbourhood, never come to market; they affect not in the least the current specie; with regard to it they are as if totally annihilated; and consequently this method of using them sinks the proportion on the side of the commodities, and encreases the prices. But after money enters into all contracts and sales, and is every where the measure of exchange, the same national cash has a much greater task to perform; all commodities are then in the market; the sphere of circulation is enlarged; it is the same case as if that individual sum were to serve a larger kingdom; and therefore, the proportion being here lessened on the side of the money, every thing must become cheaper, and the prices gradually fall.

By the most exact computations, that have been formed all over EUROPE, after making allowance for the alteration in the numerary value or the denomination, it is found, that the prices of all things have only risen three, or at most, four times, since the discovery of the WEST INDIES. But will any one assert, that there is not much more than four times the coin in EUROPE, that was in the fifteenth century, and the centuries preceding it? The SPANIARDS and PORTUGUESE from their mines, the ENGLISH, FRENCH, and DUTCH, by their AFRICAN trade, and by their interlopers in the WEST INDIES, bring home about six millions a year, of which not above a third goes to the EAST INDIES. This sum alone, in ten years, would probably double the ancient stock of money in EUROPE. And no other satisfactory reason can be given, why all prices have not risen to a much more exorbitant height, except that which is derived from a change of customs and manners. Besides that more commodities are produced by additional industry, the same commodities come more to market, after men depart from their ancient simplicity of manners. And though this encrease has not been equal to that of money, it has, however, been considerable, and has preserved the proportion between coin and commodities nearer the ancient standard.

Were the question proposed, Which of these methods of living in the people, the simple or refined, is the most advantageous to the state or public? I should, without much scruple, prefer the latter, in a view to politics at least; and should produce this as an additional reason for the encouragement of trade and manufactures.

While men live in the ancient simple manner, and supply all their necessaries from domestic industry or from the neighbourhood, the sovereign can levy no taxes in money from a considerable part of his subjects; and if he will impose on them any burdens, he must take payment in commodities, with which alone they abound; a method attended with such great and obvious inconveniencies, that they need not here be insisted on. All the money he can pretend to raise, must be from his principal cities, where alone it circulates; and these, it is evident, cannot afford him so much as the whole state could, did gold and silver circulate throughout the whole. But besides this obvious diminution of the revenue, there is another cause of the poverty of the public in such a situation. Not only the sovereign receives less money, but the same money goes not so far as in times of industry and general commerce. Every thing is dearer, where the gold and silver are supposed equal; and that because fewer commodities come to market, and the whole coin bears a higher proportion to what is to be purchased by it; whence alone the prices of every thing are fixed and determined.

Here then we may learn the fallacy of the remark, often to be met with in historians, and even in common conversation, that any particular state is weak, though fertile, populous, and well cultivated, merely because it wants money. It appears, that the want of money can never injure any state within itself: For men and commodities are the real strength of any community. It is the simple manner of living which here hurts the public, by confining the gold and silver to few hands, and preventing its universal diffusion and circulation. On the contrary, industry and refinements of all kinds incorporate it with the whole state, however small its quantity may be: They digest it into every vein, so to speak; and make it enter into every transaction and contract. No hand is entirely empty of it. And as the prices of every thing fall by that means, the sovereign has a double advantage: He may draw money by his taxes from every part of the state; and what he receives, goes farther in every purchase and payment.

We may infer, from a comparison of prices, that money is not more plentiful in CHINA, than it was in EUROPE three centuries ago: But what immense power is that empire possessed of, if we may judge by the civil and military establishment maintained by it? POLYBIUS tells us, that provisions were so cheap in ITALY during his time, that in some places the stated price for a meal at the inns was a *semis* a head, little more than a farthing! Yet the ROMAN power had even then subdued the whole known world. About a century before that period, the CARTHAGINIAN ambassador said, by way of raillery, that no people lived more sociably amongst themselves than the ROMANS; for that, in every entertainment, which, as foreign ministers, they received, they still observed the same plate at every table. The absolute quantity of the precious metals is a matter of great indifference. There are only two circumstances of any importance, namely, their gradual encrease, and their thorough concoction and circulation through the state; and the influence of both these circumstances has here been explained.

In the following Essay we shall see an instance of a like fallacy as that above mentioned; where a collateral effect is taken for a cause, and where a consequence is ascribed to the plenty of money; though it be really owing to a change in the manners and customs of the people.

34. David Hume: *Of Interest* (1752)

NOTHING is esteemed a more certain sign of the flourishing condition of any nation than the lowness of interest: And with reason; though I believe the cause is somewhat different from what is commonly apprehended. Lowness of interest is generally ascribed to plenty of money. But money, however plentiful, has no other effect, if fixed, than to raise the price of labour. Silver is more common than gold; and therefore you receive a greater quantity of it for the same commodities: But do you pay less interest for it? Interest in BATAVIA and JAMAICA is at 10 *per cent* in PORTUGAL at 6; though these places, as we may learn from the prices of every thing, abound more in gold and silver than either LONDON or AMSTERDAM.

Were all the gold in ENGLAND annihilated at once, and one and twenty shillings substituted in the place of every guinea, would money be more plentiful or interest lower? No surely: We should only use silver instead of gold. Were gold rendered as common as silver, and silver as common as copper; would money be more plentiful or interest lower? We may assuredly give the same answer. Our shillings would then be yellow, and our halfpence white; and we should have no guineas. No other difference would ever be observed; no alteration on commerce, manufactures, navigation, or interest; unless we imagine, that the colour of the metal is of any consequence.

Now, what is so visible in these greater variations of scarcity or abundance in the precious metals, must hold in all inferior changes. If the multiplying of gold and silver fifteen times makes no difference, much less can the doubling or tripling them. All augmentation has no other effect than to heighten the price of labour and commodities; and even this variation is little more than that of a name. In the progress towards these changes, the augmentation may have some influence, by exciting industry; but after the prices are settled, suitably to the new abundance of gold and silver, it has no manner of influence.

An effect always holds proportion with its cause. Prices have risen near four times since the discovery of the INDIES; and it is probable gold and silver have multiplied much more: But interest has not fallen much above half. The rate of interest, therefore, is not derived from the quantity of the precious metals.

Money having chiefly a fictitious value, the greater or less plenty of it is of no consequence, if we consider a nation within itself; and the quantity of specie, when once fixed, though ever so large, has no other effect, than to oblige every one to tell out a greater number of those shining bits of metal, for clothes, furniture or equipage, without encreasing any one convenience of life. If a man borrow money to build a house, he then carries home a greater load; because the stone, timber, lead, glass, &c. with the labour of the masons and carpenters, are represented by a greater quantity of gold and silver. But as these metals are considered chiefly as representations, there can no alteration arise, from their bulk or quantity, their weight or colour, either upon their real value or their interest. The same interest, in all cases, bears the same proportion to the sum. And if you lent me so much labour and so many commodities;

by receiving 5 *per cent* you always receive proportional labour and commodities, however represented, whether by yellow or white coin, whether by a pound or an ounce. It is in vain, therefore, to look for the cause of the fall or rise of interest in the greater or less quantity of gold and silver, which is fixed in any nation.

High interest arises from three circumstances: A great demand for borrowing; little riches to supply that demand; and great profits arising from commerce: And these circumstances are a clear proof of the small advance of commerce and industry, not of the scarcity of gold and silver. Low interest, on the other hand, proceeds from the three opposite circumstances: A small demand for borrowing; great riches to supply that demand; and small profits arising from commerce: And these circumstances are all connected together, and proceed from the encrease of industry and commerce, not of gold and silver. We shall endeavour to prove these points; and shall begin with the causes and the effects of a great or small demand for borrowing.

When a people have emerged ever so little from a savage state, and their numbers have encreased beyond the original multitude, there must immediately arise an inequality of property; and while some possess large tracts of land, others are confined within narrow limits, and some are entirely without any landed property. Those who possess more land than they can labour, employ those who possess none, and agree to receive a determinate part of the product. Thus the landed interest is immediately established; nor is there any settled government, however rude, in which affairs are not on this footing. Of these proprietors of land, some must presently discover themselves to be of different tempers from others; and while one would willingly store up the produce of his land for futurity, another desires to consume at present what should suffice for many years. But as the spending of a settled revenue is a way of life entirely without occupation; men have so much need of somewhat to fix and engage them, that pleasures, such as they are, will be the pursuit of the greater part of the landholders, and the prodigals among them will always be more numerous than the misers. In a state, therefore, where there is nothing but a landed interest, as there is little frugality, the borrowers must be very numerous, and the rate of interest must hold proportion to it. The difference depends not on the quantity of money, but on the habits and manners which prevail. By this alone the demand for borrowing is encreased or diminished. Were money so plentiful as to make an egg be sold for sixpence; so long as there are only landed gentry and peasants in the state, the borrowers must be numerous, and interest high. The rent for the same farm would be heavier and more bulky: But the same idleness of the landlord, with the higher price of commodities, would dissipate it in the same time, and produce the same necessity and demand for borrowing.

Nor is the case different with regard to the second circumstance which we proposed to consider, namely, the great or little riches to supply the demand. This effect also depends on the habits and way of living of the people, not on the quantity of gold and silver. In order to have, in any state, a great number of lenders, it is not sufficient nor requisite, that there be great abundance of the precious metals. It is only requisite, that the property or command of that quantity, which is in the state, whether great or small, should be collected in particular hands, so as to form considerable sums, or compose a great monied interest. This begets a number of lenders, and sinks the rate of usury; and this I shall venture to affirm, depends not on the quantity of specie, but on particular manners and customs, which make the specie gather into separate sums or masses of considerable value.

For suppose, that, by miracle, every man in GREAT BRITAIN should have five pounds slipt into his pocket in one night; this would much more than double the whole money that is at present in the kingdom; yet there would not next day, nor for some time, be any more lenders, nor any variation in the interest. And were there nothing but landlords and peasants in the state, this money, however abundant, could never gather into sums; and would only serve to encrease the prices of every thing, without any farther consequence. The prodigal landlord dissipates it, as fast as he receives it; and the beggarly peasant has no means, nor view, nor ambition of obtaining above a bare livelihood. The overplus of borrowers above that of lenders continuing still the same, there will follow no reduction of interest. That depends upon another principle; and must proceed from an encrease of industry and frugality, of arts and commerce.

Every thing useful to the life of man arises from the ground; but few things arise in that condition which is requisite to render them useful. There must, therefore, beside the peasants and the proprietors of land, be another rank of men, who receiving from the former the rude materials, work them into their proper form, and retain part for their own use and subsistence. In the infancy of society, these contracts between the artisans and the peasants, and between one species of artisans and another are commonly entered into immediately by the persons themselves, who, being neighbours, are easily acquainted with each other's necessities, and can lend their mutual assistance to supply them. But when men's industry encreases, and their views enlarge, it is found, that the most remote parts of the state can assist each other as well as the more contiguous, and that this intercourse of good offices may be carried on to the greatest extent and intricacy. Hence the origin of merchants, one of the most useful races of men, who serve as agents between those parts of the state, that are wholly unacquainted, and are ignorant of each other's necessities. Here are in a city fifty workmen in silk and linen, and a thousand customers; and these two ranks of men, so necessary to each other, can never rightly meet, till one man erects a shop, to which all the workmen and all the customers repair. In this province, grass rises in abundance: The inhabitants abound in cheese, and butter, and cattle; but want bread and corn, which, in a neighbouring province, are in too great abundance for the use of the inhabitants. One man discovers this. He brings corn from the one province and returns with cattle; and supplying the wants of both, he is, so far, a common benefactor. As the people encrease in numbers and industry, the difficulty of their intercourse encreases: The business of the agency or merchandize becomes more intricate; and divides, subdivides, compounds, and mixes to a greater variety. In all these transactions, it is necessary, and reasonable, that a considerable part of the commodities and labour should belong to the merchant, to whom, in a great measure, they are owing. And these commodities he will sometimes preserve in kind, or more commonly convert into money, which is their common representation. If gold and silver have encreased in the state together with the industry, it will require a great quantity of these metals to represent a great quantity of commodities and labour. If industry alone has encreased, the prices of every thing must sink, and a small quantity of specie will serve as a representation.

There is no craving or demand of the human mind more constant and insatiable than that for exercise and employment; and this desire seems the foundation of most of our passions and pursuits. Deprive a man of all business and serious occupation, he runs restless from one amusement to another; and the weight and oppression, which he feels from idleness, is so great, that he forgets the ruin which must follow him from his immoderate expences. Give him a more harmless way of employing his mind or body, he is satisfied, and feels no longer that insatiable thirst after pleasure. But if the employment you give him be lucrative, especially if the profit be attached to every particular exertion of industry, he has gain so often in his eye, that he acquires, by degrees, a passion for it, and knows no such pleasure as that of seeing the daily encrease of his fortune. And this is the reason why trade encreases frugality, and why, among merchants, there is the same overplus of misers above prodigals, as, among the possessors of land, there is the contrary.

Commerce encreases industry, by conveying it readily from one member of the state to another, and allowing none of it to perish or become useless. It encreases frugality, by giving occupation to men, and employing them in the arts of gain, which soon engage their affection, and remove all relish for pleasure and expence. It is an infallible consequence of all industrious professions, to beget frugality, and make the love of gain prevail over the love of pleasure. Among lawyers and physicians who have any practice, there are many more who live within their income, than who exceed it, or even live up to it. But lawyers and physicians beget no industry; and it is even at the expence of others they acquire their riches; so that they are sure to diminish the possessions of some of their fellow-citizens, as fast as they encrease their own. Merchants, on the contrary, beget industry, by serving as canals to convey it through every corner of the state: And at the same time, by their frugality, they acquire great power over that industry, and collect a large property in the labour and commodities, which they are the chief instruments in producing. There is no other profession, therefore, except merchandize, which can make the monied interest considerable, or, in other words, can increase industry, and, by also encreasing frugality, give a great command of that industry to particular members of the society. Without commerce, the state must consist chiefly of landed gentry, whose prodigality and expence make a continual demand for borrowing; and of peasants, who have no sums to supply that demand. The money never gathers into large stocks or sums, which can be lent at interest. It is dispersed into numberless hands, who either squander it in idle show and magnificence, or employ it in the purchase of the common necessaries of life. Commerce alone assembles it into considerable sums; and this effect it has merely from the industry which it begets, and the frugality which it inspires, independent of that particular quantity of precious metal which may circulate in the state.

Thus an encrease of commerce, by a necessary consequence, raises a great number of lenders, and by that means produces lowness of interest. We must now consider how far this encrease of commerce diminishes the profits arising from that profession, and gives rise to the third circumstance requisite to produce lowness of interest.

It may be proper to observe on this head, that low interest and low profits of merchandize are two events, that mutually forward each other, and are both originally derived from that extensive commerce, which produces opulent merchants, and renders the monied interest considerable. Where merchants possess great stocks, whether represented by few or many pieces of metal, it must frequently happen, that, when they either become tired of business, or leave heirs unwilling or unfit to engage in commerce, a great proportion of these riches naturally seeks an annual and secure revenue. The plenty diminishes the price, and makes the lenders accept of a low interest. This consideration obliges many to keep their stock employed in trade, and rather be content with low profits than dispose of their money at an under-value. On the other hand, when commerce has become extensive, and employs large stocks, there must arise rivalships among the merchants, which diminish the profits of trade, at the same time that they encrease the trade itself. The low profits of merchandize induce the merchants to accept more willingly of a low interest, when they leave off business, and begin to indulge themselves in ease and indolence. It is needless, therefore, to enquire which of these circumstances, to wit, *low interest or low profits*, is the cause, and which the effect? They both arise from an extensive commerce, and mutually forward each other. No man will accept of low profits, where he can have high interest; and no man will accept of low interest, where he can have high profits. An extensive commerce, by producing large stocks, diminishes both interest and profits; and is always assisted, in its diminution of the one, by the proportional sinking of the other. I may add, that, as low profits arise from the encrease of commerce and industry, they serve in their turn to its farther encrease, by rendering the commodities cheaper, encouraging the consumption, and heightening the industry. And thus, if we consider the whole connexion of causes and effects, interest is the barometer of the state, and its lowness is a sign almost infallible of the flourishing condition of a people. It proves the encrease of industry, and its prompt circulation through the whole state, little inferior to a demonstration. And though, perhaps, it may not be impossible but a sudden and a great check to commerce may have a momentary effect of the same kind, by throwing so many stocks out of trade; it must be attended with such misery and want of employment in the poor, that, besides its short duration, it will not be possible to mistake the one case for the other.

Those who have asserted, that the plenty of money was the cause of low interest, seem to have taken a collateral effect for a cause; since the same industry, which sinks the interest, commonly acquires great abundance of the precious metals. A variety of fine manufactures, with vigilant enterprising merchants, will soon draw money to a state, if it be any where to be found in the world. The same cause, by multiplying the conveniencies of life, and encreasing industry, collects great riches into the hands of persons, who are not proprietors of land, and produces, by that means, a lowness of interest. But though both these effects, plenty of money and low interest, naturally arise from commerce and industry, they are altogether independent of each other. For suppose a nation removed into the Pacific ocean, without any foreign commerce, or any knowledge of navigation: Suppose, that this nation possesses always the same stock of coin, but is continually encreasing in its numbers and industry: It is evident, that the price of every commodity must gradually diminish in that kingdom; since it is the proportion between money and any species of goods, which fixes their mutual value; and, upon the present supposition, the conveniencies of life become every day more abundant, without any alteration in the current specie. A less quantity of money, therefore, among this people, will make a rich man, during the times of industry, than would suffice to that purpose, in ignorant and slothful ages. Less money will build a house, portion a daughter, buy an estate, support a manufactory, or maintain a family and equipage. These are the uses for which men borrow money; and therefore, the greater or less quantity of it in a state has no influence on the interest. But it is evident, that the greater or less stock of labour and commodities must have a great influence; since we really and in effect borrow these, when we take money upon interest. It is true, when commerce is extended all over the globe, the most industrious nations always abound most with the precious metals: So that low interest and plenty of money are in fact almost inseparable. But still it is of consequence to know the principle whence any phenomenon arises, and to distinguish between a cause and a concomitant effect. Besides that the speculation is curious, it may frequently be of use in the conduct of public affairs. At least, it must be owned, that nothing can be of more use than to improve, by practice, the method of reasoning on these subjects, which of all others are the most important; though they are commonly treated in the loosest and most careless manner.

Another reason of this popular mistake with regard to the cause of low interest, seems to be the instance of some nations; where, after a sudden acquisition of money or of the precious metals, by means of foreign conquest, the interest has fallen, not only among them, but in all the neighbouring states, as soon as that money was dispersed, and had insinuated itself into every corner. Thus, interest in SPAIN fell near a half immediately after the discovery of the WEST INDIES, as we are informed by GARCILASSO DE LA VEGA: And it has been ever since gradually sinking in every kingdom of EUROPE. Interest in ROME, after the conquest of EGYPT, fell from 6 to 4 *per cent* as we learn from DION.

The causes of the sinking of interest, upon such an event, seem different in the conquering country and in the neighbouring states; but in neither of them can we justly ascribe that effect merely to the encrease of gold and silver.

In the conquering country, it is natural to imagine, that this new acquisition of money will fall into a few hands, and be gathered into large sums, which seek a secure revenue, either by the purchase of land or by interest; and consequently the same effect follows, for a little time, as if there had been a great accession of industry and commerce. The encrease of lenders above the borrowers sinks the interest; and so much the faster, if those, who have acquired those large sums, find no industry or commerce in the state, and no method of employing their money but by lending it at interest. But after this new mass of gold and silver has been digested, and has circulated through the whole state, affairs will soon return to their former situation; while the landlords and new money-holders, living idly, squander above their income; and the former daily contract debt, and the latter encroach on their stock till its final extinction. The whole money may still be in the state, and make itself felt by the encrease of prices: But not being now collected into any large masses or stocks, the disproportion between the borrowers and lenders is the same as formerly, and consequently the high interest returns.

Accordingly we find, in ROME, that, so early as TIBERIUS's time, interest had again mounted to 6 *per cent* though no accident had happened to drain the empire of money. In TRAJAN's time, money lent on mortgages in ITALY, bore 6 *per cent*; on common securities in BITHYNIA, 12. And if interest in SPAIN has not risen to its old pitch; this can be ascribed to nothing but the continuance of the same cause that sunk it, to wit, the large fortunes continually made in the INDIES, which come over to SPAIN from time to time, and supply the demand of the borrowers. By this accidental and extraneous cause, more money is to be lent in SPAIN, that is, more money is collected into large sums than would otherwise be found in a state, where there are so little commerce and industry.

As to the reduction of interest, which has followed in ENGLAND, FRANCE, and other kingdoms of EUROPE, that have no mines, it has been gradual; and has not proceeded from the encrease of money, considered merely in itself; but from that of industry, which is the natural effect of the former encrease, in that interval, before it raises the price of labour and provisions. For to return to the foregoing supposition; if the industry of ENGLAND had risen as much from other causes, (and that rise might easily have happened, though the stock of money had remained the same) must not all the same consequences have followed, which we observe at present? The same people would, in that case, be found in the kingdom, the same commodities, the same industry, manufactures, and commerce; and consequently the same merchants, with the same stocks, that is, with the same command over labour and commodities, only represented by a smaller number of white or yellow pieces; which being a circumstance of no moment, would only affect the wagoner, porter, and trunk-maker. Luxury, therefore, manufactures, arts, industry, frugality, flourishing equally as at present, it is evident, that interest must also have been as low; since that is the necessary result of all these circumstances; so far as they determine the profits of commerce, and the proportion between the borrowers and lenders in any state.

35. David Hume: *Of the Balance of Trade* (1752)

It is very usual, in nations ignorant of the nature of commerce, to prohibit the exportation of commodities, and to preserve among themselves whatever they think valuable and useful. They do not consider, that, in this prohibition, they act directly contrary to their intention; and that the more is exported of any commodity, the more will be raised at home, of which they themselves will always have the first offer.

It is well known to the learned, that the ancient laws of ATHENS rendered the exportation of figs criminal; that being supposed a species of fruit so excellent in ATTICA, that the ATHENIANS deemed it too delicious for the palate of any foreigner. And in this ridiculous prohibition they were so much in earnest, that informers were thence called sycophants among them, from two GREEK words, which signify figs and discoverer. There are proofs in many old acts of parliament of the same ignorance in the nature of commerce, particularly in the reign of EDWARD III. And to this day, in FRANCE, the exportation of corn is almost always prohibited; in order, as they say, to prevent famines; though it is evident, that nothing contributes more to the frequent famines, which so much distress that fertile country.

The same jealous fear, with regard to money, has also prevailed among several nations; and it required both reason and experience to convince any people, that these prohibitions serve to no other purpose than to raise the exchange against them, and produce a still greater exportation.

These errors, one may say, are gross and palpable: But there still prevails, even in nations well acquainted with commerce, a strong jealousy with regard to the balance of trade, and a fear, that all their gold and silver may be leaving them. This seems to me, almost in every case, a groundless apprehension; and I should as soon dread, that all our springs and rivers should be exhausted, as that money should abandon a kingdom where there are people and industry. Let us carefully preserve these latter advantages; and we need never be apprehensive of losing the former.

It is easy to observe, that all calculations concerning the balance of trade are founded on very uncertain facts and suppositions. The custom-house books are allowed to be an insufficient ground of reasoning; nor is the rate of exchange much better; unless we consider it with all nations, and know also the proportions of the several sums remitted; which one may safely pronounce impossible. Every man, who has ever reasoned on this subject, has always proved his theory, whatever it was, by facts and calculations, and by an enumeration of all the commodities sent to all foreign kingdoms.

The writings of Mr GEE struck the nation with a universal panic, when they saw it plainly demonstrated, by a detail of particulars, that the balance was against them for so considerable a sum as must leave them without a single shilling in five or six years. But luckily, twenty years have since elapsed, with an expensive foreign war; yet it is commonly supposed, that money is still more plentiful among us than in any former period.

Nothing can be more entertaining on this head than Dr SWIFT; an author so quick in discerning the mistakes and absurdities of others. He says, in his *short view of the state of* IRELAND, that the whole cash of that kingdom formerly amounted but to 500,000 *l*.; that out of this the IRISH remitted every year a neat million to ENGLAND, and had scarcely any other source from which they could compensate themselves, and little other foreign trade than the importation of FRENCH wines, for which they paid ready money. The consequence of this situation, which must be owned to be disadvantageous, was, that, in a course of three years, the current money of IRELAND, from 500,000 *l.* was reduced to less than two. And at present, I suppose, in a course of 30 years it is absolutely nothing. Yet I know not how, that opinion of the advance of riches in IRELAND, which gave the Doctor so much indignation, seems still to continue, and gain ground with every body.

In short, this apprehension of the wrong balance of trade, appears of such a nature, that it discovers itself, wherever one is out of humour with the ministry, or is in low spirits; and as it can never be refuted by a particular detail of all the exports, which counterbalance the imports, it may here be proper to form a general argument, that may prove the impossibility of this event, as long as we preserve our people and our industry.

Suppose four-fifths of all the money in GREAT BRITAIN to be annihilated in one night, and the nation reduced to the same condition, with regard to specie, as in the reigns of the HARRYS and EDWARDS, what would be the consequence? Must not the price of all labour and commodities sink in proportion, and every thing be sold as cheap as they were in those ages? What nation could then dispute with us in any foreign market, or pretend to navigate or to sell manufactures at the same price, which to us would afford sufficient profit? In how little time, therefore, must this bring back the money which we had lost, and raise us to the level of all the neighbouring nations? Where, after we have arrived, we immediately lose the advantage of the cheapness of labour and commodities; and the farther flowing in of money is stopped by our fulness and repletion.

Again, suppose, that all the money of GREAT BRITAIN were multiplied fivefold in a night, must not the contrary effect follow? Must not all labour and commodities rise to such an exorbitant height, that no neighbouring nations could afford to buy from us; while their commodities, on the other hand, became comparatively so cheap, that, in spite of all the laws which could be formed, they would be run in upon us, and our money flow out; till we fall to a level with foreigners, and lose that great superiority of riches, which had laid us under such disadvantages?

Now, it is evident, that the same causes, which would correct these exorbitant inequalities, were they to happen miraculously, must prevent their happening in the common course of nature, and must for ever, in all neighbouring nations, preserve money nearly proportionable to the art and industry of each nation. All water, wherever it communicates, remains always at a level. Ask naturalists the reason; they tell you, that, were it to be raised in any one place, the superior gravity of that part not being balanced, must depress it, till it meet a counterpoise; and that the same cause, which redresses the inequality when it happens, must for ever prevent it, without some violent external operation.

Can one imagine, that it had ever been possible, by any laws, or even by any art or industry, to have kept all the money in SPAIN, which the galleons have brought from the INDIES? Or that all commodities could be sold in FRANCE for a tenth of the price which they would yield on the other side of the PYRENEES, without finding their way thither, and draining from that immense treasure? What other reason, indeed, is there, why all nations, at present, gain in their trade with SPAIN and PORTUGAL; but because it is impossible to heap up money, more than any fluid, beyond its proper level? The sovereigns of these countries have shown, that they wanted not inclination to keep their gold and silver to themselves, had it been in any degree practicable.

But as any body of water may be raised above the level of the surrounding element, if the former has no communication with the latter; so in money, if the communication be cut off, by any material or physical impediment, (for all laws alone are ineffectual) there may, in such a case, be a very great inequality of money. Thus the immense distance of CHINA, together with the monopolies of our INDIA companies, obstructing the communication, preserve in EUROPE the gold and silver, especially the latter, in much greater plenty than they are found in that kingdom. But, notwithstanding this great obstruction, the force of the causes above-mentioned is still evident. The skill and ingenuity of EUROPE in general surpasses perhaps that of CHINA, with regard to manual arts and manufactures; yet are we never able to trade thither without great disadvantage. And were it not for the continual recruits, which we receive from AMERICA, money would soon sink in EUROPE, and rise in CHINA, till it came nearly to a level in both places. Nor can any reasonable man doubt, but that industrious nation, were they as near us as POLAND or BARBARY, would drain us of the overplus of our specie, and draw to themselves a larger share of the WEST INDIAN treasures. We need not have recourse to a physical attraction, in order to explain the necessity of this operation. There is a moral attraction, arising from the interests and passions of men, which is full as potent and infallible.

How is the balance kept in the provinces of every kingdom among themselves, but by the force of this principle, which makes it impossible for money to lose its level, and either to rise or sink beyond the proportion of the labour and commodities which are in each province? Did not long experience make people easy on this head, what a fund of gloomy reflections might calculations afford to a melancholy YORKSHIREMAN, while he computed and magnified the sums drawn to LONDON by taxes, absentees, commodities, and found on comparison the opposite articles so much inferior? And no doubt, had the Heptarchy subsisted in ENGLAND, the legislature of each state had been continually alarmed by the fear of a wrong balance; and as it is probable that the mutual hatred of these states would have been extremely violent on account of their close neighbourhood, they would have loaded and oppressed all commerce, by a jealous and superfluous caution. Since the union has removed the barriers between SCOTLAND and ENGLAND, which of these nations gains from the other by this free commerce? Or if the former kingdom has received any encrease of riches, can it reasonably be accounted for by any thing but the encrease of its art and industry? It was a common apprehension in ENGLAND, before the union, as we learn from L'ABBE DU BOS, that SCOTLAND would soon drain them of their treasure, were an open trade allowed; and on the other side the TWEED a contrary apprehension prevailed: With what justice in both, time has shown.

What happens in small portions of mankind, must take place in greater. The provinces of the ROMAN empire, no doubt, kept their balance with each other, and with ITALY, independent of the legislature; as much as the several counties of GREAT BRITAIN, or the several parishes of each county. And any man who travels over EUROPE at this day, may see, by the prices of commodities, that money, in spite of the absurd jealousy of princes and states, has brought itself nearly to a level; and that the difference between one kingdom and another is not greater in this respect, than it is often between different provinces of the same kingdom. Men naturally flock to capital cities, sea-ports, and navigable rivers. There we find more men, more industry, more commodities, and consequently more money; but still the latter difference holds proportion with the former, and the level is preserved.

Our jealousy and our hatred of FRANCE are without bounds; and the former sentiment, at least, must be acknowledged reasonable and well-grounded. These passions have occasioned innumerable barriers and obstructions upon commerce, where we are accused of being commonly the aggressors. But what have we gained by the bargain? We lost the FRENCH market for our woollen manufactures, and transferred the commerce of wine to SPAIN and PORTUGAL, where we buy worse liquor at a higher price. There are few ENGLISHMEN who would not think their country absolutely ruined, were FRENCH wines sold in ENGLAND so cheap and in such abundance as to supplant, in some measure, all ale, and home-brewed liquors: But would we lay aside prejudice, it would not be difficult to prove, that nothing could be more innocent, perhaps advantageous. Each new acre of vineyard planted in FRANCE, in order to supply ENGLAND with wine, would make it requisite for the FRENCH to take the produce of an ENGLISH acre, sown in wheat or barley, in order to subsist themselves; and it is evident, that we should thereby get command of the better commodity.

There are many edicts of the FRENCH king, prohibiting the planting of new vineyards, and ordering all those which are lately planted to be grubbed up: So sensible are they, in that country, of the superior value of corn, above every other product.

Mareschal VAUBAN complains often, and with reason, of the absurd duties which load the entry of those wines of LANGUEDOC, GUIENNE, and other southern provinces, that are imported into BRITANNY and NORMANDY. He entertained no doubt but these latter provinces could preserve their balance, notwithstanding the open commerce which he recommends. And it is evident, that a few leagues more navigation to ENGLAND would make no difference; or if it did, that it must operate alike on the commodities of both kingdoms.

There is indeed one expedient by which it is possible to sink, and another by which we may raise money beyond its natural level in any kingdom; but these cases, when examined, will be found to resolve into our general theory, and to bring additional authority to it.

I scarcely know any method of sinking money below its level, but those institutions of banks, funds, and paper-credit, which are so much practised in this kingdom. These render paper equivalent to money, circulate it throughout the whole state, make it supply the place of gold and silver, raise proportionably the price of labour and commodities, and by that means either banish a great part of those precious metals, or prevent their farther encrease. What can be more shortsighted than our reasonings on this head? We fancy, because an individual would be much richer, were his stock of money doubled, that the same good effect would follow were the money of every one encreased; not considering, that this would raise as much the price of every commodity, and reduce every man, in time, to the same condition as before. It is only in our public negociations and transactions with foreigners, that a greater stock of money is advantageous; and as our paper is there absolutely insignificant, we feel, by its means, all the ill effects arising from a great abundance of money, without reaping any of the advantages.

Suppose that there are 12 millions of paper, which circulate in the kingdom as money, (for we are not to imagine, that all our enormous funds are employed in that shape) and suppose the real cash of the kingdom to be 18 millions: Here is a state which is found by experience to be able to hold a stock of 30 millions. I say, if it be able to hold it, it must of necessity have acquired it in gold and silver, had we not obstructed the entrance of these metals by this new invention of paper. Whence would it have acquired that sum? From all the kingdoms of the world. But why? Because, if you remove these 12 millions, money in this state is below its level, compared with our neighbours; and we must immediately draw from all of them, till we be full and saturate, so to speak, and can hold no more. By our present politics, we are as careful to stuff the nation with this fine commodity of bank-bills and chequer-notes, as if we were afraid of being overburthened with the precious metals.

It is not to be doubted, but the great plenty of bullion in FRANCE is, in a great measure, owing to the want of paper-credit. The FRENCH have no banks: Merchants bills do not there circulate as with us: Usury or lending on interest is not directly permitted; so that many have large sums in their coffers: Great quantities of plate are used in private houses; and all the churches are full of it. By this means, provisions and labour still remain cheaper among them, than in nations that are not half so rich in gold and silver. The advantages of this situation, in point of trade as well as in great public emergencies, are too evident to be disputed.

The same fashion a few years ago prevailed in GENOA, which still has place in ENGLAND and HOLLAND, of using services of CHINA-ware instead of plate; but the senate, foreseeing the consequence, prohibited the use of that brittle commodity beyond a certain extent; while the use of silver-plate was left unlimited. And I suppose, in their late distresses, they felt the good effect of this ordinance. Our tax on plate is, perhaps, in this view, somewhat impolitic.

Before the introduction of paper-money into our colonies, they had gold and silver sufficient for their circulation. Since the introduction of that commodity, the least inconveniency that has followed is the total banishment of the precious metals. And after the abolition of paper, can it be doubted but money will return, while these colonies possess manufactures and commodities, the only thing valuable in commerce, and for whose sake alone all men desire money.

What pity LYCURGUS did not think of paper-credit, when he wanted to banish gold and silver from SPARTA! It would have served his purpose better than the lumps of iron he made use of as money; and would also have prevented more effectually all commerce with strangers, as being of so much less real and intrinsic value.

It must, however, be confessed, that, as all these questions of trade and money are extremely complicated, there are certain lights, in which this subject may be placed, so as to represent the advantages of paper-credit and banks to be superior to their disadvantages. That they banish specie and bullion from a state is undoubtedly true; and whoever looks no farther than this circumstance does well to condemn them; but specie and bullion are not of so great consequence as not to admit of a compensation, and even an overbalance from the encrease of industry and of credit, which may be promoted by the right use of paper-money. It is well known of what advantage it is to a merchant to be able to discount his bills upon occasion; and every thing that facilitates this species of traffic is favourable to the general commerce of a state. But private bankers are enabled to give such credit by the credit they receive from the depositing of money in their shops; and the bank of ENGLAND in the same manner, from the liberty it has to issue its notes in all payments. There was an invention of this kind, which was fallen upon some years ago by the banks of EDINBURGH; and which, as it is one of the most ingenious ideas that has been executed in commerce, has also been thought advantageous to SCOTLAND. It is there called a BANK-CREDIT; and is of this nature. A man goes to the bank and finds surety to the amount, we shall suppose, of a thousand pounds. This money, or any part of it, he has the liberty of drawing out whenever he pleases, and he pays only the ordinary interest for it, while it is in his hands. He may, when he pleases, repay any sum so small as twenty pounds, and the interest is discounted from the very day of the repayment. The advantages, resulting from this contrivance, are manifold. As a man may find surety nearly to the amount of his substance, and his bank-credit is equivalent to ready money, a merchant does hereby in a manner coin his houses, his household furniture, the goods in his warehouse, the foreign debts due to him, his ships at sea; and can, upon occasion, employ them in all payments, as if they were the current money of the country. If a man borrow a thousand pounds from a private hand, besides that it is not always to be found when required, he pays interest for it, whether he be using it or not: His bank-credit costs him nothing except during the very moment, in which it is of service to him: And this circumstance is of equal advantage as if he had borrowed money at much lower interest. Merchants, likewise, from this invention, acquire a great facility in supporting each other's credit, which is a considerable security against bankruptcies. A man, when his own bank-credit is exhausted, goes to any of his neighbours who is not in the same condition; and he gets the money, which he replaces at his convenience.

After this practice had taken place during some years at EDINBURGH, several companies of merchants at GLASGOW carried the matter farther. They associated themselves into different banks, and issued notes so low as ten shillings, which they used in all payments for goods, manufactures, tradesmen's labour of all kinds; and these notes, from the established credit of the companies, passed as money in all payments throughout the country. By this means, a stock of five thousand pounds was able to perform the same operations as if it were six or seven; and merchants were thereby enabled to trade to a greater extent, and to require less profit in all their transactions. But whatever other advantages result from these inventions, it must still be allowed that, besides giving too great facility to credit, which is dangerous, they banish the precious metals; and nothing can be a more evident proof of it, than a comparison of the past and present condition of SCOTLAND in that particular. It was found, upon the recoinage made after the union, that there was near a million of specie in that country: But notwithstanding the great encrease of riches, commerce and manufactures of all kinds, it is thought, that, even where there is no extraordinary drain made by ENGLAND, the current specie will not now amount to a third of that sum.

But as our projects of paper-credit are almost the only expedient, by which we can sink money below its level; so, in my opinion, the only expedient, by which we can raise money above it, is a practice which we should all exclaim against as destructive, namely, the gathering of large sums into a public treasure, locking them up, and absolutely preventing their circulation. The fluid, not communicating with the neighbouring element, may, by such an artifice, be raised to what height we please. To prove this, we need only return to our first supposition, of annihilating the half or any part of our cash; where we found, that the immediate consequence of such an event would be the attraction of an equal sum from all the neighbouring kingdoms. Nor does there seem to be any necessary bounds set, by the nature of things, to this practice of hoarding. A small city, like GENEVA, continuing this policy for ages, might engross nine-tenths of the money of EUROPE. There seems, indeed, in the nature of man, an invincible obstacle to that immense growth of riches. A weak state, with an enormous treasure, will soon become a prey to some of its poorer, but more powerful neighbours. A great state would dissipate its wealth in dangerous and ill-concerted projects; and probably destroy, with it, what is much more valuable, the industry, morals, and numbers of its people. The fluid, in this case, raised to too great a height, bursts and destroys the vessel that contains it; and mixing itself with the surrounding element, soon falls to its proper level.

So little are we commonly acquainted with this principle, that, though all historians agree in relating uniformly so recent an event, as the immense treasure amassed by HARRY VII (which they make amount to 2,700,000 pounds) we rather reject their concurring testimony, than admit of a fact, which agrees so ill with our inveterate prejudices. It is indeed probable, that this sum might be three-fourths of all the money in ENGLAND. But where is the difficulty in conceiving, that such a sum might be amassed in twenty years, by a cunning, rapacious, frugal, and almost absolute monarch? Nor is it probable, that the diminution of circulating money was ever sensibly felt by the people, or ever did them any prejudice. The sinking of the prices of all commodities would immediately replace it, by giving ENGLAND the advantage in its commerce with the neighbouring kingdoms.

Have we not an instance, in the small republic of ATHENS with its allies, who, in about fifty years, between the MEDIAN and PELOPONNESIAN wars, amassed a sum not much inferior to that of HARRY VII? For all the GREEK historians and orators agree, that the ATHENIANS collected in the citadel more than 10,000 talents, which they afterwards dissipated to their own ruin, in rash and imprudent enterprizes. But when this money was set a running, and began to communicate with the surrounding fluid; what was the consequence? Did it remain in the state? No. For we find, by the memorable census mentioned by DEMOSTHENES and POLYBIUS, that, in about fifty years afterwards, the whole value of the republic, comprehending lands, houses, commodities, slaves, and money, was less than 6000 talents.

What an ambitious high-spirited people was this, to collect and keep in their treasury, with a view to conquests, a sum, which it was every day in the power of the citizens, by a single vote, to distribute among themselves, and which would have gone near to triple the riches of every individual! For we must observe, that the numbers and private riches of the ATHENIANS are said, by ancient writers, to have been no greater at the beginning of the PELOPONNESIAN war, than at the beginning of the MACEDONIAN.

Money was little more plentiful in GREECE during the age of PHILIP and PERSEUS, than in ENGLAND during that of HARRY VII: Yet these two monarchs in thirty years collected from the small kingdom of MACEDON, a larger treasure than that of the ENGLISH monarch. PAULUS AEMILIUS brought to ROME about 1,700,000 pounds Sterling. PLINY says, 2,400,000. And that was but a part of the MACEDONIAN treasure. The rest was dissipated by the resistance and flight of PERSEUS.

We may learn from STANIAN, that the canton of BERNE had 300,000 pounds lent at interest, and had above six times as much in their treasury. Here then is a sum hoarded of 1,800,000 pounds Sterling, which is at least quadruple what should naturally circulate in such a petty state; and yet no one, who travels in the PAIS DE VAUX, or any part of that canton, observes any want of money more than could be supposed in a country of that extent, soil, and situation. On the contrary, there are scarce any inland provinces in the continent of FRANCE or GERMANY, where the inhabitants are at this time so opulent, though that canton has vastly encreased its treasure since 1714, the time when STANIAN wrote his judicious account of SWITZERLAND.

The account given by APPIAN of the treasure of the PTOLEMIES, is so prodigious, that one cannot admit of it; and so much the less, because the historian says, that the other successors of ALEXANDER were also frugal, and had many of them treasures not much inferior. For this saving humour of the neighbouring princes must necessarily have checked the frugality of the EGYPTIAN monarchs, according to the foregoing theory. The sum he mentions is 740,000 talents, or 191,166,666 pounds 13 shillings and 4 pence, according to Dr ARBUTHNOT'S computation. And yet APPIAN says, that he extracted his account from the public records; and he was himself a native of ALEXANDRIA.

From these principles we may learn what judgment we ought to form of those number-less bars, obstructions, and imposts, which all nations of EUROPE, and none more than ENGLAND, have put upon trade; from an exorbitant desire of amassing money, which never will heap up beyond its level, while it circulates; or from an ill-grounded apprehension of losing their specie, which never will sink below it. Could any thing scatter our riches, it would be such impolitic contrivances. But this general ill effect, however, results from them, that they deprive neighbouring nations of that free communication and exchange which the Author of the world has intended, by giving them soils, climates, and geniuses, so different from each other.

Our modern politics embrace the only method of banishing money, the using of paper-credit; they reject the only method of amassing it, the practice of hoarding; and they adopt a hundred contrivances, which serve to no purpose but to check industry, and rob ourselves and our neighbours of the common benefits of art and nature.

All taxes, however, upon foreign commodities, are not to be regarded as prejudicial or useless, but those only which are founded on the jealousy above-mentioned. A tax on GERMAN linen encourages home manufactures, and thereby multiplies our people and indus-try. A tax on brandy encreases the sale of rum, and supports our southern colonies. And as it is necessary, that imposts should be levied, for the support of government, it may be thought more convenient to lay them on foreign commodities, which can easily be intercepted at the port, and subjected to the impost. We ought, however, always to remember the maxim of Dr SWIFT, that, in the arithmetic of the customs, two and two make not four, but often make only one. It can scarcely be doubted, but if the duties on wine were lowered to a third, they would yield much more to the government than at present: Our people might thereby afford to drink commonly a better and more wholesome liquor; and no prejudice would ensue to the balance of trade, of which we are so jealous. The manufacture of ale beyond the agriculture is but inconsiderable, and gives employment to few hands. The transport of wine and corn would not be much inferior.

But are there not frequent instances, you will say, of states and kingdoms, which were formerly rich and opulent, and are now poor and beggarly? Has not the money left them, with which they formerly abounded? I answer, If they lose their trade, industry, and people, they cannot expect to keep their gold and silver: For these precious metals will hold proportion to the former advantages. When LISBON and AMSTERDAM got the EAST INDIA trade from VENICE and GENOA, they also got the profits and money which arose from it. Where the seat of government is transferred, where expensive armies are maintained at a distance, where great funds are possessed by foreigners; there naturally follows from these causes a diminution of the specie. But these, we may observe, are violent and forcible methods of carrying away money, and are in time commonly attended with the transport of people and industry. But where these remain, and the drain is not continued, the money always finds its way back again, by a hundred canals, of which we have no notion or suspicion. What immense treasures have been spent, by so many nations, in FLANDERS, since the revolution, in the course of three long wars? More money perhaps than the half of what is at present in EUROPE. But what has now become of it? Is it in the narrow compass of the AUSTRIAN provinces? No, surely: It has most of it returned to the several countries whence it came, and has followed that art and industry, by which at first it was acquired. For above a thousand years, the money of EUROPE has been flowing to ROME, by an open and sensible current; but it has been emptied by many secret and insensible canals: And the want of industry and commerce renders at present the papal dominions the poorest territory in all ITALY.

In short, a government has great reason to preserve with care its people and its manufactures. Its money, it may safely trust to the course of human affairs, without fear or jealousy. Or if it ever give attention to this latter circumstance, it ought only to be so far as it affects the former.

36. Joseph Harris: *An Essay upon Money and Coins* (1757–58)

PART 1, CHAPTER 2: OF MONEY AND COINS

XI. Money Finds Its Own Value, According to the Whole Quantity of It in Circulation

The quantities of all commodities are proportioned, as near as may be, according to the demand or vent for them and their ultimate prices include the prime cost, and the profits taken by the several dealers, thro' whose hands they pass: If the quantity of any commodity exceeds, or falls short of that proportion, its price will fall or rise accordingly; and sometimes, a change of fashion, or humour, may reduce the price of a particular commodity, almost to nothing. The prices of things in general are proportioned sufficiently near, according to the above rule; or, according to their prime cost to the manufacturer, and the progress they make from him to the consumer. But some things, as above observed, are subject to be reduced by caprice much below this standard; whilst others are raised much above it, by the arts and avarice of monopolizers. And although the silver and gold mines, are in few hands; yet, perhaps, there is nothing whose value is so little in the power of men to regulate, or that keeps so even a pace with the quantity sent to the great market of the world, as bullion.

For, Money, exchanging universally for all commodities, the demand for it is without any limits; it is every where coveted, and never out of fashion: And therefore, on the one side, the whole quantity of money, cannot exceed the whole demand; and on the other side, the whole demand must not exceed, or it must rest satisfied with, the whole quantity. For money, is not like food, cloaths, and other things, that must be proportioned to our bodies.

Therefore, as soon as money becomes properly diffused throughout any community the value of the sum total of it in circulation, will be equal to the whole quantity of commodities in traffic, in that country: For so much money and goods as lie dormant, or are out of currency and traffic, fall not within the present consideration. And so far as gold and silver, make the money of the world, so far, the whole quantity of these metals in circulation, may be said to be equal in value to all the commodities of the world, exchangeable by them: And as the total of the one, is to the total of the other; so will any given part of the one, be to a like part or proportion of the other.

And hence, the value of a given quantity or sum of money, in any country, will be less or more, according as the sum total, or the whole quantity of money in currency, is greater or less, in proportion to the whole of the commodities of that country, exchangeable for money: Or, the value of a given sum of money will be always, pretty exactly, in a reciprocal proportion to the sum total, or the whole quantity in circulation; that is, the more money there is in currency, the less will be the value of a given sum in proportion to other things; and vice versa. Hence again, it naturally follows, that, if, in any country, the whole quantity of money in circulation be either increased, or diminished; the value of a given sum will be accordingly lessened or increased and that in proportion, as the said sum becomes thereby, a lesser or a greater part, of the whole stock in currency.

The above proposition, is a very fundamental one as to the property of money; and the doctrine it contains is undoubtedly proved, as far as the nature of the thing will admit of, by universal experience: Nor is there room for any doubt to remain, when it is considered that money, by its very institution, is an exchange for all commodities; and applicable, as money, to no other purpose whatsoever. Money being universally diffused, no one hath the power to command the market, or to settle the prices of things; and every one being desirous to have his share of things, according to his income; all the money, in the long run, will be brought into the great market of the world; and its value, or the prices of things, will naturally be adjusted, notwithstanding any efforts to the contrary, according to the proportions above explained.

XII. Laws Cannot Regulate or Alter the Value of Money

Silver being made money, and thereby becoming, as it were, a commodity universally coveted; wherein every one deals, and to which every one hath a right, according to his respective share of property: No set of men have it in their power to settle, alter, or in any wise regulate the value of money; nor can laws do any thing in the case, otherwise than as by their influence, they may increase or diminish, the whole quantity in circulation; and so affect the value of a given sum, or the prices of things.

The prices of particular commodities are every day subject to change, from natural causes; and the same may be brought about, by artificial means. But to alter the value of money, would be to alter uniformly and universally, the prices of all commodities; a thing manifestly out of the reach of laws, and no other way to be accomplished, than by altering the proportion between the sum total of the one, and the sum total of the other; and this, perhaps, is continually done, though gradually and insensibly, by the common course of things.

It is the business of laws to establish rules for coining; that is, to fix a standard, both as to weight and fineness, for coins having certain denominations; and a standard being fixed, it would be difficult to shew, why it should be afterwards deviated from. For, do what you can; coins, as soon as they are out of the mint, are quite free throughout their whole progress, to find their own value, according to the quantity of pure metal they contain; that is, to purchase as much of any thing, as the market-price will allow. And it seems quite a paralogism to say, which yet I have often heard said, that in any country, money is either too cheap or too dear; or, that its value is in any wise subject to legal restraints or regulations, otherwise than as such regulations might affect the quantity of the whole stock in currency.

...

XIV. A Nation Having No Foreign Commerce Will Not Stand in Need of Any Specific Quantity of Money

In a country having no foreign commerce, any quantity of money will, in a manner, be sufficient for all purposes; and any increase or diminution of the original stock, if it be but gradual and slow, will scarce be attended with any consequences of moment. This, although to many it may seem a paradox, yet clearly follows from what hath been already shewed. But as a farther illustration of this subject:

Let us suppose that many ages ago, a certain nation consisted of half a million of people, and that they had in the whole a million of pounds sterling; and that afterwards the mines or the mint were no farther worked, than to keep the money exactly to the same or the original quantity of a million. We may suppose also, that a regular government, and all the necessary arts, were established amongst them; and likewise that all the money was distributed betwixt them, in due proportion according to their several ranks; so that the hire of a labourer, we will suppose, was ten-pence a day. By degrees, they increase in number one tenth; and with the people, all sorts of commodities, naturally increase in proportion: But the whole quantity of money remaining the same, its value increased also one tenth; and nine-pence now going as far as ten-pence would before, the wages of a day-labourer is reduced one penny: But this he doth not feel the want of; and he hath as much plenty of all sorts of necessaries now, as he had formerly.

In process of time, and that before they had any foreign commerce, the people are increased to five millions; and the price of labour, which at first was ten-pence, is now reduced to a penny a day. All this while, there were no complaints of the want of money, though every one's share came to but a tenth part of what his ancestors possessed. On the contrary, by the improvements of the arts they had set out with, and the inventions of many new ones; all ranks of people lived more comfortably, with more ease and affluence than their fore-fathers had done.

By these improvements of the arts, the whole stock of commodities was increased beyond the increase of the people; and each particular commodity bore less than a tenth part of its antient price: More people in proportion could be spared from labour, for particular services and professions; for in many of the arts, one man could perform now, more than two men could formerly. With the increase of the people, the taxes on each individual grew naturally lighter; and yet the government grew daily more powerful and splendid: Altho' rents and all other things, sunk in their nominal values; yet a greater affluence and splendor of living, was every where to be seen. So true it is, that numbers of industrious people, and not money, is what enriches a country.

Had the money increased with the people, that would have made no manner of difference in the values of things with respect to one another; nor would it have been very material, if the original stock of money had decreased upon their hands; the only difference which that would have created, would have been in the nominal prices of things with respect to money. Had the money increased faster than the people, suppose 24 times; the price of labour would have become then 20 Shillings a day, and yet the workman would have been no ways benefited by that greatness of wages.

The case above supposed of the quantity of money remaining invariable, whilst the people increased, is the very same in effect, as if we had supposed the number of people to have continued the same, whilst the original stock of money had continually decreased.

XV. Any Sudden Fluctuation of Money, Would Be Pernicious

Money as such, though very useful and necessary in all sorts of traffic, yet scarce falls within the idea of riches. Money in its very institution, is professedly of no use, but to measure the value of, and as an exchange for, things that are useful: It is so much coveted, not for its own sake, but for what it will bring; and it is very manifest, that in a regular and well-established community, a greater or less stock of money doth scarce at all affect its wealth and prosperity. The greatest effect of money is in its fluctuation, and this if it be sudden will be generally pernicious in its consequences.

If money be a flowing in, some branches of trade will be enlivened, and in reality great numbers of individuals will grow richer; as what they pay in taxes, rents, and for natural products, will be less or of less value than before; till you come to the lowest class, who, though their wages are raised, will yet find little or no advantage by this torrent of money. On the other hand, the government will grow weaker, the nobility, and in general all who live upon estates and established stipends, will become poorer; till by an increase of taxes, advancement of rents, &c. things can be re-established. But before this can be accomplished, many and great alterations will naturally happen: The government being thus weakened and distressed, disorders will inevitably arise; as peace and good order cannot be preserved, unless the strength of the government bears a due proportion to that of the governed: The nobility must change their fashion of life, and abate of their antient splendor; new debts will be contracted, increased, lands mortgaged; and before the antient owners have a right understanding of the cause of their distresses, many must part with their estates, and give place to new comers.

And this is a natural consequence of a sudden flux of money; the enriching of one part of the community, at the expence of the other; a change of manners amongst all ranks, some perhaps for the better, and some for the worse; until, this tide having spent itself, things are again resettled, tho' perhaps in quite a new form.

On the other hand, if the tide of money is a running out; during this ebb, trade will stagnate, some merchants and shopkeepers will break, some manufactures will be laid aside, many hands will be unemployed, and murmurs and complaints will be heard among all sorts of people concerned in trade. These distresses will continue, till by an abatement of taxes, lowering of rents, of wages, of stipends, &c. a due equilibrium among the different ranks of people is again restored; and then, altho' a great part of the money is gone, riches, plenty, and good order, will again abound.

Thus it is manifest, that a sudden fluctuation of money, would be pernicious whilst it lasted, and for some time afterwards; and that whether the tide be flowing in or going out. But whilst it glides and circulates smoothly and freely, in its natural course and channels, money is not only a harmless but a beneficial thing; it cherishes and invigorates the whole community, and this equally, whether the stream be large or slender.

    . . .

XVIII. Any Artificial Methods of Increasing Tale-Money, Pernicious

Any artificial methods of increasing the quantity of tale-money in circulation, beyond its natural bounds, will be attended with pernicious consequences; and this effect is perhaps not the least evil of our great national debt. As the values of all things are measured by money, it is, I think, by this time sufficiently manifest, that their prices will be in a certain proportion to the whole quantity of cash in circulation. If this quantity be greater in proportion to the trade of the nation, than in foreign countries; things manufactured at home will become too dear for foreign markets, as is the case of Spain and Portugal. As we have no mines, trade will keep, as before observed, real money to a proper level; but yet this level may be exceeded by artificial substitutes, as paper-bills, having no bullion locked up in their stead, and light coins having less value than what they pass for; and by both these methods the nation is injured: By making all things dearer at home, the public is not only, defrauded of so much bullion as these substitutes amount to; that is, to the whole amount of the paper above the bullion locked up in its stead; but it also suffers by the loss of the whole deficiency upon the light coins.

Although this subject hath been in effect illustrated before, yet is it of that importance as to deserve to be farther exemplified. Let us suppose that one tenth of the whole stock of circulating cash in this country, and 'tis not material to our argument what the specific sum amounts to, is some way lost or destroyed: If no artificial substitutes be made to intervene; it has been before shewed, that trade will gradually restore this supposed loss of bullion; as, till this be accomplished, bullion will be dearer or fetch more commodities here, than in other countries.

On the other hand, supposing the sum total of money, real and fictitious, now annually circulating in this country, to be 100 millions; 20 millions of which is in cash, and the rest in paper credit both public and private: If this paper credit be increased, by the creating of more bills, suppose to the amount often millions; one of the following will necessarily be the consequence: Either all our commodities will rise ten per cent, in their nominal value, which will render them too dear for foreign markets; or, this addition of paper-bills will drain away ten millions of our cash, and so impoverish us in reality to that whole amount; or, the effect most likely will be, partly the one, and partly the other; but which ever it is, the nation will be equally endamaged. May this be ever a caution to statesmen, how they listen to projects that must clog our trade, banish our coin, and in the end bring on a general bankruptcy.

XIX. Of Banks

The several banks now subsisting in Europe, are of a modern date; but it is not my intention here to meddle either with their histories or particular constitutions. In great trading cities, a public bank that issued no bills without an equivalent in real treasure, whether in cash or bullion it matters not much, must needs, I think, be very convenient; as therein, merchants and others may safely deposite large sums, and thence again draw their money out at such times, and in such small parcels, as may suit with their several occasions. Such a bank may be also of some support to national credit, as the great sums known to be there locked up, would be ready upon an emergency. Bills of undoubted credit, are of great conveniency in large payments, and besides, save the wear of coin. But their extent should be restrained within due bounds: Should they increase much beyond the real stock of bullion that ought to be in their stead, they would prove mischievous two ways; by increasing in effect the quantity of circulating cash beyond its natural level; and by endangering, in a cloudy day, their own credit. But the profits to be made by lending, as I may say, of credit, are temptations too strong to be resisted; and it may be questioned, if any of the banks now subsisting, keep exactly within the above rule, tho' some of them are formed upon the very model here laid down.

The oldest bank now in Europe, I think, is that of Venice; and the chief, if not all, of the rest, were instituted in the last century, and much upon the same model. The bank of Amsterdam was established in 1607; that of Hamburgh in 1619, and that of Nuremburgb in 1621.

It appears, that the main if not the sole design of erecting these banks, was for the fixing a kind of an indelible standard of money; and thereby, to secure merchants and others from losses by bad coins, whether base or light; and from the dire effects of adulterating the standards of monies, either at home, or by the neighbouring states. These banks have answered admirably well the ends of their institution; and it were to be wished, that those ends had been more regarded in the establishment of our own.

...

PART 2, CHAPTER 2: THE ESTABLISHED STANDARD OF MONEY SHOULD NOT BE VIOLATED OR ALTERED, UNDER ANY PRETENCE WHATSOEVER

II. Established Standards Should Be Inviolably Kept and More Especially That of Money

The standard measures of a country being once established and known, any deviations from these afterwards could answer no good purpose; but, on the contrary, they must needs be attended with mischievous consequences; they would disturb the arithmetic of the country, confound settled ideas, create perplexities in dealings, and subject the ignorant and unwary to frauds and abuses.

But of all standard measures in any country, that of money is the most important, and what should be most sacredly kept, from any violation or alteration whatsoever. The yard, the bushel, the pound, &c. are applied only to particular commodities; and should they be altered, the people would soon learn to accommodate themselves in their bargains to the new measures; and it is but rare, that these have any retrospect to preceding contracts. But money, is not only an universal measure of the values of all things; but is also at the same time, the equivalent as well as the measure, in all contracts, foreign as well as domestic.

The laws have ordained, that coins having certain denominations, well known to every body, should contain certain assigned quantities of pure or fine silver. This makes our standard of money; and the public faith is guaranty, that the mint shall faithfully and strictly adhere to this standard. It is according to this standard, and under this solemn guaranty, that all our establishments are fixed; all our contracts, public and private, foreign and domestic, are made and regulated.

Is it not self-evident then, that no alteration can be made in the standard of money, without an opprobrious breach of the public faith with all the world; without infringement of private property; without falsifying of all precedent contracts; without the risque at least of producing infinite disorders, distrusts and panics amongst ourselves; as all men would become thereby dubious and insecure as to what might farther be done hereafter; without creating suspicions abroad, that there is some canker in the state; without giving such a shock to our credit, as might not afterwards be easily repaired?

37. A.R.J. Turgot: *Reflections on the Formation and Distribution of Wealth* (1766)[1]

71. NATURE OF THE LOAN

The owners of money balance the risk their capital may run, if the enterprise does not succeed, with the advantage of enjoying a definite profit without labor, and regulate themselves thereby to require more or less profit or interest for their money, or to consent to lend it for such interest as the borrower offers. Here another opportunity is open to the owner of money; lending at interest, or the trade in money. Let no one mistake me here, lending at interest is nothing but a commercial transaction, in which the Lender is the man who sells the use of his money, and the borrower is a man who buys; precisely as the proprietor of an estate and a farmer sell and buy, respectively the use of a piece of land which is let out. The Latin term for a loan of money at interest expresses it exactly, *usura pecuniae*, a word which, translated into French has become hateful by consequence of false ideas being formed as to the interest of money.

72. FALSE IDEAS ABOUT THE LENDING AT INTEREST

The price of the loan is by no means founded, as might be imagined, on the profit the borrower hopes to make with the capital of which he purchases the use. This price, like the price of every commodity, is determined by the chaffering of seller and buyer; by the balance between the offer and the demand. People borrow for all kinds of purposes, and with all sorts of motives. One borrows to undertake an enterprise which will make his fortune, another to buy an estate, another to pay a gaming debt, another to make up for the loss of his revenue, of which some accident has deprived him, another to keep himself alive, while waiting for what he can get by his labor; but all these motives which influence the borrower are quite immaterial to the lender. The latter is only concerned with two things: the interest he is to receive, and the safety of his capital. He does not trouble himself about the use the borrower will make of it, any more than the merchant concerns himself with the use the buyer makes of the commodity he sells him.

73. ERRORS OF THE SCHOOLMEN REFUTED

It is for want of having examined the lending at interest in its true light, that moralists, more dogmatic than enlightened, have endeavored to have it looked upon as a crime. The scholastic theologians have concluded from the fact that money does not produce anything by itself that

---

[1] Translated by Peter Groenewegen.

it was unjust to exact interest from money placed on loan. Full of their prejudices, they have believed their doctrine was sanctioned by this passage from the Gospel, *mutuum date nihil inde sperantes*. Those theologians who have adopted more reasonable principles on the subject of interest, have endured the harshest reproaches from Writers of the opposite party.

Nevertheless, it needs but a little reflection to realise the lack of depth in the pretexts which have been used to condemn the taking of interest. A loan is a reciprocal contract, free between the two parties, which they make only because it is advantageous to them. It is evident that, if the lender finds it to his advantage to receive something as the hire for his money, the borrower is no less interested in finding the money he needs, since he decides to borrow and to pay the hire of this money. Now on what principle can a crime be discovered in a contract advantageous to two parties, with which both parties are satisfied, and which certainly does no injury to anyone else? To say that the lender takes advantage of the borrower's need of money to demand interest, is as absurd an argument as saying that a baker who demands money for the bread he sells, takes advantage of the buyer's need for bread. If in this latter case, the money is an equivalent for the bread the buyer receives, the money which the borrower receives today is equally an equivalent of the capital and interest he promises to return at the end of a certain time; for, in short, it is an advantage for the borrower to have, during the interval, the use of the money he needs, and it is a disadvantage to the lender to be deprived of it. This disadvantage is capable of being estimated, and is estimated: the interest is the price of it. This price ought to be higher if the lender runs the risk of losing his capital by the insolvency of the borrower. The bargain therefore is perfectly equal on both sides, and consequently just and honest. Money considered as a physical substance, as a mass of metal, does not produce anything; but money employed in advances in enterprises of agriculture, manufactures, commerce, procures a definite profit; with money an estate can be purchased, and a revenue procured thereby; the person, therefore, who lends his money, does not only give up the barren possession of such money, but deprives himself of the profit or the revenue he would have been able to procure by it, and the interest which indemnifies him for this loss cannot be looked upon as unjust. The schoolmen, compelled to acknowledge the justice of these considerations, have allowed that interest may be taken, provided the capital is alienated, that is, provided the lender renounced his right to demand the repayment of his money in a certain time, and leave the borrower free to keep it as long as he wished while paying only interest. The reason for this toleration was that then it is no longer a loan, for which an interest is taken, but a rent which is purchased with a sum of money, just as an estate is purchased. This was a petty subterfuge to which they had recourse in order to concede the absolute necessity of loans in the course of transactions of society, without clearly acknowledging the falsity of the principles upon which they had condemned it. But this condition of the alienation of capital is not an advantage to the borrower, who remains no less burdened with the debt until he has repaid this capital, and whose property is always destined as security for this capital. It is even a disadvantage, as he finds it more difficult to borrow money when he needs it; for persons who would willingly consent to lend for a year or two a sum of money which they had destined for the purchase of an estate, would not lend it for an indefinite period. Moreover, if it is permissible to sell money for a perpetual rent, why would it not be permissible to let it for some years in return for a rent which only continues for that number of years? If a rent of a thousand francs per year is equivalent to the sum of twenty thousand francs in the case of a man who keeps this sum in perpetuity, a thousand francs will be the amount for the possession of that sum for one year.

74.   TRUE FOUNDATION OF THE INTEREST OF MONEY

A man then may let out his money as lawfully as he may sell it; and the owner of money may do either one or the other, not only because money is equivalent to a revenue, and a means of procuring a revenue, not only because the lender loses, during the time of the loan, the revenue he might have procured by it, not only because he risks his capital, not only because the borrower can employ it in advantageous acquisition, or in enterprises from which he may draw large profits; the owner of money may lawfully draw the interest of it by a more general and decisive principle. Even if all the foregoing were not the case, he would none the less have the right to require an interest for his loan simply because the money is his property. Since it is his property he is free to keep it, nothing obliges him to lend; if then he does lend, he may attach conditions to the loan as he sees fit. In this he does no injury to the borrower, since the latter agrees to the conditions, and has no right of any kind over the sum lent. The profit that may be procured by the use of money is doubtlessly one of the commonest motives influencing the borrower to borrow on interest; it is one of the means which facilitates his payment of the interest, but this is by no means what gives the lender the right to require it; it is enough for him that his money is his own, and this right is inseparable from property. He who buys bread does it for his support, but the right the baker has to ask a price is quite independent of the use of the bread; it is the same right he would have to sell him stones, a right founded on this principle alone, that the bread is his own, and no one has any right to force him to give it for nothing.

75.   REPLY TO AN OBJECTION

This reflection makes us realise how false and how distant from the meaning of the Gospel, is the application which the dogmatists made of the passage *mutuum date nihil inde sperantes* (lend without expecting gain). The passage is clear, as interpreted by moderate and reasonable theologians, as a precept of charity. All mankind are bound to assist one another; a rich man who would see his fellow creature in distress, and who instead of providing for his wants, would sell him what he needed would be equally deficient in the duties of Christianity and those of humanity. In such circumstances, charity does not only require us to lend without interest, she orders us to lend, and even to give if necessary. To convert the precept of charity into a precept of rigorous justice, is equally repugnant to reason, and to the sense of the text. Those whom I attack here do not claim that it is a duty of (Christian) justice to lend their money; they must then agree that the first words of the passage, *mutuum date*, contain only a precept of charity; now I ask why they seek to extend the close of the passage into an obligation of (Christian) justice. What, shall the lending itself not be a strict precept, and shall only its accessory, the condition of the loan, be made one! This is in effect what men would have been told:

> You are free to lend or not to lend, but if you do lend, take care you do not require any interest for your money, and even when a merchant shall require a loan of you for an enterprise from which he hopes to make large profits, it will be a crime for you to accept the interest he offers you; you must absolutely either lend him gratuitously, or not lend to him at all. You have indeed one method of making interest lawful, that is to lend your capital for an indefinite term, and to give up the right of demanding its repayment allowing your debtor to do so when he pleases or when he can. If you find any inconvenience on the score of security, or if you foresee you will need your money in a certain number of

years, you have no other course to take but not to lend: it will be better to cause this merchant to miss a precious opportunity, than to commit a sin in helping him to take advantage of it.

This is what has been seen in these five words; *mutuum date nihil inde sperantes*, when they have been read with the prejudices created by a false metaphysics. Everyone who reads this text without prejudice, will soon find its real meaning; that is,

> as men, as Christians, you are all brothers, all friends: act toward each other as brethren and friends; help each other in your necessities; let your purses be open to one another, and do not sell the assistance which you owe each other by requiring interest on a loan which charity commands you to make.

This is the true sense of the passage in question. The obligation to lend without interest, and that to lend, are evidently connected together; they are of the same order, and both inculcate a duty of charity, and not a precept of rigorous justice, applicable to all cases of lending.

76. THE RATE OF INTEREST OUGHT TO BE DETERMINED JUST LIKE THAT OF ALL COMMODITIES, BY NOTHING BUT THE COURSE OF TRADE

I have already said that the price of money is regulated like that of all other commodities, by the balance of offer and demand: thus, when there are many borrowers who need money, the interest of money becomes higher; when there are many owners who are ready to lend, it falls. It is therefore a further mistake to believe that the interest of money in trade ought to be fixed by the laws of princes. It is a current price, determined like that of all other commodities. This price varies a little according to the greater or less security which the lender has of not losing his capital; but on equal security, it ought to rise and fall in proportion to the abundance and the need, and the law no more ought to fix the rate of interest than it ought to regulate the price of any other commodity which circulates in commerce.

77. MONEY HAS TWO DIFFERENT VALUATIONS IN COMMERCE. ONE EXPRESSES THE QUANTITY OF MONEY WE GIVE TO PROCURE DIFFERENT SORTS OF COMMODITIES; THE OTHER EXPRESSES THE RELATION A SUM OF MONEY HAS TO THE INTEREST IT WILL PROCURE IN ACCORDANCE WITH THE COURSE OF TRADE

It appears from this explanation of the manner in which money is either sold or let out for an annual interest, that there are two ways of valuing money in commerce. In buying and selling, a certain weight of silver represents a certain quantity of value, or of commodities of every kind; for example, one ounce of silver is the equivalent of a certain quantity of corn, or of a certain number of days' labor. In lending, and in the trade in money, a capital is the equivalent of a rent equal to a fixed portion of that capital; and conversely, an annual rent represents a capital equal to the amount of that rent repeated a certain number of times, according as the interest is at a higher or lower rate.

78. THESE TWO VALUATIONS ARE INDEPENDENT OF EACH OTHER, AND ARE GOVERNED BY QUITE DIFFERENT PRINCIPLES

These two different evaluations have much less connection, and depend much less on each other than one would be tempted to believe at first sight. Money may be very common in ordinary commerce, may have a very low value, answer to a very small quantity of commodities, and the interest of money may at the same time be very high.

Assume that there are one million ounces of silver in currency circulating in commerce, and that an ounce of silver is given in the market for a bushel of corn; suppose that there is brought into the state, in some manner or other, a second million ounces of silver, and that this increase is distributed to every purse in the same proportion as the first million, so that he who had two ounces before, now has four. The silver considered as a quantity of metal will certainly diminish in price, or, which is the same thing, commodities will be paid for more dearly, and it becomes necessary, in order to procure the same measure of corn which was obtained with one ounce of silver, to give a good deal more silver, and perhaps *two ounces* instead of *one*. But it does not by any means follow from this that the interest of money falls, if all this money is carried to the market and employed in the current expenses of those who possess it, as by supposition the first million ounces were; for the interest of money falls only when there is more money to be lent, in proportion to the wants of the borrowers, than there was before. Now the money which is carried to market is not for lending; it is the money which is placed in reserve, the accumulated capitals, that are lent, and so far from the increase of the money in the market, or the diminution of its price in relation to commodities in the ordinary course of trade infallibly, and as an immediate consequence, bringing about a decrease in the interest of money, it may, on the contrary, happen that the very cause which increases the money in the market, and which increases the price of other commodities by lowering the price of money, is precisely that which increases the hire of money, or the rate of interest.

Indeed, suppose for a moment that all the wealthy people in a nation, instead of saving from their revenues or from their annual profits, spend the whole of it; suppose that, not satisfied with spending their revenue, they spend their capital; suppose that a man who has a hundred thousand francs in money, instead of employing them in a profitable manner, or lending them, consumes them piecemeal in foolish expenses; it is evident that on the one hand there will be more money employed in current purchases, in satisfying the wants and humors of every individual, and that consequently its price will fall; on the other hand there will certainly be much less money to lend, and, as many people will ruin themselves, there will probably also be more borrowers. The interest of money will consequently increase, while money itself will become common in circulation, and fall in price, and precisely for the same reason.

We shall cease to be surprised at this apparently peculiar result, if we consider that the money brought into the market for the purchase of corn, is that which is daily spent to satisfy one's needs, and that which is offered on loan, is precisely that which is saved from one's daily expenditure to be laid by and formed into capitals.

79.   IN THE VALUATION OF MONEY WITH REGARD TO
        COMMODITIES, IT IS THE MONEY CONSIDERED AS
        METAL THAT IS THE SUBJECT OF THE ESTIMATE. IN
        THE EVALUATION OF THE PENNY OF MONEY, IT IS THE
        USE OF THE MONEY FOR A DEFINITE TIME THAT IS THE
        SUBJECT OF THE ESTIMATE

In the market a measure of corn is equivalent to a certain weight of silver; it is a quantity of silver that is purchased with the commodity; it is this quantity which is valued and compared with other different values. In a loan on interest, the object of the valuation is the use of a certain quantity of value during a certain time. It is no longer the comparison of a quantity of silver with a quantity of corn; it is now a quantity of values which is compared with a definite portion of itself, which becomes the price of the use of this quantity for a certain time. Let twenty thousand ounces of silver be equivalent in the market to twenty thousand measures of corn, or only to ten thousand, the use of those twenty thousand ounces of silver for a year will none the less be worth in the money market the twentieth part of the principal sum, or one thousand ounces of silver, if interest is at the twentieth penny.

80.   THE PRICE OF INTEREST DEPENDS DIRECTLY ON
        THE RELATION BETWEEN THE DEMAND OF THE
        BORROWERS AND THE OFFER OF THE LENDERS, AND
        THIS RELATION DEPENDS CHIEFLY ON THE QUANTITY
        OF MOVEABLE WEALTH ACCUMULATED BY THE
        SAVING OF REVENUES AND OF ANNUAL PRODUCTS TO
        FORM CAPITALS, WHETHER THESE CAPITALS EXIST IN
        MONEY OR IN ANY OTHER KIND OF EFFECTS HAVING
        A VALUE IN COMMERCE

The price of silver in the market is relative only to the quantity of this metal used in current exchanges; but the rate of interest is relative to the quantity of values accumulated and laid by to form capitals. It does not matter whether these values are in metal or other effects, provided these effects are easily convertible into money. It is far from being the case, that the mass of metal existing in a state is as large as the amount of the values lent on interest in the course of a year; but all the capitals, in furniture, merchandise, tools, and cattle, take the place of silver and represent it. A paper signed by a man who is known to be worth a hundred thousand francs, and who promises to pay a hundred thousand francs at a certain date, is worth a hundred thousand francs until that date: all the capitals of the man who has signed this note are answerable for the payment of it, whatever the nature of the effects he has in his possession, provided they have a value of a hundred thousand francs. It is not therefore the quantity of silver existing as metal which causes the rate of interest to rise or fall, or which brings more money into the market to be lent; it is simply the sum of capitals to be found in commerce, that is to say, the current sum of moveable values of every kind, accumulated, saved gradually out of the revenues and profits, to be employed by the owner to procure himself new profits and new revenues. It is these accumulated savings which are offered to the borrowers, and the more there are of them, the lower the interest of money will be, at least if the number of borrowers is not augmented in proportion.

38. Étienne Bonnot de Condillac: *Commerce and Government Considered in Their Mutual Relationship* (1776)[1]

CHAPTER 14: OF METALS CONSIDERED AS COINAGE

When in earlier chapters I posited measures, it was only to speak more precisely about the relative value of the goods being exchanged. It appears that at the origin of society the tribes had none; nowadays several tribes still do not have any. It is the case that whenever people are not concerned to look closely, they are happy to estimate the quantity of goods at a glance.

Let us move to the time when, in the absence of merchants, the settlers were exchanging their surplus foodstuffs among themselves; and let us look at two settlers, one who has a surplus of corn and lacks a certain quantity of wine, the other who has a surplus of wine, and lacks a certain quantity of corn. To simplify, I assume that they are each furnished with everything else they need.

With this assumption, it is clear that the man who has corn to deliver would not look closely at the size, or the number, of his sacks. Since this corn would have no value for him if it was left on his hands, he considers it well paid for when, by an exchange, he gets for himself all the wine he needs.

The man who has a surplus of wine reasons in the same way. So they exchange without measuring; indeed, it is enough for them to judge on sight, the one the amount of wine he needs, the other the amount of corn.

It is not the same when the settlers make their exchanges through the medium of merchants. Since the latter want to make a profit at one and the same time from the person from whom they buy and the person to whom they sell, they are concerned to judge the quantity of goods more precisely. So they will think of ways to ascertain what they have gained each time they buy and resell.

Now, when instead of judging goods in a rough and ready fashion they have got used to measuring them, one will assume that their value is treated like their quantity, for which there is a fixed measure. We will be all the more likely to assume it, as values will seem to vary like measures. So people will come to make misconceptions. They will speak of value and price without thinking what they are saying: they will forget that the notions they make of them can only be relative; and they will assume that they are absolute.

---

[1]   Translated by Shelagh Eltis.

It is the merchants who will above all have occasioned this misunderstanding: as they were concerned to estimate goods more accurately, they seemed to give them an absolute value. "This measure is worth so much," they said, and people no longer saw an idea of relativity in this language.

Besides, they were not in the same position as the settlers who, in the days when they traded directly, attached no value to the surplus, except in so far as they could provide themselves with the goods they needed by giving it up.

The surplus with which the merchants' trade had belonged to the settlers who gave it up to them. But for the merchants it is not a surplus; it is a useful good they expect to profit from. And so they appreciate it to the full; and the more they claim to appreciate it, the more they seem to give it an absolute value. Metals, used as money, will especially create this illusion.

Iron disintegrates: exposure to the air, however little humidity there is in it, gradually decomposes it. Copper destroys itself too. Only gold and silver keep without corruption.

Each of these metals has a value, which stems from its scarcity, its adaptability and its lasting qualities. Gold is more valuable than silver, silver than copper, and copper than iron.

It has probably always been impossible to calculate exactly the relative and proportional value of these metals; all the more so because this proportion must vary each time some of them become scarcer or more plentiful. They were estimated roughly, sometimes more, sometimes less, according to the quantity of them appearing in trade. A metal had more value when there was little of it on sale, and when people wished to buy a lot. It had less value in the opposite case. We shall deal with their respective value elsewhere.

As soon as it was appreciated that metals have a value, it was found useful to give a piece of metal in exchange for what one was buying; and as this custom took hold, metals became the common measure of all values. Then a merchant was no longer forced to cart wine or some other foodstuff to the settler who had corn to sell. He gave him a piece of metal, and this settler bought everything he needed with the same metal.

Iron was the least suitable for this use. As it corrodes day by day, the person who received it in exchange would make a loss each day. Besides, one is only accustomed to make use of metals as a common measure, because they make commerce easier. Now iron would facilitate it less than the other metals since, as it is the least valuable, we would have to cart it about in greater quantities. Copper, which keeps better and which is more valuable, would deserve its preference. Every nation uses it; however, since its value is still very limited, it is only useful when one buys low-price goods retail.

So it was gold and silver which were bound especially to be chosen for use as a common measure. They are indestructible; they have great value. The value is found in due proportion in each part; and so one can find, in each part, depending on whether it is larger or smaller, a measure of any sort of value.

So it is not following a convention that gold and silver have been introduced into commerce as a convenient means for exchanges; it is not by whim that they have been given a value. They have, like all other merchandise, a value based on our needs; and because this value, larger or smaller according to the amount of metal, does not perish, they have, for that reason alone, become the measure of all others, and the most convenient.

We have seen that trade increases the amount of wealth, because by facilitating and multiplying exchanges it gives value to those goods which had none. We see here that trade must increase this quantity of wealth still further when it has, in gold and silver considered as merchandise, a common measure of all values, since exchanges are then made easy and multiply ever more.

But this measure had to be fixed and determined. However, it is probable that, in the early days, people judged volume by sight, and weight by hand. This uncertain regime doubtless caused damage and complaints. The need to avoid them was felt: people set about it, and scales were invented to weigh metals. So an ounce of silver, for instance, was the price of a septier of corn or of a cask of wine.

This innovation succeeded in confusing all ideas on the value of things. When people believed they were seeing price in a measure which, like an ounce of gold or silver, was always the same, they did not doubt that they had an absolute value, and no longer entertained other than confused ideas on this subject.

All the same there was a great advantage in being able to determine the weight of each piece of gold and silver; because if previously what we call price was a vague estimate without precision, you can understand that people must have found in these metals, weighed and cut up, the more exact price of all other merchandise, or a surer measure of their value.

It is as merchandise that gold and silver circulated, when the buyer and the seller were reduced to weighing the quantity they needed to hand over as the price of other merchandise. This practice, which was general, still carries on in China and elsewhere.

However, it was inconvenient always to have to carry scales, and that was not the only drawback: one also had to make sure of the degree of purity of the metals, a degree which affects the value.

Public authority came to the help of trade; it had the gold and silver circulating assayed: it determined what one calls the standard, that is the degree of purity. It then made separate portions which it weighed; and it stamped on each a mark which attested the standard and the weight.

Here we have money. One knows its value at a glance. It prevents fraud, it injects confidence into trade and consequently makes trade still easier.

Gold and silver coin would not have been suitable for the small purchases one makes daily: one would have had to cut it up into tiny pieces which could scarcely have been handled. That is why copper coin was introduced. Copper coin even seems to have been the first in use; it sufficed on its own, when the tribes only had things of small value to exchange.

In becoming coin, metals have not ceased to be merchandise; they have an extra imprint and a new denomination; but they are still what they were, and they would not have a value as coinage if they did not continue to have value as merchandise. This observation is not as pointless as it might seem, because people would say, in the common reasoning on money, that it is not merchandise, and yet they do not have much to say about what it is.

Gold and silver coinage reveals that there are things of high price in trade. It is therefore a proof of wealth. But it is not so by virtue of its quantity: because commerce can make do with less as with more. If it were eight times more plentiful, it would have eight times less value, and one would have to carry a mark to market instead of an ounce. If it were eight times scarcer, it would have eight times more value, and one would only have to carry an ounce instead of a mark. It is therefore a proof of wealth by the mere fact that it is used. It is that in having a great value on its own, it proves that there are articles in trade which also have great value. But if it became as common as copper, it would lose its value; and then, in exchanges, it could serve as a measure of value for the nations which seem to us the poorest. When we deal with the circulation of silver we shall see how one judges its abundance and its scarcity.

Used as coin, gold and silver had a new use and new utility. These metals thus acquired fresh value. An abundance of gold and silver is thus an abundance of articles which have value, and consequently it is wealth.

But whatever value one places on gold and silver, the first and main wealth is not at all in the plentifulness of these metals. This wealth is only in the abundance of products which are consumed. However, because with gold and silver one can lack for nothing, one soon comes to regard these metals as the sole wealth, or at least as the principal wealth: that is an error. But it would also be an error to say that an abundance of gold and silver is not true wealth. We must confine ourselves to distinguishing two types of wealth.

I shall note in finishing this chapter that those who consider coins as representative signs of the value of things express themselves too inexactly; because they seem to regard them as arbitrarily chosen signs, which only have value by convention. If they had noticed that metals were merchandise before they became money, and that they have continued to be merchandise, they would have recognised that they are only suited to be the common measure of all values because they have value in themselves, and independently of all convention.

CHAPTER 15: THAT SILVER, USED AS A MEASURE OF VALUE, HAS BROUGHT MISUNDERSTANDING ABOUT THE VALUE OF THINGS

We have noticed that when trade comes about through the exchange of goods in surplus, everyone gives something which had no value for him, because he has no use for it, for something which does have a value for him, because he can use it, and that, consequently, everyone gives less for more. Now that is how it would have been natural to work out value in every case, if one had always traded through barter and without minted coin.

But once money had been accepted as the common measure of value, it was just as natural to reckon that one was giving equal value for equal value in exchanges, all the goods one exchanged were each considered equal in value to an identical quantity of money.

It was seen that through the medium of money one could determine, with some precision, a respective value between two quantities of a different nature, for example between a quantity of corn and a measure of wine. From then on, in these respective values, only the quantity of money which was the measure of them was noticed: every other consideration was removed; and because this quantity was the same, it was reckoned that in exchanges one gave equal value for equal value.

However, when I give you a quantity of corn, valued at ten ounces of silver, to get from you a quantity of wine at the same price, it is not certain that this exchange is equally advantageous for you and for me, although these two quantities seem to be the equivalent of each other.

In fact, if the corn which I have given you is absolutely essential to me, and if the wine you have given me is surplus to your needs, the advantage will be on your side and the disadvantage on mine.

Therefore, it is not enough to compare quantity in money with quantity in money, to work out who gains, you or I. There is another consideration which must come into the calculation; that is to know whether we are both exchanging a surplus for a necessary good. In such a case, the advantage is the same for both parties, and we each give less for more; in every other case it cannot be equal, and one of us gives more for less.

We have noticed that, in exchanges, goods are reciprocally the price of each other. We shall note here that if money is the measure of the value of the goods one buys, the value of the goods one buys is reciprocally the measure of the value of money. For example, to suppose that with six ounces of silver one can buy a muid of corn, is that not to suppose that a muid of corn is the measure of the value of six ounces of silver?

So when money has been taken as the common measure of all value, it is solely, as we have seen, because of all tradable goods it is the most suitable for this purpose; and that does not infer that it cannot itself have, as a measure, the value of the goods against which it is exchanged. On the contrary, it is clear that the value of what one buys is always the measure of the value of the money one gives.

But once people have taken money as a common measure, they soon come to see it as an absolute measure: that is to say, as a measure that is a measure by itself, independently of any connection, or as a good which, by its nature, measures all others, and is not measured by any of them. This misapprehension could not fail to spread much confusion. It has also made us see an equal value in the goods we exchange, and we have made a principle of commerce out of this equal value.

However, if what I am offering you was equal for you in value, or, which comes to the same, in utility, to what you are offering me; and if what you are offering me was equal for me to what I am offering you, we should each of us stay with what we have; and we should not make any exchange. When we make an exchange, then you and I judge that we each receive more than we give, or that we give less for more.

Let us remember the time when Europeans began trading in America, where, for things to which we attach little value, they received other goods to which we attach the greatest value.

Following our line of argument, you will agree that they gave less for more when they gave a knife, a sword or a mirror for an ingot of silver or gold. But we cannot deny that the American also gave less for more when he gave, for example, an ingot of gold for a knife: because he was giving something to which people attached little value in his country because it was useless, in exchange for something to which they attached value, because it was useful.

So people said that the Americans did not know the price of gold and silver. They spoke as though these metals must have an absolute value. People did not think that they only possess value in relation to man's uses, and that in consequence they have no value for a tribe that has no use for them.

Inequality of value following the customs and opinions of peoples: that is what has created trade and what supports it; because it is what produces the situation that in exchanges each person has the advantage of giving less for more.

However, because we are not inclined to believe that money can be overplentiful, however much of it one has, we will find it difficult to understand that, when we give money for something we buy, we have the advantage of giving less for more, especially if the good is what we call expensive. So let us see how money can be considered as a necessary good, or as a surplus good.

All your property is in land, and you have produce of all kinds, more than you can consume. It is clear that, in giving up the produce which is surplus to your consumption, you are giving up something which is useless to you; and however little utility you find in what you receive in exchange, you will have given less for more.

I only have rents, and all my income is in money. Now I cannot live off this money, as you can with your produce. On its own it is thus useless to me, and it would always be so if I could not exchange it with you or with someone else. When I hand it over, I therefore abandon something which is useless to me for something I need, and I give less for more. But we find ourselves in very different situations; because in the product of your lands, it is only the produce surplus to your consumption that is useless to you; while in the product of my rents, if I do not manage to exchange it, all is useless to me, since there is nothing for my consumption.

So money, which is useless on its own, because with money alone one could not subsist, only becomes useful because, having been chosen as a common measure of all value, it is accepted as the price of the goods one buys.

Now, the amount of money which I need to supply me with everything necessary for my subsistence is for me the equivalent of the foodstuffs you are obliged to set aside for your subsistence. If I give up that money for things that are useless for my consumption, I should make an unfavourable exchange; I should be giving an essential good for a useless good, I should be giving more for less.

But the money I have left, when I have set aside all that I need for my subsistence, is a surplus for me; just as the produce which you do not need to consume is a surplus for you.

Now, the more confident I am of being able to subsist in accordance with the needs I have created for myself, the less this money surplus is of value for me. So I shall not scrutinise it too closely; and even when I give some of it for frivolities I should like to enjoy, I shall believe I am giving less for more.

It will be the same for you when, after you have made ample provision of products of every kind, nothing can be lacking for your subsistence. Then what you have left is a surplus which you will give happily for a frivolity which seems worthless.

It will follow from this that the value of essential goods will always be estimated more accurately than the value of superfluous goods; and that these values will never be in proportion to each other. The price of essential goods will be very low compared with the price of superfluous goods, because everyone is concerned to estimate them as exactly as possible. In contrast, the price of superfluous goods will be very high compared with the price of necessary goods, because the very people who buy them are not concerned to estimate them with precision. But in the end, at whatever price one buys them, or however dear they appear, the person who purchases them with surplus money is always considered to give less for more.

CHAPTER 16: OF THE CIRCULATION OF MONEY

Each year, at appointed times, farmers bring the entire price of their leases into the towns: each market day, they sell some produce, and so they carry back to their village, in small amounts, the sums they have paid the landowners.

In the course of the year, the merchant receives in individual sales the price of the goods he bought wholesale; and the artisan, who bought his raw materials wholesale, sells them retail, when he has worked on them. So it is that day by day sales reimburse in small sums the large sums which have been used for payments or purchases in gross; and, when this reimbursement has been made, people pay out or buy again with large sums to have themselves reimbursed by new retail sales.

Money is thus constantly moving around, to be collected later as into reservoirs, from which it spreads through a mass of small channels which bring it back into the first reservoirs; whence it spreads out again, and to which it returns again. This continual movement, which collects it to distribute it, and distributes it to gather it up again, is what we call circulation.

Do I need to point out that this circulation assumes that, at each movement the money makes, there is an exchange; and that when it moves without causing an exchange, there is no circulation? For example, the money which comes from taxes has gone through many hands before it reaches the Sovereign's treasury. But that is not circulation, that is only transport, and often very costly transport. It is important that, through circulating, money changes itself in some way into all the goods which are needed to support life and strength in the body politic. Thus money from taxation only begins to circulate when the sovereign exchanges it for products or works.

All the money in commerce circulates from the reservoirs to the channels, and from the channels to the reservoirs. If any obstacle holds up this circulation, commerce languishes.

I say all the money in commerce, and I do not say all that is in the state. There is always a certain amount which does not circulate at all, for example what one puts aside to have a standby in case of misfortune or to improve one's position someday: such also are the savings of misers, who cut back on their needs.

That money does not circulate at all at present. But it is not very important whether there is more or less in circulation; the main point is that it should circulate freely.

We have seen that money is only a measure of value because it possesses value itself; that if it is scarce, it has greater value; and that it has a smaller value if it is plentiful.

If there is twice the amount of money in commerce, we will give for a good two ounces of this metal instead of one; and if there is half the quantity of money, we will only give half an ounce instead of a whole ounce. In the first case, an owner who would put out his land to farm for fifty ounces, would let it for a hundred; and in the second he would let it for twenty-five.

But with a hundred ounces he will only do what he did with fifty; just as with fifty he will only do what he did with twenty-five. So he would be deceiving himself if he thought himself richer in one of these cases than in the other. His income is always the same, whether the coin is smaller or greater. Whether one counts it at a hundred ounces, or fifty, or twenty-five, nothing is changed; since with these various ways of counting, one can only ever make the same consumption.

So one sees that it is fairly unimportant whether there is plenty of money, and that it would even be a good thing if there were less. Indeed commerce would be carried on more conveniently. Would it not be dreadfully awkward if silver were as common as iron.

All products come from cultivated land. So one can consider farmers as the first reservoirs of all the money that circulates.

They spread some on the lands for the expenses of cultivation, another part, at different times, is carried bit by bit to the towns, where the farmers buy worked materials which they cannot find in their villages. Finally, a last portion is carried to the towns, in large sums, for the payment of the leases.

The landowners therefore form other reservoirs, from which money spreads among the artisans who work for them; among the merchants from whom they buy, and among the farmers who come to the town to sell their foodstuffs.

The merchant, who plans to make bulk purchases, becomes in his turn a reservoir as he sells his goods; and it is the same with the artisan, who needs to build up a stock in order to be able to supply himself with raw materials.

I agree that the merchant and the artisan can buy on credit, to pay later at different dates. But whether they pay when they buy, or only pay later, they must necessarily keep back a proportion of what they sell each day, if they do not want to fail to meet their undertakings. They therefore have to accumulate.

It would be beneficial for the use of credit to become established, since then a merchant and an artisan, without money, could keep an inventory, the one of merchandise, the other of raw materials; and, consequently, a larger number of actively occupied men would join together in advancing trade. For that to happen good faith must bring confidence. This is especially what happens in republics which have, shall we say, habits of simplicity and frugality.

The merchant and the artisan can do nothing without money, or at least without credit. The same does not hold true of the farmers. If they need the one or the other for the goods they buy in the town, they do not have the same need in providing for the expenses of cultivation; because they can pay all the country-dwellers who work for them with the grain they harvest, with the drinks they make, with the animals they raise. Custom sets the wages they owe, and the foodstuffs they hand over are valued at the market's prices.

So one spends no money in the country, or one spends little; and as one can only earn on the one side what someone spends on the other, it must be the case that those who work for the farmers earn little money, or earn none at all. Money thus circulates less in the countryside than elsewhere.

The consequence is, in the last analysis, that the towns form large reservoirs which money enters and from which it issues by a self-sustaining movement, or one which constantly renews itself.

Let us suppose that half our tribe lives in the town, where we have seen that the landowners consume more than they did in their villages, and where, in consequence, they will consume more than half the product of the land.

To settle our ideas, let us value the produce of all the land at two thousand ounces of silver. On this assumption, since the inhabitants of the town consume more than half of all products, they will need more than a thousand ounces of silver to buy everything necessary for their subsistence. I make the assumption that they need twelve hundred, and I say that if this sum is enough for them, it will be enough to support commerce throughout the tribe. That is, it will pass to the farmers to return to the landowners; and as this cycle will only finish to begin again, it will always be with the same quantity of money that exchanges are made in the town and in the country. From that fact one could speculate that the amount of money that commerce needs depends mainly on the amount of consumption in the towns; or that this amount of money is almost equal to the value of the products that the towns consume.

It is at least certain that it could not be equal in value to the product of all the lands. Indeed, although we have evaluated this product at two thousand ounces of silver, it would not be enough to give our tribe these two thousand ounces to give it a value in silver equal to the product of all its lands. Silver would lose all the more of its value as it became more available:

the two thousand ounces would only be worth twelve hundred. So it is in vain that one would put a larger amount of silver into trade. Whatever this quantity was, it could only ever have a value roughly equal to the value of the products consumed in the towns.

Indeed, as the wealth of the countryside is in products, the wealth of the towns is in silver. Now, if in the towns, where we assume that at the end of each year consumption had been paid for with twelve hundred ounces, we suddenly spread out another eight hundred, it is clear that the silver will lose its value in proportion to its increased plentifulness. So people will pay twenty ounces, or near enough, for what they used to pay twelve; and consequently the two thousand will only have the value of twelve hundred, or near enough. I say near enough since these proportions do not fix themselves by exact, geometric calculations.

The amount of silver needed for trade must also vary according to circumstances.

Let us assume that the payment of leases and that of everything on credit takes place once a year; and that to liquidate them, the debtors need a thousand ounces of silver; there would have to be, in relation to these payments, a thousand ounces of silver in circulation.

But if these payments were made half-yearly, half this amount would be enough, because five hundred ounces, paid twice, equal a thousand paid once. One can see that if these payments were made in four equal terms, two hundred and fifty ounces would suffice.

To make the calculation easier I am omitting the small, daily disbursements which are made in ready money. But people will no doubt say that I am establishing nothing precise about the quantity of money in circulation. I would reply that my sole purpose is to show that internal trade can be conducted, and it is, following the customs of countries, with less money in circulation as with more; and it is not otiose to comment on it, in these days when people imagine that a state is only rich in proportion as it has more money.

Often little money is needed in trade, and credit takes its place. Established in different countries, the traders or dealers send each other goods which command a higher price in the places to which they are carried, and in continuing to sell the goods they stock, each for his own account, they all sell for each other's accounts the goods they have received. By this means they can make an extensive trade without requiring silver to circulate between them. Because in valuing the merchandise entrusted to them, according to the current price, they will only have to pay for whatever some have supplied beyond that; yet again one can meet obligations towards them by sending them other merchandise. So it is that the largest enterprises are often those where silver circulates in the least quantity.

But money is needed for daily expenses: it is needed to pay the wages of artisans who live by work from day to day. It is needed for the small merchants who only buy and sell retail and who need their capital to come back to them continuously.

It is in small channels that circulation takes place more perceptibly and more rapidly. But the faster it is, the more the same pieces of coin pass and pass again frequently through the same hands; and as, in such a case, one coin takes the place of many, it is clear that this smaller trade can carry on with a quantity of coin which gets less as the circulation speeds up. So, in small channels one needs little money because it circulates rapidly; and in large ones even less is needed, as often it hardly circulates at all.

We may conclude that it is impossible to say anything with confidence about the precise amount of money circulating which is, or which should be, in commerce. I might have put it far too high when I supposed it roughly equal to the value of the products which are consumed annually in the towns. Since at the beginning of January each citizen certainly does not have all the money he will need in the course of the year; but because, as he is spending it, he is earning it, one can appreciate that, at the year's end, the same coins have come back many times into the towns, just as they left them a good many times.

The circulation of money would be very slow if one always had to change it at great expense in the distant places where one might need it. Therefore it would matter to be able to make it pass in some way over very great distances. This is what one achieves by means of exchange which we are going to deal with.

...

CHAPTER 18: OF LENDING AT INTEREST

A farmer, who takes land on a lease, exchanges his work for a part of the product, and gives the other part to the landowner, and that is in the order of things.

Now would the borrower be in the same position as the farmer? Or does money have a yield of which the borrower owes the lender a part?

A septier of corn can produce twenty, thirty or more according to the goodness of the soil and the hard work of the cultivator.

Indubitably money does not reproduce itself in the same manner. But it is not with corn that we should compare it: it is with land, which does not reproduce itself any more than money.

Now in commerce, money yields a return according to the effort of the person who borrows it, just as the land yields one according to the hard work of the farmer.

Indeed, an entrepreneur can only maintain his trade in so far as the money, with which he makes advances, comes back continuously to him with a return in which he finds his subsistence and that of the workers he employs, that is to say, a wage for them and a wage for him.

If he were alone, he would make the most of the demand people had for the articles he sells, and he would bring this return to the highest point.

But as soon as many entrepreneurs carry on the same trade, forced to undercut each other, they make do with a smaller wage and those whom they employ are reduced to smaller gains. Thus competition regulates the return they can reasonably draw from the advances they have made; advances which are for them what the expenses of cultivation are for the farmers.

If commerce could only be carried on by entrepreneurs who were rich enough to provide the capital for it, a small number would carry it on exclusively. Less under pressure from competition to sell at a discount, they would put their wage at a rate that would be all the higher because they would be less pushed to sell their goods, and because it would be easy for them to get together to wait for the moment when they could take advantage of the citizens' needs. Then their wage could be taken to 100 per cent or more.

But if in contrast commerce is carried on by entrepreneurs to whom people have given advances from their stock, they will be under pressure to sell in order to be able to pay out as their obligation falls due. It will therefore not be in their power to await, from one day to the next, the moment when people will have the greatest need of their goods, and competition will force them all the more to make do with a smaller wage because, being more numerous and for the most part under pressure to make money, it will be harder for them to take concerted action. One cannot doubt that it is desirable for commerce to be carried on by such entrepreneurs.

Now I assume that, having subtracted all the expenses of commerce, there is a general net residue, to form the wage of each entrepreneur, of 15 to 20 per cent.

How will a man manage who has no property, and yet who could with hard work carry on some branch of commerce? He has only two openings. Someone must lend him a stock of merchandise, or someone must lend him the money to buy it, and it is clear that these two possibilities come down to the same thing.

He approaches a rich businessman who says to him: "I am going to advance you what I should have given you for one hundred ounces of silver if you had been able to pay me in ready money, and in a year you will give me one hundred and ten ounces for it."

He accepts this offer, in which he sees a profit of 5 to 10 per cent for himself out of the 15 to 20 per cent that one may customarily earn when one owns one's own capital.

No one will condemn this transaction, which is freely made and is at one and the same time advantageous to both contracting parties, and which, by multiplying the number of merchants, increases competition, an absolute necessity if trade is to benefit the state.

No one will deny the rich businessman the right to demand interest for advances which he runs the risk of losing. He counts, as a matter of fact, on the honesty and the hard work of those to whom he has made them; but he can be deceived: he is sometimes: it is necessary for those who pay him to compensate him for the losses he makes with the others. Would it be fair to condemn him to make advances on which he would often lose, without his ever being able to compensate himself? He would certainly never make the advances.

Besides, you cannot deny that a merchant who advances a stock of merchandise has a right to reserve to himself a share in the profits which this stock must produce; he who before advancing the stock had the sole right to the profits.

Now we have just noted that to advance an entrepreneur a stock of merchandise, or to advance him the money he needs to buy that stock is the same thing. If one is in the right to demand interest in the first case, one then has the same right in the other case.

It is a fact that the interest-bearing loan sustains commerce. It has besides been shown that it increases the number of merchants; that in increasing them, it increases competition; that in increasing competition, it makes commerce more profitable to the state. The loan at interest is therefore equitable, and must be allowed.

I know that the casuists condemn it when it is made in money; but I also know that they do not condemn it when it is made in goods. They allow a businessman to lend at 10 per cent, say, merchandise to the value of a thousand ounces of silver; but they do not allow him to lend, at the same interest rate, the thousand ounces in kind.

When I say that the casuists allow the loan of goods at 10 per cent I do not wish to accuse them of using this language, "to lend at 10 per cent": they would be contradicting themselves too palpably. I mean to say that they allow a businessman to sell for 10 per cent more the goods that he advances for a year. One can see that the contradiction is less palpable.

Our legislators, if that were possible, reason even worse than the casuists. They condemn the loan at interest, and they allow it. They condemn it without knowing why, and they allow it because they are forced to. Their laws, the outcome of ignorance and prejudice, are useless if they are not observed; and if they are observed they damage trade.

The error into which the casuists and the legislators fall comes uniquely from the confused notions they have formed. In effect, they do not blame the exchange market, and they blame the loan at interest. But why should money have a price in one that it does not have in the other? The loan and the borrowing, are they anything other than an exchange? If, in the exchange market, one exchanges sums of money where the loan or the sum borrowed are separated in place, cannot one exchange sums of money which are separated in time? And because these distances are not of the same kind, must one conclude that the exchange in the one case is not an exchange in the other? So one does not see that to lend at interest is to sell; that to borrow at interest is to buy; that the money one lends is the goods which are sold; that the money one must give back is the price which is paid; and that the interest is the profit to the seller. Certainly, if one had only seen in the loan at interest, goods, sale and profit, one would not have condemned it; but one has only seen the words loan, interest, money; and without reflecting too much on what they mean, one has judged that they should not go together.

Interest at 10 per cent is only an assumption that I make, because I needed to make one. It can be higher, as it can be lower: it is a matter on which the legislator must not reach any decision if he does not want to harm liberty. Custom, which regulates this interest, will cause it to vary, according to circumstances, and the variations must be allowed. Observe how it must of necessity rise and fall in turn.

It will be high, however plentiful money may be, if there are many people wanting to borrow, and if there are few who want to lend.

If those who have money, or who own most of it, need it themselves to support enterprises in which they are engaged, they will only be able to lend by abandoning their enterprises, and it follows that they will only lend when they are assured of a profit equal to, or larger than, the one that they would have made. One will therefore have to give them a lot of interest.

But, even at a time when money is scarce, the rate of interest will be low if money is mainly in the hands of a large number of economical landowners who seek to place it.

Interest rises and falls in turn, in the proportion that the money that people wish to borrow is to the money on offer for loan. Now this proportion can vary all the time.

In a time when rich landowners make very great outlays of every kind, one will borrow more; firstly because the landowners will themselves often be forced to contract loans; and secondly, because to provide for all the consumption they make, a larger number of entrepreneurs will be established, or of men who for the most part need to borrow. That is one of the reasons why interest is higher in France than in Holland.

On the other hand, in a period when more economical landowners spend less, there will be fewer borrowers: for instead of their having to contract loans themselves, they will have money to lend; and since they will consume less, they will reduce the number of entrepreneurs and, consequently, of borrowers. There you have one of the reasons why interest is lower in Holland than in France.

If a new kind of consumption gives rise to a new branch of commerce, entrepreneurs will not fail to multiply in proportion as they believe they can promise themselves much greater profits; and the interest on money will go up because the number of borrowers will be greater.

If this branch of trade collapses the money will come back to those who lent it, they will seek to place it a second time, and the interest rate will go down, because the number of lenders will have grown.

If entrepreneurs carry on their business with as much careful management as hard work, they will bit by bit become owners of the sums they borrowed. So they will have to be removed from the number of borrowers and added to the number of lenders when they have gained more than the money they need to carry on their commercial activities.

Finally, laws will increase the number of lenders when they permit interest-bearing loans. Today, in contrast, they tend to reduce the number.

But it is pointless to seek to provide an exhaustive account of all the factors which cause variation in the ratio of the demand for money to borrow to that on offer for loan: I have said enough to show that interest rates must sometimes be higher, sometimes lower.

Just as prices settle themselves in the market place, following the haggling of sellers and buyers, so the rate of interest, or the price of money, is fixed in the places of trade following the haggling of borrowers and lenders. The government recognises that it is not its function to make laws to fix the price of goods which are sold in the market; why then should it think it ought to fix the rate of interest or the price of money?

To make a wise law on this subject, it would need to grasp the ratio of the quantity of money available to lend to the demand for borrowing. But since this ratio forever varies it will not grasp it, or it will only hold it for a moment and by chance; it will therefore need to keep on making new regulations without ever being sure it is doing good: or if it persists in wanting to enforce those it has made, because it does not know how to make others, it will only disturb commerce. People will escape these regulations in secret markets; and the interest rate, which it claimed the right to fix, will rise all the more, as the lenders, having the law against them, will lend with less security.

In contrast, in commercial centres, interest will always regulate itself well, without interference, because it is there that the offers of lenders and the demands of borrowers make apparent the ratio of money to lend to money to borrow.

Not only can interest rates vary from one day to another, they also vary according to the type of trade. That is what we still have to examine.

A merchant who has borrowed to raise the stock for a shop has to earn, over and above his subsistence, the wherewithal to pay the interest he owes. If he has formed a large concern, which he directs with hard work, his outlay to maintain it will be small beer compared with the profits he can make. He will therefore be all the more in a position to pay what he owes: one will therefore run fewer risks in lending to him; one will therefore lend to him with more confidence, and, consequently, at lower interest rates.

But if, with a trade that produces little, he barely earns his subsistence, then what he needs for his subsistence is a high proportion of what he earns. There is therefore no longer the same security in lending to him. Now it is natural that the interest which lenders demand increases in proportion as their confidence falls.

In Paris, the retailers from the Halles pay five sols interest a week for an écu of three livres. This interest puts up the price of the fish they sell in the streets; but the people prefer to buy from them than to go to the Halles to stock up.

On a yearly basis this interest comes to more than 430 per cent. However exorbitant it is, the government puts up with it, because it is profitable for the retailers to be able to carry on their trade at this price, or perhaps again because it cannot stop it.

However, the price that the lender places on his money, and the profit that the retailer makes, are out of all proportion. That is why this interest is hateful; and it becomes all the more open to abuse as the loans are made secretly.

It is not the same with loans made to entrepreneurs who carry on a large-scale business. The interest demanded, proportional to the profits they make, is regulated by custom; because money in the commercial centres has a current price, just as corn has one in the markets. People deal openly, or at least do not hide themselves, and a person sells his money as one would sell any other good.

It is only in the commercial centres that one can learn what rate of interest one may draw from one's money. Every loan which conforms to that rate of interest is honest because it is in line.

If you ask me what is usury nowadays, I say that there is none in the loans of which I have just spoken, and which adjust themselves to the price that the dealers themselves have placed on the money, and have placed freely.

But the loans made to the retailers of the Halles are usurious, because they are without rules and underhand, and the greed of the lender rides roughshod over the need of the borrower.

In general, every loan between merchants and dealers is usurious when the interest that is extracted is higher than the rate which has been publicly fixed in the commercial centres. But when loans are made to individuals who do not carry out any trade or business, by what rule can one judge the interest one may extract from one's money? The law. It is here, I think, that the government can without inconvenience set interest. It even ought to do it, and it would be an act beneficial to the state if it made borrowing more difficult. Let it only allow loans at the lowest rate of interest to owners of lands; fathers of families would have less scope to ruin themselves, and money would flow back into trade. Let it tax usury, or let it cover with a still more stigmatizing note every loan, even at 1 per cent, made to a son who borrows without his family's consent. Let it forbid underhand loans; or, if it cannot prevent them, let it give help itself to the entrepreneurs who are in the lowest class of merchants. In a word, while leaving the freedom to borrow in commercial centres, let it check it wherever it can degenerate into abuse. Doubtless it would not be easy to carry out this design but it would be useful to concern itself with it.

When one considers the loans in these two extremes, it is easy to understand where usury lies: it will not be as easy to determine where it begins, if one considers in this interval the different prices money can have. Because, in commercial centres, this price is fixed between dealers who know each other to be solvent, would that be a reason to lend at the same price to a merchant whose affairs are in disorder? If so, no one will lend to him, and he will be utterly ruined. It seems that in such a case the risks one runs allow one to demand a higher price than that of the market place. Now what is this price? It is bound to vary according to the degree of confidence that the borrower's honesty and hard work inspire. It is therefore impossible to predetermine it, and the government must leave well alone.

If trade were perfectly free, secrecy, which is the hallmark of a dishonest action, would be the true character of usury, and the fear of being found out would be the biggest restraint on it. Nowadays, when the law forbids an interest rate that it ought to allow, secrecy means nothing, since one only hides from a law which is held in contempt. People avoid it openly, they are even forced to. Usurious loans, as defined by this law, are authorised by practice which regards them as legitimate, and they are well known in all sorts of loans: people no longer fear opprobrium, and they end up demanding interest publicly.

But is it only the price of money that can be usurious? Cannot the price of every other good be equally so? Is not a merchant a usurer when he abuses my trust or my need in order to gain from me more than he should? Doubtless he is, and he is so with impunity. Now why does the government wish that it should only be the money merchants who cannot take interest, and why nevertheless, contradicting itself, does it allow it to the bankers? It would do better to tolerate in every instance what it cannot prevent.

Index

abundance or scarcity
  of goods 103–4, 121
  of money 122, 241
  of silver 113, 217
accounting distortions 54, 73, 80–81, 83, 96, 100,
  119, 129, 145, 152, 189
Albert the Great
  commentary on *Nicomachean Ethics* 2,
    14–20
  commentary on *Politics* 3, 21–8
  as one of three founding fathers of monetary
    theory 3
  opening door for Renaissance 1
alchemy 56, 71
alloy 71, 77, 83, 89, 96–8, 101, 176, 186–7, 193
alteration of money
  alternate ways of 58–60, 90–92
    form 74, 79, 90–92
    material 56, 58, 60, 77, 82, 90
    name 75–6, 90
    quantity 262–3
    ratio 74–5
    value 73–4, 75, 76, 81, 94, 176, 182,
      183, 247, 264, 284
    weight 76
  causes for lawful 91–2
  community
    ability of 83
    disadvantages to part of 82–3
    disadvantages to whole of 81–2
    for good of 60, 65
  compound 77–8
  copper
    advantages derived from 147–8
    disadvantages derived from 151–4
    major disadvantages derived from
      154–8
  denomination 75–6, 186–7, 214–16, 264
  established standards of money 288
  frequency of 145–7
  in general 73–4
  gold 161–3
  inability of law to 284
  king

debasement of money by changing
  weight or quality without
  consulting subjects 142–3
demanding tribute from subjects without
  their consent 140–42
helping in need 163–7
ownership of subjects' goods 138–9
knight and doctor case 117–19
lawfulness 54–5, 58–62, 80, 85
loss for public 193
making restitution for 91–5
maravedis and their values in Castile 148–51
and prince 58, 61, 74, 78, 81, 84–7, 93–4
profit
  injuring whole royal succession 87–8
  unjust 78
  unnatural 79
  as worse than usury 79–80
silver 158–61
see also debasement
Angel Gabriel Model 214, 232, 244, 267, 269,
  275, 293, 298
Angelus 90, 92, 94–5
Aquinas, Thomas
  on altering money 145
  commentary on *Nicomachean Ethics* 2,
    29–33
  commentary on *Politics* 3, 34–40
  as one of three founding fathers of monetary
    theory 3
  opening door for Renaissance 1
Aristotle
  brief history 1–2
  on cause and effect 55, 114
  on civil matters 88
  on coinage 11–12, 23, 25, 35–6, 73, 119
  on consequences of errors 83
  on currency as measure 33
  on exchange 3, 8–24, 27–8, 30–37, 47–52,
    105, 143–4
  on features of tyranny 61, 84, 86–7
  on human need
    as natural measure of exchanges 47–8,
      52
    price measured by 52, 94, 104

Printed and bound by CPI Group (UK) Ltd, Croydon, CR0 4YY

16/04/2025

14658495-0002